THE LIFE OF

# ST. IGNATIUS OF LOYOLA

Dearest Lord, teach me to be generous.
Teach me to serve Thee as Thou deservest;
To give and not to count the cost;
To fight and not to heed the wounds;
To toil and not to seek for rest;
To labor and not to seek reward, save that of
  knowing that I do Thy will, O God.

*—St. Ignatius of Loyola*

St. Ignatius Loyola
Founder of the Society of Jesus
1491-1556

# THE LIFE OF
# ST. IGNATIUS OF LOYOLA

*by*

FATHER GENELLI
*of the Society of Jesus*

*"I am come to cast fire on the earth: and
what will I, but that it be kindled?"*
—Luke 12:49

TAN BOOKS AND PUBLISHERS, INC.
Rockford, Illinois 61105

Nihil Obstat:   Arthur J. Scanlan, D.D.
                Censor Librorum

Imprimatur:   ✠ John Cardinal Farley
                Archbishop of New York
                New York
                March 20, 1917

Library of Congress Catalog Card No.: 88-50847

ISBN: 0-89555-345-7

Printed and bound in the United States of America.

TAN BOOKS AND PUBLISHERS, INC.
P.O. Box 424
Rockford, Illinois 61105

1988

# TABLE OF CONTENTS.

## THE FIRST PART.

### CHAPTER I.

The family of St. Ignatius and the Castle of Loyola. His birth—his name in baptism—his education. He is placed at Court, and there forms acquaintance with a lady whose name he does not give. He devotes himself to feats of arms and reading romances of chivalry. In 1517 he takes part for the first time in the war against Navarre. The revolt of the towns—it is suppressed. In 1521 Francis I. renews hostilities. Henry d'Albert conquers Navarre and besieges Pampeluna. The garrison wishes to capitulate, but is prevented by Ignatius, who after a courageous defence is severely wounded. He is treated with honor by the enemy, and sent back to his own country. His health becomes worse—he prepares for death, and is suddenly cured. He undergoes a second operation. The reading of some pious books makes him feel the necessity of choosing between the world and the service of Jesus Christ. He decides on choosing the latter. His desire to please God. The Blessed Virgin appears to him with the Infant Jesus. He thinks of becoming a Carthusian

### CHAPTER II.

Ignatius quits his country, notwithstanding the representations of his elder brother, and departs for Mont Serrat. He meets an unbeliever. He prepares himself in the church of Mont Serrat for his new life. Gives away all he possesses, and takes the habit of

## CHAPTER VI.

## CHAPTER VII.

## CHAPTER VIII.

## CHAPTER XV.

## CHAPTER XVI.

# THE SECOND PART.

## CHAPTER I.

# THE AUTHOR'S PREFACE.

In undertaking to write a new Life of St. Ignatius at a time by no means favorable to him or his Society, I do not purpose to gain the good-will of the public by setting it forth in a manner suitable to their tastes, at the expense of truth. Nor am I led by the motive of a narrow-minded, exclusive devotion towards the great man whose child I have the honor to be, for I am well aware that such a sentiment, shown imprudently and out of season, would be more prejudicial than advantageous to his memory. I have been led to take this work in hand through a taste for that method of historical pursuit which by close observation of facts throws clearer light upon the character of times and of persons. I have observed that the Lives of St. Ignatius, hitherto published, have kept rather to the surface of things, without endeavoring to trace out their connection or to dive into the motives which actuated this great man, or into the world of thought which was awakened in his soul. I would have preferred to hear him speak for himself, and I often regretted that so little use had been made of his letters at a time when it would have been comparatively easy to have done so. For it cannot be disputed that every man is the best painter of his own portrait, and this more especially in his letters. The progress made in historical research within late times has made these deficiencies more observable, and as no one, even the most prejudiced against St. Ignatius, can deny that he is one of the greatest characters who figure in modern times, I cannot be taxed with having undertaken a useless task in endeavoring to fill up this void.

Another object, and one to my mind still more important, is the refutation of the unfounded supposition made by those who pretend that the Society of Jesus is not what it was when St. Ignatius founded it, but that its present state is the work of Lainez and Acquaviva. This prejudice threatens, indeed, to become a fixed idea, and while it is repeated from mouth to mouth no one seems to give himself the trouble to inquire into its truth. Nor is this merely an involuntary mistake advanced by some Protestant author who, as a stranger to Catholic usages and institutions, misinterprets all that he reads, sees, and hears, but it is a wide-spread opinion which is continually cropping up in books and conversations. Were this only a literary error it would not so much matter, but the design is evidently to represent Ignatius as a pious enthusiast, who would have been incapable of establishing the Society of Jesus such as it subsequently showed itself to be. It is insinuated that the Society has been constituted as an after-thought by Lainez and Acquaviva, without the cognizance of the Church and without its co-operation, and that it is governed by secret and mysterious rules, and has some concealed object in view.

Accordingly some would make a comparison between the Society of Jesus and the Order of Templars, and treat its Constitutions as resembling the mysteries of that Order. And therefore Ignatius himself must be set at the lowest figure, and be represented as a simple man, for since *his* Constitutions are known and have been approved by the Church, this hidden poison cannot be found in them. But they say the change was introduced later on, pretending that the same happened to the Society of Jesus as to the Order of the Templars, which latter had been holy and glorious in its beginning, till secret and wicked doctrines and the worship of the devil crept in under the Grand Master Thomas Berard, or perhaps even under Odo de Saint-Amand. Falsehood, together with the employment of the most unlawful measures, accomplished in the fourteenth century the deed of violence and wrong; and not only so, but it has in such a manner blackened the character of its victims, that history has never been able, even through the course of four centuries, to clear or justify them.

The attempt, successful then, was renewed in the eighteenth century, and although calumny had not quite the same success, violence accomplished the same results. It is therefore the duty of history to make a loud protest against every calumnious charge, or the assumption of facts without ground, and thus prevent the tissue of falsehood from being repeated by the writers of the time. For instance, when M. de Raumer sought to give to his historical researches the reputation of diplomatic precision by rummaging old State papers and quoting the gossip of some ill-informed politician, was he justified in making a vague statement that, " The mysteriousness of their institutions might well give umbrage even to a Catholic Government "? *   For by this insidious phrase he would arouse the fears, not of Catholic Governments, which have never been alarmed by the mysteries of which he speaks, and which do not exist, but of his own unguarded readers, since he knows how natural suspicion is to the mind of man.

This expression has evidently the design of misleading public opinion; it renders the Jesuits objects of suspicion, and that for the moment is enough. But I ask, " Have not the Constitutions of the Society of Jesus been printed from the first? are they not known to all Governments? and if there be other secret ones besides these, have not the sudden persecutions and imprisonments of the Jesuits afforded ample opportunities for their discovery?" Their archives, their houses, have they not fallen into

* *Papers for a Modern History*, t. iii., p. 95.

the hands of their enemies?   Well, have they found anywhere any traces of secret instructions, of *Monita Secreta*,
or anything else of the kind?   What a shout of triumph
would not have been raised at such a discovery!   Would
it not by itself have sufficed, not only for the actual but
for the moral annihilation of the Jesuits?   Their lot would
have been the same as that of the Templars in the fourteenth century, and deservedly so.   Let us hear no more
then of secret statutes and designs as proving the guilt
of the Jesuits.   Their true crime in the eyes of their enemies is their inviolable fidelity to the Catholic Church and
to its Head, the Vicar of Jesus Christ upon earth, and this
crime had its source in the Constitutions given by St.
Ignatius, and sealed and confirmed by so many Popes.
This is the true crime of the Jesuits, and if they are to
be attacked for this, they have at least the right to demand
that their enemies attack them fairly and openly.   But
this crime, so great in the eyes of the friends of incre-
dulity, was first committed by St. Ignatius, and then he
had for his accomplices Popes, and Bishops, and kings.
The conduct of the Jesuits in all times was laid down
from that day to the present in the original Constitutions
of St. Ignatius, and it is ridiculous to refuse him the title
of the Father of his own spiritual children.

In addition to the two motives which have induced me
to undertake the work, there is another, namely, that
although the German mind is so much distinguished for
its historical research, there has not yet appeared in
German any original Life of St. Ignatius drawn from
authentic sources.   A taste for collecting and appreciat-
ing facts especially suits the character and mind of our
people.   This quality, it is true, is not in itself sufficient
for an historian, it must be accompanied by other talents
necessary for labors of the kind, and these I am very far
from attributing to myself.   The thought of my own
incapacity would have deterred me, had I not been again

encouraged by the opportuneness of the present time, in which one may venture to say with perfect freedom what could formerly be only hinted at consistently with prudence and the interests at stake.

The sources from which I have taken my work are, first, the Lives already published, and secondly, the Life by Mariani, composed from the Bollandists and hitherto unknown in Germany, but chiefly the records of these last and the collection of St. Ignatius' letters, of which the Bollandists make mention indeed, but of which they could not avail themselves ; and lastly, certain letters sent to me from Spain by a person of consideration. The Saint's letters have in the course of time fallen into different hands, which makes it very difficult to collect them. This explains the fact that for a long time they have had at Rome only authentic copies of them, or some abstracts which they preserve in the archives of the Professed House, under the title of " Traslados de cartas que escrivio Nuestro Santo Padre ; " a part only of these letters has been published from time to time, either as fragments or in a collective form, but almost always in a Latin translation, in which, for the sake of style, the sense as well as the idiom of the original has been sacrificed ; and even these translations are now very difficult to obtain. The latest and most considerable collection was made by a Spanish Jesuit, Father Roch Menchacha, who after the dissolution of the Society brought with him to Italy a number of these letters, and published them anonymously at Bologna, in 1804. But unfortunately he confines himself to a Latin translation, and the Spanish text corrected from the originals has never yet been printed, though extant in Spain in the hands of a private person. *

* The author gives at the end of his book a portion of these letters in the original ; but as they have been translated in the course of the work we thought it unnecessary to reproduce them, especially as the greater part is in Spanish, a language known only to a small portion of readers.

Father Menchacha has prefaced his collections with some remarks showing great learning and accuracy, and from these I have taken many valuable points to which I have drawn attention. In fine, this Life of St. Ignatius has received additions from various quarters which have helped much to its accuracy and exactness.

The first portion of the work contains fewer letters than the latter part, because in the early life of St. Ignatius his letters were not preserved by those to whom they were addressed with the same care as they afterwards were. And as those few which remain contain for the most part matters of little interest, I have not thought proper to insert them. The second part enters at greater length than previous Lives of the Saint have done into what he did as Founder and Superior of his Order, and it contains a far greater number of his letters, in which the reader will find many things quite new to him.

Among the documents of which I have made use are some which I could not myself consult, owing to the shortness of my stay in Rome, but the correctness of their historical information has not suffered from this. I think it right to add a few words on the Life of St. Ignatius by Father Louis Gonzalez, being the most ancient one we have, and often quoted in this work. In the Saint's later years, frequent endeavors were made to obtain from him authentic accounts of what he had done in his lifetime, and Gonzalez, who enjoyed his confidence, took upon himself the difficult task of drawing out from him this information. He had great difficulty in succeeding, and only obtained from him very scanty particulars, as the Saint contented himself with purposely recounting less important matters and touching very lightly on the most interesting events of his life, whether private or public, as though he wished that they should not be spoken of. Still these notices are precious, and hold, without doubt, the first rank as original matter, since they came from the Saint's own mouth. Gonzalez had a very retentive memory, and immediately committed to writing what he had heard from him, which was the easier as the Saint's recitals were repeated at various times. The first half of the work of Father Gonzalez is in Spanish, the second in Italian. This diversity arises from his having had at Rome a Spanish secretary to whom he dictated the notes he was taking as he obtained them. But having been obliged to leave suddenly for Portugal, he finished his work at Genoa, where he stayed awhile upon his road, and where he had only an Italian secretary at his disposal. The Bollandists* treat at length of this document and how it came to be written, and give it entire in the Latin translation of Father Annibal Codretti ; but it has never been printed in the original.

When I have been obliged to translate some fragments, especially of the letters of St. Ignatius, I have made it a rule to follow as closely as possible the expressions of the original, though the style of writing in the sixteenth century has but little resemblance to the polished phrase of modern times. But it is pleasant to hear historical personages speak in their own words, and these also form an essential element in their true portraiture, which the reader would be sorry to lose.†

---

\* July 7th.

† *French Translator's note.*—I have thought it my duty to imitate the exact fidelity of Father Genelli, and to preserve as much as possible, not only the sense, but the construction and the mannerism of the phrase of St. Ignatius. I have chosen to sacrifice the beauty of a free translation to the preservation of the original, so that the reader in perusing it may recognize, not only the meaning of the author, but his very spirit and way of expressing it. Such is the only merit aimed at in this translation, and I have done it not only out of respect for the great Saint whose life I here give, but for the love of truth, and for the advantage of those readers who like to find in the words of great men, and of Saints especially, the peculiar stamp which distinguishes their character.

# PREFACE OF THE FRENCH TRANSLATOR.

Amongst the most celebrated men of the sixteenth century stands forth prominently St. Ignatius of Loyola, whilst few have exercised a more profound and lasting, and at the same time more beneficial influence upon modern times. All the secret of his greatness lay in his power to discern the wants of the age, and in that genius which foresaw the dangers certain to accrue to the Church from the rise of heresy which was to deny the very basis of her authority. The history of St. Ignatius is the history of the Society which he founded. This was the work of his life; and this is the best title which he has to renown before God and man. But in order to understand the nature of the mission intrusted to him, and the spirit of the Society which he founded, we must take a retrospective view of the times in which it was established and observe narrowly the circumstances which determined the character of his Institute.

Though the Church is ever the Spouse of Christ, without spot, which never admits one shadow of change in the deposit of the truths which He has committed to her to interpret, nor of the inheritance of sanctity and virtues which He has purchased for her at the price of His Blood: yet He permits in His mysterious providence that, according to time and place, she should more prominently develop the truth of virtue of which mankind has then and there more special need, and which is more particularly ignored by the children of men. He commonly makes use for this purpose of some Religious Order, which He animates and penetrates with His Spirit, so that the truth to be imparted to the world shines forth in it brightly and conspicuously. Each one of the Religious Orders may be regarded as a branch of the Church into which the mysterious sap that circulates through the whole living tree flows more freely and abundantly, there to take some special form and throw out some particular fruit of benediction and salvation suitable to each successive age. For God, by an admirable condescension of His love, vouchsafes to accomodate His gifts of grace, not only to our wants, but even to our natural tastes and dispositions, so as to secure for them more easy access to our minds and hearts; and although one and the same in essence, His grace is of all things the most supple in its motions and most varied in the form of its exterior manifestations. So that the Apostle, describing it in its distinctive character and giving it in a manner its own true title, styles it the " multiform grace of God."

Thus in the sixth century, when the West, devastated by the inroad of barbarians, presented everywhere a scene of ruin ; when force had taken the place of right, and the corruption of the expiring Roman Empire was mingled with the rude and savage manners of newly risen and victorious nations ; when the minds of men were most averse to labor and penance, God raised up a man and a Religious Order to recall to a forgetful world this double obligation, to arouse it from the sleep of sloth and inactivity, and to save the sweet germ of gentleness and Christian charity that was in danger of being utterly destroyed amidst the angry passions of incessant war. St. Benedict and the Benedictine Order, his children, **under** the movement of the grace of God and of His

Holy Spirit, saved not only the souls for whose good and everlasting salvation they labored, but they saved civilization also, and may be justly considered as the fathers and founders of the constitutions of modern nations.

Again, in the thirteenth century, when socialism made its first appearance in Europe, and when the poor, having lost the spirit and true glory of their condition, were demanding, in the name of Jesus Christ and of the Gospel, a share in the goods of this world, which they had no longer the wisdom to despise, and were rising in many parts against the rich and powerful, whose baneful example had taught them to set their hopes and affections on the things of this world, then did God confirm His gifts of grace to the fresh exigencies of the times and to the wants of the Church, and raise in its beauty the flower of Evangelical poverty and bid it bloom. In the sight of an astounded world He exhibited its most perfect pattern in that man of sublime simplicity, whose folly confounded the world's wisdom and extorted from it a cry of admiration. To this day the children of St. Francis have retained the same ardent love of poverty which characterized their holy Founder, and still show how truly his lineaments can be distinguished in them. It is remarkable that by the marvellous designs of God each Founder of a Religious Order gives to the family of which he is the parent characteristic features, which neither time nor circumstance can wholly efface. All Religious Orders have not preserved their first fervor, some have needed a reform ; but even in the most relaxed the type imprinted by their Father can be traced, as though it were more indelibly marked than even those which have their source in relationship of flesh and blood. After the lapse of thirteen centuries St. Benedict can recognize his children, and St. Francis after six hundred years can acknowledge his own spiritual family.

At the epoch of the sixteenth century the Church found

itself assailed by one of the most furious tempests it had ever encountered.   It was not merely one of its doctrines that it was called upon to defend, but the very basis and warrant of them all—its own divine authority or infallibility.   If this be once overthrown, faith itself is at an end.   And as faith is the root of supernatural life, the world was in peril of falling back into the darkness and corruption of heathenism, had not God given succor to His Church.   Luther and Calvin, after having exaggerated the effects of original sin, which they held to have made a complete and radical change in human nature, after having stripped reason and free-will of the prerogatives most essential to their being, and having in a thousand ways asserted that the first is involved in such utter darkness that it cannot see the least glimmer of truth, and that the second has not strength to make the slightest movement towards good in co-operation with the grace of God ; after having, in a word, reduced man to the state of a brute beast, they preposterously claimed for him the right of choosing for himself the doctrines which were to regulate all his actions and thoughts. After having made him an inert and passive thing, they put the Bible into his hands and said to him, " Open and read.   What seems to thee good shall be the truth, and what thou likest shall be thy good. "   The contradiction is evident ;  and it is easy to see the logical consequence of so false and absurd a principle.   If a man, in fact, has no power to co-operate with divine grace, either in knowledge of truth or in doing good, if he is reduced to an absolute impotency, and God must do all in him, and even in spite of him, to what purpose is all the working of the Church, with its teaching to aid the weakness of our understanding, and its Sacraments and maternal love to succor our feebleness ?   Why speak to one who has no ears to hear ?   Man's justification is a new creature, and therefore the sole and unaided work of God, which man by his co-operation would only spoil or hinder. Thus were Luther and Calvin forced to the conclusion that the intervention and authority of the Church must be rejected, and thus, whilst degrading man beyond the bounds of truth, they unfettered his pride and made him the arbiter of his own salvation. The authority of the Church once subverted, all other authority must by degrees succumb, and nothing remains at last but the maxim of heathen times—that might is right.

Such were the circumstances of the times in which St. Ignatius was raised up by Almighty God, to exemplify in a special manner, and to personify in the Society which he founded, the practice of that truth of Christian doctrine which heresy had obliterated. The mission of this great man was to restore the principle of authority ignored by the innovators, and to give back to Christian obedience its glory and beauty. Possibly without a full consciousness of the work in which under God he was engaged, but guided by that heavenly light which conducts the Saints, he pursued a method of procedure the very reverse of that of the Reformers. They, in order to shake the authority of the Church, sought to degrade human nature by depreciating its two constituent powers, the reason and the will. St. Ignatius, to rehabilitate the principle of authority, seeks to restore the dignity of humanity ; and, before he asks of his Religious the sacrifice of their judgment and their will in the obedience which he prescribes, he labors to make them understand the value both of the one and the other, that he may thus enhance the value of the sacrifice and its merit. He would have man act in the work of his salvation as if the success entirely depended upon his own exertions, and at the same time he would have him look for all from God, as though he himself were nothing. Taking human nature as it is after the sin of Adam and the Redemption, with its ignorances and its weaknesses, but also with its relics of ancient majesty and with the dignity which Christ has conferred upon it, he would not suppress or stifle any of its constituent elements, but subjecting nature to grace, he would make the first serve to the triumph and the working of the second, and thus confine himself to the correction of its faults, the guidance of its wanderings, the strengthening of its weaknesses, and the development of its capabilities. The maxim that guides him in the direction both of himself and of others, is the sentence of St. Thomas—" That grace does not destroy nature, but perfects it."

It must always be remembered that St. Ignatius addresses Christians whose reason is formed by the teaching of the Church and by its own dictates, and whose will is strengthened both by the operations of grace and by due exercise of its own powers. Having conducted his exercitant by prayer and meditation to the solemn moment when he must choose between God and the world, and having first led him step by step through the whole range of Catholic truths, he leaves him with all the elements of good in him developed, and supplied with all the means which grace and nature can give him, to deliberate in the presence of God and his own conscience upon a choice never to be repented of. This method of proceeding, which seems at first sight derogatory to the power of grace and for the exaltation of nature, does on the contrary, by a slow and gradual, but almost infallible process, break and soften nature, rendering it docile and obedient to grace, while it gives it that force and energy which God does not fail to bestow upon the soul which He has regenerated.

The idea we would represent of St. Ignatius is that of a man who in all his life, and even in his least actions, is perfectly master of himself, always self-possessed, always keeping nature under control, and never for one moment letting it loose. He does not act until he has deliberated long and maturely; he takes no resolution until he has weighed and balanced carefully the reasons for and against it. You would say that he is a man who counts only upon himself, and yet he reckons on nothing but on God. All his deliberations and mental labors were sanctified, assisted, and elevated by prayer, to which he never failed to have recourse in the least difficulty, recommending the matter to God and putting all his confidence wholly in him. His letters and conversation exhibit the same character; they give evidence of the same ruling and sober reason, the calm wisdom which knows always how to keep between the two extremes, and, when directing others, the watchful care to guide in the way most suitable to the given nature, taking account of the dispositions of mind and of the affections, so as to draw these out and develop them to the best issue for the glory of God—that being the sole end which he had before him in all his actions. In his relations with temporal Princes or with Bishops he is always full of respect, always deferential and submissive, refusing them nothing but what his conscience and the rules and end of his Institute do not permit him to accord to them. With regard to the Pope and the Holy See, what more can be said than that he bound his Religious by a special vow to put themselves at the entire disposal of the Sovereign Pontiff, to go whithersoever he should send them.

Such was St. Ignatius; and such was, and is to the present day, the Society which he founded. The resemblance between the Father and the sons is so complete, that the former may be known by beholding the latter. The same spirit, the same method of direction, the same manner of acting, may be traced in them also. Like their Father, the sons of St. Ignatius have ever respected human nature, and have sought, like him, to develop what is good and noble in it, rather than to crush it; they have always taken careful account of individual dispositions, varying their direction according to the differences of character, and endeavoring to bring into play all the several powers of the soul and to engage the whole man in the work of his salvation. In all the disputes which have arisen as to the rights of reason and the power of the human will, they have always warmly advocated the cause of both, and have sought to conciliate opposite opinions by moderate, reasonable, and ingenious explanations, conceding invariably to human nature all that Catholic teaching allows to be given to it. Like their Founder, they have been uniformly the firm supporters of the Holy See ; they have defended its rights with admirable constancy and vigor, both in their writings and in their conduct ; and the manner in which they received the blow which it inflicted on them at the close of the last century is perhaps the most glorious proof of their obedience and devotion to it. They have shown the same fidelity and submission to the Governments which have received them, and history has never found them engaged in the conspiracies plotted against the power of temporal Princes.

The object of Father Genelli has been to show this marvellous resemblance between St. Ignatius and his children, and to prove by facts to the opponents of the Jesuits that they have always remained the same as when they first came forth from the hands of their Founder ; that they have not degenerated ; that they have still his spirit ; that the Constitutions are the same as he made them ; and that they have not been modified, either by Lainez, the Saint's immediate successor, or by Acquaviva, as some have pretended. This object explains the main feature of the book, and distinguishes it from other Lives of St. Ignatius. Wishing to show the resemblance between the Jesuits of the present day and their Founder, he has been obliged to bring out into clear relief the principal traits of his character, so as to give us in some sort his photograph ; and as a person is ordinarily best painted by himself, he has compiled his work in a great measure from the Saint's own letters, many of which have hitherto been unknown.   For the same reason he touches less upon the miracles and the mystical part of the life of St. Ignatius, as serving less directly to the object he has in hand.   Whoever reads this book with an unprejudiced mind will recognize in St. Ignatius the Religious of the Society of Jesus at the present day. For my own part, I openly avow that these have been the characteristic features of those of the Society with whom I have been acquainted in France and elsewhere, and I am happy to be able, while undertaking this trans- lation, to give this public testimony to my admiration of this illustrious Order and of my veneration for its present General. *   The kindness and affection with which he honored me long ago, when he was far from imagining the high honor which awaited him, has left in my mind a remembrance which my heart will cherish as one of the best and sweetest of my earlier life.

CHARLES SAINTE-FOI.

* Father Roothaan.

# THE LIFE

OF

# ST. IGNATIUS OF LOYOLA.

## 𝕿𝖍𝖊 𝕱𝖎𝖗𝖘𝖙 𝕻𝖆𝖗𝖙.

## CHAPTER I.

### THE EARLY LIFE OF ST. IGNATIUS TO THE TIME OF HIS CONVERSION.

THE old Castle of Loyola stood at a little distance from the small town of Azpeytia, in the province of Guipuscoa, and occupied a gently-rising eminence commanding the flat of a narrow vale, enclosed by mountains and watered by the little stream of Urola.   These mountains are rich in iron ore, and the mines are worked by the inhabitants of the two neighboring towns, Azpeytia and Azcoytia, about a mile distant from each other.   The castle was anciently used as a fortress in the wars that frequently raged between the lords of the province, and was only one amongst a number of similar fastnesses.   These were destroyed by order of Henry IV., King of Castile, but the Castle of Loyola escaped the decree of demolition.*   At one time it could boast of a domain so con-

---

\* It came into the possession of the Society of Jesus through the liberality of Anne of Austria, who purchased it from the heirs of the family title, the Margraves of Alcanizes, that a college might be added over which the King should have right of patronage.   Her son, Charles II., confirmed this foundation, but forbade the destruction of the old family castle, which was therefore enclosed within the College buildings, and now adjoins one side of the great church.   No essential change has been made in its interior, but it has been adorned with a magnificence suitable to its present purpose.   In the court-yard opposite

siderable as to form a noble inheritance, which, in the thirteenth century, fell by right of marriage to the ancient family of the Lopez of Recalde, a house which, in wealth and noble blood, ranked among those called in that country the *Parientes Mayores*, or nobles who have the privilege of being invited by the King of Spain himself to render solemn homage to him.

The parents of St. Ignatius were Don Bertram Tañez and Dona Marina of the house of Saenz, of Licona and Balda, whose union God had blessed with eight daughters and three sons. It is not known for certain what precise place in the order of the family St. Ignatius held, but he was the youngest of the sons. The day and month of his birth are also unknown ; but the acts of his life show that he was born in the year 1491. Some authors have stated that his mother, out of humility, chose a stable in which to give him birth ; but this tale is disproved by the Bollandists, from the fact that St. Francis Borgia, as related in the Spanish Life written by Ribadeneira, kissed, during the lifetime of St. Ignatius, the floor of the chamber in which he was born. As the Castle of Loyola was both temporally and spiritually of the town of Azpeytia, he was baptized in the parish church of that

the entrance, where the stables formerly stood, is a chapel and place of interment for the inmates of the College. To the right the staircase leads to a chamber where confessions were heard, and from it a tribune looks into the chapel, in which St. Francis Borgia said his first Mass. The upper story is divided into a sacristy and oratory on the left hand, while on the right is the room in which St. Ignatius lay sick, and which is now a chapel, occupying the whole side of the building towards the town of Azpeytia. It is low, but ornamented with great magnificence, the pavement being laid in marble mosaic-work, the beams of the ceiling being gilt, and the walls covered with frescoes. The present main staircase of the College, on the north side of the old house, pierces the wall by the gateway, and leads to a tribune commanding a view of the chapel by two apertures. The lower portion of the building is of hewn stone, the upper part of brick. Its measurement is fifty-six feet high by fifty-eight feet in width. Above the old entrance gate are the family arms, rudely carved in stone, representing two lions rampant and lambent, having between them a caldron, or something similar, suspended by a chain. The great church, which is circular, is 131 feet in diameter and 200 feet high, and is faced with costly and different colored marbles, but remains still unfinished, giving rise to a common saying of the country : "It will be finished about as soon as the Church of Loyola."
—*Este projecto, se adificara tan pronto come el templo de Loyola.*

place, dedicated to St. Sebastian, and received the name of Eneco, which he changed afterwards for that of Ignatius.*

Ignatius, whilst still a child, was placed with one of his aunts, Doña Maria de Guebara, who resided in the Castle of Arevalo, in the diocese of Avila. He there received a Christian education, and afterwards entered as a page into the Court of Ferdinand the Catholic.

It was there, no doubt, that, according to the customs of the times, he devoted himself to the service of some lady as her knight, and he touches on this circumstance of his life in a passing way in some of his communications, speaking of it as quite a worldly folly, but at the same time saying of this lady that she was "more than a Countess or a Duchess." In such a case Ignatius could not have seriously entertained a hope of marriage ; but as he was of a noble character and incapable of being attracted by anything base, this affection could only have inspired him with a desire of undertaking some grand enterprise, and so lessen, by feats of valor and renown, the distance that lay between him and the lady whom he loved. It contributed, doubtless, to give him that constancy and perseverance of mind which he showed afterwards in so different a career.†

* The name Eneco has been changed by the Spaniards into Inigo, and for this several curious reasons are given. But Eneco and Inigo are the same names, as Father Menchacha proves in his Preface (p. 13) from incontestable documents, and so disposes of what is said by Father Pinius the Bollandist (p. 403, n. iii.), who, without giving any reasons, rejects the name of Eneco. Menchacha derives the word from the old Cantabrian dialect, in which it means "mine own." The name of Ignatius has no connection with these two names, and was before unknown in Spain. The Saint signed his name sometimes Inigo, sometimes Ignatius. All his Latin letters are signed with the latter, but almost all the letters in Spanish are signed with the first name, up to the date 1546, after which the Spanish and Italian letters are both signed with Ignacio but never Ignatio. He took the name of Ignatius out of reverence and devotion to the holy Martyr St. Ignatius, Bishop of Antioch, as he himself declares to St. Francis Borgia, in a letter written in the year 1546.

† Without wishing to risk conjecture, I cannot help remarking that, at the time spoken of, there were at the Court of Spain only two ladies to whom the Saint's words could apply. Of these one was the young widow of Ferdinand the Catholic, who died January 23, 1516, cousin of Foix, and daughter of the Viscount John of Narbonne, and

It is not surprising that at this time he wrote some poetry ; and although the greater portion of his lays and sonnets were addressed to the lady to whom he was attached, yet religion found a place in his affections by the side of the profane Muse, and inspired him to compose an entire poem in honor of St. Peter, to whom he was to render a more lasting service in the persons of his successors than the perpetuity of his verse, of which no piece remains.*  Attention to such objects as these preserved him from many dissipations to which young persons at Courts are exposed when left to follow their own inclinations.  Amongst other things it is told of him that he never gave himself to gambling, that ruling passion among Spaniards.  On the other hand, he delighted in reading *Amadis de Gaul,* a wearisome romance in twenty-four books, and other tales of chivalry, to the rage for which, as well as to the influence they exerted in Spain, Cervantes has long since put an end.  It is also said, with great likelihood, that Ignatius was very expert in all the accomplishments of war and chivalry.

He probably passed his time in this way at Court till the age of twenty-six, for he does not seem to have achieved anything of note before that time.  He then, however, attached himself to the household of his kinsman, Don Antonio Manrique, Duke of Najera, under whom he had first learned to carry arms, and who was

Mary, sister of Louis XII. of France.  The other was the Princess Catherine, born in 1507, who was the Daughter of Queen Joanna, but lived entirely secluded from the Court.

---

* A sonnet, attributed in Spain to St. Ignatius, and which Menchacha also says is his, probably is of a later date.  We give a translation of it for the benefit of the reader—

> 'Tis not the joys of Heaven to prove,
> My God, that fires my heart with love ;
> Nor fear that keeps me, lest I dwell,
> A sinner, in the flames of hell ;
> It is Thy Cross, on which I see
> That pierced Thou art and nailed for me,
> Until Thy death upon the tree.
> Thy love is still my soul within,
> Though Heaven were none for me to win ;
> Thy fear does in my bosom reign,
> Although there were no hell of pain.
> I love Thee and I love Thee so,
> That all beside I can forego ;
> And I would love Thee as I love,
> Though I had naught to hope above.

now the Viceroy of Navarre. Ferdinand had wrested this province from its rightful sovereign, John III., to unite it to the crown of Spain. But immediately after the death of Ferdinand and under the regency of Cardinal Ximenès, John endeavored, with the aid of France, to recover this kingdom, the greater part of the inhabitants of which were favorable to him. He besieged S. Juan Pied de Port, but Ximenès quickly sent troops thither under the command of Villalva, who beat and drove back the French. Ximenès then dismantled all the petty castles and fortresses of Navarre, that the enemy might have no place to hold, and began to fortify Pampeluna, and by this wise measure he continued to preserve Navarre to Spain. Ignatius had taken part in this expedition, and so entered upon his first campaign, and mention is made in particular of his attack upon the little town of Najara, on the frontiers of Biscaya. Courageous in battle, he was never greedy of plunder, and took no part in the pillage of the town after it had been taken by storm. Renown was what he sought, and success seemed to crown his hopes. Soon a more favorable opportunity of distinction offered itself, and to understand the whole affair we must recall in brief the circumstances which led to it.

The young King Charles had brought with him from the Low Countries, in the year 1517, his advisers and an army of mercenaries, who treated Spain as a conquered country, wounding the national pride by their oppressions, as they had the Government in their own hands. Ximenès, too, had deprived the nobles of many of their rights and exorbitant privileges, and had made use of the towns to humble them the more. They, however, remained quiet, though partaking of the general discontent against the strangers. But when Charles, having become in 1520 Emperor of Germany, being desirous of quitting Spain, demanded considerable subsidies of the Cortes, which he had assembled, contrary to custom, at Compostella instead of Valladolid, the burgesses of the great towns, jealous of their privileges, began to stir up opposition, and demand redress of their grievances before they granted the supplies. As, however, the majority of the Cortes was in favor of the King, he left without paying any attention to the complaints made to him. Upon this disturbances broke out at Segovia, and Cardinal Adrian, Governor of Valladolid, sent troops under the command of Ronquillo against the town. These were defeated by John de Padilla, who alone of the high nobility had, along with Don Pedro of Giron, taken the side of the towns, and, to retrieve this loss, fresh troops were sent under the command of Antonio Fonseca. The latter, having reduced Medina del Campo to ashes, by this outrage drove the other towns to form an alliance at Avila, under the name of the Holy Junta, which dismissed Adrian as a foreigner, and made itself master of the person of Queen Joanna at Tordesillas. This body then removed its seat from Avila to the latter place, and undertook the Government in the name of that unfortunate Princess. Charles offered pardon to the rebels if they would lay down their arms, but summoned to the defence of the throne the nobles who had hitherto remained tranquil. He appointed at the same time, as assistants to the Governor, Don Frederigo Enriquez and the Constable of Castile, Don Inigo de Velasco, with all the powers necessary to crush the rebellion. The Junta responded by a manifesto declaring its grievances, some of which were well founded, though others were dictated by the bigotry of the burgesses and by a revolutionary spirit. The nobility, seeing clearly that its destruction was designed, took part with the King, whom it had hitherto held in but little esteem, from its dislike to the foreigners. The Regency gathered all its troops, especially from Navarre, at Rio Seco, the seat of Government, and gave the command of them to the Count de Haro, the Constable's son, who, by a bold march, surprised Tordesillas, and got possession of the Queen Joanna, with a considerable number of the members of the Junta. This was a death-blow to the rebels, who thus lost the moral support of the Queen's name, and suffered all the evil consequences of being mere numbers without a head. Compelled to give battle, they were completely worsted by Don Haro near Villalva, on the 23d of April, 1521, and Padilla was taken and executed the following day, with two other ringleaders. A few days after the greater part of the army marched towards Navarre, which the French had entered without resistance, and had already passed the frontiers of Castile, being invited by the rebels to Toledo.

Their entry had been brought about by the following circumstances. Charles had concluded, on the 13th of August, 1516, a treaty at Noyon with Francis I., King of France, by which he bound himself to recover the rights of the heirs of John d'Albert or De Brit, and in case he gave them no satisfaction Francis was to aid them with all his power. In consequence of this treaty the heirs of John had often demanded back the kingdom that belonged to them, but in vain ; and so, when Francis began war against Charles V., his army entered Navarre in the name of Henry d'Albert. It was a favorable moment, for the towns in rebellion against Charles wished well to his enterprise, the country was denuded of troops, and the whole population well disposed to the family which had been dispossessed. But the commander of this expedition, Andrew de Foix de l'Esparre, kinsman of Henry, was not capable of conducting it, being but a young man. He made himself, it is true, within a few days master of all the open country, and advanced to the walls of Pampeluna, the fortifications of which, only commenced by Ximenès, were not yet very complete, and were supplied with neither artillery nor troops sufficient for their defence. He quickly took this town, and would have pushed on further, but having unadvisedly encountered the army of Castile, he was routed and made prisoner, along with the principal officers of his force, and thus lost all the country he had conquered within less time than he had taken to gain it.

Returning now to St. Ignatius, we do not know whether he had been engaged at first in combating the rebels in Castile, and then went to succor Pampeluna, upon the attack of the French, or whether he was already posted at that place. The wavering disposition of the inhabitants and the desperate condition of the small Spanish garrison sufficiently explain why the magistrates did not think of defence, but considered this a favorable opportunity for securing the best terms for themselves by a voluntary surrender, and so regaining their nationality by the return of their ancient royal family, the more so as Spain did not seem to be in a condition to recover what the victorious enemy had gained by conquest. But Ignatius was not of this opinion, and knowing how important it was that the citadel should hold out until the arrival of the Viceroy, he had resolved on resistance. As he could not single-handed defend the town, on account of the disposition of the inhabitants, he tried to persuade the Commandant of the fortress at least to stand on the defensive, and gave him such good reasons for it that he brought him completely over to his side, and, in opposition to the advice of all the other gentlemen present, it was resolved to hold out against the French, although the want of resources afforded but little hope, and had given rise to the adverse opinion. The enemy, having got possession of the town itself without opposition, then summoned the citadel to surrender, and prepared to assault it with vigor. The Commandant decided upon a parley, and went to the quarters of the French General, accompanied by three others, one of whom was Ignatius. The besiegers, knowing that the fortress could not hold out long, and wishing to strike more terror into their enemies, laid upon them the hardest conditions. Even these, however, the Spaniards would have accepted, had it not been for the vehement remonstrances of Ignatius. The conditions were refused, and they had to prepare themselves for a fierce assault from the enemy, all the more enraged at the rejection of the terms proposed. Upon the commencement of the siege, Ignatius, as was often done by the brave knights of the middle ages when in danger of death, made a confession, as he himself tells us, to one of his companions in arms—a gentleman like himself, with whom he had often engaged in combat, probably in tournaments. This confession, made to a layman in default of a priest, was an act of penance and humiliation, and shows that the warriors of those times did not consider it a weakness to think of their soul in the hour of danger. The attack and the defence were both alike hotly contested. The French endeavored to open a breach with their cannon, and then mount and take the place by storm. The wall was already crumbling and about to fall under the fire of their artillery, at the very spot where Ignatius stood fighting with the courage of a lion and with no intention of retreat, when* a ball of the enemy, passing between his legs, broke the front bone of the right leg and severely wounded him in the flesh of the left one. He fell, and with him fell the courage of the defenders of the citadel, so that the French quickly made themselves masters of it. But the valor with which he had fought in the defence of his post won for him the admiration of his enemies, and instead of treating him as a prisoner, they carried him to his quarters in the town, where he remained some twelve or fifteen days, attended by the French physicians.

The date of an event so important in its consequences was the 20th of May, the second day in Pentecost week, not the 19th, as was believed before the time of the Bollandists, for in the year 1521 Easter Day fell upon the 31st of March. The fortress which St. Ignatius had so gallantly defended was afterwards demolished, but in remembrance of this action a chapel, dedicated to St. Ignatius, was subsequently built upon the site, as may be seen by an inscription on the wall, showing that, in place of the chapel, there had been previously a memorial of another form, and that the chapel could not have been erected prior to the year 1606.

The state of Ignatius' wound required more exact care than he could receive at Pampeluna, in the midst of strangers. He had reason a second time for gratitude to his captors, as they gave him permission to retire to his own country, and had him conveyed thither in a litter. Whether it was that his journey was undertaken too soon, or that the bandages had not been well put on, it was found on examination that the parts of the broken bone were not adhering straight together, and the surgeons declared that the bone must be broken again before the parts could be replaced in their natural position. Ignatius consented and endured this terrible

---

* Gonzalez does not speak of a spent ball as Bartoli does.

operation without any other sign of pain than that of clenching his hands. But his health, instead of mending, grew worse; fever followed, along with such weakness and loss of appetite that he was reduced to great extremity. Made acquainted with the danger in which he lay, he wished to prepare himself for death by receiving the last Sacraments. On the eve of the Feast of SS. Peter and Paul the physicians declared that there was no hope unless a change for the better took place that night. The crisis, in fact, occurred at midnight, and by the aid of St. Peter, to whom he always had special devotion, and who, as all the historians of his life assert, appeared to him, promising that he should recover, his cure began. From that moment a sensible change for the better showed itself, and the wound healed up. Still, it was afterwards found that, from the mismanagement of the physicians, one of the reunited bones overlapped the other, so that the right leg was shorter than the left, while he could not walk without halting, nor even stand straight upon both feet. A disfigurement so painful to a man of the world, and one who wished to cut a figure in it, was deemed insupportable by the ardent temperament of Ignatius. He inquired of the surgeons whether any remedy could be found. They replied that they knew of no other than to cut away the protruding bone, but that the operation would be exceedingly painful. As, however, he feared nothing so much as to appear in his deformed state before the eyes of the world, he submitted with unheard-of constancy to the martyrdom he had determined to endure, not even allowing himself to be tied, and held his leg without wincing under the saw, so that his brother, Don Martin, who was present, declared in astonishment that he himself could never have had the courage to undergo such pain. This operation took away, it is true, the crookedness of the limb, but could not prevent one leg from being shorter than the other, and though Ignatius put himself for a long time to the torture of having it stretched out by machinery, yet, in spite of everything, he remained a little lame all his life.

Whilst remaining so long an invalid time hung heavily

on his hands, and he sought for some amusement suitable to the disposition of his mind. He regarded the apparition of St. Peter and the cure which followed it as an especial favor from Heaven, intended rather to enable him to continue the life which he had hitherto pursued than to suggest his changing it for another. This view filled him with new hopes, and he was very far from suspecting the true designs of Providence with regard to him, even at the moment when they were on the point of being actually begun in him. He, on the contrary, gave himself up for whole hours to the reveries of his imagination, and to the dreams of happiness with which it supplied him. He says of himself that the thought of the lady of his affections incessantly occupied his mind, and that for three or four hours together he represented to himself how he would soon go to see her, how he would address her, and what mots * or pleasantries he would discourse of with her, and the feats of arms he would perform in her presence. In order to entertain more fully these agreeable fancies he asked for books of knight-errantry, but as none were to be found in the Castle of Loyola, they gave him instead the life of Jesus Christ and of the Saints. †

We may easily suppose that this style of reading would not be very agreeable to one who was thinking only of diverting himself, since the lives set before him could only recall lessons of mortification and self-abnegation. St. Ignatius tells us little of this important period of his life, nor explains at all how the thought of changing his life and of imitating the Saints, whose histories he read, was suggested to his mind. He only speaks of the difference he found between thoughts of the world and those suggested by faith. He says that, when the hopes and pictures of the world had charmed his phantasy for a while, upon their disappearance they left behind them a certain void, a trouble, and an interior discontent, which he did not find when he thought of the imitation of the Saints, for that then, on the contrary, he felt an un-

* A *mot* is a saying with a double or hidden meaning.
† The title of the book was *The Lives of the Saints in Romaunt,* that is to say, in the old Castilian tongue.

speakable calm and peace ; that during a considerable time he did not remark this difference, but having one day observed it he gave it his deep attention.  From the effects he proceeded to examine the causes, and thus learned to distinguish the different spirits that acted upon his soul.

It seems certain that, after this, the reading of these books speedily made an impression on the mind of Ignatius, for he very soon began to think of renouncing the world, notwithstanding all the ties and strong inclinations which bound him to it.  Although the accounts of his life give us very few precise dates of the rise and progress of this interior change leading him on to a supernatural life, yet we may endeavor in the following way to trace how it was brought about.  He is in love with a lady whom he cannot hope to espouse.  The affection is a pure one, which inspires noble thoughts and high desires to distinguish himself by actions of renown ; it preserves him from many falls, at an age which is liable to be led astray by its passions.  In the midst of his plans and his hopes he is struck by a cannon-ball, which leaves his life, but disfigures him.  With his heart still full of his former inclinations, he tries every means to be rid of the deformity, and endures intolerable pains that he may realize his prospects of earthly happiness. But all these incidents come to him from a supporting hand above, which he does not yet recognize, and which is guiding him, though his will is tending in quite an opposite direction.  It is in the midst of this very struggle between the wishes of his heart and the exterior circumstances which prevent their accomplishment, that a new life wakens within him from the perusal of a book. But with the dawn of this life commences also within him an intestine war.

Those who have experienced it know what sufferings it causes and what a sacrifice it requires, simply to give up *hopes*, for does not the happiness of man in this world consist in a great measure in hopes ?  Ignatius had sought an earthly happiness, which had fled before him, enticing him on anew by treacherous illusions of which he never saw the realization.  The lives of the Saints made him acquainted with another kind of happiness, that gives all that it promises, which makes us rich by foregoing all superfluities, and happy by renouncing ourselves. He had hitherto dreamed only of battles, love, and earthly glory. Suddenly the hand of God arrests him in his career, and discovers to him a new world which he had not so much as thought of. He is introduced into the new lore of the high deeds of the warriors of God. There also he finds love, but a love pure and disinterested, the imperishable love of God, which raises its sweetest songs amid those pains and sorrows that prove it, and which, kindling its heavenly sparks in the hearts of these holy men, and inflaming them with celestial fire, drives them to the solitude of the desert, there to cultivate their souls and make them a garden of virtues ; while the world, with its selfishness and egotism, renders the soul a wilderness.

But here too there is war of another kind—the spiritual combat ; a struggle, not between two forces which, if equal, can make a compromise, or two friends who may be reconciled, but between two parties whose enmity is to the death, and whose opposition is complete. The prize of victory is the heart of man, and the combatants are good and evil, light and darkness, the kingdom of God and the kingdom of Satan. Two adversaries these of which the one is Life and gives it, the other, so far from giving the life which it has not to give, quenches it. The histories of the Saints taught him the science of this battle of life, and how to gain the victory, and he saw that there is no other glory but the glory which makes the soul pure and like to God, for there is no other that is immortal.

No sooner had St. Ignatius grasped in his mind this principle of a new life, than he read these books, not with indifference, but with the most lively interest. The thoughts which had before engrossed his mind vanished in proportion as the new ideas arising in it became more vivid. But grace, like nature, does nothing by sudden starts or by violence; it does not create new elements, but makes use of those which it finds ; it develops them and grows with them. The moment that Ignatius had discovered by their effects the difference between his former thoughts and those which had taken their place, he cast this light in reflection upon his past life, and took good note of the end to which he was tending. His reflections freed him from many illusions, and served at the same time to confirm him in the new path he had taken, and this the more rapidly in that he had naturally a vigorous intellect and a determined will. Thus to the regret for the past was added an ardent desire to lead another life for the future, of which he saw before him the model in the lives of the Fathers of the desert and in the Saints, in those especially who had been distinguished for their austere penitence; and this feeling was in complete accordance with the degree to which he had arrived in the progress of spiritual life.

The conversion of St. Ignatius is full of instruction, because it was not the effect either of a sudden emotion of the heart, or of any exterior event, but was the result of the internal strife of two contending principles—the world, namely, and the kingdom of God, and it is only after maturely weighing the nature of both of these, that he decides for the latter. Now it is this mental process which most completely transforms the whole man, and elevates him to the highest degree of spiritual growth in the Christian sense of the word, and so we find in it the main outlines of the *Spiritual Exercises,* which wholly turn upon the choice of the paths to pursue. The economy of divine grace is none the less admirable and instructive as seen in this event, and as exhibiting its power to draw such important issues from beginnings apparently so inconsiderable. The little ray of light, which gave St. Ignatius an insight into the difference between heavenly and earthly affections, was to him like the grain of mustard-seed in the Gospel, which grew with him, and became in the experiences of his after-life a great tree.

The extraordinary ways by which God was calling him were accompanied with remarkable circumstances and phenomena, that convinced him how direct was the interference from Heaven, and how Providence was working in him its own mysterious designs. In fact, no sooner had the important moment passed in which the human will weighs and deliberates before deciding, and in which St. Ignatius had fully fixed his resolve in favor of God and of His service, than he entered immediately upon ways where God took him, so to speak, by the hand, and Himself became his director, a favor that was to be declared to him by sensible manifestation. One night, as he was praying with more than usual fervor before the picture of our Lady, and was offering himself with tears to God through her hands, he felt the shock of an earthquake shake violently the house, and especially the chamber in which he was, so that the wall was rent asunder, and the frames of his windows were broken. It pleased God to give him a sign that He accepted his offering, and that he would make use of him for His glory, as indeed was confirmed by the result which followed, and corresponded exactly with what was taking place in his interior ; for he too had been completely moved and transformed by what had passed within him, and was changed both in soul and body. The combat was over, and the world was conquered within him, and divine consolations began to visit him. From this time forward he felt within a power that urged him to disentangle himself from all earthly ties that united him to the world, in order that his life without might correspond to the state of his soul within.

A sweet vision closed this period of his purgative life. His true Benefactress and the real object of his affections, she who had assisted him all the while in an invisible manner, and as a mother had led him by the hand, now showed herself to him to teach him how much he owed to her, how much she had done for him. Our Blessed Lady appeared to him one night with the Child Jesus in her arms, and remained some time visible before him without speaking to him, but still long enough to fill his heart with the sweetness of her presence. On leaving him, she conferred upon him a still greater benefit, for he was henceforth so confirmed in the grace given him, that all earthly inclinations of sense were extinguished in him, and he was preserved for the remainder of his life in angelical purity.

For the future Ignatius was to walk in the path in which alone we can truly follow the footsteps of the God made Man; and as the Son of God concealed His glory, in order that He might take upon Himself the humiliations prompted by His love, together with the miseries and the chastisements which we have deserved; as the Son of God, when ministering to us, would be clothed in no human dignity or state, but left all that is in heaven or on earth to win for us eternal happiness, so he also that would be His disciple must divest himself of all that can divide his heart.   In the grade of the spiritual life to which Ignatius had then attained, grace imparts to the soul the desire of penitence and retirement in solitude, in order to purify itself more by penitential tears, and to hasten the development of the germ of the new life which it has received.   But in the state of excitement in which he was, he could not resolve upon his future course with certainty ; and so for the present he thought of nothing more than making a pilgrimage to the Holy Land, that he might give himself to a penitential life in imitation of Our Lord.   He proposed on his return to enter into the Carthusian monastery of Seville, and there live unknown in the continual practice of mortification. His resolve on this point was still hesitating, as he feared he might not be permitted to give himself up to penance so much as he desired.   However, he commissioned a servant of the house, who was going to Burgos, to obtain exact information of the Rule of the Chartreuse.   And although the information which the servant brought back to him pleased him, as he himself relates, it did not lead him to the full execution of his purpose, but only to a sincere reciprocal amity between St. Ignatius and his own Order, and the children of St. Bruno.

Notwithstanding the care which he took to conceal from others what was passing in his soul, the retirement in which he lived, his prayers, and meditations, and spiritual colloquies, drew upon him the notice of those about him.   Instead of vain and worldly pastimes as before, he was only occupied in reading pious books and noting down the lights he received in prayer.   His chief delight was to gaze upon the heavens at night spangled with stars, and by the beauty of the visible to raise his thoughts to the invisible world, or to fly thither on the wings of prayer, where his heart desired to be. This practice was always dear to him, and he was seen often in his later years to lift his eyes to heaven and weep at the sight for joy, saying, " Oh, how vile this earth seems when I look on Heaven." Such was the first preparation of St. Ignatius to obey the call of God, who designed by means of him to recall a great number of souls to the Gospel truths. This was his first Exercise, and the foundation of those that followed. It was his spiritual awakening, and wherein he received light to understand that the end of man is not to serve the creature but God the Creator, and Him alone.

# CHAPTER II.

THE spring of the year 1522 had come, when Ignatius found himself well enough to undertake a journey. He therefore declared to his eldest brother, Don Martin Garzia, as head of the family, his intention of leaving Loyola, to pay a visit to the Duke of Najera. His family had, without doubt, ere this observed the change which had taken place in him, but they had kept silence until he himself should avow it. As he avoided doing so, his friends thought that they ought no longer to conceal their suspicions. Accordingly his elder brother considered it his duty to caution him against doing anything to the prejudice of the honor of the family, or of his own happiness. Don Martin, who could not be aware of what had passed in his brother's interior, looked upon things from the point of worldly fame and human prudence, and according to this view the observations which he deemed it his duty to make to Ignatius were just, although applicable only to ordinary cases, and not to his, whose unusual conduct was justified by supernatural motives. Judging of things from what ordinarily takes place, he supposed that his brother, who had hitherto advanced so courageously in the career of honor, was now disgusted by the misfortunes that had befallen him, and in order to escape them wished to pass, perhaps, in a cloister a life of greater tranquillity, but, as it seemed to him, of less glorious renown. Possibly the servant who had gone to Burgos had let slip in some degree the commission intrusted to him. Moreover, as Ignatius had hitherto been unacquainted with studies, his brother might fear, and with reason, the dangers that a man without

46

science and education for such a vocation might meet with in this new career.   However, he could do no more than represent these things to him, and as they made no impression on Ignatius, he was obliged to be content with the general assurance that he was aware of his duty, and that he would never do anything unworthy of his ancestors, or likely to tarnish the honor of his family. The Saint added that he thought himself bound to present himself to the Duke of Najera after his recovery, as he certainly must have heard of it.

Ignatius then took leave of his relatives, his brother accompanying him as far as Onate, where one of his sisters resided.   Ignatius passed the night in prayer in the church of Our Lady of Arancuz, and after having made his thanksgiving to the Blessed Virgin and commended himself to her, he departed the same night for Navarette, leaving his brother at Onate.   At Navarette, the residence of the Duke, his kinsman, he obtained a sum of money due to him from a person in the household, and after paying some debts he owed, with the remainder he caused an image to be made of the Blessed Virgin. These affairs settled, he took leave of his kinsman and sent back the two retainers who had attended on him. Then he continued his journey alone, mounted on a mule, being still too weak to travel on foot, and directed his way towards the Monastery of Our Lady of Mont Serrat.   He was inflamed with the desire of doing great things for God Our Saviour Jesus Christ, and as he himself afterwards declared, in the numerous and painful penances which he proposed, and which in fact he inflicted on himself, he had in view not so much the expiation of his sins (although he did not suppose that he had no more need of penance) as the desire to render himself pleasing to God, and to give a proof to Him by them of his earnest devotion and love.   As to the practice of this virtue with the heart, and the regulation or measure of its external manifestation, he as yet knew nothing.*   The spirit of chivalry and romance was still uppermost in his thoughts, and it was only by little and little that he laid aside this idea.

* Gonzalez, chap. iii.

While he travelled alone, engaged in his meditations, he was accosted by a man of the unbelieving Moorish race, which had once occupied almost the whole of Spain, and which, though subjugated, still remained in considerable numbers in the southern and western parts of the Peninsula, Christians in outward show, but secretly followers of Mahomet. The two travellers having saluted one another, and Ignatius having told the Moor the place whither he was going, they entered into a discussion concerning the Blessed Virgin. Though the Moor admitted that she had conceived without the loss of her virginity, he denied that she remained a virgin after the birth of her Son. Ignatius, as a good Catholic, could not comprehend how, in matters of faith, it was possible to admit one portion of the truth and reject another, and tried in vain to bring him to a better state of mind by reasons and comparisons, speaking with such vehemence that his opponent, who saw with what sort of a person he had to deal, deemed it prudent to take himself off, and so without a word more suddenly turned aside to a town that was near. Well was it for him that he did so, as Ignatius was on the point of taking him more seriously to task than he ought perhaps to have done, or than the other could have imagined. Scarce had the Moor left him, than, indignant at the blasphemy spoken against the Holy Virgin, he doubted whether he ought not even then to hasten in pursuit of him and wash out the injury in his blood. This, as he soon reflected, was to act more like the knight-errant than the apostle, and so a conflict arose within him, his feelings on the one side urging him to punish the guilty upon his own private authority, whilst reason told him on the other that he had no right to do so, and between these he knew not how to decide. In his doubt he resolved to leave the matter to God ; and having arrived at a place where two ways parted, one of which led into the town whither the Moor had gone, he let fall the bridle on the mule's neck, and left it to choose which way to go. " If it takes the road," he thought, " which the blasphemer has gone, it is a token that I ought to pursue and punish him." The mule, however, took the way towards the mountain, and thus his conscience was set at rest, and he continued his journey without further thought of vengeance. As he had been unable to lay aside an erroneous judgment based upon the interests of faith, he could not have done better than call the faith to his aid, and remit the matter into the hands of God. At the same time such a line cannot always be justified, but Ignatius' late difficulty arose merely from a false principle which he had assumed. The whole question, however, has a deeper root springing from the very bottom of the human heart. In each one of our acts we are compelled to choose, and it is not always easy to discern the true from the false. He who decides for himself is often deceived, because the human understanding cannot foresee all the consequences of an action, cannot always seize upon the proper means or the right time. On the contrary, man would often make the circumstances shape and bend to his own design, and thus fall foul of his own imagined wisdom. Most men act upon present impulse, or upon vague and uncertain feelings ; those who are clear-sighted and spiritual minded prove and examine all, it is true, but yet are not wholly guided by their own light, they ask it of Him Who sees the future or what might be in futurity, as well as that which is now present. This, perhaps, is the deep moral of the conduct of St. Ignatius on this occasion; it is thus that he acted in his after-life. Hence his maxim that we ought to employ all our powers as if everything depended on ourselves, and at the same time leave all to God, as if we could do nothing.

On his approach to Mont Serrat, Ignatius procured in a neighboring place the dress of a pilgrim, as being best suited to his design. It was a long vesture of coarse texture, with a cord for a girdle, and hempen shoes, after the fashion of the country, together with a pilgrim's staff and shell. After having laid these new accoutrements upon the housings of his mule, he took his way to the Church of Our Lady.

Mont Serrat is a lofty mountain, standing alone, and distant a day's journey from Barcelona. Underneath its highest peaks, on a plateau, is situated the well-known church, which is at once a place of pilgrimage and a

Benedictine abbey.  Its summit is composed of several ridges, ranged like teeth, which give it from a distance the appearance of a saw, and hence its name.  A steep staircase cut in the rock leads to the peaks, which have been levelled at the top.  There were formerly fifteen cells, with chapels attached, for that number of anchorites belonging to the monastery below.  On the rocky soil, at the expense of much labor, the monks had found means to cultivate some small beds of flowers and odoriferous plants.*  The rule and monastic discipline were then very exactly observed, and mention is particularly made of one among the monks, a French priest, who had come there when young upon a pilgrimage and had embraced the religious state in the monastery.  He was named, according to the Spanish way of pronouncing it, Chanones, and lived to the age of eighty-eight, in a manner edifying and useful both to his brethren in the convent and the faithful in general.  Ignatius, who wished to begin his new career with a general confession of his whole life, took for his director this holy man of so great experience in spiritual things.  He not only confessed to him with abundance of tears the sins of all his life, but communicated to him his designs and his plan of life to which, according to the light given him, he believed himself called ; for this he as yet had done to no one.†  This affair, so important for his soul, occupied him three whole days.  He also agreed with his confessor that, leaving his mule for the use of the convent, he should suspend his sword and dagger near the altar in the church :‡ and from this it is clear that his confessor approved of his resolution as coming from God, as well as the motives which actuated it.

Ignatius himself tells us that the idea of keeping the night-watch of arms, as practised by the knights of old according to the laws of chivalry before receiving their

---

* The present state of this famous monastery is sadly notorious. Spoiled of its wealth and ornaments, it is merely a deserted ruin with its few inmates.  There is nothing left of its ancient splendor but its magnificent situation, of which no hand of the plunderer could rob it.

† Gonzalez.  Quoted in the Bollandists, n. 17.

‡ This sword was afterwards removed to the Jesuit College at Barcelona, and kept in the sacristy.

spurs, came to his mind from his recollections of the romance of Amadis de Gaul. Being at Mont Serrat at the time of the feast of the Annunciation, he chose the eve of that festival for the purpose, and passed the night in watching and prayer before the altar, in honor of the great mystery of the Incarnation, wherein Mary became Mother of God most high. He took for his apparel this night, not the rich coat of arms of a noble knight, but the habit of a poor penitent man, after having given to a mendicant his rich dress, the last remaining mark that he had of the world. Wrapped in a cloth of coarse serge, and girded with a cord, his head and feet bare except a hempen shoe upon his right foot, which was not yet perfectly healed, and supporting himself with his staff, both when kneeling and standing, he forgot entirely Inigo de Loyola, and put on, so to speak, another person in the poor unknown pilgrim, as he styles himself, and so departed at break of day, after receiving holy Communion.

A memoir left by a certain John Pasquale, and published by the Bollandists,* explains to us how Ignatius passed thence to Manresa. Pasquale tells us in this memoir that his mother, Agnes Pasquale, residing at Barcelona, was then staying for some object at Manresa, and that she often went in pilgrimage to Mont Serrat, especially on Sundays, as it was only nine miles from Manresa, nor did she fail to be there on the feast of the Annunciation. She was returning in company with three women and two other young persons, when about midday, near the Chapel of the Holy Apostles, lower down the mountain, she fell in with a young man in a coarse pilgrim's dress, who was below the middle height, but of a striking appearance and modest engaging manners, and whose eyes were almost always cast downwards with a remarkably chaste expression. He seemed to be tired, and walked lame. He inquired of her whether there was any hospital in those parts to which he might go. Agnes was immediately touched with a deep sentiment of respect and compassion for him, and answered that the nearest hospital was at Manresa, where she was staying, at three leagues' distance from thence ; that if he would

* N. 45.

follow them they would give him hospitality and take care of him in the best manner they could. The pilgrim accepted the offer with gratitude. They continued their journey at a slow pace, that Ignatius might follow them, for he had refused the offer of an ass to ride on. It is probable that at this time the following circumstance occurred: An officer of justice came in haste after him, and questioned him whether it was he who had given a rich suit of clothes to a poor mendicant, as the man asserted, adding that he had been put in prison because his story was not believed. Ignatius, much distressed to find that his charity had brought this affliction on the beggar, assured the officer that he had given him the clothes, but refused to answer when questioned further about himself and about his motive in what he had done.

When the travellers came near the little town of Manresa, Agnes sent on the pilgrim with one of her companions, who was a manager of the hospital, and recommended him to special care, she herself sending him food from her own table. The hospital was named St. Lucy's, from the neighboring church, and was distant about forty yards from the town. This latter is situated on the banks of the Cardenero, a stream that flows into the Llobregat, or Red River, and at that time contained somewhat less than three thousand inhabitants, though it had once been the seat of a bishopric. The appearance of Ignatius at Manresa caused unusual sensation, as the story of what he had done at Mont Serrat had received many embellishments, and the most strange and extravagant reports of his fortune and condition had been spread. * It would be hard to imagine why St. Ignatius stopped at this place instead of departing immediately for Jerusalem, did we not know that besides his intended pilgrimage he had the design of going to hide himself in a desert to practise penance, after the example of the Fathers of old. It mattered little to him where the place was, provided he was unknown and undisturbed, and as he found what he wanted at Manresa, he had no need to seek any further. The manner of his life there was as follows. Every day he devoutly heard

* Gonzalez.

Mass, and attended at Vespers and Compline, and went to Communion regularly every Sunday. He set apart in particular seven hours for prayer, which he always made upon his knees, and these he divided between day and night. He allowed but very little time for sleep, and had for his bed the bare ground, for his pillow a stone or a piece of wood. As soon as he rose, he scourged himself to blood, and this he repeated three times a day, and sometimes oftener. He begged his food day by day, eating only once, and selecting by preference the hardest and blackest crusts ; his only drink was a glass of water. On Sundays he added a glass of wine and some vegetables, which he sprinkled, as he one day admitted to Father Lainez, with ashes to make them more unpalatable. Under his garb of coarse stuff he wore a hairshirt next his body, to which he afterwards added an iron chain as a girdle. He sought, moreover, to act in direct opposition to all he had hitherto loved and desired. For example, he took pleasure in the company of children and the poor, and imitated their expressions and actions. He served the sick in the hospital, choosing out those who had the most loathsome disorders, or the most disagreeable humors. He joined the company of beggars, neglecting his person and letting his hair grow and his beard get disordered ; but all he could do, he could not pass himself off for one of them, but, as is inevitable in such a case, received only jeers and laughter for attempting it. The children cried after him in the street when he appeared, " Here comes the man in sackcloth ! " and followed him with mockery and derision.

This was the very thing he sought, and he knew how to turn it all to the most exalted purpose, taking his delight not in these things themselves but in the virtues which they gave him occasion to practise. He bore with patience not only the contempt which was of his own seeking, but that which came upon him from an unexpected source, which was a much more trying test in a character so fiery and so sensitive in point of honor. An idle young man, from the natural opposition of vice to virtue, conceived against him so violent a hatred that he endeavored, not only to make him pass for a hypo-

crite, but turned into ridicule his whole manner and
behavior, and after thus making game of him, loaded
him with every species of abuse.  This conduct he
repeated every time Ignatius entered the town ; and
when we remember the former life of the Saint, we cannot sufficiently admire his heroic virtue in conquering
himself under such circumstances.  On one occasion,
while he was in the hospital attending the sick, the
sensibilities of nature awakened for a moment to show
what strength still remained in them, had they not been
brought into subjection to grace.  He felt suddenly an
unconquerable aversion to all that is most painful to
sense—the ill-humor, the rude manners, the disgusting
maladies, and the coarse habits of the mendicants.  But
reflecting at once that it was the love of God which had
from the first led him to seek such things, he would not
allow himself to be deterred by such motives, but courageously pursuing the course directly opposed to that
which was counselled him by flesh and blood, he immediately mixed with the company of some of the poor-
est, and, by embracing them, stifled the temptation in its
first beginning.

Ignatius, however, was not always destined to remain
in the narrow sphere of an attendant in a hospital and in
the company of mendicants, nor was he to confine himself to giving to such a small circle as this an example
of self-abnegation and piety.  This was not enough for
a man whom God called to a loftier scene of action ; it
was therefore necessary that he should pass through
other trials.  Whether it was that his mind, so thoughtful
and well regulated, perceived of itself that a new period
of the spiritual life was necessary for its development, or
whether it was an inspiration of grace directing a deep
feeling of the wants of his soul, or perhaps a combina-
tion of these motives, but, after having spent about four
months in the manner above at the hospital of Manresa,
he came to the resolution of seeking a more retired and
complete solitude.

# CHAPTER III.

IGNATIUS RETIRES INTO A CAVERN NEAR MANRESA. HIS SICKNESS, HIS TEMPTATIONS, AND HIS REVELATIONS. HE RESOLVES ON QUITTING MANRESA.

TWO HUNDRED PACES from Manresa, at the foot of the rocky sides which inclose the delightful valley called by the people of the country the Vale of Paradise, stands a dark and lonely cave. Not far from it runs the stream of the Cardenero, between the cavern and the highway, to Manresa. This cave is twenty-six spans long, eight wide, and eleven in height, but at the further end the level of the floor is much lower.* Towards Mont Serrat is a fissure in the rock, through a crevice of which that mountain may be seen. As the cave was unused its entrance was overgrown with brushwood, through which Ignatius had to make a passage. Here he redoubled his prayers and penances, passing sometimes whole nights in meditation and three or four days without food, scourging himself to blood, or, like St. Jerome, beating himself on the breast with a stone. He was, moreover, exposed to the dampness of the floor on which he lay down to sleep or knelt in prayer. But the most trying of all his sufferings in this cave were the interior pains that he then began to experience. Hitherto he had felt continual peace and joy, and his soul was filled with delightful transports, but had these been his only experiences he would have remained still a novice in spiritual things. Suddenly a tempest arose in his soul and began to darken its serenity. A thought abruptly presented itself to his mind with a furious and violent assault, without any previous notice or occasion to give rise to it—" How canst thou endure this kind of life so austere for the forty years which thou mayest

---

* Bartoli is wrong in the distance at which he places the grotto and in its dimensions. He is corrected by the Bollandists.

perhaps yet have to live ? " Perceiving in this access of melancholy and lowness of spirits a temptation of the enemy of all good, he armed himself quickly with a holy indignation, and cut short his sophistries, exclaiming— "Wretch, canst thou promise me with certainty an hour of life ? " The lesson he had to learn on this occasion is that of all beginners. Grace had hitherto borne him upon its wings, and the rigors of penance had for him unspeakable charms. But as human nature is free it must be strengthened by the trial of its energies ; accordingly, grace withdraws its consolations, and a void ensues, so painful to the soul that, feeling its own burden and deprived of the heavenly comfort for which it sighs, it finds a disgust for its new life and for the thorny paths which are wounding it. The devil tries to regain his own in this condition of mind, and aids by his sophistries the pleadings of sensitive nature.

After this first assault followed a continual alternation of consolations and desolations. Ignatius passed from one state to the other, like a man, as he himself describes it, who changes his clothes. "What is this ? " he exclaimed. "What strange kind of life is this that is coming upon me ? " When he had conquered this revolt of the flesh against the spirit, he was assailed by a more subtle temptation still. He felt himself tempted to dwell with self-satisfaction on the merits which he had acquired by his austerities. Having fallen into a state of health which endangered his life, the devil endeavored to fill his mind with thoughts of vanity, and to persuade him that he ought to die with joy, having now merited heaven. To these suggestions he made reply by recalling all the most humiliating events in his past life, and he besought the pious persons who tended him in his sickness to say to him from time to time—"Sinner, remember all thine offences against God." But this temptation is deeply rooted in human nature, and, notwithstanding the heroic means he made use of to subdue this enemy of flattery and self-complacency, he could not gain a complete victory till after two years of hard combat.*

* The Bollandists, p. 634, in the Preface to the *Acts of Father Gonzalez.*

The course, however, of his interior trials was not yet finished. During the latter months of his sojourn at Manresa, he was assailed by a storm of scruples that wellnigh drove him to desperation. At first he had doubts as to the validity of the general confession which he had made in the Church of Mont Serrat, and to free himself from these he began to accuse himself again of the sins he had already confessed, and, lest he might have forgotten anything, he scrutinized his conscience and weighed all his past actions with the most scrupulous care. This plan, however, only entangled him the more in the labyrinth into which he had wandered, while it increased the anguish and the uncertainties of his conscience. The Priest whom he chose as confessor, and who was preacher at the principal church, tried to restore confidence to his penitent by a means that only aggravated the evil. He bade him write down all that he could remember, and then to disquiet himself no more after he had confessed it. Ignatius, taught by experience, soon perceived that his doubts arose precisely from over-scrupulousness in trying to assure himself of the validity of his confessions, and that consequently the means prescribed were prejudicial to him. But having once yielded to these sentiments of excessive distrust of himself, he rejected as a temptation the voice of reason, which pointed out the true remedy for the evil, and durst not ask his confessor to command him simply on the part of God to think no more of the sins he had confessed. His Director, therefore, only prolonged the sufferings of his penitent by telling him to confess no more of his life than what appeared to him clearly and evidently sin, for in so doing he even closed him more securely within the maze in which he was entangled. In his state of scrupulosity Ignatius mistook for sin everything, even what was most innocent, and remained incapable of forming the judgment required of him.

In this state of mental darkness and desolation he found no relief either in prayer or in practice of penance, to which he gave himself with renewed ardor ; not even in holy Communion, which, on the contrary, became for him the occasion of a new martyrdom, as he considered himself the enemy of the Saviour of souls. Some

crisis only could save him from falling into the abyss of
despair which opened at his feet. The crisis came,
brought on by the very excess of his malady, and his
piety and perseverance gained the day. On one occasion,
when he was more than usually wearied out with
doubts and darkness of mind, and had nearly yielded to
the despondency which the violence of his efforts had
brought on, he exclaimed, in sudden fear of being
abandoned, "O my God, since I find no help in man,
nor in any creature, do Thou come to my aid and show
me where to find it! If I must ask guidance, though it
were even to be had only from a dog, I would ask it."
The impatience which drew from him this exclamation
led him to an extreme course when he saw that he was
not heard. He was then at the house of the Dominicans
at Manresa. In his cell there was a large opening in
the floor* or wall, near the spot where he prayed. He
conceived that the only course left to him, since God
had abandoned him and there was no help in man, was
to precipitate himself down the opening. But he did
not succumb to this violent suggestion of despair ; on
the contrary, full of horror, he cried out, "No, I will
not ; never, O my God, never will I offend Thee so !"
At this moment, when his trouble was at its height, he
remembered to have read in the life of a solitary, that, in
order to obtain a favor from God, he resolved to fast
until such time as it should be bestowed. And as a
drowning man catches at the first floating thing that
passes, so Ignatius had recourse to this expedient, though
in fact it did not essentially differ in character from the
other penances he had already practised, and which had
availed him nothing, for this reason, that the state he was
in entered into the designs of God regarding him and
into the economy of the graces which were to form of
him a master of the spiritual life. So he fasted from
one Sunday to the following Sunday, and would have persevered longer, had not his confessor, apprised by him
of what he was doing, threatened to refuse him absolu-

* *Magnum foramen.* It seems plain that this was a hole in the
flooring of the room, which would let him fall below, and not a window,
as Bartoli and others suppose.

tion unless he immediately took his ordinary food. He instantly obeyed, and found himself for a time delivered from his state of disquietude. After three days he had a return of his fit of melancholy, but it was the last time that he suffered from it. During it a feeling arose of excessive disgust at the life he had adopted, and a strong temptation to put an end to the martyrdom he was suffering by renouncing an enterprise in which he received such a poor return. However, he withstood this last assault, the violence of which exhausted itself by its very excess, and at length came forth victorious from the perilous combat. His novitiate was over. His doubts and mental anxieties gradually ceased. The sad, gloomy thoughts, which had hung so heavily upon him, dissipated, like mists scattered before the sun, and his soul, again comforted, gave thanks to God for its deliverance. He drew from these trials his experience of the different stages of spiritual progress, and his power of discerning the action of good and bad spirits ; at the same time he learned the course of action to be pursued in such circumstances. He saw clearly that there is no portion between the natural efforts and sufferings of man and the gift of divine grace, and that man, even by the most holy life, cannot merit of himself this supernatural assistance.

After having seen the dark side of his interior life, we must now give something of its brighter aspect. Let us return for this purpose to the preceding year and the cave of Manresa. The manifestations of the powers of heaven and hell succeed each other in the lives of the saints, and make a counterpoise, one against another. They both, notwithstanding their contradictory character, serve to the spiritual growth of the soul that experiences them. Ignatius entered this school with little preparation, and having for his only guide the finger of God, which it is far from easy for man to follow. He used to say that God had treated him as a wise master does a child, to whom he gives but little to learn at a time, and before whom he does not place a second lesson until he has well understood the first. He was so inexperienced, that an aged lady of great knowledge in

spiritual things, with whom he often had pious communications, having one day said to him, " Oh, that Our
Lord Jesus Christ would only manifest Himself to you,"
" How," he exclaimed, not understanding the purport of
the words, "could it be that Christ could manifest
Himself to me ? " That he made rapid progress in the
growth in holiness is certain, and that he learned nothing
from man; but we have no certain information of the
manner in which this took place, for he has said very
little about it, and the declarations taken for his canonization could only relate what was known to the witnesses,
who knew nothing of his interior. From these two
sources we have only fragmentary and imperfect indications.

  It seems that the devil appeared to him in some visible
shape thus early in his progress, for he says, in Gonzalez'
narrative, that he remained ignorant of spiritual things
until the apparition of the serpent ; and this would not be
true, if before that he had experienced heavenly raptures.
He saw a luminous figure, which he could not perfectly
distinguish, as it was so vague and indeterminate, but it
seemed to have some resemblance to a serpent, and it had
many points or centres, like eyes, from which issued a
vivid light. This apparition was presented to him for the
first time while he was in the hospital at Manresa, and was
afterwards frequently repeated. He felt a certain pleasure at the sight, until he learned, on the occasion of which
we are about to speak, from what source it really came,
though he was at the same time being favored with celestial visions. One day, while he was seated beside the river
Llobregat, after having prayed in the neighboring Church
of St. Paul, he was rapt in spirit and filled with such
light that he learned in an instant a number of things
concerning the faith and the natural world with such fulness and clearness that, as he himself afterwards declared,
if all the communications and lights he had received from
God up to that time, at the age of sixty-two, were put
together, they would not equal the knowledge he then
obtained in a single moment. Coming to himself from
this ecstasy, he ran to a cross which stood near, at the foot
of which he had often prayed, to give vent to the feelings

with which his heart was full, when on a sudden this luminous figure appeared to him. But this time the vicinity of the cross gave it something of an unpleasant aspect, and the impression it made upon him was quite different from what he experienced before, and hence he discovered that it was an illusion of the devil. This same appearance was afterwards renewed at Manresa, at Paris, and at Rome, but after this time it always caused a painful impression, from which he speedily delivered himself by striking at it and chasing it away with his staff.

It was also requisite that Ignatius, who was called to be a firm pillar of the faith, should have the sublimest mysteries directly infused into his soul, and be wholly penetrated with them. Thus, in the ecstasies with which he was favored, he received a very clear vision of the Holy Trinity, always under images suited to our manner of conception in the present life. The first time he was rapt in this manner was on the staircase of the church of the Dominicans, while he was reciting the Little Office of the Blessed Virgin during the preparations for a procession. This vision filled him with such sweetness that during the whole ceremony he could not contain his sighs and tears, and all the rest of the day he could speak of nothing else, which he did in so striking and admirable a manner as to fill his hearers with astonishment. It is certain that after this moment he entered into a very close union, as far as a creature can, with his Creator, and intimacy with the Three Divine Persons, and that later in life the greater portion of his prayers and revelations had this sublime mystery for their object. He wrote down, then and afterwards, the lights he received, as far as they could be expressed in human language; but except some fragments that by chance escaped him, he took care to destroy all that he had written.

Another time, whilst he was in the same church, he understood by a light from heaven how God had created the world—a fact which he afterwards declared, but added that he could find no words to express what he had seen. At another time, in the same church, at the elevation of the Host, he had a vision of the Child Jesus, and learned by an interior revelation how our Divine Saviour is present in the Sacred Host after consecration.

More frequently he enjoyed the vision of Our Lord's Sacred Humanity, manifested to him in a form of splendor about the middle height, especially whilst he was in prayer. Discoursing on this subject with Father Gonzalez, he told him that this vision was quite an interior one, without any sensible discernment of the organic parts of Our Lord's Person. He added that he believed he might truly say that he had seen this vision from between twenty to forty times during his stay at Manresa. He also had visions in the same manner of the Blessed Virgin. Another ecstasy, which he had at the Hospital of St. Lucy, belongs to the most extraordinary class of the marvels which are related in the lives of the saints. It lasted for a whole week, from a Saturday to the ensuing one. During the whole time he lay as one dead, and only a slight beating of the heart told that he was alive. When he came to himself he opened his eyes like one awakened from a long sleep, and with a voice expressive of the love with which his soul was inundated, he exclaimed only the words "O Jesus! Jesus!" This fact is attested by those who were eye-witnesses, but the Saint always kept the most profound silence upon this subject, and consequently nothing is known for certain of the things communicated to him in this rapture. We may, however, conjecture that they related to the establishment of the Society of Jesus. For while he was writing the Constitutions, several times when he was asked the reason for such and such a point, he answered that he had thus seen it at Manresa. We know for certain from him that the idea of the Society of Jesus was given him in a meditation upon the kingdom of Jesus Christ. He confided in a general manner to Father James Lainez that he had learned more in an hour of prayer at Manresa than all the wise men of the world could teach him. He assured him that, although there were no Holy Scriptures, and the Catholic faith had no other proof of its truth besides what he had seen at Manresa, he would be ready to lay down his life for it, so fully had these revelations confirmed him in the faith.

St. Ignatius had, moreover, to pass through physical trials at Manresa. The excessive austerities he practised, borne on as he was by his ardent character beyond the bounds which prudence prescribes, inevitably acted injuriously upon his health, though naturally he was of a robust constitution. He had to learn, and at his own cost, the bounds to which Christian mortification should be confined, in order to be able to give, at a future time, exact rules upon this point to his spiritual children. He fell into his first sickness while he was dwelling in the cave at Manresa, and it attacked him on the occasion of one of the little pilgrimages he often made in the neighborhood. He had been to a place named Villadordis, about three miles distant from Manresa, to pray before an image of Our Lady honored in those parts, and fainted on the road home, and was found lying insensible on the ground. He was carried to the Hospital of St. Lucy, where a violent access of fever ensued, which brought him to death's door. Some pious women, who were acquainted with him, tended him with the greatest care ; and as the hospital did not appear to them a suitable place for him, they procured a lodging with a respectable townsman, named Andrew D'Amigant. It was probably in this sickness that he was tempted, as related above, with thoughts of vanity. His second illness came upon him at the approach of winter, and this time the public authorities of the place took charge of him, and had him carried to the house of one Ferrera, to be taken care of. Some of the principal ladies of the town offered themselves to watch through the night in turn and wait upon him. After his recovery there ensued a great weakness of stomach, from which he ever afterwards suffered.* He had also several returns of sickness, and one of these took place while he was living in the convent of the Dominicans, as the Bollandists relate, who add, moreover, that, as the women who tended on him could not enter the Religious House where he was without giving scandal, he was at their desire taken a second time to the house

* We have followed the account of St. Ignatius himself, as given by Gonzalez, ch. iii. Mariani's recital of the sicknesses of the Saint does not agree with this.

of D'Amigant.* Taught by experience to be prudent, towards the close of his sojourn at Manresa he began to abate a little his austerities, and to take in some degree more care of his exterior. However, he denied himself flesh meat, although a very strong inclination for eating it came one day upon him, which he resisted.

Perhaps we ought in this place, after the example of all the biographies of St. Ignatius, to speak of the book of the *Spiritual Exercises*, but it seems more convenient to speak of it afterwards, contenting ourselves for the present with remarking that, according to the evidence on all hands, the essential parts of the work were composed in the cave of Manresa; but the Saint made additions subsequently, as occasions presented themselves, and as experience suggested them. For this we have his own word. No one can be so unreasonable as to deny him the authorship of the book. It is enough to cast an eye upon the manner in which his conversion was brought about, and to compare it with the main contents of the work, to be convinced that he is the author of it, and that it would be folly to dispute it.

To complete this portion of the narrative, it remains for us to describe briefly the effect of the Saint's influence upon those around him. It was impossible that a young man, whose manners, notwithstanding his humble poverty, showed the nobility of his birth, should not in time make some impression, speaking, as he did, like an Apostle, and living like a St. John in the desert. It is not, then, a matter for suprise that the inhabitants of the place gathered around him when, standing on a stone before the hospital and discoursing like a man inspired, he spoke to them of God, giving force to all he said by his looks, which bore the impress of his words upon them; for his appearance itself preached, as it exemplified the love of God and self-abnegation. So rigorous a course of penance, such indomitable perseverance, and such profound knowledge of spiritual things must needs have appeared extraordinary to all whose hearts were touched

---

* It is possible that this sickness is the same which began at the approach of winter, and the Ferrera of whom St. Ignatius speaks may be the same as the D'Amigant of the biographers.

with the influence of divine grace. Moreover, when any one gave him an alms he joined to his thanks some words of charity for the good of the souls of those who bestowed it, and the pious, earnest manner in which he spoke could not fail to produce its effects. Accordingly the greater part of the inhabitants of Manresa, seized with the spirit which lived in him, began to fulfil with greater fervor all their duties as Christians, and to rise out of the state of indifference into which they had previously sunk. He soon found himself surrounded with a little circle of disciples, who, feeling more particularly the desire of progressing in the way of perfection, were drawn to him, because they found that by his conversation they were elevated to supernatural thoughts and courage. Some have been already named, and we shall have occasion to notice others when we come to the Saint's letters. In his conversations with them he imparted to them the lights he had received in prayer, the meditations and spiritual readings he had made, chiefly in Holy Scripture. His discourse bore witness to his familiar converse with God, and to the atmosphere of sanctity in which he lived. These outpourings of the love of God communicated to his hearers the fountain of the waters of grace from which they flowed. However, none of this small knot of followers could satisfy the desire he had of finding companions capable of apprehending his plans and of applying to their lives his rules in spiritual things. This desire sprang up in his mind more definitely after his second sickness, but neither at Manresa nor at Barcelona, during his first sojourn there, could he find men who suited his purpose. This piece of information, given us by St. Ignatius himself, shows that even thus early he thought of forming a band of companions, whom he could model according to the idea conceived in his Exercises—for the purpose of preaching the kingdom of God and extending it among the infidels in the Holy Land, this being the first enterprise designed by him. He observes, with regard to those who were then around him, that he found no one in those two towns, who was capable of making the progress he desired in spiritual life, and that the only person who seemed to him deeply versed in the secrets of heavenly things was the woman* who said to him, " Oh, that Our Lord would show Himself to you ! " Finding none to suit him, he ceased to seek with solicitude for followers, leaving the whole to the care of the providence of God.

Whilst the good at Manresa found themselves thus drawn to a course of life more comfortable to the maxims of the Gospel, the opposition of the bad became in proportion more violent. It was principally directed against Ignatius, whom they with truth regarded as the author of the change among the people, though at the same time they were embittered against all his followers. They endeavored, by casting injurious suspicions and ridicule of all kinds upon him and them, to draw them from him and thus to make him powerless. Their chief resentment fell upon the family of D'Amigant and the lady Pasquale, whom they accused of being the cause of all the disturbance and excitement of men's minds, by the favor they had shown to this stranger. All this caused the friends of the Saint to make no opposition to his departure, to which they would have otherwise consented with great difficulty. These, however, were not his only motives in deciding to quit Manresa, though he at the same time feared that by a longer stay he might bring upon his benefactors the persecution and calumnies of his enemies. He felt himself urged to accomplish his design of visiting Jerusalem, and when he learned that the obstacles thrown in the way of vessels leaving Barcelona, on account of the plague, had been removed, it was agreed that he should depart for that city. According to the paper of information left by John Pasquale, his mother sent for her brother, Antonio Pujol, a priest of the household of the Archbishop of Taragona, to come to Manresa, that she might explain to him the state of things and beg him to conduct Ignatius to Barcelona, which he accordingly did.

* Gonzalez, ch. iii. I can nowhere find the name of this person, but she is said to have enjoyed so great a reputation for wisdom and sanctity, that Ferdinand I., king of Castile and Aragon, consulted her on matters of conscience.

# CHAPTER IV.

IGNATIUS AT BARCELONA.  HE PROCEEDS TO ROME AND
VENICE.  HE EMBARKS FOR PALESTINE.  HIS ARRIVAL
IN PALESTINE.

THE stay of St. Ignatius at Manresa had lasted nearly ten months, and he quitted it in January, 1523.  He had now divested himself of all that was extraordinary in his dress, and changed the long sackcloth habit of a penitent for a shorter garment of coarse grey woolen cloth, and his head and feet were no longer bare.  He would receive nothing more than the clothes as an alms, refusing the money which was offered him.  As he could speak neither Italian nor Latin, his friends requested him to take as a companion when passing through Italy one who was acquainted with the language of the country, and whom they offered to provide for him.  But he would in no manner consent to it, and answered in his forcible, characteristic way, " That if they offered the son of the Duke of Cordova, he would not have him, and that all the company he needed was faith, hope, and charity," adding that, if he took a companion, he would be looking to him for food when hungry, and if he fell would look to him to lift him up, and would thus be learning to rest in him, whereas he desired only to love and look up to God, and put all his hope and confidence in him.  " And the Pilgrim, when he spoke thus," says St. Ignatius of himself, " spoke from his heart." *

At Barcelona, Pujol provided him with a lodging until he embarked for Italy.  He remained in this city only twenty days, during which he practised all his usual works

* Gonzalez.  Here we must remark that the Saint always speaks of himself in the third person, and calls himself the " Pilgrim "—*El Pelegrino.*

of piety, begging each day the morsel of bread which he needed, and serving the sick in the hospital, besides visiting the prisoners. He sought most earnestly for men experienced in the spiritual life, and, in the hope of finding such, visited many recluses who lived around the town, devoting their life in solitude to prayer and meditation, but his search was in vain. In the city he made acquaintance with some pious persons, with whom he maintained friendly correspondence in later life, and amongst these was one whose friendship he acquired in an extraordinary manner. As he sat one day upon the steps of an altar listening to a sermon, with a group of children round him, a lady of rank, named Elizabeth Roser, accidentally regarding him, saw his head encircled with a bright light. She began to consider him attentively with feelings of deep veneration, and desired to know more of him. Upon her return home she told her husband what she had observed, and they invited St. Ignatius to visit them. Under pretext of giving him an alms they induced him to dine with them, and, the conversation turning upon spiritual things, they had opportunity to hear and admire his great knowledge in these matters, and were accordingly edified with his discourse. Finding that he intended to sail for Italy, and that he had already taken his passage on board a small vessel, they begged him to delay his voyage and take advantage of a larger ship about to sail, on which a bishop, a relation of Madame Roser, was to embark, and whose company he might join. He consented, being doubtless led to his decision by this circumstance, though we note in it the hand of Divine Providence, inasmuch as the other vessel encountered a violent storm shortly after it had left the port, and foundered with all on board.

Ignatius begged in the name of God for a free passage upon the second vessel, and the captain gave it him, on condition that he brought with him his provisions for the voyage. The Saint, who had purposed living upon alms asked on shipboard, as he had done at Barcelona, and who had taken a resolution never to be solicitous about any temporal concern, thought that he could not accept of this condition without infringement of his resolve, since, instead of leaving all care to God, he would be providing for himself. In this state of doubt he had recourse to his confessor, who assured him that in so doing he would show no want of confidence in God. Upon this he began to beg bread sufficient for the voyage, although the Lady Roser offered him all he could need, but he would not accept of it. When asked where he was going, he answered—" To Rome," through fear, as he afterwards said, of some feeling of vanity, had he mentioned Jerusalem as the object of his journey, such a pilgrimage being at that time dangerous and very rarely undertaken. A lady of rank, to whom he made this answer, supposing him to be one of the ordinary pilgrims, whose motives are often very mixed, said to him with some displeasure—" To Rome? Those who go to Rome seldom come back the better for their visit." This circumstance is related by himself. It is doubtful whether this occurrence is the same as that mentioned by Bartoli, who tells us that the Saint, having applied to a lady named Cepilla when begging for provisions for his passage, met with a very bad reception, and was treated as a good-for-nothing vagabond, for the lady had a son who, after quitting her, led a wandering life, and she looked upon Ignatius as the counterpart of her unhappy son, with his poor habiliments yet noble bearing. Bartoli goes on to say that the Saint received her bad treatment with thankfulness and joy, when she, perceiving her mistake, asked his pardon and gave him abundant alms. Later on she acknowledged her hastiness with regret, and on St. Ignatius' return put herself under his spiritual direction.

Before he embarked Ignatius laid upon the stone steps near the quay five or six pieces of money called *biancas*, as an alms for the first person into whose hands they should fall, for there chanced to be no poor person present to whom he could offer them, and yet he had firmly resolved to take no money along with him. The passage was made quickly by help of a strong west wind, which carried him in five days, though not without considerable danger, to the port of Gaieta, in the kingdom of Naples. From Gaieta he travelled on foot to Rome, in company with three persons who, like himself, were begging their way. These were a young man and a mother with her daughter, the latter being in man's clothes, to avoid the dangers to which she might be exposed. On arriving at a certain village they found some people round a large fire, who invited them to warm themselves and gave them food. They then offered as lodging an upper chamber to the mother and her daughter in disguise, and to the young man and St. Ignatius a stable underneath. At midnight Ignatius heard a great noise overhead, accompanied by loud cries for help. Ascending in all haste, he met the mother and her daughter in flight from their apartment, declaring that an attempt had been made upon their virtue. As Ignatius raised his voice, and cried out in a tone of the highest indignation that such a shameful outrage was past being endured, the villain, deterred from his abominable design, fled in the obscurity of the night. It was to all appearance the young man who had travelled in their company, for Ignatius and the two others, leaving the place the same night, could not find him. * They arrived late the next evening at the gates of a little town, which they found closed, so that they were forced to pass the night in a chapel outside the walls. In the morning, when they presented themselves at the gate, they were refused entrance, for fear they might be infected with the plague. They were therefore obliged to go to beg for food in a village at some distance, where Ignatius stayed, as he was too weak to proceed, while his companions pursued their journey to Rome. The lady to whom the place and the country round it belonged having come by chance to the village where the Saint was, he went with the inhabitants to meet her on her entrance, and asked permission to pass through the town the gates of which had been shut upon him, assuring her that he was not suffering from the plague, but from exhaustion and weakness. Having obtained permission, he entered the town and begged alms, and after a rest of two days was able to continue his journey.

* It is clear, from the account of Gonzalez (ch. iv.), that he is the person spoken of by St. Ignatius. He had learned on the road the disguise assumed by the daughter.

Arriving at Rome on Palm Sunday, he found there some fellow-countrymen, through whom he obtained from Pope Adrian VI. a passport to Jerusalem ; and, having visited during Holy Week the churches of the Stations and some of the principal sanctuaries, he continued his way to Venice, having first received the Pope's blessing as a pilgrim to the Holy Land.* Thus he stayed only nine days in Rome. His compatriots, having in vain attempted to dissuade him from his purpose, had in a manner forced him to accept of seven or eight pieces of gold, on the ground of the impossibility of obtaining a passage on shipboard without money. But scarcely had he left the city than he began to feel compunction, as being guilty of a fault against poverty, for which he asked pardon of God. In the first impulse of regret he threw down the money in the road, but upon second thoughts he took it up and gave it to the first poor man he met.

In this journey, as in the preceding one, the plague which was breaking out in Italy caused him much difficulty and embarrassment. His feeble steps, his pale and emaciated looks, marked him out as one stricken with the plague, and this was enough to make all fly from him and refuse to take him in. On his road he fell in with others travelling like himself, but on arriving at Chioggia they were told that no one was permitted to enter Venice without a bill of health. They resolved, therefore, to go to Padua, where they could obtain a certificate to show that they came from a part of the country which was not infected. His fellow-travellers hastened on at so quick a pace that the Saint could not keep up with them, and had to pass the night in the open air. Abandoned by human aid, and in the most pitiable condition, he was not left desolate by Him for Whose sake he suffered all these hardships. Our Lord manifested Himself to him in the manner in which He ordinarily appeared to him, and promised His special protection, of which he soon experienced evident proofs. For on the next day, not only was he able to enter the city without being stopped, but

* Gonzalez (ch. iv.) says that he left the eighth or ninth day after Palm Sunday, so it could not be, as Bartoli says, the day after Low Sunday.

also to pass out of it free, to the great astonishment of his companions, whom he rejoined, and who knew that he had no certificate of health.    They were much more surprised to observe that, on arriving in Venice, where all were taken and examined by the officers of the board of health, their certificates were demanded, whereas the presence of the Saint did not seem to be even noticed.

Having now arrived at Venice, but without knowing where to find lodgings for the night, he resolved to pass it the best way he could beneath the arcades of the public commissioners on the Piazza of St. Mark.    While he lay thus upon the pavement to sleep, forsaken apparently by man, God again took him under His own care.    A devout senator, Mark-Antonio Trevisani, well known for his liberalities and charities to the poor, was startled from his sleep by hearing a voice, that said to him—"What! art thou sleeping at ease on thy bed, while My dear servant and poor pilgrim is lying near thy door in the open air upon the pavement?"    The friend of the poor rose quickly, filled with astonishment, and eager to discover who this could be to whose assistance he was summoned in a manner so extraordinary, and who was so singularly honored by God.  He found Ignatius and took charitable care of him, giving him food and lodging.    But, either because he paid too much attention to his guest, or, with a pious curiosity, sought to know too much of his hidden virtues, or for some other reason, the Saint thought it unsuitable to his condition as a pilgrim to remain longer in the senator's palace.*   He therefore refused his proffered hospitality, for reasons as holy as those which prompted the pious servant of God to invite him.

One day, whilst Ignatius was passing through the city, he met a rich merchant of Biscaya, who recognized him and asked him whither he was going.  The Saint informed him, and he invited him to dine with him.   Ignatius relates of himself that it was his custom on these occasions never to speak during meals  except when asked  a ques-

---

* This saintly man received the poor and lodged them in his own palace, and would have spent on them all his fortune, had he not been hindered by his nephews.   He was elected Doge in 1553, without his own consent, and died at an advanced age, whilst hearing Mass.

tion, and to listen to what others said, that he might take occasion from it, when the repast was over, to lead the conversation to some pious subject for the spiritual good of the hearers. His entertainer was so much pleased that he wished to persuade Ignatius to give up his intended voyage and remain with him. Unable to succeed, he gave proof of his friendship by rendering him the service of introducing him to Andrea Gritti, the Doge, and obtaining for him an audience. The Doge, at the request of the Saint, gave him a free passage to Cyprus on a Government vessel, which was about to convey thither the new magistrates of the Republic. Ignatius remained at the merchant's house until the vessel sailed.

There were very few pilgrims this year for Jerusalem, on account of the plague, and besides, after the fall of Rhodes, Dec. 25, A. D. 1522, the Turkish ships made the voyage very perilous.* The friends of Ignatius tried to avail themselves of this circumstance, and still more a violent attack of fever which seized him some days before his departure, to dissuade him from the enterprise. But nothing could deter him, neither danger nor sickness. His soul, superior to these considerations, and putting all things human aside, regarded only the higher principle within, which urged him forward, and placed implicit confidence in it as the voice of God, which must be obeyed. He expressed these sentiments in his usual forcible manner when replying to the expostulations of his friends, "That, if he could not find a ship in which to embark, he was confident that he could pass the sea safely on a plank."

Upon the day fixed for his departure, he was so ill that the physician, on being asked by the people of the house whether he could set sail in such a state, answered, "Yes, if he wishes to die on the passage." However, he hastened on board at the signal of a gun fired for sailing, and quitted the harbor for Jerusalem on the 14th of July. The voyage had so salutary an effect upon his health, that after the usual sea-sickness he was cured of the fever. But the ribald and wicked behavior of some of the pas-

---

* The ship which bore the pilgrims had only thirteen of them on board, and had already sailed. Eight more were to sail with Ignatius.

sengers and crew caused him greater pain and grief than the fear of corsairs. He continually rebuked them for their vile language, and this in bolder and more menacing terms than such rough and violent men would brook, for they had no regard for anything sacred upon earth. Some Spaniards among the passengers, having taken notice of this, advised him to be more cautious. In fact, the sailors had agreed among themselves to take their revenge on this preacher out of season by landing him and leaving him on a desert island that was near. But as they approached it a contrary wind sprung up, which made it impossible to land, and carried them quickly to the Isle of Cyprus. There Ignatius was informed that the ship with the pilgrims which had left Venice before him was lying in the harbor at Salina, thirty miles distant. He went thither with the other eight pilgrims on the ship with him, and thus they happily reached the coast of Syria after a passage of forty-eight days. From Joppa, where they landed, they took their departure for Jerusalem mounted upon asses, according to the custom of the country. When they were coming near to the Holy City, a Spanish gentleman, Don Diego Nuñez, devoutly said that as soon as they came in sight of the walls of Jerusalem it would be well to enter into their hearts and examine themselves in silence. The pilgrims all assented, and soon after seeing the Franciscan Brothers coming to meet them with the cross, they dismounted from their beasts to make the rest of the road on foot. They entered in procession, about midday, on the 4th of September, that city in which the Expectation of the Nations was seen visible in the flesh.

# CHAPTER V.

EVERYTHING tends to show that Ignatius, in making the journey to Jerusalem, had no other object than to take up his abode near the sepulchre of Our Lord, and there labor to extend the kingdom of Christ, and to make war upon His enemies. It was not, then, a simple pilgrimage that he was making, for the East had been his first thought after his conversion. He had the idea of at once establishing, on the very spot sanctified by the presence of Our Lord in the flesh, a Society of Jesus, composed of apostolic evangelical laborers, whose spiritual warfare, in the midst of the children of Mahomet, should open a way to new triumphs of the Catholic Church. This was without doubt a noble conception, which the swords of the Christian chivalry of Europe had not been able to realize by the efforts and enthusiasm of centuries. That this was the real design of St. Ignatius is proved by the pains he took to gain a footing in Palestine, and of these I shall speak in the proper place, contenting myself with remarking here that to the last years of his life he thought seriously of securing at least an entrance for the Society into Jerusalem, an idea which may be considered as one of the characteristic elements of the Exercises, though this is not a place in which to dwell on the connection.

Ignatius certainly did not conceal his design from the Fathers resident in the Holy Land, as his biographers have asserted without proof. On the contrary, from what he himself states we may conclude that he confided to them his plan, with the hope that, ignorant as he was of the true state of things there, he might obtain their counsel and assistance. His silence could have served no purpose, for if he had remained in Jerusalem his plans could not have been executed in secret. The Franciscans, who knew the state of things, could not act otherwise than they did, though the threat of excommunication in case he remained at Jerusalem seems like an excessive measure, unless we can justify it by supposing that they did know the whole plan of the pilgrim, and that they considered it so prejudicial to the interests of Christianity in the Holy Land, as to oblige them, in case of necessity, to have recourse to so severe a measure. Under this supposition, moreover, we can understand the prudent and evasive reply of the Father Guardian, to whom the Saint communicated his purpose of remaining at Jerusalem. The Father Guardian did not absolutely refuse him the permission which he asked, but made it dependent on a condition that Ignatius could not fulfil. He told him that it might possibly be permitted if he could maintain himself upon his own resources, but that he must await the return of the Provincial, who was then at Bethlehem, for it was he who must decide the question. This answer, though in truth an evasive one, appeared to the Saint like a real promise in his favor, and considering the whole thing to be certain, he wrote in the joy of his heart to his friends at Barcelona.*

Ignatius visited several times all the holy places in Jerusalem and in its environs, both alone and with other pilgrims ; and we may picture to ourselves with what fervor of devotion he would propose to consecrate himself entirely to the service of God, and to walk in the footsteps of his crucified Saviour. On the day on which the other pilgrims were to depart Ignatius was unexpectedly summoned into the presence of the Provincial, who had returned from Bethlehem, and he was apprised, to his great astonishment, that he must leave with the rest on the morrow, as his design of remaining and fixing

---

* If these letters could be found they would inform us how matters passed. Mariani (p. 52), according to the Bollandists, speaks of a letter written to Doña Pasquale as still extant. The Bollandists mention only to whom the letters were addressed, and speak of them in the past tense, not as now existing. In fact, I have found none such in any collection, either printed or MSS., at Rome or elsewhere.

his residence at Jerusalem would be good neither for himself nor for the interests of the convent. Several times already, he was told, had the pilgrims, having imprudently passed the bonds prescribed them, fallen into the hands of the Arabs and had been even killed by them ; that the convent had been obliged to ransom them at great expense, which had fallen heavily upon them. Ignatius, disconcerted by this unexpected declaration, which seemed to defeat all his plans, answered that he feared neither slavery nor death for Jesus Christ, and that if taken he did not ask to be redeemed ; at the same time, with a modest assurance, he declared his intention to remain if he could do so without offence to God. He added this proviso with confidence, being persuaded that his purpose was agreeable to Him. But, however good his purpose might be, it was not the appointment of Divine Providence that he should execute it then and there; for God made use of the Provincial, who was the spiritual Superior of Ignatius, to make known His will. He informed St. Ignatius that he had received powers from the Holy See to allow whom he pleased to stay at Jerusalem, and to send others away, and that whoever resisted his orders would fall under excommunication, offering at the same time to show the Bull of the Pope which conferred on him these powers.*

Ignatius did not require the Pope's Bull to be shown to him, but submitting himself to the divine will, declared to the Father Provincial that his word was enough, and that he would obey his orders. Before leaving, however, he wished once more to visit the Mount of Olives. Now it must be observed that visiting the holy places beyond the walls of Jerusalem was at that time very dangerous for persons, whether alone or with other pilgrims, unless they were accompanied by a Turk as guard, whom it was necessary to pay. Ignatius ventured to attempt it, and arrived without being observed at the summit of the Mount, where, according to the tradition, the prints of

---

* This declaration shows that it was not Ignatius' stay at Jerusalem which the Franciscans disapproved of, but only his intention of preaching to the infidels. And this they could very well forbid him to do without giving him the reasons of their conduct.

our Saviour's Feet as He mounted to heaven are left
upon the rock.   As he had to purchase permission of the
guards to pay his respects to the holy place, he gave them
his pocket-knife in order to obtain it.   When on his return into Jerusalem he had reached the spot which once
was Bethphage, it came to his mind that he had not
observed to which point of the compass Our Lord's footsteps were turned.   He therefore went back and purchased again the permission to satisfy his devotion by
giving to the guard a pair of scissors, and so found his
way back to the city.   As, however, an eye was kept on
his movements, his absence from the convent was soon
discovered, and they sent after him an Armenian servant,
who, as soon as he perceived him, threatened him with his
stick, and reproaching him for his rashness, dragged him
roughly by the arm back to the convent.   Ignatius bore
this rude treatment with patience, and during the whole
time of it saw Our Lord as he was accustomed to behold
Him, appearing close beside him in the air.   The following day he departed with the other pilgrims for Europe,
having stayed about six weeks in Jerusalem.

They found at the point of embarkation, which probably was Joppa, three ships ready to sail, of which one
was a Turkish vessel and the two other were Venetian.
Of the Venetian ships one was large and sound, the
other but small and leaky.   Since the winter was approaching, when storms are frequent, the pilgrims chose
the safer ship, and begged of the captain to take Ignatius
for nothing, on account of his poverty, saying that they
looked upon him as a saint.   The captain refused, and
only laughed at their request, remarking that, if he was
a saint, he had no need of a ship, but could walk over
the water like St. James.   He met with a better reception on the smaller vessel, which set sail early next day,
in company with the two others, under a favorable wind.
But towards evening a violent gale arose, which separated the three vessels.   The Turkish ship foundered at
sea, with goods and all on board.   The larger and sounder
Venetian vessel was wrecked upon the rocky coast of
the Isle of Cyprus, though the goods and passengers were
saved.   The little barque which bore the Saint was the

only one that weathered the storm, and, after being tossed by the tempest, escaped the perils of the sea and came safe to land in Apulia, where it put in to repair damages, and then continued its voyage to Venice, at which place it arrived towards the middle of January, 1524, after a passage of altogether two months and a half. Ignatius stayed there only a few days to rest after his long fatigue, and it is probable that the good merchant who had treated him so kindly the previous summer offered him again friendly hospitality.*

Thus ended the journey of St. Ignatius, from which he had looked for so successful an issue. And, we may ask, had it been for him only an ordinary pilgrimage ? He certainly must have asked himself this question, when he found himself obliged to seek a new way of reconciling the plan of life he had formed with the wants of the times. He had by experience found that the East contained no elements suitable for his design ; and he was now convinced that, to labor with fruit for the good of souls and of the Church, he must first of all prepare himself in the ordinary way, and not neglect the human means prescribed by Providence of acquiring the necessary learning and of embracing the ecclesiastical state. The position in which he was placed brought these things forcibly before him, and he kept these thoughts continually in his mind during the voyage. It was then that he laid down a plan for the future, which, indeed, seemed to postpone indefinitely the accomplishment of his object. But, like a valorous knight who has essayed an enterprise without calculating his powers and has failed, he showed still greater courage and energy in resolving to begin anew, and as a child learn the first elements of the sciences, that so, being better prepared, he might return to his work after a long novitiate or probation. His strong will resolutely embraced what reason pointed out as necessary to be done. He determined to

* Bartoli, and all who follow his account, make Cyprus the scene of the captain's refusal to take the Saint on board, and suppose, without proof and contrary to probability, two passages from Cyprus to Joppa, and again from Cyprus to Venice. I have followed Orlandini, who speaks but of the one embarkation on the coast of Syria.

return and study at Manresa, where he could count upon
the aid of the friends whom he had left.    Thus, after a
few days' rest, he took his way from Venice, while the
season was still wintry and severe, in scanty clothing,
and having many dangers to pass through, for his route
lay by Genoa, and he was obliged to traverse the theatre
of the war then raging in Upper Italy between France
and Spain.    At Ferrara, while he was praying in the
cathedral, a mendicant asked of him an alms, and received
from him a piece of silver instead of the small coin which
he expected.    Scarce had the first quitted him when a
second presented himself, and then a number more
pressed around.    His friends at Venice had forced him
to accept of about fifteen crowns, which he probably
intended to distribute to the poor, and he gave them, entire
as they were, with a smiling air, and when he had no
more to give he expressed his sorrow at sending away
the rest who came empty.    Such liberality from a man
who appeared as poor as themselves seemed marvellous to these poor people, and when he left the place,
they began to cry after him, thinking perhaps he was
some saint who had appeared under this form, "See the
Saint ! the Saint !"    Ignatius, thus reduced to extreme
poverty, had to continue his journey begging and before
he arrived at Genoa experienced considerable danger
from the armies engaged in the war.

One time he was stopped by a Spanish sentinel on the
road near a walled town, and as he had passed the lines
alone, they conducted him as a suspicious person to the
gate of the town, where they began to question him.
Then they searched him carefully, lest he might be the
bearer of important papers, and even stripped him of his
clothes.    On his protesting that he was innocent, and as
they found nothing on him to inculpate him, they conducted him, half-stripped, to their officer, to know what
they should do with him.    Ignatius' first thought while
they were conducting him was to imagine to himself Our
Lord led in shame through the streets of Jerusalem; and
his first emotion was that of joy in being treated as Our
Lord was.    But when he reflected on the consequences
that might follow from his position if they took him for

a spy, he asked himself the question whether he ought to declare himself to the officer who and what he was, and speak to him according to his rank, or should continue to express himself like a person of low condition, as he had been doing for the sake of concealment. Upon reflection he rejected this new thought as a piece of weakness inspired by the desire of making an impression upon the commander, and so escape the disgrace of being put in prison, or of suffering, perhaps, even worse. Full of holy indignation against himself, he said, " No, I will not behave to him as a great lord, nor make low obeisance, nor even take off my hat to him." In fact, he conducted himself as a simpleton, not answering the questions put to him, or else making answers not to the purpose. When asked, however, if he was a spy, he answered that he was not. The commandant soon perceived that his men had made a mistake, and reprimanded them sharply for having brought before him a half-witted creature as a spy. The soldiers, angry at his reprimand, vented their ill-humor upon the Saint, beating and maltreating him in a brutal manner. A subaltern officer, pitying his condition, gave him lodging and food. The following day things seemed to take no better turn, for Ignatius, having walked all day till nightfall without hindrance, was seen by a French sentinel of a garrison in a fortress, and conducted to the presence of the captain. Here, however, he was treated more humanely, and the very reverse happened of what he might have expected when, on their asking who he was, he replied that he was a Spaniard, and of Guipuscoa. In fact, the captain was himself a native of that country, and treated Ignatius as a fellow-countryman, taking care of him, and freely allowing him to continue his journey the next day. At Genoa he quickly found an opportunity of crossing over to Spain, having met in the commander of the galley a friend, Don Rodrigo Portundo, whom he had known at the Court of Spain, and who took him on board of one of his ships. Here again he found himself in the midst of that warfare which once he had sought so eagerly, but which now had no longer any charms for him, nor any laurels for him to win.

The Spanish fleet was pursued and closely pressed by the famous Admiral Andrea Doria, who at this time was in the service of France. However, Ignatius reached the harbor of Barcelona at the end of February or the beginning of March, in the year 1524.

# CHAPTER VI.

As soon as Ignatius arrived at Barcelona he hastened
to communicate his new plan to his pious benefactress,
Doña Isabel Roser, who approved of it entirely. He was
also encouraged in his design by a certain Jerome Ardebal, a man who feared God, and kept a public school
of the Latin language. Both these offered him their
assistance: the first engaged to provide him with support,
and the second to give him gratuitously the lessons
he required. But Ignatius, having made acquaintance
at Manresa with a Cistercian of great experience in the
spiritual life, of whose counsels he had resolved during
his voyage to avail himself, would not accept the kind
offers of these two friends unless he could make his
studies at Manresa. In fact, he went there with this design, but finding the Religious whom he sought no
longer alive, he returned to accept the generous offers of
his friends, and they faithfully fulfilled their promises.
Agnes Pasquale provided him with lodgings, and her
brother Pujol, the parish priest, lent him the books he
required. By degrees the circle of his acquaintance and
benefactors increased, owing to the spiritual advantages
derived from his company and conversation, and from
his experience in spiritual things. Amongst others the
names are recorded of Doña Stephana de Requesens,
Doña Isabella de Bajadox, Doña Guiomar Gralla, Doña
Elizabeth de Sosa, and others besides, several of whom
belonged to distinguished families. His circumstances
here assumed a condition similar to that in which he'
had lived at Manresa. The good were drawn to him with
a powerful attraction, while, on the other hand, he roused

the strong opposition of the bad, and they poured out
against him the hatred they felt against piety and virtue.
They treated him in the most outrageous manner, and
having learned that he was of noble extraction, as his
manners and appearance indicated, they tried to make
him pass for a man who had quitted his home to live as
an idle vagabond.   Not content with this, they tried to
frighten him by menaces, but the Saint took no notice of
their words, and preserved a serene and smiling countenance, proceeding on his path with firmness, and counting
his antagonists as men who did him a true service.   The
manufacturers and people employed in the house of his
benefactress took part in this ill-usage of him, and, by
way of revenge, before he left, he obtained their conversion by his prayers.*

Ignatius had now become, at the age of thirty-three,
a scholar studying the rudiments of the Latin tongue,
amongst boys who surpassed him in quickness of learning
and in the progress they had made.   This act of his
proves that he possessed a strength and magnanimity of
soul for a parallel to which we may look in the old histories of Grecian worthies, some few of whom have
gained a glorious celebrity by less than what he did, for
he had to triumph over greater difficulties, and to overcome the humiliation and wearisomeness of a study so
little agreeable to his ardent character or his former
habits of life.   But the greatest obstacle arose from the
irresistible drawing of his mind to prayer and contemplation of heavenly things, and this tendency became
stronger than ever, and so constantly occupied his mind
as to lead him to neglect his studies and his lessons.
He soon became aware that he must put a salutary re-
straint upon his inclination, and had recourse for this
purpose to decisive measures, binding himself to keep
his resolution by a vow.   For one day he begged his
preceptor to come with him into the Church of Our Lady

---

* The house in which Ignatius lodged was in the street of the cot-
ton-spinners, the last upon the left hand as you go down to the sea.
He inhabited a little chamber at the top of the staircase in the middle
of the upper story.   It is plain, from what can be gathered, that the
Pasquale family were opulent manufacturers.

of the Sea, which was close by, and there, falling upon his knees, he asked pardon for his past negligence, and promised him under vow to apply himself with all possible diligence for the future, and earnestly besought him that, if at any time he failed in his promise, he would punish him as he would a child, in the presence of the scholars. This act of heroic humility increased still more the esteem his master had for him, and all those who were acquainted with him, and, at the same time, it caused him to make greater progress in his studies. Nor was the lesson which he thus learned by experience by any means a fruitless one, seeing that it served afterwards to help him to prescribe those exact rules regarding the studies of the Society and the practices of piety which were to accompany them, that the one might assist the other. Upon this subject he thus writes in aftertimes, when General of the Society—"We must not be surprised if our studies do not always derive from the holiness of their object that unction which we could desire, for He to Whom alone it belongs to grant this grace dispenses it to whom He will, and only when it seems good to Him; so that, when we do not feel it, we ought to think that it is Divine Providence that would deprive us of these sensible consolations during the time of our studies, which generally present many difficulties to the mind, and for the reason that these sensible delights, as they give great pleasure to the soul, so they tend to enfeeble the body. Besides, the study of the sciences has commonly the effect of stilling the sentiments of piety and drying up the feelings. But, notwithstanding, study undertaken for the sole sake of pleasing God is an excellent exercise of piety. Provided that the solidity of virtue suffers no detriment, and that the time prescribed by the constitutions is given to prayer, sensible consolations are of little importance; we must not be disquieted at the loss of them, but accept from the hand of God all that he pleases to send us, and keep our eye upon the main thing, which is patience, humility, obedience, and charity." *

* Bartoli, i., 26.

Ignatius lived at Barcelona in the same manner as he had done at Manresa, if we take into account the difference of circumstances. He practised the same austerities, giving to prayer the greater part of the night, since he could not give to it much of the daytime. He was poorly dressed, and wore shoes without soles to them, and begged his daily bread, giving to other poor people the best of what he received, whether in food or other alms. Being found fault with for this, he would reply— " What, then, would you do if Christ Our Lord asked of you an alms? Would you be content to give Him of the worst? " As to what passed in his prayer during the night, we have declaration upon oath taken from an eye-witness, John Pasquale, the son of his hostess, who often, out of curiosity, watched the Saint through a crevice of the door. He observed that from time to time the room was lit up by a bright light, which seemed to proceed from the Saint in prayer; that, when on his knees, he was often raised from the ground, and that in his ecstasy he would gently say, in a scarcely audible voice—" O Lord, if men only knew Thee! "   And another time, speaking of himself, he said—" My God, Thy goodness is infinite in bearing with so miserable a sinner." He was once also in public raised from the ground in a rapture. He often visited the church of the Nuns of the Order of St. Jerome, and these saw that one day, having prayed three hours motionless and with a glistening countenance at the altar of St. Matthew, he was raised in the air in a kneeling posture, and remained so a long time.*

Ignatius prayed for the interests of the kingdom of God, and not for his own individual consolation, but we have only scanty evidence to show the number of those to whom he did good during this period of his life, and we are left to little more than conjectures. We may gather, however, this much from his written life. Out-

---

* He appears to have held some communication with the Nuns of this convent, for one of them, Antonetta Strada, received a reliquary from him, containing a little earth and a pebble from the Holy Land. This relic was still kept, in 1800, on the high altar of the church, and under it was written, in the Saint's own handwriting—" For a keepsake." (Menchacha, *Comm. prat.*, l. i., p. 2.)

side of the walls of the town, between the Porta Nueva
and the Porta San Daniele, was situated a convent of
Dominican nuns, bearing the name of the "Holy Angels," into which, through neglect of inclosure, a worldly
life had so far found entrance that, to the great scandal
of the faithful, the parlor was frequented by men who
visited the convent. The Saint was aware of this dis-
graceful state of things, and resolved upon putting an
end to it. Accordingly he made a visit daily to the
church of the convent, and prayed for the conversion of
the nuns. After he had continued to do so for some
time the sisters took notice of him, and could not but
admire the fervor of his prayers, the expression of his
countenance, and the tears which he shed. The novelty
excited their curiosity, and when they heard it reported
that he was a saint they wished to hear him, and so invited him to an interview. This was what he desired.
He began at once to put before them, in the liveliest and
most striking manner, the holiness of their vocation,
and the consequences which the life they were leading
would entail upon them, the wrong they did to God, the
scandal they gave to men, and the loss of grace they
incurred. In the course of his conversations he laid before them the grand truths of religion on the end of
man—especially when consecrated to God by vows,—sin
and the chastisements of God upon it, and the chief
points of the Spiritual Exercises. He then taught them
to meditate on these subjects and on the life of Jesus
Christ, and by these means wrought such a change in
them, that not only was strict inclosure re-established,
but they returned to the full spirit of their rule. This
improvement was displeasing to those with whose dised-
ifying visits it interfered, and roused their anger against
the author of it, which they soon made him feel. They
resolved to deter him from his visits, and twice they
caused him to be beaten on his road. Seeing, however,
that he persevered, they suborned two Moorish slaves,
with orders to kill him. These awaited him at the gate
of St. Daniel, as he was returning from the convent, in
company of a good priest named Puyalto, who was assisting him in the work of the conversion of the nuns.

The assassins fell upon them with such fury that they were left for dead upon the ground, and the priest died a few days after from the effect of the blows. Ignatius was found in this condition by a miller, who, out of compassion, laid him on his mule and conveyed him to his lodging. There his death was hourly expected, and for about thirty days it was uncertain whether he would live or die, but, notwithstanding his sufferings and extreme exhaustion, he would not leave off wearing his hairshirt, until his confessor, a Franciscan, commanded him to do so. During his convalescence he received from all of every rank marks of the most sincere respect and regard. Ladies of the highest station of life were eager to visit him and wait on him, and the poor surrounded his bed, offering all that they could, namely, their prayers and their tears. Nor were these offered up in vain, for, to the joy of all but his wicked enemies, he recovered. As soon as he could leave his sick bed his first visit was to the convent of the Angels, in spite of the remonstrances and entreaties of the Señora Pasquale, to whom he replied that he desired nothing so much as to die for the glory of God and the good of his neighbors. However, he not only received no harm, but had soon the satisfaction of seeing the author of the outrage against him come as a penitent to beg forgiveness. This man was one Ribera, a merchant, who, being touched with remorse, came to discover himself to the Saint, as he returned from the convent of the Angels, and, while he promised amendment of life, declared that he had had no intention of killing him, but only of putting him in fear.

It happened at the same time that, in his return from the convent, he passed through the street of Belloc, and saw a great crowd assembled, from which loud cries and lamentations proceeded. Hastening to the spot whence they came, he found that a man named Lissani had hanged himself in a fit of desperation at having lost a lawsuit with his brother. Ignatius drew near to the body, which had been cut down, and hoping that the poor man might not be quite dead, endeavored to recall him to life. Seeing that his efforts were in vain, he fell upon his knees and poured forth tears and prayers in behalf of one who had died such a miserable death. Many of the by-standers united their prayers with his, and he then arose and pronounced aloud over him the holy name of Jesus. The dead man instantly opened his eyes, came to himself, and had time to express his sorrow for what he had done before he closed his eyes forever. Some documents declare that he had time to make his confession. His body, by the bishop's permission, to whom all the circumstances of the fact were given, was buried in consecrated ground. The by-standers, who had attentively observed all that the Saint did, were deeply moved at the spectacle of which they were eye-witnesses. *

As we have said above, St. Ignatius had long desired to find some companions animated with sentiments like his own, and calculated to aid him in his undertakings for the sake of God and the good of the Church. He endeavored to carry this intention into effect at Barcelona, and out of a number who presented themselves he made choice of three, whom he judged to be the most suitable, but who had not yet completed their studies. The first, by name Calisto, had, by counsel of the Saint, made a pilgrimage to Jerusalem—perhaps Ignatius wished to put him on his trial. He speaks of him in a letter written at this time to Agnes Pasquale—

My Sister in Our Lord Jesus Christ,—
     I have thought it my duty to write to you, on account of the desire which I know you have to serve Our Lord, and because I think you are in affliction at the loss of your daughter, the gracious child whom it has pleased God to take to Himself, and at the troubles raised up against you by your many enemies through your service to

* This account is taken from the acts of the Canonization of St. Ignatius. Much has been said for and against the reality of the death of Lissani, as may be seen in the Bollandists. According to the opinion of the by-standers and of John Pasquale, he was really dead. The latter, however, could not affirm positively that he recovered his speech or made his confession, but he was sure that he gave signs of repentance. The first Fathers of the Society leave us in uncertainty about the fact. The juridical informations were taken too late to ascertain from the proofs then existing as to whether Lissani was really dead, and whether, if dead and resuscitated, he recovered the full use of his senses for a short time, so as to be able to repent.

God, as well as the temptations of the common enemy of mankind, who never ceases to lay snares for us. I assure you, by the love of Our Lord God, in which you daily endeavor to make progress, avoiding everything that may be an impediment to it, this temptation will have no power to hurt you, if you have a care to prefer above all things the glory of God, as you are bound to do, especially seeing that He does not ask of you to undertake anything that may be injurious to you by the efforts it may require, but would have you, on the contrary, rejoice in Him, and give your body what is necessary for it. Let Him be the end of all your thoughts, words, and actions. As to temporal affairs, be occupied in them in such a manner as always to prefer to them the commands of Our Lord, for such is His will and desire, and whoever considers it well will find that this life is more sad and full of pains. *

There is here at present a pilgrim, named Calisto, with whom I should wish to treat on the matter relative to you, for it may be that you will find in him more than he at first appears to give promise of. Let us then, for the sake of the love of God, take courage in Our Lord, to Whom we owe so much, and let us exhort each other to receive His gifts with the same generous will as He bestows them. May our Blessed Lady intercede with her Son Our Lord for us sinners, and obtain for us His blessing on our endeavors, that our hearts and minds may rise up from all feebleness and discouragement to strength and joy, for His greater glory.

Barcelona, St. Nicholas' Day. †

The second disciple who joined St. Ignatius was named Artiaga, and the third was Diego de Cazeres, who held a situation at the Court of the Viceroy of Catalonia. Among those refused by the Saint was a certain Rodis, to whom he addressed these prophetic words—" You cannot follow me, but one of your sons will enter the Order which, by the grace of God, I shall found." This double prophecy was verified, for within sixteen years from this date the Society of Jesus was publicly acknowledged, and afterwards a son of Rodis—Michael Rodis, a distinguished lawyer—entered the Society, and has mentioned that he heard from his father the words we have related. §

In these occupations two years had elapsed, and Ardebal, the preceptor of Ignatius, as well as others who were

---

* We could not decipher the words that follow and close this sentence.

† The year is not given, but it can be no other than the year 1525, for the year following he was a student at Alcala.

§ The Bollandists cite the authentic testimony of Father Francis de Caspez, who declared that he had often heard this prophecy from the mouth of Father Michael Rodis.

interested in him, thought that he ought not to study Latin any longer, but proceed at once to philosophy. Ignatius, wishing neither to follow his own light nor to reject the opinion of others, requested to be subjected to an examination, that he might be assured that he was fit to pass to higher studies. A distinguished theologian examined him and declared him to be sufficiently well prepared, upon which he resolved to go for his studies to the University of Alcala, which had been lately founded by Cardinal Ximenès, and already enjoyed a high reputation. He arrived there at the beginning of August, in the year 1526, preceding his three companions, who were to follow him. The impression which he had made at Barcelona was such, that fifteen years after his departure the remembrance of his stay there was still fresh, so much so that, when a near relative of the Saint, Antonio d'Araoz, who had lately entered the Society, came to this city, he was in a manner besieged in his house by a crowd of people who came to hear news of Ignatius, and who recounted to him at the same time what they had seen and heard of Ignatius during his stay at Barcelona.

The Saint pursued at Alcala the same kind of life which he had led at Barcelona, dividing his time between study, prayer, and the works of charity to which he was prompted by his zeal for the salvation of souls. He lodged at first at a hospital,* where, in waiting upon the sick, he made acquaintance with a young Frenchman named John, a page in the household of Don Martin of Cordova, Viceroy of Navarre, who was suffering from a wound received in a quarrel a little time before, when his master passed through Alcala. Ignatius gave all the attention to his wants, both corporal and spiritual, that charity could suggest; and God blessed his labors, for this young man, quitting the world, put himself into the hands of St. Ignatius, and thus became his fourth disciple. He joined the three others when they came to Alcala, and they

---

* He afterwards quitted this abode for the new hospital, where he was lodged in a room haunted by evil spirits. He was not informed of this, and the first night was much alarmed by the noises he heard, but he quickly took courage and commanded the infesting spirits to disturb the place no more. After which they never returned.

lodged in the house of a printer, Diego d'Eguia, with whose brother Ignatius was previously acquainted. *

The members of this little Society lived on alms, and wore the same dress, a long habit of light grey and a cap of the same color, so that the people called them the *ensacados*, or men in sacks. They put in practice all the works of mercy, but our Saint desired always to live unknown, as the following circumstance shows. A rich merchant of Azpeytia, named Martin Saez, having come on business to Alcala, heard speak of his countryman as a saint, and as he had seen him before in his own country, he wished to renew his acquaintance with him. Accordingly he waited for him one day as he came from school, and following him unobserved he saw him enter a poor dwelling, and not long after come out again. When Ignatius had quitted it he also went in, and finding there a poor, old, sick woman, asked her who that student was who had just left the house, and whether she was acquainted with his name. She replied that she was not, but that he was a saint who came every day to see her and bring her alms, and also comfort her with his pious discourse. Saez desired her to tell the unknown on his return that, if he had any need of assistance for himself or others there was one who would abundantly supply him. She gave the message, but Ignatius, finding that he was observed, came there no more, saying to the old woman—"Good sister, I have hitherto taken care of you, but God will henceforth provide for you in some other manner, and to His care I commend you."

Our Saint's zeal for the good of souls was still greater. When he gave an alms he never failed to accompany it with suitable lessons and exhortations to virtue and the fulfilment of religious duties. These he gave not only in private, to individuals, but in public, to all who were willing to hear them. He set before them the great truths of religion, which are of themselves so powerful to move

* He afterwards entered the Society, and at that time assisted the Saint with alms for the sick and the poor. One day, when Ignatius had recourse to his generosity, and he had no money to give, he opened a chest and offered him some bed-coverings, and some torches and other articles, which Ignatius took away enveloped in a cloth, and sold for the poor.

the feelings, and were made more so by the manner in which he explained them, as set forth in the Exercises, enlightened by his own ardent piety and lively faith. His teaching consisted chiefly of popular exercises, which he and his disciples subsequently developed. He held conferences of the students, teaching them the means of progress in perfection, and conversing with them on pious subjects. Two characteristic points were peculiarly his own; on the one hand, entire disregard of all human considerations, and abandonment of self to the operations of grace, and, on the other, the employment of all human means in disposing souls to receive it. These two principles were developed in his own conduct in proportion as he advanced in the paths of perfection, and he has left them as an inheritance to his children, prescribing them as a rule of conduct, in which the forces of heaven and earth are combined in a manner conformable to the state of man in this world, so as to attain happily to the end of creation. Thus that schism caused by sin, which weakens our strength by division and exposes us to strife and danger, is remedied; weakness and inconstancy give way to strength and confidence; union takes the place of division; search becomes possession, and trouble and disquietude are changed into certainty and repose.

We may well conjecture that, here as elsewhere, the efforts of the Saint were crowned with success, and that numerous conversions were made which remain unrecorded; it is certain that he sowed seeds which afterwards sprang up. It was only natural that a soul like his, touched with divine grace, and coming into contact with men of all kinds, should draw many of them by its influence, and work in them a salutary reformation. But in this work he was distinguished by the characteristic difference between him and the false reformers of the time—that he built up in the Church and with the Church. Like salt which retains its savor, he renewed that which was beginning to decay, and, by the virtue of the teaching of the Gospel, infused fresh vigor into spiritual life and attachment to the Church. A fact is recounted of him which shows how gifted he was in converting souls most deeply sunk in vice. It was then the custom, and continued so a long time afterwards, that young ecclesiastics, who, though not priests, yet held preferments in the cathedral churches, should go to the universities to complete their studies. There was at Alcala at that time one of these young clergy, a canon of one of the principal churches in Spain. Having made acquaintance with some disorderly students, he led a life little in conformity with his vocation and very scandalous to others. Ignatius undertook his conversion. After having implored light and assistance from Heaven, he went to the canon's house, and, arming himself with courage and patience, sent in a message that he desired to have an interview with him. The canon received him with a look that plainly showed that such people as Ignatius were not welcome at his house. However, he observed the ordinary forms of politeness, so much so that, when the Saint expressed a wish to speak with him alone, he dismissed his attendants. Ignatius addressed himself to his conscience, speaking respectfully but forcibly, and telling him plainly the opinion entertained of him commonly in the town, but which his flatterers had concealed from him. Wounded in his pride and transported with anger, the canon interrupted him by a torrent of abuse, and ended by threatening to have him thrown out of the window. The servants, hearing loud words. hastened to the room, but before they entered Ignatius had time to address some words to him which calmed his anger, though what he said or how it took such effect upon him is a mystery. The servants, on entering, saw only that their master was advancing towards Ignatius with signs of singular respect, and received orders to prepare a repast for himself and the visitor. To complete the good work begun, the Saint consented to remain, with such happy result that the canon not only changed his whole life and continued always a friend and protector of Ignatius, but used his great influence with others, and so was able to render him a double service.

Trials and contradictions could not fail to find out Ignatius at Alcala, as they had found him at Barcelona and Manresa; and the more so, as the sphere of his action was enlarged, and his position as a student brought him into closer connection with the authorities. At first his conduct found no opponents, with the exception of some private individuals of little note, who looked merely to exterior things and took scandal at seeing a young man of condition professing a mendicant life. Among these were some clerics of different colleges. But subsequently, when it was noticed that he and the persons under his direction communicated regularly every week and on all festivals, a thing then unhappily very rare, the unfavorable opinion with which he was regarded began soon to be shared by persons in a higher position, so that even the canon of the college church of St. Just publicly refused holy Communion to him and his companions, blaming their frequent reception of it as too great familiarity with God. However, this was a plea that could not be long maintained, and the worthy canon, convinced no doubt by Ignatius himself, changed his whole disposition in his regard and became his friend. Still greater sensation was caused by his instructions, and various reports were spread concerning his book of *Spiritual Exercises*, and he was soon denounced to the Inquisition at Toledo. But before we see what were the consequences of this denunciation, we must close the chapter with a few words on the immediate object of his residence at Alcala—namely, his studies. It cannot be matter of surprise that he made less progress in these, while occupied in exterior labors sufficient to engage an apostolic missioner. Moreover, with the object perhaps of shortening the time and becoming a priest sooner, he studied philosophy and theology at the same time, and thus drew little benefit from either, overtaxing his mind by the multiplicity of subjects on which it was engaged.

# CHAPTER VII.

THE INQUISITION PROCEEDS AGAINST ST. IGNATIUS. HE
IS DECLARED INNOCENT, AND GOES TO SALAMANCA.
PERSECUTED THERE ALSO, HE RESOLVES TO QUIT SPAIN
AND GO TO PARIS.

AT this period of time, when the world was running
after novelties, and there was much excitement and confusion of ideas, we need not wonder that the conduct of
St. Ignatius appeared to many strange, and therefore suspicious, for men of superficial minds are apt to look with
distrust on all that they do not at once understand. Such
men as these, remembering that a few years previously, in
1523, a secret society of fanatics, calling themselves the
"Illuminati"—*Los Alumbrados*, had been discovered in
the dioceses of Seville and Cadiz, now confounded the
unknown student of Alcala with these, equally unknown
to them, and accordingly denounced him to the Inquisition
at Toledo.*

After a denunciation of this kind, which could only be
made from persons on their oath, the Tribunal was obliged
to act, more especially as in such dangerous times the
authorities were forced to redouble their vigilance in order
to preserve to the Church countries not yet infected with
the poison of heresy. It is true that suspicion fell in this
case on the man who was to be the very firmest support

---

* The sect of the "Illuminati" was not entirely destroyed at its first
appearance. It existed forty years after in Andalusia. The Tribunal
of Cordova condemned it in 1565, and declared that its principles were
contrary to the spirit of Jesus Christ and the Church, and of the saints.
Its partisans were given to a false spirituality and a false mysticism.
They pretended to receive illumination from Heaven in the prayer of
quietude. They may be considered from these indications to have
been the precursors of Quietism.

of the Apostolic See ; but he himself was very far from blaming their conduct, though he had so much to suffer from it. We ought, indeed, to recognize in it an appointment of Divine Providence, since, besides the other advantages derived by St. Ignatius from the inquiries and examinations to which he was subjected, it gave him opportunity to manifest to all that the spirit with which he was animated came really from God.

The Tribunal of the Inquisition commissioned Don Alonzo de Mechia to go to Alcala, and, assisted by Dr. Michael Carasco, canon of the College of St. Just, to take exact information on the life and conduct of the accused. The inquest was held in secret, on the 19th of November, and the persons of the house, as well as those who were acquainted with Ignatius, were examined. As nothing deserving of blame was found in him, the Judge thought his own presence no longer necessary, and charged the grand vicar of the Archbishop of Toledo, Dr. John Figueroa of Alcala, to proceed, if necessary, against Ignatius. The Doctor, after some days, caused him and his companions to be sent for, and informed them of what had passed, adding that he found nothing to blame in them either as to faith or morals, and that they might continue their pious practices as before. But he added, that, as they did not belong to any Religious Order, it was not right for them to wear a uniform habit, and bade them at least vary the uniformity of color: for example, that Ignatius and Artiaga might assume the color of black, while Calisto and Cazeres wore brown. They all obeyed this order, and were equally submissive when the vicar some time after bade them make use of shoes and no longer go barefoot.

On the 6th of March, the following year, 1527, a new charge was made against Ignatius. He ordinarily engaged the persons whom he directed in visiting the hospitals and in exercising other works of mercy. Thus a lady of high quality and much devoted to the Saint, being desirous of following this practice, gave ground for an examination, which, however, turned entirely to his credit. All cause for disquietude seemed to have disappeared, when a new incident raised a more serious disturbance. Ignatius had gone to Segovia to take care of his disciple Calisto, who had fallen very sick there, and had scarcely returned to Alcala after leaving his companion convalescent, than he was visited at his lodging (for he stayed no longer at the hospital) by an officer of justice, who conducted him to the prison for clerics, where he was to take up his abode, though not under close confinement, until it should be decided what was to be done with him; meantime he was not told the reasons of this harsh proceeding.*

The following circumstance was the cause of the Saint's imprisonment. Two ladies of rank, a mother and her daughter, both widows, had put themselves for some considerable time under his direction, and were among the most fervent of his disciples. The daughter, still young and remarkably beautiful, was named Doña Louisa Velasquez, and the mother, Maria del Vado. Led by female impetuosity, they were not content to keep within the limits prescribed to tnem by their director, but they would traverse the country as mendicants, and go from one hospital to another to serve the sick. They communicated their design to Ignatius, who strongly disapproved of it, and represented to them the dangers to which they would necessarily expose both their virtue and their reputation. They gave up this purpose, it is true, but towards the close of Lent, in the absense of Ignatius, they took it into their heads to make a pilgrimage on foot and beg their way to the holy cloth of St. Veronica, at Jaën, and Our Lady of Guadaloupe. They carried out their design, accompanied by a single servant-maid, taking the precaution to confide their secret only to a small circle of intimate friends. These persons, however, were obliged to reveal the truth, when after the departure of the ladies the most sinister rumors were spread concerning them. As soon as the object of their secret journey was known, the indig-

---

* It was on his way to this prison, according to Bartoli, that he met the young Francis Borgia, seventeen years of age, accompanied by a grand retinue. Scarce twenty years after, the same Francis, then duke of Candia and viceroy of Catalonia, humbly cast himself at the feet of Ignatius, at Rome, and asked of him to be admitted into the Society.

nation of the public fell upon Ignatius, whom they accused of being the instigator of these extravagances. The Dr. Peter Cirvello, guardian of the two ladies, was especially furious against him, and he was a man held in high esteem, for Ximenès had lately given him the first chair of theology in the newly-founded University of Alcala. In order to free from blame the ladies under his care, as it fell in some sort indirectly on himself, he laid the most unfounded accusations against Ignatius, declaring that by his extravagances he drew away from their duty persons of all ranks and condition, and led them into indiscretions to which it was time to put an end. Not content with this, he addressed himself to the Grand Vicar Figueroa, setting aside the rector of the University, whose duty it was to judge of the faults against discipline committed by the students. But as the rector, Matthew Pasquale of Catalonia, was favorable to the Saint, and as they had extended the accusation to points of faith, as the interrogatory proves, the affair was carried before the spiritual authorities.

Ignatius, not being under close confinement in his prison, was visited by a great number of persons, with whom he could hold his usual spiritual conferences, now made the more impressive by the position in which he was placed, for he was preaching by his own example the doctrine which teaches us to suffer affronts and persecutions for the sake of Jesus Christ. Among these persons was the Dr. George Navero, first professor of exegesis in the University, who was so touched by his discourse that he forgot the hour of his lecture, and when he entered the room where his audience was waiting for him he said to them, like a man out of himself, " I have seen Paul in chains ; " thus expressing the force and spirit of the words of Ignatius, and the constancy of his character. Many ladies of the highest rank interested themselves about him, among whom were Eleanora de Mascareña, who was soon afterwards appointed governess of Philip II., and Doña Teresa de Cardeña, who often sent him messages offering to take him out of prison. But he made reply to her, " He for Whose love I am here can easily deliver me if it be His good pleasure." He feared so little an inquiry, that when Calisto, whom he had left at Segovia, returned to Alcala upon the news of his imprisonment before he was fully restored to health, that he might enter into voluntary confinement with him, Ignatius sent him to the grand vicar to inform him of all he knew against his .master. On account of Calisto's feeble health the Saint obtained his enlargement, through the interposition of a friend, a professor of the University. The prisoner was heard for the first time on the 18th of May. Figueroa came to him with a notary and put several questions to him. He asked him among other things whether he observed the Sabbath. To this question Ignatius replied, " Yes, without doubt ; I observe the Saturday in honor of the Blessed Virgin. For the rest, I know nothing of the usages of the Jews, for there are none in my part of the country." The Grand Vicar having asked him if he was acquainted with the two ladies who had gone away secretly, he replied that he was ; but when he was asked whether he knew of their design before they carried it into execution, he said, " Upon the oath which I have taken before this interrogatory, No." This reply gave great satisfaction to the Grand Vicar, who said to him with a smile, and giving him a tap on the shoulder, " Be of good courage, for this is the only cause of your being here. However," said he, " I should be better pleased if you avoided all novelties in your discourse." Ignatius replied with modesty, and at the same time with firmness, " Sir, I should never have believed that it was a novelty among Christians to speak of Jesus Christ." All the declarations having been set down in the protocol, the Vicar General went away satisfied, awaiting the return of the two absentees to terminate the affair. They on their return having declared that they had gone of their own accord, there was no further reason for detaining Ignatius in prison, where he had been kept forty-two days. On the 1st of June he had to appear before the Vicar General Figueroa, who announced to him the decision of the tribunal, to the effect that he should be set at liberty, because they had found nothing in him contrary to faith or morals, but that it was enjoined on him and his companions to abandon within the space of ten days their long habits, and to assume the ordinary costume of students ; moreover, that he was forbidden to hold public assemblies and discourses, either in public or in private, until he had completed his four years of philosophy ; and that, if he broke these injunctions, he should be excommunicated and banished the kingdom.

This decision seemed to contradict itself, for it approved and forbade the same thing at the same time. On the one hand it declared the accused not guilty in what he had done, and on the other menaced him with penalties in case he did it again. But if we consider things more critically we shall find the explanation of this extraordinary conduct in the coarse-minded, material conceptions of Christianity then prevalent. It was supposed to be limited within certain fixed boundaries, which none might cross without being at once guilty of error and temerity. Such was the state of things generally in Europe. That living spirit of charity, which alone imparts a true knowledge of the faith, having been lost in a great proportion of men, the interior emptiness of their minds showed itself on the first assault of the spirit of falsehood. In Spain, it is true, the iron hand of the Inquisition had prevented the evil from appearing, but in the long run the means which it employed would not have sufficed, as the sequel has shown but too clearly, had not our Saint renewed the true spirit of Christianity, and restored the faith to its vigor by rendering it practical. He it was who, by recommending meditation on the truths of the faith, gave reality and an object to the want that was felt after the minute study of the dogmas of religion; whilst in the North the faith, delivered over by the doctrine of free inquiry to the fancies of the human intellect, degenerated into empty formulas, mostly false, and finally succumbed to the seduction of sensuality. The same danger manifested itself among those nations which remained Catholic, for the continual increase of the spirit of the world had so weakened the principles of Christian life among the faithful, that the pastors themselves looked upon those whose faith was more lively, and who approached frequently the sacraments, as belonging to the new sects. This remark is of importance, and shows what we owe to St. Ignatius.

He submitted to the sentence of the Inquisition, but observed that he was too poor to buy new clothing for himself and his companions. The Grand Vicar recommended him to a charitable priest named Luzena, whose whole life was given to works of mercy, and who immediately offered to accompany Ignatius through the city to beg for money to procure the new clothing. On their way they saw a gentleman of the name of Don Lope Mendoza playing at ball in front of his house with a great number of friends; Luzena saluted him and asked him for an alms in behalf of his companion. But Lope, to whom Ignatius had on a previous occasion given a salutary piece of advice as to the life he was leading, angrily refused. "Now," said he, "are you not ashamed to go begging for such a worthless fellow and hypocrite as that: if he does not deserve a pile of faggots, may I be burned alive." These words caused a general feeling of disgust among those who were present; but still more of fear, when the malediction which he had called down on his head actually befell him. For shortly afterwards news of the heir-presumptive, Philip II., having arrived, every one did his utmost to manifest his joy by firing guns or by display of fireworks. Lope, mounting on a tower at the top of his house, began firing salutes, when a match fell upon a powder-barrel, which exploded and burned the unhappy man so fearfully that, shrieking out in sudden agony and despair, he expired before he could obtain any help. This calamity, falling upon him like a judgment of God, made a profound impression on those who had possibly conceived some unfavorable ideas with regard to the Saint. The affront, if it may be so called, put upon Ignatius, or rather this trial to which he was subjected, was amply repaid even during his life, when his disciples showed in this same city what their master had been, for here St. Francis Borgia, among others, lectured on Holy Scripture, and after the death of St. Ignatius the most celebrated theologians taught theology, amongst whom were Vasquez and Suarez.

It was impossible for our Saint, considering the spirit with which he was animated, to become on a sudden, as they wished, a mere ordinary student. A soul like his could not be content with slow degrees in becoming victor of the world. As he found himself urged by a superior law within to continue his labors for the spiritual good of his neighbor, and yet could not do this at Alcala without resisting authority, he resolved to leave the city, after having been a little more than a year in it, and to go to Salamanca to continue his studies there, having first sent on his two companions before him. *

On his way to Salamanca he had an interview at Valladolid with the Archbishop of Toledo, Alphonso de Fonseca, concerning the conduct of the Inquisition in his regard. But the Prelate, notwithstanding his good disposition towards him, could alter nothing in his case, and the Saint would not appeal to the Archbishop's tribunal. Besides, it was the will of God that the Saint should be conducted by other ways to the high mark of his vocation, for which the common and purely human means were not sufficient. The Archbishop approved of his design, and encouraged him to continue his studies at Salamanca, and after giving him an alms for his journey, dismissed him. Arrived at Salamanca, without, however, knowing where to find his companions, he went into a church to pray. A pious woman, who was present, recognized him from the description she had heard from them, and coming up to him asked him his name, and conducted him to the friends whom he was seeking.

Being now in another diocese, he was no longer bound by the inhibition of the Vicar General of Alcala. He continued therefore, as before, to labor for the spiritual and corporal welfare of his neighbor. High and low, clergy and laity alike, felt the effects of his zeal. But communications with regard to him soon followed him

* He came to Alcala in the month of August of the year 1526. He was freed from prison on the 1st of June, 1527, and, supposing that his stay at Alcala after this, together with his journey to Salamanca, occupied some months, he must in any case have reached the latter town by the autumn. He cannot therefore have resided at Alcala eighteen months, as Bartoli and Mariani say, for he was in Paris at the beginning of February of the year 1528.

from Alcala, sent either by the spiritual authorities, or by private persons, possibly with the best intentions. At all events, his fame everywhere either preceded or accompanied him, and soon drew attention to him; so that he had scarcely been a fortnight in Salamanca when a new inquiry and accusation was set on foot against him. We relate the account which he himself gave to Father Gonzalez. About twelve days after his arrival, Ignatius received from his confessor, a Dominican of the convent of St. Estevan, an invitation to a spiritual conference with some of the Religious of the house, who desired to hear him. He answered that he would attend him " in the name of the Lord." The Dominican then invited him to come to dine the Sunday following, adding that many questions would be put to him. Ignatius kept the appointment, and came with Calisto. After the repast the superior, accompanied by the confessor and another Father, conducted him to a chapel, where all were assembled. The sub-prior expressed then his astonishment at the dress and appearance of Calisto, who, being very tall, wore clothes too short and too small for him, which he had begged here and there ; besides, he still carried with him his pilgrim's staff. Ignatius replied that Calisto had given to a poor priest, for the love of God, the habit which he had, for the love of God, received at Alcala. Of this the Dominican disapproved, but yet, turning to Ignatius, said with an air of affability that he saw with pleasure that he and his companions went through the cities like the Apostles, to draw the people to God. At the same time he desired to know what studies they had made. St. Ignatius replied that he had studied more than the rest, but that he did not know very much, having not been very solidly grounded. " How is it, then, that you preach ? " said the Dominican. " We do not preach," replied Ignatius, " but we hold spiritual conferences on the virtues and vices, and we endeavor to excite those who hear us to the love of the one and the hatred of the other." " But," said his questioner, " to speak suitably of the virtues and vices, one must have either studied in the schools, or must be taught by the Holy Ghost Himself. Now, you have not been taught in the schools, you must be therefore taught by the Holy Ghost."

The good Father seemed well satisfied with his argument, though Ignatius would not admit the conclusion he drew from it. The Dominican, by this dilemma, did wrong in some sort to Gospel truth, or at least to the common-sense view of Christianity, which certainly it is impossible to have without a knowledge of the law of Jesus Christ. For, in order to know the duty of a Christian, and, consequently, what is morally good and bad, it is not necessary to have studied in the universities. Now, Ignatius spoke of the virtues and vices, and, consequently, of the life of a Christian, solely in a practical point of view, while his opponent supposed that he taught them speculatively, as in the schools, and so his dilemma fell to the ground. Ignatius probably wished to cut short the discussion, seeing that, from their opposite points of view, there was little likelihood of their coming to an understanding. Having, therefore, well weighed his reply, he said to them : " I have already sufficiently explained myself on this point." But the Father, not content with this answer, pressed him again. Ignatius contented himself with saying : " My Father, I have already said enough, and I will say no more except before my superiors, who have a right to interrogate me." " Well," replied the sub-prior, " since it is so, you must remain here ; we shall know how to oblige you to speak." And immediately leaving the chapel, along with all his company, he ordered the gates of the convent to be closed, and lodged Ignatius and Calisto in separate cells. Here they remained for three days, during which the Religious made frequent visits to the Saint, to hear him speak on his method of prayer and meditation, and to converse with him on pious subjects. But they were divided in their judgments of him ; some unreservedly approved, saying that he might without danger be allowed to act freely, while others, though doing justice to his character, regarded it as dangerous to allow a layman to teach. Meanwhile the affair had been reported to the vicar-general of the bishop, who, on the third day, sent a notary with orders to conduct Ignatius and his companion to prison. They were not thrown, it is true, among ordinary malefactors, but they were put into a horrible chamber, situated underneath the common prison, and having in its centre a pillar which supported the arch. To this was attached a chain, about four ells long, with two ends, to each of which one of the prisoners was fettered by the foot, so that when either of them moved the other must follow him. They passed the first night praising God and singing canticles. The next day all the town became acquainted with what had passed, and food, bedding, and other necessaries were brought or sent to him and to his fellow-prisoner from all parts, in the extreme want to which they were reduced. The Saint took advantage of these visits to give lessons and salutary advice to each one that came. Francis de Mendoza, who was afterwards cardinal and archbishop of Valencia, came among others, accompanied by the vicar-general Frias, and asked him in a friendly manner "if the prison and the chains were very painful to him?" "Do you think it," he replied, "to be so great an evil to be in prison and in chains? I assure you, there are not in Salamanca so many handcuffs and chains that I would not gladly wear them all for the love of Our Lord." The prisoners were each separately examined by the vicar-general, and the Saint had to deliver up his manuscripts, and more especially the little book of the *Spiritual Exercises*, to be rigorously examined by three censors. He gave, of his own accord, the names of his three other companions, that they might also be called to account. They were arrested and put in prison, with the exception of John, on account of his youth, and were confined in lower chambers, that they might have no communication with Ignatius. He had a second time to submit to an examination, in which he had to answer a great number of questions, not only on his book, but on important matters concerning the faith. He acknowledged that he did not possess sufficient learning to teach, and he submitted the whole to the judgment of the Church. However, he gave such satisfactory answers that the judges were astonished. He replied also in a very proper manner to a question which Frias put to him

in canon law. The judges then told him to explain the
first commandment of God in their presence, as he was
accustomed to explain it to the people. He chose the
precept enjoined by it of the love of God, and spoke on
it in so lively and penetrating a manner, that the judges
perceived clearly that he was full of the matter of his
discourse, and that he spoke from his own actual feelings. Although he had satisfied them on every point,
they did not fail to reproach him with having attempted,
without the requisite knowledge, to give rules for distin-
guishing venial from mortal sin, a thing difficult even for
theologians. "It is for you to examine whether what I
have said on the point is true or not," he replied, "and
then, if I am wrong, to reject it." But this would have
been a very delicate undertaking, and they were very
far from attempting it. *

At that time a circumstance occurred, extremely favorable to Ignatius and his companions in captivity. All
the prisoners contrived one night to effect their escape,
and none remained but only the disciples of the Saint,
who could have escaped with the rest. This was an
evident proof of their innocence, and when viewed along
with the results of the examination, determined the
judges to remove them to a large building adjoining the
prison, that they might remain there in chains until the
conclusion of the matter, an event not long delayed, for
on the twenty-first day of their imprisonment they were
summoned to hear the sentence pronounced, which declared them to be without reproach as regarded faith
and morals, and allowed them as before to consecrate
their labors to the service of their neighbor. Nevertheless a clause was added, by virtue of which they were
forbidden to endeavor to distinguish between mortal
and venial sin until they should have completed the
course of their theology. Although this sentence was
more gently couched in its terms than that of Alcala, it
did not essentially differ from it. For, in fact, conversion

* The place of which there is question here, and which, with the
rest of the book, has received the Church's approval, is to be found in
the article " Gen. examen of Conscience."—*De Cogitatione.* The
great theologian Suarez has completely justified it.

must have for its foundation the knowledge of sin, and since all the measures which God has taken for the salvation of man have reference to sin as the cause of our ruin, it is impossible to touch upon any question without coming to this fundamental relation. And besides, how can sin be spoken of without indicating the difference between mortal and venial sin ? and the more so, as Ignatius took the matter in its practical point of view. He therefore at once comprehended the purport of this restriction, and, as he had probably already taken his resolution in case they laid it on him, he declared that he submitted to this order only so long as he was under the jurisdiction of his judges; that, having been found to be without blame in all things, it seemed to him scarce conformable to justice to forbid him to consecrate himself with all his power to the salvation of souls, and that consequently he should take such measures for his conduct in future as he should deem convenient. Frias clearly perceived that he meant to indicate by this his intention of quitting the city, and as he desired to gain his affection, he endeavored to soften the impression which the sentence had made upon him, and showed his esteem and the interest he took in him, but without being able to change his purpose. And not only Frias, but many others, and among them men who enjoyed the highest repute, as the Saint himself says,* were desirous of his remaining at Salamanca, but their wishes did not prevail over the strong reasons he had for leaving it. He had formed the resolution of going to Paris, to give himself more fully to study in that foreign city, and with the hope, also, of finding in a central place, where men of talent from all nations flocked together, companions suitable to his design. He communicated his purpose to the disciples who had hitherto followed him, but, either from fear of the risks, or from uncertainty as to how they should live at Paris, they had not the courage to undertake this distant journey, or it may be that for these motives Ignatius would have them wait until he had provided for their subsistence at Paris, and so it was

* Gonzalez, ch. vi.

resolved that he should depart alone, and they should meanwhile continue their studies at Salamanca. In any case, they were to remain united in spirit, until such time as they could afterwards rejoin him. He therefore took leave of them, about fifteen or twenty days after they came out of prison, and went on foot to Barcelona, where he was received with joy by his old friends. They endeavored to dissuade him from his purpose, and, in fact, the journey to France was at that time very dangerous, for, besides that the winter was setting in, the war between the two countries was raging more fiercely than ever. The frontiers were infested by brigands, and he was going to travel on foot and alone, without knowing either the roads or the language. Seeing that none of these reasons made any impression on him, they wished at least to facilitate his journey as much as they could, and, through Elizabeth Roser, they made him accept of a sum of money, partly in specie and partly in bills of exchange. He quitted Spain about the end of that year, or in the first days of the ensuing year, 1528.

# CHAPTER VIII.

SPAIN was not destined, any more than the Holy Land,
to receive the newly-planted Society which Ignatius was
to form.  For some time past this country had been
spreading its dominions at a distance from Europe.
Occupied with the conquests of the New World, it had
no space for other thoughts, and took no interest in the
solution of the great religious and social questions which
agitated and divided the Old World at this time.  All
that it did was to avoid them as much as possible.  But
Ignatius was called to exercise a considerable influence
on the events of the age, and to form a Society keeping
in relations with the development of mental progress, and
capable, at the same time, of defending the inviolable
sanctuary of religious truths.  His country could not
supply him, even in his individual capacity, with the
elements necessary for so vast a work, nor a sphere wide
enough for the plan he had conceived.  Divine Providence conducted him then to Paris, where the two
epochs—that which was concluding and that which was
commencing—were both alike represented, and where he
himself could complete his own individual preparations
for the accomplishment of the designs of God in his
regard.  In order to introduce the reader more intimately
to the thoughts which occupied his mind, we will here
give the faithful translation of some letters, which he
wrote from Paris, and which have been preserved to us.
The first is addressed to Agnes Pasquale—

May the true peace of Our Lord Jesus Christ be with our souls and
keep them.  Considering the good will and charity in the Lord which

you have always had for me, I have thought it my duty to write to you at present, and give you an account of my journey since I left you. By the grace and goodness of God Our Lord I arrived here in Paris the 2d of February, having favorable weather and being in perfect health, and I shall study here until it please the Lord to dispose of me otherwise. I should be very glad to have heard from you whether Fonseca has answered your letter, or you have spoken with him. A thousand (kind) things to John, and say to him to be always obedient to his parents, and to keep the Feast-days with devotion. If so, he shall live long here on earth and hereafter in Heaven. Remember me [here there was an omission]. I have received your letters, and see that your good will and charity for the love of Our Lord do not fail towards me. May the Lord of all things repay you, and may He of His infinite goodness dwell in our souls, so that His will and desires may be always done in us.

YNIGO, little in good.

Paris, March 3, 1528.

The second letter is addressed to his brother, Don Martin de Loyola—

You say that you are rejoiced beyond measure that I have broken the silence I have hitherto kept with you. You must not, however, be surprised at the line of conduct I have pursued. To heal a deep wound a different ointment must be used at the first from that which is applied when it is nearly cured. At the beginning of my course a certain remedy was necessary for me. Later I may try another without harm; at least, if I find it prejudicial, I shall take care not to employ it a second or a third time. It is not surprising that it has happened so to me, when St. Paul himself, shortly after his conversion, says—" A sting of the flesh has been given me;" and again —" I find another law in my members." And he found in his soul such an opposition that he said—" The good that I would I do not, and the evil that I would not that I do; what to do I know not." Later and at another time he says—" I am certain that neither death nor life, nor things present, nor things to come, nor any other creature, shall be able to separate me from the love of Our Lord Jesus Christ." At the commencement I have been not unlike him. May the goodness of God later and at the end refuse not to grant me the fulness of His holy grace, that I may imitate and be the servant of all His true servants ; and if I should have the misfortune to offend Him in anything whatsoever, or fall into any remissness in His holy praise and service, may He rather take me out of this world. To explain somewhat more, I will say that I would have written to you more frequently some five or six years since, if two things had not hindered me. First, my study, and the numerous relations in which I have been engaged, not however of this world ; the second is, that I had no probable and sufficient reason to suppose that my letters would serve to the glory of God Our Lord, and the good of my kindred and relatives according to the flesh, so that we should be kindred also in spirit, and aid one another in those things which endure for all eternity. For, in truth, I cannot love any one in this life who does not his whole duty in the service and praise of the Lord Our God, seeing that God does not love entirely him who loves anything in the world for its own sake and not for the sake of God. So that, when two persons serve God in the same degree, of whom one is related to us and the other not, He would have us feel warmer affection and attachment towards our natural father than towards any one else, and to a kinsman or benefactor rather than to one who is neither of these. Thus, too, we love and honor the Apostles more than saints less holy than they, because they always loved and served the Lord Our God in a greater and higher degree. For charity, without which we cannot attain to everlasting life, is called dilection, and it is by it that we love the Lord Our God for His own sake, and all other things for the sake of Him. As the Psalmist says, we must " praise Him in His saints." I desire very much, and more than very much, if I may be allowed the expression, that this true charity may be perfected in you, my relations and friends, and that you may consecrate all your powers to the service and praise of the Lord Our God; that so I may love you and ever serve you the more, since it is my triumph and my glory to serve the servants of my Master. And it is the sincere feeling of this pure charity which makes me say and write and admonish you, as I desire and from my whole heart would gladly be admonished and corrected —always, that is, with just judgment, and not for the motive of worldly or profane glory. Whoever in this life is occupied with the cares of much building, and of extending the limit of his domains and increasing his income and estate, and of leaving after him a name upon earth and a great memory, such a one I do not venture to condemn; but I cannot commend him, because, according to St. Paul, we ought to use these things as if we used them not, and possess them as though we possessed them not, and that even those who have wives should be as though they had them not, for the " figure of this life passes quickly away." If so be, as I would desire, you have already known, or in part do now know, these things, I conjure you, by the fear and love of God, to employ all your efforts in acquiring glory in Heaven and a name and a good remembrance before the Lord, who will one day be our Judge ; for He has given you temporal goods in abundance, that by means of these you may acquire eternal goods, and that you may give to your children and to your servants, and all over whom you have charge, good example and salutary lessons, to the former exercising just strictness, though without anger or offence, and to the latter giving recompense according to their labor, and attaching them to your family, doing good also in much alms to the poor, and providing for orphans and those in necessity. It becomes us not to be sparing when the Lord Our God has been so liberal towards us. We shall find one day peace and happiness in proportion as we shall have bestowed alms and done good in this life. And now, since you can do much in the country in which you live, I again conjure you, by the love of Our Lord Jesus Christ, to urge yourself not only to meditate on these things but to will and do them.

Paris, 1532.*

* The date of the month is not given in this letter, but it must have been written at the end of June, since he concludes by saying that he has received his brother's letter on the 20th of this month of June.

## Letter to Elizabeth Roser—

To my dear Sister in Jesus Christ, E. R.

I have received through Dr. Benet three letters from you and twenty ducats. May the Lord our God reckon them to your account and repay you for me at the Day of Judgment, as I hope in His divine goodness He will, and that in money of the best and highest worth. I trust in Him, that He will not have to punish me hereafter as an ungrateful servant, and that He will make me in some degree worthy to praise and serve His Divine Majesty. In your first letter you tell me that God's holy will has been done in regard of your separation for this life from the lady Las Canillas. It is not on her account that I feel sorrow, but for ourselves, who remain in this place of banishment, pain, and misery, because, having known her in this life as a soul dear and precious in the eyes of her Master and Creator, I readily believe that He has given her a blessed mansion of rest, and that she has no longer need of the palaces, the riches, or the vanities and magnificence of this world. You express also the apologies made to me by our Sisters in Our Lord Jesus Christ. They owe me nothing, and it is I who am their eternal debtor. In short, if I am not at present able to repay my obligations as I ought, I have no recourse but to pray God to share among those to whom I owe so much all the merits I may acquire, always with His grace, in the sight of His Divine Majesty, giving to each according to the services they have rendered me, and to you above all, to whom I owe more than to any other person in the world. In your third letter you speak of the false, treacherous, and wrongful dealing that you are surrounded with on all sides. I am not astonished at it, and if you had much more to suffer I should not be surprised, for since the time that you resolved to seek with your whole endeavors the glory, honor, and service of the Lord our God, you took for your portion war against the world; you lifted up the standard against it, you prepared yourself to combat all that is lofty by embracing what is lowly, and by forcing yourself to be indifferent both to greatness and to littleness, to honor and dishonor, to riches and to poverty, to pleasure and to displeasure—in a word, to all esteem and all contempt of this world. We ought not to think much of the wounds which may be inflicted on us in this life as long as they only come to words, for these cannot hurt so much as one hair of our head. Injurious and offensive words and innuendoes cause neither pain nor pleasure when once they are made welcome; but as long as we seek for the honor and glory of men we are not firmly established in God, and so, when men affront us, we cannot escape being wounded. If, then, I have rejoiced to learn that the world afflicts you, I cannot endure to think that you seek to find help and remedies against the sufferings and ill-treatment that you receive from it. May the Mother of God obtain for you perfect patience and perseverance, and enable you to reflect how much greater were the affronts and the sorrows which Our Lord Jesus Christ has suffered for our sakes. May she obtain for you still greater humiliations, provided always it be without sin of others, that so you may daily gain greater merits. If we do not find in ourselves this patience, we have the more reason to lament our sensitiveness and our carnal dispositions when we see that we are not dead to ourselves and to the things of the earth. as we ought to be. It is of ourselves, then, that we ought to complain much more than of those who humble us, for they give us thereby the means of acquiring treasure of far more value than any that can be gained in this life, and riches which far surpass all that can be amassed on earth. I see that Artenga, and many others at Alcala and Salamanca, continue with great perseverance in the service of Our Lord God, and I return Him for it infinite thanks.

Paris, November 10, 1532.

## Letter to Agnes Pasquale—

It is now a year since I received your letter by Dr. Benet, may he have his recompense in Heaven, and I received at the same time the alms and the supplies which he brought me from Barcelona. I perceive, both from your letter and from his report, how great is your solicitude for me as well as the good will you have always shown me. You declare that you are ready to exhibit towards me for the time to come the same zeal and the same care, and you would have me to be your debtor, not only for the past, but for the future. May God our true Lord repay you. Though I have already answered your letter, I write a second time, because I know that you desire it, and because I am in want of the means necessary for making more rapid progress in my studies than I have hitherto done. I have this Lent attained the grade of Master, and so have been obliged to incur more expense than I either wished or could well bear. I have fallen thereby into great difficulties, and it is very necessary that God Our Lord come to help me. It is on this account I write to the lady Cepilla, who in her letter has offered to help me in every way that she can, begging me to tell her what I am in want of. I write also to Elizabeth Roser, but say nothing to her on the subject of money, as she has written that she cannot any longer assist me, through the pressure of her own wants. I believe what she says is true, and I venture to say that she has done more for me than she could afford to do; and consequently I owe her more than I can repay. I am of opinion that you should not let her know in what necessity I am placed, as she would be too much afflicted at having been unable to assist me. Since my departure, the wife of Gralla has many times promised to support me during my studies, and she has always done so. It is the same with Doña Elizabeth Sosa and Doña Aldonza de Cordova, who have in like manner assisted me. I do not write to them, that I may not seem too troublesome. Please to give them my remembrances. I always think that if Señora Gralla knew of my want she would contribute her share to the alms sent me. Arrange the thing with her and the others as you shall judge to be best, in which light I will take whatever is decided on and shall be content, always acknowledging myself the debtor of those who do me a service. The bearer of this letter will relate to you in detail all that has been done here; and you may believe him in every particular as you would myself.

Paris, June 13, 1533.

These letters cover a period of five years, and we see by them how small was the assistance which the Saint received from his own country, so that he was obliged to seek help elsewhere, more particularly as from the very first he had found himself in the greatest difficulty. He had exchanged at Paris a bill for twenty-five Spanish crowns received by him from Barcelona, and this had been squandered by a Spaniard who lodged with him. He therefore obtained free lodging at the Hospital of St. James immediately after Lent, as Gonzalez relates, and lived upon alms which he went to beg, with considerable injury to his studies, for not only were his lodgings at a great distance from the college, but the lectures began before the hospital doors were opened and did not finish till after the gates were closed. In this unpleasant position, he took a resolution which shows how great his humility was. Aware that many poor scholars, without any detriment to their studies, acted as servants to the professors, and by way of recompense received food and lodging within the college, he sought to procure a situation of this kind with a professor, whom he could wait upon as he would upon Our Lord Jesus Christ Himself. He could not, however, succeed, notwitstanding the efforts made by two of his friends, one of whom was the Bachelor de Castro and the other a Carthusian. Either the last-mentioned or some other Religious advised him to go to the Netherlands, and beg from the Spanish merchants there sufficient to live upon for the year. He followed this advice, and employed the vacations of three successive years in going to Flanders. During the third year he also visited London, where he received more assistance from his fellow-countrymen than he had in the Flemish towns. After he had once made himself known in this latter city, he was saved the trouble of returning thither again, as his friends sent each year to him in Paris the sum they had contributed for him. In this way he found himself in a condition to assist others, among whom were not only Peter Faber and Bobadilla, who afterwards became his companions, but many other persons also who were in distress. This manner of living upon alms drew on him much opposition from his fellow-countrymen in Paris. One of them, by name Madera, fancied that he saw even sin in it, as by it he dishonored his family. To assure him on this point, Ignatius consulted several theologians of the Sorbonne, putting to them the question—Whether a gentleman who had renounced the world for the love of God could beg without dishonor to his family? The decision was, of course, unanimous in his favor, that there was nothing wrong in it, and that the objections made were without any foundation.

We now turn to consider the studies of the Saint, beginning by some remarks upon the ancient University of Paris. The city was divided into three parts, one of which was simply called the University, because it contained many colleges, which had been founded for the sake of the schools, and where resided the masters, the professors, and a great number of scholars who had obtained burses, or who waited on the professors and were boarded in their houses. The greater part of the students also lodged in this part of the city, and came together in such great numbers that, at the period of which we treat, there were supposed to be from twelve to sixteen thousand in residence. There were also a great many professors, who were in general but poorly paid. The greater part of the scholars were also poor; but the schooling was gratuitous. Each college had a prefect at its head, who was called the primarius. The scholars and the masters of arts, as those who had finished their philosophy were called, were divided into four nations—the French (comprehending the Spaniards, the Portuguese, and the Navarrese), the Picards, the Normans, and the Germans. There were also schools for humanities, as well as for philosophy and theology. Ignatius frequented for eighteen months one of these last schools—from February, 1528, to the end of the scholastic year 1529—that he might acquire more profound knowledge in these matters, and to prepare himself for the higher studies. He had seen before this that his haste in passing through his studies in Spain had been of little advantage to him. The house he had attended was called the college of Montague. He began his course of philosophy at the college of St. Remy, on the 1st of October, 1529, and continued it during three years and a half, with such success that his professor, Peña, insisted on himself presenting him for his degrees. The examination for the philosophy was at that time most severe, the students calling it the *examen lapideum,* as being the test of the head. The diploma of Doctor of Philosophy, which he received at the University, shows with what success he passed this examen. It ran as follows—

To all to whom the present letters shall come, the Rector and the University of Paris, health in the Saviour of all men.

Whereas all who hold the Catholic faith are bound, both by the natural law of justice and by the divine law, to give faithful witness to the truth, it is, moreover, fitting that ecclesiastics, especially professors of the various sciences, whose duty it is to search into the truth in all things and teach it to others, should in nothing deviate from the path of truth and reason, either through love or favor, or from any other motive whatsoever. Desirous, therefore, to give thereby witness to the truth, we make it known by tenor of the present letters, to all and each whom it may concern, that our well-beloved and learned Doctor Ignatius of Loyola, of the diocese of Pampeluna, Master of Arts, has with honor and glory obtained the degree of Doctor, in the illustrious Faculty of Arts at Paris, after having passed through severe examinations, in the year of Our Lord 1534, after Easter, according to the statutes and customs of the said Faculty of Arts, and with the usual solemnities. In attestation of which we have set our grand seals to the present letters.

Given at Paris, in our Assembly General, solemnly held at St. Mathurin, in the year of Our Lord 1534, the 14th of the month of March.

LEROUX.

The University began its year with the Feast of Easter, and hence its dates, not agreeing with the ordinary manner of reckoning, took the form of "before" or "after Easter." The original of this diploma is in the archives of the Professed House at Rome.

Ignatius, after receiving his doctor's degree, passed on to the study of theology, and attended the course of the Dominican convent. The distance he had to walk was very troublesome in the winter, as the lectures began before sunrise. He was not able to finish his course at Paris, and only studied theology for a year and a half, as appears from an attestation dated October 14th, 1536, at which time the

Saint was at Venice. He probably required this document, and caused it to be sent to him from Paris. As he left Paris shortly after the 25th of March, 1535, he must have commenced his theology at the latest in the autumn of 1533.

During the course of these seven years, Ignatius, with his mind now matured, had to contend with great difficulties, for very many obstacles presented themselves in the way of his designs. Moreover, he felt rising within him again that attraction to a life of contemplation and prayer which had been such a hindrance to his progress at Barcelona, and in order to overcome it he was obliged to employ the same means to which he had recourse then. For the same reason, during the latter part of his course of philosophy, he abstained from giving his book of the *Exercises* to any great number of persons, but limited himself to some few young men who joined him. Not to put any hindrance in the way of study, he had made an agreement with his companion in his room, Peter Faber, that during the time appointed for it they should hold no converse on spiritual subjects, because these had too powerful an attraction for him. Faber repeated with him the lectures in philosophy. Besides, after having for some time enjoyed good health, in the latter half of his residence at Paris he suffered from very grievous infirmities, partly because he had redoubled his austerities, which at first he had diminished, partly because the climate disagreed with him. If we add to this the pains and privations of his poverty, the persecutions he had to endure, the repugnance which these dry studies must have caused at his age, the humiliations which could not but attend them, it is impossible not to be struck with admiration at the perseverance and the vigor of soul in this great man. Looking back, later on, upon this part of his life, he let fall the following words, the truth of which it would be difficult to dispute —"That he would much question whether another but himself, having to struggle with so many difficulties and obstacles in the course of his studies, would have given so long a time to the acquisition of the sciences." Had a man of the world devoted so much labor to the world and its service, it would never cease to praise him, in season and out of season, and would propose him as an example to all others; but the world does not even deign to notice what Ignatius did in this regard, for it takes no account of anything that is done for God.

# CHAPTER IX.

CHARITY OF IGNATIUS FOR HIS NEIGHBOR. HE IS DE-
NOUNCED AND PERSECUTED. HIS FIRST DISCIPLES
FORSAKE HIM. PETER FABER BECOMES HIS FIRST
COMPANION.

SOME indications which have been preserved to us, relative to this period, enable us to comprehend how much the idea of founding a new Order occupied the mind of Ignatius, and how strongly he felt the vocation of God to this work. During one of his visits to Flanders he received hospitality in the house of a Spanish merchant, named Cuellar, and there met a young man, also a merchant, of the name of Peter Quadrato, of Medina del Campo. One day, as they were seated together in the company of several merchants, and were at the moment a little removed from the other guests, Ignatius took him aside and said, " Since you are to be at a future time one of the benefactors of my Society, it is but right that we should make friends with one another. I wish you to know that I shall be much indebted to you, for you will one day found a college for the Society of Jesus." This fact has been affirmed on oath by persons present, and, in verification of it, Peter Quadrato later on actually founded in his country a college of the Society. Another circumstance shows, though less distinctly, what were at this time the intentions of St. Ignatius. He had been much befriended, while at Bourges, by Louis Vivès, a man of considerable learning. It is likely that in some of his conversations with him he had given hints of his design, for Vivès remarked one day to some of his friends, " This man is a saint, who will for certain found a new Order."

There is little doubt that Ignatius, soon after his

arrival at Paris, sought for new disciples, with a view to carrying out this object. He at first addressed himself to his fellow-countrymen, of whom there were a great number at the University, and with whom community of language made relations more easy for him. He followed the same course with the students at Paris that he had done in Spain, seeking to gain them by spiritual entertainment, and then to form them by the Exercises. He succeeded quickly in influencing three young persons, of whom the first, John de Castro, of Toledo, a man of distinguished talents, was already doctor of the Sorbonne. The second, still a student, was named Peralta ; and the third was a young Biscayan gentleman of the family of the Amadori. These three resolved to renounce the world and to consecrate themselves to God in entire poverty. They accordingly sold all that they had, and gave the money to the poor. They then took lodgings at the Hospital of St. James, and lived by begging alms. This sudden change excited the astonishment and the anger of all their compatriots, and especially of a Portuguese named Govéa, a professor of some note, whose lectures Amadori attended. This man was so exasperated at such conduct, as to declare publicly that if St. Ignatius showed himself at his College of St. Barbara, he would have given him, for decoying away this youth, a public correction of a most humiliating nature, which was called *aulam dare*, or the " giving a hall."

The chief cause of scandal was the sight of the new converts begging alms in public, which was considered a disgrace to their families. It is true that all those who had as yet made the Exercises had begged alms in imitation of Our Lord's example ; but this was not the main object proposed by the Saint. Some opposition, therefore, was useful to set bounds to these exterior manifestations—which in themselves, and without the proper motive to inspire them, are of no value—lest they should become, in persons of an enthusiastic turn, the chief and only object. Ignatius' adversaries did indeed render him this service by their opposition, so that the disciples who joined him afterwards were warned by it to avoid all extravagance, and to keep always in view the main object of the Exercises—namely, the renovation of the spirit of Christianity. But as the principle on which these exterior practices were carried out wholly escaped the notice of the authorities, to whom, as being men imbued with the ordinary ideas of the world, these practices were very displeasing, they could attribute them only to bad motives, and thus suspected Ignatius of bewitching those who frequented his company. This suspicion easily became exaggerated into a formal accusation of sorcery, and from this into a denunciation to the tribunal of the Inquisition. Add to this that letters came from Spain to the same purport, in corroboration of the suspicions already conceived. The opponents of Ignatius, filled with zeal not according to knowledge, clung to their prejudices against him all the more firmly the less they knew of him, and thought they were justified in disseminating these calumnious reports concerning him, which, though incredible to all not predisposed against him, were but too greedily received by those who are ready to listen to anything that people say. Many persons were led by these reports to keep aloof from the Saint, and to avoid all kind of connection with him, through the imaginary fears engendered in their minds. But we must not be too severe on his contemporaries, since at the present day, in the midst of the so-called enlightenment of civilization, the same phenomenon may be observed. While these reports were flying about, Ignatius, after the example of his Divine Master preserving the peace of his soul, quietly continued on his course, and left it to his own conduct to answer the charges against him.

In the midst of this effervescent feeling he had the opportunity of showing what he truly was. The fellow-lodger who had squandered the Saint's little means of support, when making his way back to Spain, was obliged to stop at Rouen on accout of a grievous malady, which seized him at the moment when he was about to embark. In his distress he could think of no better expedient than that of writing to the man to whom he had been so ungrateful, and telling him the extreme necessity he was in.

Ignatius, immediately upon receiving this letter, betook himself to the church of the Dominicans to consult with God and consider whether he ought to go to the succor of this unfortunate man, for, anticipating what was to ensue, he felt a kind of repugnance for the journey; this feeling, however, left him during his prayer. The next day, at the moment of rising, the same feeling returned, and it was accompanied with so great bodily weakness that he could hardly stand. In spite of this he had the courage to set out, barefoot, before sunrise, and arrived at Argenteuil without having broken his fast. There, after he had mounted a little rising ground, he suddenly felt himself so revived and strengthened in body and mind that he could make the journey to Rouen without feeling hunger or fatigue, although it took him three days. The first night he passed in a hospital, and the second in the open air, upon straw. He tended the sick man until he recovered, when he procured for him a passage in a vessel to continue his voyage, and gave him letters of recommendation to his disciples and friends in Spain. But before he quitted Rouen he received a letter from one of his friends in Paris, telling him that during his absence he had been denounced to the Inquisition, owing to the rumors spread about him, and on account of the three students whom he was accused of having led from their duty. He was in the street when the messenger gave him this letter, and immediately went with him to a notary, that he might obtain a certificate, signed by two witnesses, attesting that he had set out for Paris immediately on the receipt of the letter. He then set out on his road, accompanied for some way by the notary and the witnesses, and no sooner had he arrived in Paris than he went straight to the Inquisitor to submit himself of his own accord to an inquiry, after showing his certificate to him. For he wished to prevent suspicion, and to prove to his opponents that the object of his journey had not been to escape from the prosecution laid against him.

Matthew Ori, the judge, a Dominican and doctor of divinity, had set aside the accusation of sorcery as without foundation, and had up to that point abstained from proceeding against Ignatius. His quick return and ap-

pearance before him confirmed him in his good opinion,
and he dismissed him, saying that he had nothing to fear.
The unreasonable zeal of his opponents thus met with a
check from the good sense and understanding of the
judge.   But they were more successful with the scholars
whom they looked upon as deluded by the saint.   These
resisted the entreaties and representations of their friends
so long as they confined themselves only to words and to
threats; but when they came to actual measures and dismissed them from the hospital, under pretext that they
must first finish their studies, and then might act as they
pleased, they began to yield by degrees, and ended by
quitting Ignatius.   John de Castro was afterwards a
preacher in Spain; but, ashamed of advising others to renounce the world, which he himself had not had the
courage to do, he soon entered into the house of the
Carthusians at Valencia, and remained always bound in
close ties of union with his former master in the spiritual
life.

These events occurred while Ignatius was repeating his
rhetoric, in the year 1529.   When, during his study of
philosophy, this storm against him abated, one of his intimate friends, the Dr. Fragus, said to him, "see how
they have changed their sentiments in your regard—those
who were your adversaries have become your warmest
partisans: how can you account for that?"   Ignatius replied, "Wait till I am freed from these bonds and have
finished my philosophy, and then you will know the reason
of this calm.   My opponents are quiet, because I am
quiet; but as soon as I move again I shall stir up new
tempests, and they will attack me on all sides."   These
words came true sooner even than he had expected.   He
had ceased, it is true, to give the Spiritual Exercises to
the scholars, but he took the practical way, making use of
these to exhort them to live a Christian life, and to join
piety to knowledge, and holding with them conferences
on spirituality, recommending them at the same time to
approach the Sacraments every Sunday and holiday, and
to avoid all irregularity.   He soon had at his conferences
more scholars and masters than the professors of the
College.   It was then a custom that the students held

public academies on the mornings of holidays, but these sittings were becoming less frequented, because so many of the scholars were making their devotions in the churches on these days. Peña, one of the professors, was displeased at this, and several times warned Ignatius not to meddle in what did not concern him, by busying himself with the students, otherwise he would have him for his enemy. But as he could not oblige his pupils to neglect their Christian duties to attend exercises the time of which had been ill-chosen, his threats had little effect upon Ignatius. The professor then had recourse to the principal of the college, Govéa, and they both agreed to give another warning to the Saint officially, threatening him with the chastisement of the " aula," and as this notification was to no purpose, they resolved to proceed to its actual infliction. This punishment was as follows: The delinquent had to present himself in the public hall, where the academies were held, and at the sound of the bell all the masters and students were assembled, the former carrying rods with which they touched the shoulders of the culprit, for the chastisement was rather humiliating than painful, and he who had once been subjected to it was avoided by all the others. This was the affront which they would inflict on Ignatius as a disturber of the studies, because he had exhorted the scholars, who were one day to be the leaders and pastors of the people, to keep the Commandments of God; and the persons who were to inflict it were the masters and the clergy—the real disturbers of the divine service. And so we may ask ourselves, whence came the troubles and divisions of these sad times, but from the vineyard of the Lord having been left so long lying waste without culture, and from the entrance of profane science into the place of the sanctuary? The reformers of those days were not assuredly wanting in what are called the humanities, they were over much scholars, but they were in want of true piety, and therefore the lamp of the sanctuary was in danger of being extinguished.

When the hour had come for receiving this chastisement, the Saint found different sentiments arising within him. He felt at first extreme joy at having it in his power to suffer an

affront for the sake of God, but to this feeling soon succeeded an excessive horror of the humiliation which would
follow from it.   However, as this last thought sprang
evidently from self-love, he quickly rejected it, saying to
himself in angry reproof—" What, you mule, will you kick
against the goad ?   Plunge as you will, you cannot break
the traces.   On, then, with good will, and if not, at least
perforce."   Nevertheless, considering the thing more
narrowly, and becoming convinced that the affront to
which he was about to submit would injure the work he
had begun more than it would injure himself, his resolution was forthwith taken.   The official being sent to his
room, as he was then  residing in the College of St.
Barbara, he declared himself ready to follow him, but
wished first to speak with the rector, Govéa, who had  not
yet left his chamber.   Full of the sense of the rectitude
of his cause, as representing that of God, he courageously
set before him that, for his own part, he could desire
nothing more precious than to have to submit to blows
and affronts for the sake of Jesus Christ,  having already
in the same cause suffered prisons and chains ; but,
since the loss of his honor would result in great danger
to the salvation of a large number of souls, he begged
him to judge for himself whether it was conformable to
his duty as a Christian to punish as disobedient one to
whose charge no crime could be laid excepting that of
conducting souls to God ; whether it was just to disgrace
him in order to separate from him those who were
attached to him solely by the desire of progress in perfection ; and that, if he was culpable in any other point,
he had but to be told of it.   Govéa had never considered
the matter from this point of view, and the plain truth set
before him sufficed to scatter the cloud which had hitherto
blinded him with regard to Ignatius.   Each word pierced
his very heart, and he saw that, in persecuting the Saint,
he had persecuted that which he himself esteemed above
all things—Christian virtue, and he resolved immediately
to repair the wrong that he had done.   Without saying a
word he took Ignatius by the hand and conducted him into
the hall, and there, in the presence of all, discoursed in a
touching manner in praise of him whom he had slighted,

declaring him free from all blame, which he took entirely upon himself. Then, throwing himself at the feet of Ignatius, while the tears fell from his eyes, he entreated his pardon for the wrong which he had done him. It may be well imagined what was the impression produced on the assembly by so honorable a reparation, and the high esteem which accrued to Ignatius from this unlooked-for change. He henceforth made disciples, not only among the scholars, but among the masters, and Peña was the first to be reconciled to him. Other professors wished also to attend his instruction, and acknowledged him for their spiritual master. One of these, named Martial, who was a member of the faculty of Divinity, discerning in him a theologian of a superior order, proposed conferring on him a doctor's degree, but Ignatius would not give his consent to the proposal.

His zeal for souls was not, however, limited to the students, and although his want of acquaintance with the language of the country did not permit him to exercise the same influence upon the public as he had done in Spain, he availed himself of every possible occasion to succor those who were in suffering or exposed to danger, either by giving them alms—which he found means to bestow notwithstanding his poverty—or by other works of charity. He had the natural gift of winning hearts, and he knew how to deal with and manage all characters, dissembling with tact the wrongs done to himself, and condescending to the wishes and inclinations of every one, so long as they were within the limits of what is right. In this manner he won back many persons who, through ignorance, had allowed themselves to be seduced by the false opinions of the time. After having instructed them with the greatest charity he led them to confessors, in whose hands they abjured their errors without publicity.

The following details are given as an instance of his inventive charity. He learned that a certain person, probably a Spaniard, was engaged in an intrigue with a married woman. He took occasion to represent to him his conduct in terms calculated to move him, but found him quite deaf to remonstrance by reason of his passion.

Ignatius knew that, in making his visits, this victim of his own passion must pass by a certain bridge. Thither, therefore, he betook himself one evening, and just before the other passed by took off his habit and placed himself in the water up to his neck, though it was winter time, offering this penance to God for the conversion of the sinner. As the man came by, buried in his own thoughts, Ignatius suddenly awakened him from his reverie, crying out aloud, with a voice at the same time trembling from cold—" Go, take your sinful pleasure, regardless of the danger to soul and body. Meanwhile I will do penance for you here : every night, as you pass by, you will find me here, until you are converted or until I die." At these words, and still more at this spectacle, the man, who had been blinded by passion, was restored to his senses, and his soul, so besotted up to this, was sobered by the Saint's example. Ignatius, standing thus plunged in the water, bade him remember that he too was plunged deeper in the sink of sin, till, feeling that compassion for himself which the Saint had felt for his soul, he ended by taking compassion on his own miserable state, and was converted. Thus ended also the Saint's voluntary penance, and he shortly completed the reformation of the soul which he had drawn out of perdition.

Another act, by which he converted a Religious who was living in a manner little in conformity with his vocation, is still more remarkable, as being a singular case in the manner of dealing with souls. Since he saw that, having as a layman to deal with a priest, he could not succeed by way of representations and remonstrance, he had recourse to another device. He presented himself one Sunday morning at his confessional, and made a general confession to him of his whole life. This he did in a manner so open, and with signs of such extraordinary sorrow, that the Religious could not help admiring so great tenderness of conscience in a layman, while he, notwithstanding the sanctity of his vocation, made so little account of sin. The shame which he felt awakened contrition within him. He saw at the same moment the great efficacy of grace and the admirable penitence of Ignatius, and began to feel a desire of these two things.

which he had hitherto little thought of. After giving
absolution to the penitent who knelt before him, he, in
his turn, discovered to him the state of his soul, and,
recognizing in him a master in the things regarding salvation, asked his counsel and assistance. Thus the Saint
had attained his object, and he completed his work by
inducing the Religious to make the Spiritual Exercises.

A third instance, less well known, proves on the one
hand the tact with which the Saint seized upon every
occasion to bring souls to God, and on the other the
continual assistance of supernatural aid given him. He
entered one day, upon matters of business, the house of a
Frenchman, a doctor of divinity, whom he found engaged
in playing at hazard. Invited to take part in the game,
he excused himself, saying that he was not acquainted
with it. But as the other would take no excuse, the Saint
suddenly felt himself inspired to accept the offer, and
said—" Well, sir, I accept your proposal ; but as I have
nothing to risk at play but myself, let us agree that, if I
lose, I become your servant for a month, and if I win,
you shall do what I shall ask you, for your own advantage." The conditions being accepted, the game was
commenced, and Ignatius won. The doctor having asked
what he required of him, the Saint replied that he only
asked him to make the Spiritual Exercises under his
direction, which he did, to the great benefit of his soul.

The facts just related belong to the later years of his
studies at Paris, but we must retrace our steps and return to the year 1530, to see how he gained the first of
those disciples who remained faithful to him. At the
close of this year Peter Faber was his companion in his
chamber, and repeated the lectures with him. He was
born in the year 1506, at Villaret, in Savoy, of the diocese of Geneva. From his early childhood, while he
kept his father's flocks, he showed precocious talents for
study and the ecclesiastical state. Accordingly he was
placed under a good master for the study of the classics.
Pushed on by a desire of learning, he went to Paris,
where he made such rapid progress that he received the
degree of doctor of divinity in 1530, and was so well
versed in the Greek language that he equalled his pro-

fessor, Peña, in the explanation of Aristotle.  He lived
for a long time with Ignatius before there arose between
them intimate friendship.   At last interior sufferings obliged him to enter into closer acquaintance with his
companion, who was his senior in years.  Faber, from
the age of twelve, had made a vow of chastity, and was
assaulted with the most violent temptation against this
virtue.  Shame, on the one hand, closed h's lips, and on
the other he had satisfied himself that fasting and a
vigorous resistance were enough to defeat the enemy,
but these seemed only to give new strength to the foe.
Besides these troublesome attacks, he found himself
tempted to vanity, and to the love of the pleasures of
the table.   In a state like this, wherein a man without
experience and interior light can neither counsel nor
direct himself, he soon fell into faint-heartedness and
scruples of conscience.

Freethinkers can smile at such afflictions, and accuse
those who suffer from them of weakness of mind.  But
what remedy have they against such temptations except
to yield to concupiscence?   That is easy enough, no
doubt, but by giving away to excess we sacrifice all that
gives dignity to human nature, and remain still slaves.
Faber, as a rational being, sought, in the conquering of
his temptations, a true escape from the labyrinth in
which he was involved.   But when he could not succeed
by his own unassisted efforts, the completeness of his misery compelled him to surmount that natural pride which
would lead him to conceal the state of his heart from
the eyes of another, and endeavor rather to escape from
others, and from self also, were it possible, into a solitude, where he might combat with the importunate enemy
by penitential austerities.   In a happy hour he discovered to Ignatius, with a blush upon his face and with
tears in his eyes, the secrets of his soul, and exposed to
him the wound which had festered within because it
could find no issue.   In making this avowal he at once
felt relieved, and wise treatment soon sufficed to cleanse
the sore and complete the cure.   Ignatius proceeded
with gentleness, a proof to us what progress he had
made in the sublime science of dealing with souls.   From

this time forward, in fact, we find him ever advancing
with slow and gentle steps, conforming himself to the
several characters of those with whom he dealt, and
making skilful use of their natural dispositions, contenting himself with assisting nature to act where it is of
itself too feeble, until, strengthened by an appropriate
rule of life, it has gained power to make advance for itself.

It was in this manner he treated Faber. He did not
require of him to engage all his enemies at once, with
the risk of conquering none, but taught him to vanquish
them in detail, and to aim at the root of the evil—in a
word, he made him practise the particular examen, which
is an essential part of the Spiritual Exercises. When
Faber's mind had become more tranquil he advised him
to make a general confession of his whole life, and to
approach the Sacraments every eight days. He treated
him after this method for nearly two years. * During
the whole of this time Faber remained undecided as to
the kind of life he should embrace, feeling only a great
desire to consecrate himself entirely to God, without any
endeavor on the part of Ignatius to give to this disposition a determined direction. But at the commencement
of the year 1534, the time being come for Faber's ordination to the priesthood, he took occasion to speak to him
of the Exercises, and to recommend them as a preparation for ordination. He gave him, at the same time, an
insight into his own design of going to the Holy Land,
to labor there at the peril of his life for the conversion
of the infidels. These suggestions came on Faber's
mind like a sunbeam of light. He saw clearly a future
course before him which he had hitherto sought to know
in vain, and that Ignatius was sent to him by God to
discover it to him. He threw himself upon his neck and
embraced him, offering to be a companion in all the
labors he should undertake. Ignatius joyfully received
him as the first-fruits of his long endeavors. It was

* Ribadeneyra speaks of four years, but this is wrong, unless he
includes all the time which had elapsed since they first formed acquaintance. Bartoli and those who have followed him are more exact
on this point.

agreed that the Exercises should be made, and they entered upon the work—the one as master and the other as disciple. But before we proceed, this appears to us the proper place in which to give the reader a general idea of the Spiritual Exercises, to enable him to understand well the course of the narrative ; and that we have not done so already is because we desired to put before him in a living picture their practice and their theory, both together.

# CHAPTER X.

## THE IDEA, THE END, THE OBJECT, AND EFFECT, OF THE SPIRITUAL EXERCISES OF ST. IGNATIUS.

UNDER the name of Spiritual Exercises is to be understood in general the most perfect method of prayer. I say the most perfect method, because this kind of intercourse with God has for its end the creation within the soul of a life like the divine life, and accordingly it embraces in its exercise all that is most important and most sublime in man. Our Lord, in recommending us to pray in spirit and in truth, teaches us to desire eternal and heavenly goods, and it is this prayer which purifies the soul, which makes it holy and unites it with God. He would have us, then, in prayer, know God with our understanding, and bring our will into conformity with His divine will ; and as guidance is needed in everything, so the practice of this implies a holy art, the rules of which St. Ignatius gives in a method quite his own. To make this clearer to the reader, and treat the subject with all the completeness requisite, I will endeavor here to explain the general idea, end in view, subject-matter, and effect of the Spiritual Exercises.

If we would have an exact definition of them, they may be said to be " an exercise of the soul, by which, in the presence of God, a man meditates in silence and retreat upon the eternal truths, and by the light of these examines his spirit, with a view to correct what is wanting, and give that direction to his life which shall be most agreeable to God and most useful toward his salvation." Accordingly, we may express the general idea of the Exercises by saying that they refer to God all the concerns—both temporal and eternal—of man, whom He has redeemed. He who makes them endeavors, by a method suitable to his purpose, to comprehend clearly and dispose in order what he has learnt to be the divine will in his regard. The Exercises have, therefore, for their main object, not only to discover to man what is wanting in him, but, over and above, to conduct him to the greatest perfection of which he is capable. And since this cannot be attained except in that particular state to which God calls us, the Exercises dispose us to make good choice of that state, or else to draw more fruit from it if our choice be already made. Their idea, then, must include within its scope all the degrees of Christian perfection up to the highest—that is, the perfection of the Gospel, such as Our Lord commended to His disciples both by counsel and example. For which reason it includes the general and ordinary perfection of all Christians, according to which they keep the commandments of God. And in this point of view the Exercises instruct each one in particular what he ought to do, or to leave undone, for the attainment of his end ; but the scope of the Exercises also, and principally, includes the formation of apostolic men in the highest degree of perfection, by the close imitation of Our Lord Jesus Christ. Their general scope is, therefore, the development of the life of the God made Man in us, up to the measure of either of these degrees, and that through the exercise of the understanding and the free choice of the will.

They have also in this, their idea, a relation to history, and deserve to be studied in this point of view. Protestantism arose precisely at the time when the most important developments of European progress were beginning. The leaders of this great apostasy, taking up a merely human position outside of the Church, laid it down as a principle that the reading of the Scriptures, together with human faith built upon them, is all that is requisite for salvation. What allowed this error to spread so easily and quickly was, in great measure, the low moral standard which the circumstances of the times had fostered. The life of the Church, which is sustained by the Sacraments, was extinguished in great numbers, and so their faith had become dead. As they did not accept the Gospel in a practical point of view, and so its influence was hardly felt at all upon men's lives, the dissemination of the dead letter and the perusal of the mere text of Scripture electrified indeed men's minds, but left only illusory and unreal effects. The Providence of God, however, had taken measures to meet the evil, and produced within the bosom of the Church herself a remedy suitable for the sickness of the age, though undiscoverable by human error, when she brought out into full bloom the flower of deep and true spirituality. Men began to take a nearer view of the Gospel, to scan more closely its mysteries, and make the influence of its spirit and of its faith more felt, but it was reserved for the Church completely to solve the problem. God converted Ignatius by the truths contained in the Gospel, by that living Word which is sought for in vain in the dead letter, by meditation on the life of Our Lord, which enkindled the desire of imitating Him. And thus, while God formed of him a new apostle, He, at the same time, inspired him to compose the book of the *Exercises*, as a means of forming others also after the same model.

The development of the idea of the Exercises shows us at the same time their especial aim and purport. They tend entirely to discover to us the one end necessary to man in time and in eternity, and the means of attaining it in the best and surest manner that is possible in our present condition. We give the words in which the Saint expresses himself with regard to his Spiritual Exercises. Their end is "to prepare the soul, and properly dispose it to lay aside all inordinate affection, and then to inquire and discover how God would have it set its life, in order for gaining eternal salvation." So that man has to apply his mind to know the end for which God has created and redeemed him, nor may he consider the question as a purely speculative one not personal to himself, but he must find it verified with him, for it consists in the accordance of revelation and of moral and dogmatic truth with the wants of the human soul, which takes place when it no longer allows itself to be seduced by the illusions and cheats of the senses, but hearkens to the voice of conscience, giving us a knowledge of the truth and leading us to union with God.

To reach this last point, he who makes the Exercises must pass through several stages, each of which brings him to a separate conclusion. These stages form in respect of time the four divisions called weeks, and correspond, as to the end they have in view, to the three ways—the purgative, the illuminative, and the unitive. The sinner needs purification, and every one requires to know what sin is, and what are its consequences. The whole of the first division or week, which may occupy more or less time than an ordinary week, is devoted, according to the wants of each, to the accomplishment of this object through the exercise of the powers of the soul, producing in it repentance and hatred of sin as the fruit of the Exercises of this first part. The second and third weeks comprise the paths in which the soul must walk after having been purged from the vices which made it sick, in order to obtain that perfect health which consists in the knowledge and practice of the will of God. It is then that it makes choice of the state in which God would have it serve Him, or reforms its life in the state of which it has already made choice. These meditations, in their turn, prepare the soul for the concluding stage, contained in the last week of the Exercises, the object of which is to unite the heart indissolubly and forever to God after it has become detached from the love of this world.

The subject-matter of the Exercises accords with their idea and with the end they have in view. In order to build on a solid foundation, they begin by a meditation on the end of man, since this final cause must exist before the being which is created for it. The first question which man ought to ask himself is, "Why am I in this world?" The Exercises begin by answering this question. They tell us, "Man is created to praise God, that is, to honor Him and serve Him, and so to save his own soul. Everything that is upon the earth has been made for man, that it might aid him in attaining to this end for which he has been created." If one tries to give any other answer to this question, truth will soon force us to confess that no other reply can satisfy us. It is not art, nor science, nor power, it is neither riches nor enjoyment, which can be the end of man, for were it any of these all men ought to have the same aptitude for them, the same rights, and the same portion in these things, and the inequalities which actually exist in the division of gifts, both of body and soul, would be an inexplicable and an irremediable injustice. The Positivist gains nothing by setting aside this question, since, after infinite windings and wanderings, he must return to the answer given above, or else, by sinking into a stupid indifference, must neglect the most important affair of his being, and wilfully reduce his soul to inaction. Still, the generality of men substitute the means for the end, because they do not reflect, nor ever carry their thoughts back to this high consideration. The real stumbling-block is to be found in the irregular passion for enjoyment and material happiness. Sin having detroyed the original happiness of man, derived from God, he turns to seek it in that which pleases the senses, and thus becomes the slave of material things. And since many ancient Greek philosophers* have acknowledged this to be a true disorder in man, with how much greater reason may we say that it is irreconcilable with Christianity.

In order that we may make good use of created things, our mind ought to be in a state of indifference in their regard, as they in themselves are indifferent in their intrinsic value; for in themselves they are neither good nor bad, but they become the one or the other only in our relation to them, according as we use them in a manner that is conformable or in a manner that is contrary to the divine will. Seeing that this is a wholly practical and wholly fundamental question, on account of the consequences that may follow from it, the meditation on this truth, called the foundation, because the whole of the rest is built upon it, must be continued until the mind becomes thoroughly imbued

---

* We will content ourselves with citing a passage from the *Phædo* of Plato. " The body," he says, " weighs down the soul, and prevents its arriving at the truth and at wisdom. The care which it requires for its entertainment is the source of infinite hindrances to us. The maladies to which it is subject hinder us also in the search of truth. It fills us with the passions of love and of fear, and with desires and foolish fancies. Is it not the body and its wants that are the cause of wars, of rebellions, and contentions ? For cupidity is the parent of all troubles, and this would be unknown to us without those innumerable wants to which the body is subject."

with it, and can draw from it the practical conclusions most requisite; after which the mind can pass on to other meditations, having been sufficiently prepared for them.

The second meditation is on sin, whether original or actual, both of which consist in the preference given by man to the creature above the Creator, thereby tending, as far as in him lies, to nothingness. Sin, offending the eternal God, is eternal also, and deserves eternal chastisement. Therefore the meditation on sin is followed immediately by that on hell. Here is the issue at which man arrives by sin. He has taken the wrong road, and the facts evidently reply to the question of "Why am I here?" when he would resolve it in his own way and contrary to the will of God. Thus the mind in its meditation has examined the two opposite sides of life. In the one, man turns away from the creature, is converted from sin, and arrives at happiness ; in the other, on the contrary, he loses his end, becomes the servant of vanity, and deserves eternal chastisement.

When man, by considering to what the love and service of creatures lead, has attained during this week the first degree of conversion, namely, indifference to creatures and cleansing from sin, the second and third weeks propose for their object to advance him on the road of perfection, and make him determined to follow in the footsteps of his Saviour, the Captain of all the elect. To this end he meditates on the life of Christ, while a series of comparisons or parables, which are of the Saint's own composition and peculiar to him, singularly contribute towards winning the heart and mind to the love of Jesus Christ.

This second part begins, like the first, with a principle or a foundation, that, namely, of vocation. The old world has passed away, a new world begins. God says —"Let us redeem man." And accordingly this week commences with the meditation of the Kingdom of Jesus Christ, Who is represented solemnly inviting all men to follow Him, as subjects follow their king, on the condition of suffering nothing which He has not suffered before them. Then succeed the meditations on the life of Christ, beginning with His Incarnation and Nativity.

But here the method of meditation changes, just as in fact it did in the meditation on hell, where not so much the powers of the soul as the senses themselves were employed. Similarly, in the meditation on the Incarnation of Christ, St. Ignatius recommends us to place before our eyes the countries of the earth, their kingdoms and inhabitants, as in a grand *tableau*, and to consider the state of abasement into which sin has plunged them, their manners also, and their conduct, and at the same time to see and hear in spirit what they do and say, that we may make more distinct by contrast what God Himself is in silence doing in the mission of the Angel Gabriel, the dwelling of the Blessed Virgin, and the accomplishment of the mystery of the Incarnation. *

Meditation on the life of Christ is continued throughout the following days. On the third day comes the consideration how Jesus, at the age of twelve years, quits His parents and remains in the Temple, and it is immediately followed by the meditation of the "Two Standards." This serves as an introduction to the choice of a state in life, or it may help to perfect a man in the state which he has already chosen. It indicates progression when considered in relation to the preceding meditations, and its object is to make us advance in the imitation of Our Lord Jesus Christ. In this contemplation Lucifer, on one side, raises his throne of usurpation in the earthly Babylon, which is the image of the infernal Babel, and from thence he seeks to gain fresh partisans, who may more zealously extend his reign than do his ordinary soldiers. On the other side, within the mystical Jerusalem, sits Our Lord, of a charming beauty, in a lowly

---

* Ignatius carefully distinguishes contemplation from meditation properly so called, and assigns to each its own particular method. Meditation, being chiefly employed upon abstract matters, requires the active use of the powers of the soul. Contemplation, occupying itself with things in the concrete and with historical facts, admits of a twofold process. Either it makes use of the senses (though not in a material way), or else, as is more commonly the case, it recalls before the mind, closely and in detail, the different persons and their words and actions. In both these methods the points of first importance are the affections, the resolutions, and the practical applications, because it is these which act practically upon life.

and humble place, summoning around Him warriors who are of a disposition to do and suffer more than ordinary Christian men. The one makes promise of earthly goods and pleasures, though he is not master of them, and so in a shameful manner deceives us. The other, on the contrary, invites those who will follow Him to take upon themselves here in this world poverty, humility, affronts, and persecutions, and with these arms to assist Him in the combat in which He is engaged. The better to test whether he who makes the Exercises is truly called to this high vocation, the object of his choice is placed still more closely before his eyes in the following meditation, which presents to him three classes of men, of whom all, it is true, wish to save their souls, but do not employ the same means to attain it. The first are well aware of the obstacles which their love of, and irregular attachment to, the goods of this world put in their way, but they delay the employment of the means necessary for surmounting this affection, though they know them well, till the uncertain hour of death. The second do violence to themselves, so as to overcome their propensity towards these temporal goods, but still do not renounce their condition in life, because they prefer that God should come to them rather than that they should go to God. The third, in fine, detach their affections completely from all interior ties, and are ready to sacrifice in all reality the perishable things of earth, so soon as they know clearly that such is the will of God. Every man belongs to one of these three classes, but he who makes the Exercises is prepared by the previous meditations to embrace the third ; for everything hitherto has disposed and invited him to it, and it now remains for him to choose. At this decisive moment it often happens that he is assailed by opposing feelings. The clearness of his understanding is obscured, and his mind has no power over it to determine it. For this state of mind St. Ignatius gives rules that have reference to the several affections of the soul ; and these rules discover a profound knowledge of the human heart, and a wonderful tact in the discernment of spirits, and in direction, but the full exposition of them would detain us too long.

On the fifth day, when the will ought to decide, the first meditation represents Our Saviour quitting the house of His Mother at Nazareth, and going towards the Jordan, to commence His public life ; and during the whole day the mind is engaged in considering the three degrees of humility, which are like a compendium of the three preceding meditations, and which place before the eyes that perfection which we are called upon to embrace. In the first degree we can live in the world, and with possessions, without offending God grievously. The second degree excludes from the possession of earthly goods even all venial sin—and consequently both the one and the other presuppose to a certain extent freedom of the soul from the power of the senses. But 'we only attain to the third degree when we are equally disposed to serve and glorify God in riches, in honor, in poverty, and humiliations, at the same time that we even prefer the latter, as making us more like Jesus Christ Himself. This degree is the mark of the highest perfection, and gives singular assistance to the full practice of it. Perfect humility consists in this detachment from earthly goods, but it includes interior self-renunciation, so that the affections of this world form no longer the principles of our thoughts and actions, and the influences of grace are supreme. This is the core or kernel of the Exercises. It contains also the perfection of the Gospel, and the doctrine which Our Saviour counselled those to embrace who can and will follow close after Him. And, therefore, he who makes the Exercises always has this Divine Model set before his eyes.

Finally, having triumphed over the hallucinations and enchantments of the senses, the exercitant has taken the resolution of following Jesus Christ in earnest. He has entered into the stream of living water which springs up to eternal life, and which leads into it. He learns the sublime art of raising his mind above all created things, and enjoys the unspeakable happiness which the soul experiences in waking from the dreams of this earthly existence. But he must not forget that he is enrolled in the army of Jesus Christ, and that he serves and fights under a King crowned with thorns, that terrible engagements await him, and that he must be ready even to lose his life, if called upon to do so. He then enters upon the third week with the meditations on the Passion of his Divine Master, whence he is to draw the strength and energy he will need in combating the enemies of his salvation, and the power from on high which will confirm and seal the choice which he has made. But in the two preceding weeks he has learned that it is better to follow God made Man in poverty and pain, and be united with Him here and hereafter, than to serve under the standard of one who was a murderer from the beginning, to take part with whom is to condemn oneself to hate and to suffer for eternity. On this consideration he falls back in order to support with perseverance the sufferings that await him. One sentence will recapitulate to us all the meditations of this week: " The love of God for man is a love crucified, and therefore the love of man for God ought to make him ready to suffer all things, and so to enter into His glory, for such is the vocation of man redeemed by Jesus Christ."

The fourth and last week is set aside for the meditation on this vocation and this glory. In it the exercitant is engaged in considering the mysteries of Our Lord risen from the dead until His ascension. In these he learns how the spiritual man is perfected and completed. And he concludes by meditating, not, as might be imagined, on the union which we shall one day enjoy with God in glory, but upon the means of attaining charity, which is the practical object and corollary of the Exercises, and the constant aim of our efforts in this world. St. Ignatius endeavors above all to impress upon the mind that love consists more in works than in words ; that it consists in the mutual interchange of the things which the Lover— that is, God—and man, the object of His love, can do and can give to one another. And what man gives to God in this exchange is himself, and this giving of himself is, according to the Saint, the most perfect fruit of the Spiritual Exercises, as he expresses so well in this admirable prayer : " Take and keep, O Lord, all my liberty, my memory, my understanding, and my whole will—all that I am, and all that I possess. Thou hast given them

to me, O Lord, and to Thee I give them back.   It is all
Thine; dispose of it according to Thy good pleasure.
Give me only Thy love and Thy grace, and it is enough
for me."

Such is the subject-matter of the Exercises of St.
Ignatius, and we will only add here some considerations
on the effect they produce.   As to their manner of affect-
ing the interior soul, they procure for man an exact and
intimate knowledge of himself.   They are as a lamp to
enlighten the most concealed and obscure corners of the
soul ; and as a probe which penetrates to the bottom of
those wounds which corrupt it.   The exercitant sets himself to work to eradicate the noxious weeds which he had
permitted, up to this time, to grow undisturbed, and the
difficulties of the undertaking no longer deter him.   The
Exercises both enligthen and purify, and so do a work
much needed amongst all kinds of men, and at all times,
though attempted in these latter days only by means of
exterior light and cleanliness.   But it may be asked, how
did the Exercises of St. Ignatius bring about such marked
effects as to render their name so famous?   They are,
after all, only meditations on the old grand truths of
Christianity, which have long since unfortunately ceased
to make an impression on a vast number of men, whether
they meet with them in sacred books, or have them presented before them in any other way.   Why is it that
these same truths have always had, and even at the present
day still have, so powerful an effect on those who make
the Exercises, that more than once the ignorant attributed
it to magic ?   Are there any secret artifices brought into
play in them, in order to excite and cheat the imagination?
Quite the contrary.   Every allusion and every object
which can come between us and the truth, and so darken
the understanding, is put aside, so that no created thing
can take the place in our heart which belongs to God and
to the truth.   What alone gives to the Exercises their
wonderful efficacy, is that they are an active prayer, and
a practical meditation of the fundamental truths, which
simply read or heard would make a much more feeble
and superficial impression.

Here, on the contrary, man *brings home* to himself these

truths which have to him a personal interest, and this one
object he keeps always before him.   We must also look
for the cause of their wonderful efficacy in the study of
them in detail, and in the order and arrangement given
to these truths in their relation to the wants of the soul, so
that no other form or method than this could well be
employed, if things are to be as they should.   The exact
analytic and deductive process is one of the greatest
importance, as experience shows in all human sciences.

Every man knows the human body by sight, but what
a difference there is between one who has studied ana-
tomy and one who has never studied it.   The one knows
only the surface and some external phenomena which he
does not seek to explain, while the other perceives the
slightest motions and smallest deviations which escape the
notice of the unscientific.   Knowing the interior mechan-
ism, he can give account of the external manifestations,
and the more he has studied the most delicate fibres of
the human frame, the more he has divided and analyzed
them, the more he knows of the life which is the result
of these primal causes.   The same takes place in revealed
truth.   The deeper we dig into this mine, the purer is the
metal and the richer the vein of gold upon which we strike;
the heart finds itself more powerfully drawn, the mind
more disengaged from its ignorance and its ties to earth,
the will is detached from the senses, and the soul is more
like to God.   But these wonderful effects are not merely
the result of human activity, they take place because God
is faithful to His promises that He will go before where
the creature aspires after and seeks the truth, that He only
waits for it to make use of the means to which He attaches
the gift of grace.   Now one of these means is to be found
in the Spiritual Exercises we are speaking of, which
introduce into the soul, through prayer and meditation,
the fundamental truths of Christianity, and make them
penetrate the soul, like a principle of divine life, with infinite fruit to itself, because he who meditates has always
a positive and definite object.   In this manner these great
truths, which have been in all times the object of the research and investigation of the mind of man, become not
merely exteriorly applied to us, like foreign substances,

as is the case in human sciences, but they are made to enter within us, as things which most intimately concern us.

We must not forget that the Society of Jesus owes to the Exercises its rise and preservation, its spread and its organization. St. Ignatius would have the novices receive their first lessons in spiritual life from them, and plant in them the foundation of their progress in the perfection suitable to their state. One may go further still, and apply this observation to the life in general of the whole Order, to its rules and all its constitutions, for throughout them the spirit of the Exercises is to be found, of which they are in some manner the development and offshoot, so that the life of the whole and of each of the constituted parts derives from them its origin and its form. The meditation with which every Jesuit begins the day, the examen of conscience, and all the other practices, are but a continuation of the Exercises. The thought which St. Ignatius has chosen as the motto and abridgment of the spirit of the Exercises is found embodied at every turn— " For the greater glory of God."

It would require a volume to show the influence they have had on all states and conditions outside of the Society. But it is not our present scope to write a history of the Exercises. The celebrated Spanish theologian, Torres, explains in these terms how they could have so great an effect upon learned men, who take them in good faith and in earnest: " In my first studies," he says, " I had for my object the gaining of knowledge; but I made the Spiritual Exercises, in order that I might practise them, for there is a great difference between knowing a thing for the sake of knowing it, and knowing it for the sake of doing it." One may say the same of the influence they have exerted upon bodies of people to whom they are given in a more plain and simple manner, according to their power of apprehension and condition of life.

I conclude with this remark, very important in an historical point of view—that the Exercises of St. Ignatius produce a true reformation, for they reform our lives, and we know that there is always something to be corrected in us. Nor is this an imaginary want, but a real and true one, and this reform is the fruit neither of an error in the understanding, nor of a dream of the affections, nor of a corruption of morals. It does not consist in a revolt against the dogmatic truths which man has not invented, but which God has given for our guidance, our consolation, and our salvation. In a word, St. Ignatius was for those times, and is still for ours, a true reformer in all that truly needs reformation.

# CHAPTER XI.

FIRST BEGINNINGS OF THE SOCIETY. ST. IGNATIUS AND HIS COMPANIONS MAKE THEIR FIRST VOWS AT MONTMARTRE. HE IS OBLIGED TO LEAVE PARIS FOR HIS HEALTH.

FABER, being well prepared and having come now to the decisive moment of his life, was capable of undertaking the task of the Spiritual Exercises, and could not fail of aiming at the highest mark they propose—namely, the third degree of humility and the honor of combating in the first ranks under the standard of Christ. As it is to be expected that the sinner, when recalling with sorrow his past life, and the innocent, when he perceives in himself an inclination drawing him towards sin, should both feel the need of mortification and of doing penance, St. Ignatius has so arranged this part of Christian asceticism that, on the one hand, he is urged to do works of penance, but, on the other, is kept within due bounds, according to the spiritual and bodily dispositions of each individual. Faber had withdrawn alone into a retired house in the Rue St. Jacques, where his master came frequently to visit him and give him spiritual counsel. Led on by the thoughts which were the subject of his meditations, he gave himself up with ardor to the spirit of penance, which is so necessary and so efficacious for the purification of the soul. Although the winter was so severe that, from the thickness of the ice, loaded wagons could cross the Seine, he meditated by night in the open air, in order that the sight of the heavens might draw him from the earth. He neither ate nor drank anything for six days, and he would have continued his fast still longer, if Ignatius had not prevented it. This heroic act cured him forever of the habit which he had formed of taking too much food.

He was ordained priest shortly after making the Exercises, and said his first Mass on St. Mary Magdalene's day, the 22d of July, 1534.

St. Ignatius lodged at the college of St. Barbara, in the same apartment with a young man belonging to Navarre, of a noble and ancient family, whose name was Francis Xavier. He had resided at Paris since the year 1527, and had been public professor on the text of Aristotle since the month of October, 1530. Full of talent, and passionately fond of philosophy, it was his ambition to acquire, by the fame of his learning, that distinction which Ignatius had sought to reach by feats of arms. He therefore looked with contempt on the poor and humble life of his fellow-countryman, the exterior lowliness of which scandalized him, and therefore carefully avoided his company. Ignatius, however, soon perceived in him a soul capable of great things, and readily forgave his conduct, for, though not in conformity with the maxims of the Gospel, yet it was dictated by a motive that was noble in itself. Xavier had fallen into the error of supposing that Ignatius had chosen this kind of life, not from the pure desire of Christian perfection, but simply from the want of any higher aspirations. Ignatius, on the other hand, perceived the weak side of the young professor's character, as betrayed in his love of glory, and availed himself of this to overcome the antipathy with which Xavier avoided him. He began by making a show of friendliness and zeal in procuring more scholars for him, and so removed the prejudice which he had against him. Xavier saw clearly that Ignatius, so far from being, as he had suspected, a man of poor spirit, was possessed of a great mind, which could bear contempt with fortitude; and characters of this stamp always exercise a powerful influence over others. He changed completely his view of the life led by Ignatius, though he could not as yet fully comprehend that of which he had hitherto no experience. Ignatius tried to persuade him how necessary it was to prefer eternal interests to those of time; while Xavier, on the other hand, full of the aspirations of this world, defended with warmth what appeared to him to be the noblest ambition of man on earth. But he found his weapons too weak, and he felt his heart growing ill at ease, and his mind filling with doubts, as Ignatius repeatedly pressed him with the words of Our Saviour—"What doth it profit a man if he gain the whole world and lose his own soul?" Xavier could fight no longer against God. His arms fell from his hands, and he was compelled to give in; but it was only after a severe and deadly conflict, with his wounds still fresh and bleeding, that he at last gave himself up wholly into captivity to the spirit of Christianity. This, however, once done, it was impossible that man could be nobler or more generous in his sacrifice, or could with greater abandonment open his heart to the influence of divine grace. When, in fact, we consider the extraordinary career he afterwards ran, we are tempted to ask if there was at that time in the world another like Xavier. The meeting of these two men was certainly a marvellous event, and the victory gained by Ignatius over Xavier casts a vivid light upon his greatness. As Xavier could not make the Exercises in a retreat, on account of his engagements, our Saint contented himself with giving him, during the hours he was at liberty, what he could of direction and method for his spiritual life; and as the heart of the disciple was disposed in the best of manners, he made rapid progress in arriving at the height of perfection which the master himself had attained.

The conversion of one so remarkable in every respect produced a great sensation, especially among his friends, men full of the spirit of the world. One of these, named Michael Navarre, either from a desire of gaining the good graces of his fellow-countryman by getting rid of the author of his conversion, or from other low and sordid motives, conceived the detestable idea of assassinating Ignatius. He had lived hitherto in Paris at Xavier's expense, and perhaps feared lest, in imitation of Ignatius, he too might renounce his worldly goods, and so withdraw from him his supplies. Whatever was his reason, he one day provided himself with a poniard, with the purpose of entering the chamber of Ignatius at a time when he knew that he would be alone. But on his way to it he heard a voice suddenly exclaim to him,

" Miserable man, where art thou going, and what wouldst thou do ? " Struck with confusion and terror, he ran to throw himself at the feet of the man whom he would have assassinated, and disclosed to him with penitence his criminal design ; later on he even made public confession of it. His conversion was not, however, a lasting one, and we shall find him afterwards at Rome, appearing against Ignatius as his accuser.

About the same time, in the year 1533, two very distinguished young men came from Alcala to Paris, to continue their studies and to make acquaintance with Ignatius, of whom they had heard at Alcala, where he had left a wonderful reputation behind him. One of these, James Laynez, * of Almazan, in Castile, then twenty-one years old, had been already for four years a graduate in philosophy, and was incontestably one of the profoundest thinkers and most distinguished men of the time. The other was Alphonsus Salmeron, from the neighborhood of Toledo, at that time scarcely nineteen years old, yet remarkable both for his talents and acquirements, and especially for his acquaintance with the ancient languages. On their arrival in Paris, when dismounting at the inn, the first person whom they saw was Ignatius. Laynez immediately guessed it was he, though he had never seen him before. He immediately went up and spoke to him, and telling him the reason which had brought him to Paris, at once gained his friendship. These two young men soon entered into the little circle of the disciples and companions of the Saint, and made the Exercises about the same time as Faber.

Ignatius gained another disciple by the temporal and spiritual services which he rendered him. This was Nicholas Alphonso, surnamed, from the place of his birth, Bobadilla. After having taught philosophy with distinction for some time at Valladolid, he came to Paris

---

* This great man, distinguished alike for his science and indefatigable zeal, refused with constancy the cardinalate which Paul IV. tried almost to force upon him. After the death of that Pope, a part of the Conclave wished to raise him to the dignity of the Holy See, and had he not himself defeated the plan, it would probably have met with success.

to study his theology under the best masters. He learned the science of divine things in the Spiritual Exercises, and engaged himself forever to serve amongst the soldiers of Jesus Christ.

Before making acquaintance with the three last named, Ignatius was already closely bound in ties of friendship with Simon Rodriguez d'Azevedo. He was a native of Buzella, near Viseu, in Portugal, and was sent to make his studies at the king's expense. To great purity of manners, preserved more than once from grievous assaults, he added great zeal for foreign missions and an especial attraction towards the Holy Land. On becoming acquainted with Ignatius he communicated to him this desire, and learned that he too entertained the same project. This brought them into relation with one another, and gained the Saint another disciple. Besides those just named, there were other young men then at Paris who entered, some sooner and others later on, into the newly-established Society. Thus Ignatius had no reason to regret the loss of the disciples who deserted him in Spain, for they were not up to the mark of the difficult enterprise he was about to begin. *

As things were now ripe for his design, and his disciples sufficiently numerous for beginning his project, the Saint resolved to put his hand to the work. He had as yet communicated his ideas to his companions only in a vague and general way, taking good care, in order to prevent all difficulties, to leave each in ignorance of what he had told the others, for experience had taught him this

* Of these we may, however, here say a few words. The Saint wrote to Doña Eleanora de Mascaregna, begging her influence with the king of Portugal to obtain for Calisto one of the burses which had been founded at Paris for Portuguese studying at that University. The lady complied with his request, and gave Calisto money to make his way to Lisbon : but he had other plans in view. He went out twice to America, and returned with great wealth to Salamanca, where every one was surprised at the change that had taken place in him. Artiaga was made first Commendator and afterwards Bishop in America. Twice he asked, as Bishop, to become a disciple of Ignatius, but was refused, as the rules of the Order did not admit of his being accepted. He died in his bishopric, having been accidentally poisoned by the inadvertence of his attendant during a sickness. John, the third on the list, a Frenchman by birth, entered into a Religious Order.

lesson. All had finished their studies and had taken University degrees. They were also inflamed with a holy desire to consecrate themselves to the service of God and of their neighbor. without knowing in what manner it was to be done. In the month of July, 1534, the Saint recommended each one to offer up prayers and perform some penances for a certain time, that God might enlighten them as to the manner of life they were to choose, and then they were to come on a fixed day to communicate to him the lights they had received ; at the same time he told each one that on that day he would meet other companions. When they had come together on the day appointed, they were agreeably surprised at meeting one another, for they were all mutually acquainted, and were delighted at the selection he had made. Their happiness was so great that they could not restrain their tears, and they fell upon their knees to give utterance in mingled prayer and thanksgiving to the joy and gratitude which filled their hearts. Then they looked at one another with eyes opened wide in astonishment, and each one was deeply affected by the solemnity of the moment. Ignatius had anticipated this result, and as he had formed each one of them with the greatest possible care, and had led them to despoil themselves of everything which could interrupt that intimate union which he desired to form amongst them, he saw before him in these men a most important nucleus for his future Community. He then disclosed to them the project he had long entertained of visiting the Holy Land, for the sake both of pious pilgrimage and of shedding their blood, if necessary, for the conversion to the Christian faith of countries in which Catholicity had once flourished, but which now for centuries had been overrun by the children of the false prophet. To this he added that, if any among them desired to follow him, he would bind himself to them to the death*—that

---

* Bartoli allows himself on this occasion, as he commonly does, to put into the mouth of those whom he describes words which, it is true, they might have pronounced, but for which we have not sufficient authority. But, however beautiful Bartoli's language may be, the simplicity and humility of St. Ignatius are still more beautiful, and these virtues are faithfully pictured in the recital of Orlandini, i., 89.

he wished to confirm by solemn promise the project which he had formed, and to consecrate himself entirely to God by the vows of chastity and poverty.

God had spoken to them by the mouth of Ignatius, and they who had not yet known in any clear and precise manner what they were called to, but had felt in general an ardent zeal for the apostolic career, accepted with joy the proposal made to them by their master. Ignatius laid before them his plan in detail, and, after having conferred together, they held council whether, in case they could neither go to Palestine nor remain where they were, they should direct their steps to other countries and preach the faith in them. It was agreed that they should all go to Jerusalem, and there recommend the thing to God, and if the majority decided to remain in the Holy Land they should all regard this decision as the will of God ; but that, if the contrary was the case, they should go to Rome and put themselves at the disposal of the Pope. That if at Venice they found no opportunity of going to Syria by sea, they decided to wait a year, after which they were to be no longer bound by the vow they had made of going in pilgrimage to Jerusalem. They fixed the 25th of January, 1537, as the day on which they should all leave Paris on their way to Venice, so as to allow time for those who had not begun their theology to make their studies.* They chose the 15th of August, the Feast of the Assumption of the Blessed Virgin, as the day on which to take their vows.

We give here first the account of Father Faber, as preserved in the narrative of his journal—

The same year, 1534, in the month of August, the Feast of the Assumption of the Blessed Virgin, after having taken the same resolution, and made the Spiritual Exercises (Master Francis had not made them yet, though he had taken the same resolution as we had), we all went to the Chapel of Our Lady, near to Paris, to make each of us the vow of going at the time appointed to Jerusalem, to put ourselves on our return into the hands of the Pope, and to quit our parents and all ties after the term agreed on, keeping only money sufficient for the voyage. There were present at this meeting, Ignatius, Master Francis, myself (Faber), Master Bobadilla, Master Laynez, Master Salmeron,

* This date is thus given by Gonzalez. Bartoli is mistaken in saying that this day was appointed for the arrival of all in Venice (ii., 23).

and Master Simon.  Le Jay had not yet arrived in Paris to this intent, and Master John and Paschasius had not yet been gained by Ignatius. The two following years we all returned on the same day to the same place, to renew our resolution, and we all found ourselves each time extremely comforted in it.  Master Le Jay, Master Codurius, and Master Paschasius were with us in the course of these two years.  I mean all these were with us the last year, 1536. †

Bartoli's account enters more into detail, and is grounded on a memoir which Simon Rodriguez, one of Ignatius' companions, wrote thirty years afterwards; of this account the Bollandists were unfortunately not able to avail themselves.  It stated that the Saint and his companions prepared themselves, during the day preceding the Assumption, by prayer and fasting, and that they made choice of this Festival in order to show thereby that they took the Blessed Virgin for their patroness.  But as they desired to have no witnesses, and to avoid being much talked about, they betook themselves to the Church of Our Lady of Montmartre, a mile and a half from the city, where was an old crypt, like those often to be found in Italy in churches dedicated to martyrs.  Faber, the only one among them who was a priest, said Mass there, with his companions kneeling around him.  Before the Communion, he turned towards them, holding in his hand the consecrated Host, and so remained until all had, one after the other, pronounced the formula of their vows, after which they communicated.  According to this formula, they renounced all possessions and dignities in this world, and made a vow of perpetual chastity.  But they fixed the term at which they were really to make the renunciation of all property, as they could not do it during the time of their studies.  They also entered into an engagement to receive no stipend for the Holy Sacrifice of the Mass.

Who can describe their happiness, or the tears of devotion and thanksgiving which they shed on this occasion ?  Whenever I call to mind this passage of the life of St. Ignatius, I feel myself profoundly affected and imagine I am present there, along with him and his companions, at this act so important in their lives, and that I

† The original is to be found in the Bollandists, sec. 18, n. 178.

share in all the hopes and all the feelings which animate them. They felt, without doubt, the solemn import of that moment and the presence of God with them; they felt that He destined them for heroic achievements, that He called them to awaken the faith and enkindle charity, in danger of extinction from the egotism of the age, and to give strength to souls falling through feebleness. Never was there seen a smaller, and yet at the same time a more courageous band gathered together for the conquest of the world.

After they came out from the church they went to a fountain which sprang at the foot of the mount, and there they partook of a simple repast of bread and water. This finished, they concerted measures to remain united in heart and spirit, since they could not under present circumstances live in community as they would have wished. Ignatius proposed to them, besides daily prayer and weekly confession and Communion, that they should renew every year, on the same day and at the same place, the vows they had lately made ; and should meet, sometimes at the residence of one, sometimes of another, for a common frugal repast, so as to keep always alive the spirit of union which was their whole strength. He exhorted them also to apply themselves to the study of theology. The manner in which they fulfilled these directions soon drew upon them general esteem, and all the students spoke of them with praise. As they increased in virtue, so also they increased in number; and before Ignatius quitted Paris the three following presented themselves as new companions—Claude Le Jay, of the diocese of Geneva; John Cordurius, of Embrun, in the Dauphiné, or, according to others, of the village of Seyne, near Aix of the Viennese; and Paschasius Brouet, of Bretancourt, near Amiens. Faber gave the Spiritual Exercises to them. From such small beginnings the Order arose, with an extraordinary rapidity, to a greatness of power and extent which soon drew the eyes of all upon it, and in these first outlines may be seen the sketch of all that it afterwards became.

About this time St. Ignatius began to redouble his penitential practices, in order both to strenghten his own

soul and to give example to others.   From time to time
he retired into a secret cave, hollowed out in a plaster-
quarry near Montmartre, that he might there give himself
unobserved to the practice of mortification and prayer.
But it would be an error to represent him to ourselves as
an anchorite, breathing only a spirit of penitence and
seeking to impose on others the imitation of this part of
his character as their rule.   Far from that, he has prescribed no corporal austerities in his Constitutions, and
forbids his Religious to do any without the consent of
their superiors.   We have often spoken of his energy and
solicitude in supplying the wants, both corporal and spiritual, of his neighbor.   At this period of his life we have
the authentic testimony of a contemporary, Dr. Peralta,
who had attentively observed him during his life in Paris,
and afterwards declared that the little he had seen of him
in that city appeared quite sufficient for his canonization.
In truth, had he not possessed those pleasing qualities
that gain men's hearts, how could he have gathered round
him such distinguished persons, some of whom had reason
to look forward to a most honorable career in the world,
while others had already won glory and renown, as the
Duke of Candia and many others, in the highest ecclesiastical dignities, or in the first chairs of the universities?
He is represented to us in the various periods of his life
as a man of admirable patience and sweetness, indulgent
to the weaknesses of others, supporting with meekness and
forgiving affronts, whether they came from friends or from
enemies, and never more sweet-tempered than when dealing with his chiefest opponents.   It appears evident that
this meekness and sweetness were the fruit of consummate virtue, and not the effect of weakness of character,
for all acknowledged and esteemed these admirable virtues as existing in him.   An anecdote, which he relates
of himself at this time, shows clearly that the violence he
did to himself to break this fiery temperament had not
the result of making him timid and faint-hearted.   As he
was one day in conversation at the house of one of his
friends, Dr. Fragus, a friar entered and besought him to
look for another lodging, as the plague then in the city
had broken out in the house where he was residing.

Upon this they immediately accompanied the Religious to the house, taking with them a person skilled in the symptoms of the plague, that he might examine if it was really there. On being told that the plague had stricken the house, Ignatius visited one of the lodgers who was taken with it, consoled him, and touched the plague-boil with his hand. When coming out he felt a sharp pain in his hand, and was seized with a sudden fear. Instantly, however, recovering his courage and exercising great strength of mind to overcome his sensations and the infection communicated to him, he put his hand into his mouth, as if ashamed of the weakness, and said, " If the plague is in your hand, you shall have it in your mouth too." The pain immediately left him, and the only bad result of his visit was, that for some days he was shunned and was excluded from the College.

During the eighteen months that Ignatius studied divinity at Paris his health was again considerably shaken. He suffered considerably from his stomach, and the sickness became so serious that the physicians declared there was no other means of cure than a visit to his native air, the climate of Paris not agreeing with him. This reason would not, perhaps, have been strong enough to induce him to interrupt his studies * if another circumstance had not helped to decide him on returning to Spain. In fact, Xavier, Laynez, and Salmeron had many affairs of business to settle in their own country, and by their vow of poverty they were bound to renounce all they could claim from their parents. To prevent exposing them to the difficulties and annoyances that might be raised against them by their families, Ignatius resolved, at their urgent request, to go himself in their stead, and to attend to their affairs as soon as his health was established.

The fellow-countrymen of the Saint, who watched all his movements, were not long in discovering his inti-

* When Ribadeneyra (ii., 5) says, in speaking of the journey of Ignatius to Spain, "Quod Ignazius eo libentius fecit," he uses an expression not strictly correct, for the Saint says himself, in Gonzalez, "Paruit tandem peregrinus sociorum consilio." The pilgrim at last obeyed the counsel of his companions. This is not " eo libentius facere."

mate relations with his little Society, and as they could
find nothing in it but what was holy, they threw themselves into the field of conjecture and suspicion, and con-
jured up matter for denouncing him.   This time it was
not publicity they laid to his charge, as they had done in
Spain ; on the contrary, it was the mystery and secrecy
which experience had taught him to preserve in the establishment of his Society.   They imagined that he
wished to found a new sect, and so was seeking for
adepts ; and as they had heard mention of the book of
the Exercises, they suspected that this work contained
pernicious doctrines.   Out of these conjectures combined they framed an accusation, which they presented
to the Inquisitor, Valentine Lievin, who supposed himself obliged by his office to take cognizance of Ignatius
and his companions.   The Saint, on hearing this, would
not take his departure until the affair was settled.   He
went to find the judge, and begged him to proceed to an
examination, representing to him that, when alone, so far
from fearing the accusations of his adversaries, he had,
on the contrary, derived benefit from them ; but that
now, having companions, he was obliged, for the sake of
God's glory, to take care of his own reputation and
theirs.   The Inquisitor told him to fear nothing, assuring him that the complaint had no foundation.   He
only asked to see the book of the Exercises, and was so
pleased with it that he asked to be allowed to take a
copy for his own private use, which the Saint willingly
granted him.   Ignatius, however, insisted on having an
authentic attestation of his innocence, even though the
judge assured him that it was needless.   He therefore
presented himself one day before the Inquisitor, accompanied by a notary and several of the doctors of the
University as witnesses, and obliged him to grant the
testimonial he requested.   A copy of it still exists, dated
in the year 1536, which St. Ignatius, at that time at
Venice, probably ordered to be sent to him for his own
security.   This was the first judgment passed on the
Exercises by a spiritual authority.   It speaks with praise
of the faith and morals of Ignatius and of his companions, and is drawn up in the following terms—

We, Brother Thomas Laurent, Professor of Theology, Priest of the Order of Friars Preachers, Inquisitor-General in France, Delegate of the Holy See, certify by these present, that, after an inquiry made by our predecessor, Valentine Lievin, and by our councillors, on the life, morals, and doctrine of Ignatius of Loyola, we have found nothing therein but what is Catholic and Christian. We know, moreover, the said Loyola, and Master Peter Faber, and some of his friends, and we have always seen them live in a Catholic and virtuous manner, without ever having seen in them anything that is not suitable to Christian and virtuous men. The Exercises, which the said Loyola distributes, appear to us also, according to the knowledge we have of them, to be perfectly Catholic. Done and given at Paris, in the Convent of the Dominicans, under our ordinary seal, the 23d of January, 1536, in presence of—

Here follow the names of the witnesses ; the signature of the Inquisitor is illegible.*

Ignatius, reassured and tranquillized on all points, could set out on his way for Spain. Before leaving Paris he recommended all his companions to be constant in their vocation, and charged Faber, who was the only one a priest, to watch over them. The precise day of his departure is not known. It appears, however, from a letter of the 25th of March, 1535, which Francis Xavier wrote to his parents, and in which he recommends to them Ignatius, who was the bearer of it, that he must have quitted Paris shortly after that date.†

* This document is to be found in Latin in the Bollandists.

† We owe to Menchacha (n. iv., p. 5) this more exact piece of information. Bartoli has given correctly the year of the departure of Ignatius (ii., 23, 26). Orlandini says—"Vergente ad exitum hujus sæculi anno quinto et trigesimo," which must be understood in the sense we have explained above.

# CHAPTER XII.

THE Saint's friends had bought him a horse, on which, on account of his feeble state of health, he made the whole journey from Paris to Spain.  The exertion of travelling and the change of air did him good.  He wished to arrive at Azpeytia without any one knowing of it, but he was recognized at Bayonne by some people of his country, who probably acquainted his brother with his arrival.  When once in Spain he left the high road, and took an unfrequented and rather unsafe way across the mountains.  He soon met two armed men, who passed near him, looked at one another, and followed him.  Supposing that they were brigands, he addressed them, and found that they were in his brother's service, as he had sent them to meet him and to act as his escort.  He refused their offer, and told them to go on before him.  But when he was near Azpeytia, several of the clergy came to meet him, and asked his permission to accompany him to Loyola.  He politely thanked them, and continued his route alone to the little town.  There he took up his lodging in the hospital, and lived on alms.  He received a great number of visitors, but he would converse with no one except on spiritual matters and things relating to salvation.  He proposed to teach the catechism in public daily, and his brother having represented to him that he would have no one to hear him, he replied that he would be content if but one came.  On the contrary, however, a large number came, and among them his brother.  He gave discourses, besides, on Sundays and holidays, and the people flocked from far and near to hear him.  He induced the authorities of the town to forbid gambling at cards, and to abolish other abuses in vogue, especially among ecclesiastics. He gave himself in a particular manner to the service of the poor, and established a regular system of rendering assistance to them.

Such is the simple recital of the facts that took place, according to the Saint's narrative, so far as he could recollect and thought fit to communicate them. But the authentic documents, of which Bartoli has made use, reveal many things to us which his humility has passed over in silence. His family and the townspeople also had done everything to prepare an extraordinary reception for him. They had sent out scouts along all the roads to give notice of his arrival, one of whom discovered him at an inn, and looking through a crevice of the door of his room, saw him absorbed in prayer. On receiving this news the clergy of the town and the members of his family came in procession to meet him. They had at first designed to give him a pompous reception, but they afterwards changed their minds, thinking that this worldly grandeur would displease him. The honor which they showed him in coming to meet him in procession gave him more pain than it would have given of pleasure to most men. He most positively refused the invitation to the paternal mansion made him by his relatives, and went direct to the hospital of St. Mary Magdalene, where they sent him a comfortable bed and refection, but he made no use of the one and distributed the other to the sick. To prevent his sleeping any longer on the floor, they were obliged to change the good bed they had sent him for a poor and ordinary one, and then he consented to make use of it. He began, as we have said, to teach the people the catechism, and this practice was from this time forward considered and employed by him and his companions as an essential part of their mission. In this they divined the true want of the people, for it is certain that the great falling away, which at this period caused such havoc in the Church, came in a great measure from the ignorance of Catholics. In one of these instructions it happened that a very ill-favored boy, who lisped a little, made some women laugh by his ungainly way and his replies. The

Saint, turning to them, said : "You laugh at this child because you judge by the exterior, but know that his soul is as beautiful as his body is ill-favored. He will be one day a great servant of God, and will do much in his country for the good of his neighbor." This prophecy, which was soon made public, was fully accomplished, and the child became afterwards a saintly priest.

Ignatius was indefatigable in preaching the Word of God. He gave instructions not only on the Sundays and holidays, but also three times a week in the afternoon, and ceased not to do so until he was attacked by a slow fever. As no church could contain the crowd of his hearers, he was obliged to preach in the open air, and what was marvellous is the fact that, though he could not, on account of his weakness, speak with a loud voice, he was heard, notwithstanding, at a distance of some hundreds of yards. It is difficult to understand how a man in such a poor state of health could have endured so great fatigues of body and mind, for his discourses were not learned by heart and delivered, but when he spoke his whole soul was in what he said ; and this explains the wonderful effect of his preaching, notwithstanding its simplicity, for he preached both by word and example. Nothing costs a man more than to make a humiliating avowal of his own faults, for our nature is so corrupt that we commit easily the most shameful sins in secret, and yet have hardly the courage to confess the smallest when they humble us. Ignatius, triumphing over his self-love, was not afraid, in the midst of the extraordinary honors that were heaped upon him, to avow publicly a fault which he had committed in his younger days. In his very first discourse he declared that he had returned to his native place in particular to repair the scandal which he had given in his early years by his bad example, and, among other things, the wrong which he had done to a person then present, whom he named. "This man," he said, "though innocent, was condemned to imprisonment and fine, for fruit stolen from a garden by me and by other thoughtless boys ; and to repair the wrong which he has suffered I here declare his innocence, and make over, as due to him and as a gift, the two acres of land which remain to me of my inheritance, and to this act I take all here present to witness."

His words also were accompanied by extraordinary marks of the favor of God.  A woman one day brought a child to him and asked him to bless it, and to pray to God to preserve it to her for her comfort.  Ignatius, having looked for a time upon the child, said to its mother, "be of good cheer, this child will live to a good old age, and will have many children."  In fact, the child, whose name was Francis d'Almar, lived to the age of eighty years, and had fifteen children.  At his prayer a man who had been a long time subject to epilepsy was cured ; and a woman who washed his linen, having an arm paralyzed, recovered the use of it.  One day they brought him a person possessed, to have the devil exorcised ; he answered them by saying that he was not yet a priest, but that he would pray for her, and she was accordingly delivered from her possession.

All these circumstances, as well as the care with which he exerted himself for the good of his neighbor, had a strong influence for good, and his words were the more powerful because it was seen that he himself did what he recommended to others.  In particular he devoted the property that belonged to him to the foundation of an establishment for the poor, the administration of which he confided to the care of the magistrates of the town, while he engaged his brother to give a dole of twelve loaves of bread to twelve poor people, on the part of the house of Loyola, every Sunday, at the church, and to keep up for ever this pious practice.  Long after his departure he was attentively solicitous for the welfare of his fellow-townsmen, as may be seen from a letter which he wrote five years later, and of which we cite here some passages : *—

The infinite wisdom of the Lord our God knows most surely how many times I have for His sake ardently desired and purposed to show kindness to every one according to my power, and in every the least

* Not having the original to refer to, I have made use of the old Latin translation which Menchacha gives (I, xi.), for though it does not present to us the style and manner of Ignatius, yet it may be considered faithfully rendered, as Menchacha has not corrected it.

thing which is allowed to me. This desire I feel still more strongly towards those amongst whom I was born, by a particular favor of God which I can never sufficiently acknowledge. It was from this feeling, inspired by God rather than by human considerations, that, after leaving Paris, I visited your town more than five years ago, not-withstanding my feeble health. You know what good came of it, if indeed I was able to do any, after having been somewhat restored to health, through the goodness and mercy of God, Who brought me among you. The same desire which I then had I have now, and this leads me to seek the means of securing your peace in this present life, and of filling your soul with true joy and calm. I often think of the time I spent among you, and of the kindness and goodwill of many in so readily and cheerfully adopting all the pious practices which I sought to introduce among them, of offering up a prayer at the sound of the bell for those in the state of mortal sin, of giving succor to persons in need, that none might be obliged to beg in the streets, and of forbidding all persons to play cards, threatening with a severe penalty those who sold or bought them.*

Ignatius then conjures them, to persevere in the good which they have begun, and recommends as an excellent means of doing so, that they should often receive the most holy Sacrament, in honor, indeed, of which they purposed establishing a confraternity. After this he continues—

In former times all Christians of sufficient age received the Euchar-ist daily. But as their zeal and piety began to cool, they received only every eight days. After considerable lapse of time the fervor of charity grew colder still, and the usage was established of communi-cating only at the three great Feasts of the year. At length things have, through our weakness and negligence, come to such a pass that we fortify ourselves but once a year with this Bread of Heaven, and little remains to us but the name of Christians, as is easily seen if you consider without prejudice what the majority of men really are. The honor and service of the Divine Majesty and the good of souls being deeply concerned, it is just that we should pay particular attention to this matter, and should stir ourselves up to renew by a pious confra-ternity of men the holy practices of our forefathers.

The trouble and fatigue which he gave himself brought on a severe sickness, during which he was attended at the hospital, as he would not allow himself to be taken to the castle of Loyola, though his family earnestly desired it. Two of his near relatives, Doña Maria d'Oriola and

* It must be remembered that in Spain card-playing was then, and is to the present day, a practice of which the people are passionately fond, and which gives occasion to a great number of abuses.

Doña Simona d'Alzaga, were with him to wait on him for some days, and it is from their testimony that we gather the following wonderful circumstance. One night, before retiring, they wished to leave a light burning in his sick room, but he opposed it, saying that God would not leave him without the light he wanted. According to his custom, he arose to pray, and his heart became so inflamed with devotion, that, unable to contain the feelings with which it was filled, he was compelled to utter frequent sighs and exclamations. The two ladies, hearing these, and supposing that he was worse, ran and opened the door with haste, and found him in prayer, surrounded with a brilliant light. He was greatly confused at being discovered in this state, and his only resource was to oblige them never to say anything of what they had seen.

His stay at Azpeytia was extended to three months, during which he only once presented himself within his paternal castle, to comply in some degree with the entreaties of his family. As soon as he recovered his health, he thought of settling the affairs with which his companions had intrusted him. When he was about to depart, and the news of it had got abroad, a great number of the laity and clergy came as a deputation to him, and besought him with tears to remain among them, and continue the good which he had begun. But he replied, with good reason, that God called him elsewhere, and that the good they desired for themselves would be exercised in a more extended sphere, yet so that they themselves would partake of it. Although the heat of summer had now set in, he wished to travel on foot and without money, but he had great difficulty in delivering himself from the attentions of his brother, who, to do him honor, desired that, all the time he should be on Spanish ground, he should be accompanied by several servants, and should travel on horseback. Ignatius was so urgent, that by a sort of compromise his brother agreed to accompany him with attendants only so far as the frontiers of the province, while he on his part promised to make the journey thus far on horseback. After this he continued his journey on foot, passing by

way of Pampeluna, Almara, and Toledo, in which towns
the families of his companions resided.  He arranged
with these the affairs which had been intrusted to him,
without, however, permitting them to put into his hands
for them the portions which fell to them, although their
parents earnestly entreated him, and saw with great pain
their sons thus renounce all their goods.*

From Valencia he went to visit his former professor
of humanities at Paris, John Castro, who had once
wished to follow him, but had been hindered by his
friends.  He was now a priest and a novice of the
Carthusian convent of Vallis Christi, in the diocese of
Segorbia.  He communicated to him the project he had
of going to the Holy Land, and spoke to him of the
Society he had begun, and recommended it to his prayers.  Castro felt again so great a desire to join in this
work, that he offered to the Saint to leave his novitiate
and to attach himself to him ; but Ignatius would not consent to it, first, because he would not so easily have him
change his vocation, and secondly, to avoid the appearance of seeking to draw their members from other
Religious Orders.

At Valencia he set sail for Italy, though the sea was
infested by a fleet of corsairs from Algiers.  He escaped
this danger by falling into another, for they were overtaken by a furious storm that threatened destruction to
their vessel.  Whilst the other passengers abandoned
themselves to terror and alarm, Ignatius spent the time
in calmly examining his conscience, which only reproached him with not having corresponded to the
graces he had received as faithfully as he deemed he
ought to have done.  The vessel escaped, though not
without damage, as it was found necessary to throw
overboard the greater part of its cargo, and put into
Genoa, the place of its destination.  From thence our
pilgrim started on foot for Venice, but he met in his
journey not less perils than those he had encountered
upon the sea.  For one day he lost his way upon the
Alps, while following the course of a torrent that led him

* Gonzalez, ch. viii., n. 90.

into a mountain-pass so narrow that he could neither go forward nor retreat without great risk of falling into the river as it roared beneath him. With the utmost difficulty he extricated himself from his perilous position by clinging with his hands and feet to the rocks and bushes in his way. He, indeed, afterwards declared that he endured in this journey greater suffering in body and mind than he had ever experienced in his life. The rains of winter had broken up the roads, and swollen the streams, so that he arrived at Bologna utterly exhausted, and to complete his mishaps, he missed his footing just as he was entering the city, and fell into the foul and miry water of the moat. The idle fellows of the town, seeing him all covered with mud, pursued him with their cries as he went through the streets, asking in vain for alms. In fact, he would have perished of hunger, had he not been assisted by some of his fellow-countrymen attending the richly endowed Spanish college, which formed part of the University of Bologna. He arrived at Venice the last day of the year 1535, as appears from a letter which he wrote on the 12th of February, 1536, to his friend Cazador, then archdeacon, and afterwards bishop of Barcelona.*

You say first that you will not withdraw from me your usual assistance. After receiving the letter of Elizabeth Roser, I thought it well to let you know that she will provide for me till next April, that I may finish my studies, and I think it best to accept her offer, in order that I may procure books and other things needful for the year. Although the expense of living here is greater, and the state of my health prevents my bearing poverty and other corporal labors beyond what study entails, I am sufficiently provided, thanks to Elizabeth Roser, who has made me draw here in her name a bill for twelve scudi, not to speak of the alms which you have directed to be sent me for the love of God. A fortnight before Christmas, I was kept in bed at Bologna by pains in the stomach, brought on by cold and fever. I then resolved to come to Venice, where I have been for six weeks, in the house of a good and learned man, so that I am persuaded nothing could be better. The desire which you express, that I should preach publicly at Barcelona, I feel very earnestly myself. It is not that I imagine I could do better than others, or attain to more than they can, but I wish to explain to the people, as one of the least among themselves, things clear and easy of comprehension, in the hope that the

* This letter is to be found translated into Latin in Menchacha (I.,2). I have not had a sight of the original Spanish.

Lord our God may support with His grace my feeble endeavors, and enable me to contribute a little to the increase of His service and glory. I reckon then, that, after having finished my studies within the space of a year, dating from this Lent, I shall not take up my abode in any city of Spain to announce there the Word of God, without our having previously seen each other face to face, as we both so much desire to do; for I feel myself beyond all doubt under much greater obligation to the people of Barcelona than to any others in the world. All this, however, must be understood in the supposition that we hit the right nail, * or, in other words, that God our Lord does not call me to some work outside of Spain, which may give me both less honor and more labor. This I know not; but of one thing I am sure, that I shall be a preacher in poverty, as soon as I shall escape from the cares and hindrances which now enthral me during my studies.

The Bollandists tell us † that Ignatius sought lodging in a hospital of which St. Cajetan of Thienna was director. This must have happened some time after the letter which we have cited; and we advert to this circumstance because it may have afterwards given occasion to the story given by Castaldi the Theatine, in the *Life of St. Cajetan*, where he says that Ignatius besought this Saint to receive him into the Order which he had lately founded, but that he refused his request, believing it to be more to the glory of God that Ignatius himself should found a different Order, wholly consecrated to the salvation of souls. But a more authentic version of the story is that the Cardinal Caraffa, associated with St. Cajetan in founding the Theatine Order, and afterwards Pope under the name of Paul IV., wished to fuse the two Orders into one. Ribadeneyra, in fact, recounts that Laynez, on his return from Venice, in the month of April, 1545, communicated to St. Ignatius in his presence the desire expressed by many of the most considerable of the Order of the Theatines that they should be received into his Society, but that the Saint replied, he thought it best for the service of God that each Order should remain as Providence had established it. In truth, it is impossible that St. Ignatius could have taken a step which would have overthrown all the plans of his life, and have thwarted the marvellous order of events arranged by God for their accomplishment. But a fact

* *Clave non errante.*        † N. 212, sec. xxii.

which more than any other proves this story to have been pure invention, is that St. Cajetan was during that time at Naples, and not at Venice. In fine, Ignatius would in this case have been obliged to forego his Spiritual Exercises, a means he looked upon as so especially efficacious in the conversion of sinners, and would have done this precisely at the time when he wrote the following letter to Miona, his former confessor at Paris—

I have a great desire to know of your welfare, which is not surprising, since I am under the obligations to you of a son to a father in spiritual matters. Besides, it is right that I should correspond to the love and devotedness which you have ever felt towards me, and which you have proved by acts. I know of no other means in this life of making some return for all that you have done for me, than to induce you to make the Spiritual Exercises for a month with the person whom I have named, and who has offered himself for the purpose. If then you have made this trial and have derived satisfaction from it, I beg you in the name of God our Lord to write and tell me of it. And if you have not yet made the Exercises, I entreat you, for His love and for the sake of His dolorous Passion and death for us, to enter on them now, and should you ever repent of having done so, I engage to submit to whatever penalty you inflict on me, and to be regarded by you as a man who mocks the clergy—to whom, indeed, I owe so much. As in writing to one I write to all, I have not yet written to you personally; but Faber will acquaint you with all you may desire to know in my regard, and you can learn this also by reading the letter which I address to him. I beg of you, twice and three times, and, indeed, as many times as I can, to do what I have asked you, for the glory of God our Lord, that I may not hereafter have to reproach myself for omitting to urge you with every argument in my power to do that which seems to me the best method of all that can be seen, thought of, or understood in this world, and the most conducive, not only to the good of each one in particular, but also to the direction of others into the way of virtue, by assisting them and being useful to them. And though you may not feel their want for yourself, you will see much to be drawn from them beyond your expectation for the good of others. I beseech the infinite goodness of God our Lord to give us the grace to know His most holy will and to accomplish it perfectly in all things—*juxta talentum omnibus commissum,* if we would not have him one day say to us, *Serve nequam sciebas,* etc.

Venice, 16 Nov., 1536.

Ignatius made still greater use of the Exercises here than he had done in Paris, and by means of them gained three new companions, James d'Hozez, of an ancient family of Cordova, and the two brothers James and

Stephen d'Eguia, whom he had known at Alcala, and who were then at Venice on their return from Jerusalem. Besides these, many others also made these Exercises without entering into the Society of St. Ignatius. Among them Peter Contarini, nephew of the cardinal of the same name, who became afterwards bishop of Paphos, in the Isle of Cyprus, and with whom Ignatius always continued to correspond by letter.

# CHAPTER XIII.

**IGNATIUS REJOINS HIS FRIENDS FROM PARIS. HE RECEIVES THE PRIESTHOOD. THEY SEPARATE AND GO INTO THE DIFFERENT VENETIAN STATES. THEIR RETURN TO VENICE. JOURNEY OF IGNATIUS TO ROME.**

THE year 1536 had not yet closed while Ignatius was thus engaged, ere he and his companions were overtaken by the war which broke out between Charles V. and Francis I., King of France, on account of the Milanese, after the death of the Duke Francis Sforza. Those who remained at Paris were in consequence obliged to leave that city before the time appointed, lest their road should be closed by the troops of the hostile armies. Accordingly they left on the 15th of November for Italy, passing through Lorraine and Switzerland. Ignatius, before hearing of their departure, wrote to the confessor of the Queen of France—" Master Faber and his company will have to make a very painful journey, and will be reduced to extreme necessities." He on this account recommended them to his care, and they had, in fact, many sufferings and dangers to encounter in a journey made on foot, in winter time, through foreign countries, disturbed by war and by religious strife. Their joy was the greater when they had the pleasure of embracing Ignatius at Venice, on the 6th of January, 1537, and of being under his paternal care.* They shared between them the two principal hospitals, that of the martyrs SS. John and Paul and that of the Incurables, where they lodged, serving the sick with a tenderness and devotion which soon drew

---

* According to Ribadeneyra and Orlandini they arrived on the 8th, but the Bollandists adduce a manuscript of Laynez, extant at Rome, in which it is said, " We arrived at Venice on the 6th of January," and we can more safely rely on this authority.

upon them the esteem and admiration of poor and rich
alike.   Ignatius and his companions, immediately after
their meeting at Venice, resolved to go to Rome, in order
to obtain from the Pope leave to pass on to Jerusalem,
and to remain preaching the Gospel there without its being in the power of any one to hinder them, and that they
might also receive Holy Orders under the title of voluntary poverty.   Their journey, however, was delayed by
the approach of winter, and did not take place until the
commencement of Lent.   Ignatius remained behind, as
there were in Rome two very influential persons whom
he thought prejudiced against him, and likely to raise
opposition to the work on his account.   He therefore
judged it to be more prudent not to go there, as we find
in the manuscript of Laynez, preserved in the archives
at Rome—" We went to Rome.   During the time we were
at Venice two persons were spoken of as opposed to us ;
one of these (Caraffa) took the side against us, and the
other (Dr. Ortiz) received us, thanks be to God, with the
greatest kindness."   Indeed, Ignatius himself names the
persons who decided him upon not accompanying his two
associates to Rome.   He had already learned at Venice
the unfavorable dispositions of Caraffa towards him, who
was created cardinal towards the close of the year 1536.
The cause of this ill-will is enveloped in obscurity, and
must be looked for, not so much in what took place
between the two, as in the irritable temper of Caraffa, to
which Ignatius gave umbrage.   The Dr. Ortiz, then one of
the most famous professors of theology at the University
of Paris, had come to Rome as procurator of the Emper-
or with the Holy See in the affair of the divorce of Catherine, the Emperor's aunt, and wife of Henry VIII., King
of England.   As he was one of those who had most contributed to render Ignatius suspected by the Inquisition
at Paris, there was good reason for mistrusting him.   But
Ortiz had laid aside his prejudices, and now showed true
greatness of soul by speaking in praise, to Pope Paul III.,
of the eminent qualities of the new-comers, and by recommending them to his notice.   By this he gave the Pope a
desire to make their acquaintance, and convince himself
of their learning by a personal interview.   Paul III. was

fond of listening to learned discussions during his repast, and accordingly invited one day to his palace the companions of St. Ignatius, to hold disputation in his presence with other Roman theologians on certain matters. After the repast was over, as the Holy Father had been greatly pleased with them, they were admitted to kiss his feet, and Paul, stretching out his arms as if to embrace them, said to them: "I am truly happy to find so much learning joined to so much humility; if I can assist you in anything, I will do so willingly." They asked his blessing and permission to go to Jerusalem. "I willingly give you permission," he replied, "but, notwithstanding, I do not think that you will go." The doubt expressed by the Pope was founded on the treaty which he had concluded with the Emperor against the Porte, and in consequence of which a war was about to break out. However, Faber presented his supplication for himself and his twelve companions, and, on the 27th of April, obtained from the Cardinal Grand Penitentiary, Antonio Pucci, permission to go to Jerusalem, and leave for those who were not yet priests to receive Holy Orders from any Catholic Bishop. They received also, as alms for their journey, from the Pope himself and from some fellow-countrymen, two hundred crowns, which they afterwards restored on finding that the journey was impossible.

On the 24th of June, 1537, Ignatius and those of his companions who had not yet received Holy Orders were ordained priests by the Bishop of Arba, Vincent Nigusanti, after having made, in the hands of the Nuncio Veralli, the vows of poverty and chastity. Ignatius resolved to devote a whole year to his preparation for saying his first Mass, and afterwards added six other months to the time, owing, perhaps, to his not having yet given up all hope of going to Jerusalem, and of celebrating for the first time the Holy Sacrifice on Calvary, or in Bethlehem at the shrine of the Holy Nativity. And the reason for thinking this is that afterwards, when in Rome, he chose for saying his first Mass the Chapel of the Holy Crib in St. Mary Major's, that there he might find his Bethlehem. But however great his desire was to go to the Holy Land, God gave him clearly to understand, by

the circumstances which followed, that this was not what
He wished of him.　The Republic of Venice was, during
this very year, at war with Soliman the Great, and so it
was impossible to cross by sea into Syria during the whole
of that time during which Ignatius and his companions
had made a vow to wait; and it was exactly after this term
had elapsed, and after they had given up the intention of
their pilgrimage, that the war ceased and the sea was
again open for the passage.　This circumstance was a
very marked indication of the will of Providence.　They
at length resolved to leave Venice, that they might prepare themselves in retreat for their first Mass, and then
begin their apostolical labors.　The Nuncio gave them in
writing, on the 5th of July, permission to say Mass, to
dispense the Sacraments, to preach, explain Holy Scripture, and absolve from reserved cases, throughout the
States of Venice, and expressed himself in terms highly
favorable to them.　They left for different places of retreat; Ignatius, Faber, and Laynez went to Vicenza,
Xavier and Salmeron to Monfelice, Le Jay and Rodriguez to Bassano, Brouet and Bobadilla to Verona,
Codurius and Hozez to Treviso.　Each was to be superior for a week in turn, and all were to wait for the end
of the year.

From Vicenza, Ignatius wrote several letters to his
friends, of which only one remains to us, but it reveals the
dispositions of his mind and the spiritual state in which
he was.　It is addressed to his noble friend, Peter Contarini, and is written half in Latin and half in Italian, a
language which he as yet knew very imperfectly—

In the letter to Don Martin Gonzaga we have spoken at length of all
our affairs, and of some things which concern your highness.　I will
therefore write only briefly, and not so much because there is any need
of doing so, as that you may not think you are forgotten.　We have
hitherto been, thanks to God, in good health, and we find every day
more the truth of those words, "Having nothing and possessing all
things."　All those things, I mean, that Our Lord has promised to give
in addition to such as seek first the kingdom of God and His justice.
If He gives all as addition to those who seek first the kingdom of God
and His justice, what shall be wanting to those who seek only the King
of kings and the justice of His Kingdom?　They have the benediction,
not of both the dew of heaven and the fatness of the earth also, but of

the dew of heaven only—I speak of those who have *both* their eyes raised towards heaven.   May we obtain this grace from Him Who, although He was rich in all things, stripped Himself of all for our instruction ; and Who, although He was in the glory of omnipotence, wisdom, and goodness, vouchsafed to submit Himself to the power, the judgment, and the will of all that is weakest.   For this is sufficient for those especially whom Christ Our Lord is pleased to raise to a higher degree of virtue, but for you it is requisite to take care, above all, that you possess the things of earth and not be possessed by them, and that you refer all to Him from Whom you have received all.   He, in fine, who cannot attend solely to the one thing necessary, must take care that the things that demand his solicitude be well regulated.   But I see that I am digressing from my point, and I return to ourselves.   We have found a convent, called St. Peter's, in Vanello, near Vicenza, about a mile from the gate of St. Cross.   It is inhabited by no one, and the monks of Our Lady of Graces at Vicenza gladly allow us to remain in it as long as we please.   We shall stay here some months, if it please God.   It only remains for us to become good and perfect, since God puts no limits to His bounty towards us.

The convent of which the Saint speaks had been destroyed in the last war, and had neither windows nor doors.   Ignatius and his companions had carried thither a little straw, on which they slept.   Their food was very poor, for they begged it, and had very little given them. They maintained for about forty days the most profound retreat, occupied solely in ascetical practices.   At the end of this time Master Codurius came to them, and they resolved to preach publicly the Word of God.   They divided among themselves the most frequented quarters of the city, and each of them, mounted on a seat or some elevated spot, invited from thence the passers-by or those who were near, by moving his hat towards them or addressing them, to listen to the discourse he was about to give.   Ignatius evidently wished to imitate in this the example of our Divine Saviour and the Apostles, who often thus preached in the open air.   In the East it was the old custom for masters to collect their disciples around them wherever it seemed good, and the people of the south of Europe are accustomed, as is well known, to live much out of doors.   But a reason which may have induced the Saint to resolve upon this manner of acting was that many people then rarely went to the church to hear the Word of God, and, besides, it was very seldom preached there.   Though they spoke very imperfectly the language of the country, they drew an audience to them by the spirit that spoke in them, and which could dispense with choice phrases. Ignatius himself, speaking of these sermons, says that they made a great sensation and caused many conversions, and the favorable dispositions felt towards them were plainly evinced by the more abundant alms which they received.

Still, the old prejudices against Ignatius followed him to Venice, even though he had come out victorious from all the probations to which he had been subjected. His adversaries wilfully turned away their eyes from the judgments which had condemned them, and supported one another in their aversion to him, endeavoring by all means in their power to hinder, if it were possible, the work which he had undertaken, hoping that, by their intrigues, and by placing facts in a false light, they might find at last some less impartial judge. For this reason they resolved to raise a storm against him while he was absent from Venice. They durst not, however, accuse him publicly, but contented themselves with spreading abroad the most odious reports and calumnies, saying that he had escaped from the prisons of the Spanish Inquisition, that he had been burned in effigy, and that he had removed from Paris for the same reason, to escape being put in prison. It appears, from the account of Ignatius and Ribadeneyra, that the Pope's Nuncio made an examination into the matter regarding him, but it is not clear whether he was secretly denounced by his adversaries or had himself demanded a trial, as he had done before at Paris and afterwards did at Rome. Of these two suppositions, the latter appears to me the more probable. Before proceeding with the narrative, I wish to state my reasons for placing this judicial inquiry in the autumn of 1537, although the biographers of the Saint have hitherto given it an earlier date, and so have ignored the second visit that Ignatius paid to Venice at this time. Three circumstances seem to me to decide in favor of this date. First, the Saint says, in Gonzalez, that he learned at Venice of the sickness of Rodriguez, which, by all accounts, took place in the month of September; secondly, the judgment, at the publication of which he was required to attend, is dated the 13th of October. But that which decides the question is a passage in a letter written by the Saint on the 19th of December, 1538, where he says, in the most positive manner, that the Vicar General of the Legate at Venice proceeded against him "after he had begun to preach in the States of Venice." * This fact, then, in the life of St. Ignatius is proved beyond doubt.

Although the accusations brought against him were sufficiently disproved by the testimony of the Inquisition of Paris, an attempt was made to hush up the whole affair. But Ignatius, who had many reasons for not being content with such a manner of proceeding, insisted with the Nuncio Veralli on having a certificate in which his innocence should be formally declared; and this he obtained, as simple justice demanded. The Bollandists give this juridical decision, which was pronounced on the 13th of October, 1537. We there read that, the information against the Priest Ignatius of Loyola having been made according to the regular form, he has presented himself before the court, and that, a term having been assigned to the witnesses, their declarations and the defence of the accused heard, and the other formalities complied with, the judges, after having weighed all the circumstances, have pronounced in conformity with justice the following sentence—

The Father Ignatius of Loyola is innocent of all the imputations and calumnies which have been laid against him before us and our tribunal : they are false and without any foundation. We then declare him by these present to be entirely justified, and command silence on all those who are concerned in this process, certifying that the said Ignatius has been and is now a priest of good and holy life, of irreproachable doctrine, and of excellent condition and character, and that he has promoted in the city of Venice purity of life and doctrine. Such is our opinion and our judgment, by which we recognize, in the best terms and manner we can, his innocence.

As to what concerns his interior life at this period, he himself declares that, while he prepared himself for the priesthood, at Venice and at Vicenza, he began again to experience more frequently the heavenly consolations

* The letter will be given in the next chapter.

with which his soul had been inundated at Manresa;
and, in consequence of the spiritual sweetnesses he
tasted, he shed abundance of tears, so that his eyes were
affected.    Supernatural states of the soul began also to
show themselves again in him, after having ceased during the time of his studies.   He was apprised of the
grievous sickness of Simon Rodriguez, who was dwelling
in a hermitage near Bassano, together with Le Jay.   Although himself suffering from fever, he left Venice,
where he was staying along with Laynez, and walked on
so fast that his companion, in his amazement, could not
keep up with him, and the Saint was often obliged to
stop and wait for him.   He assured him on the way that
the sick man would not die, and when he had come to
him, he said, as he embraced him, "Courage, Brother
Simon, for you certainly will not die of this sickness."
In fact, from that very moment he felt himself better,
and in a short time got well again.    But this good
Father fell into another danger.   The life of solitude
and the constant company of a hermit named Antonio, a
man deeply versed in the spiritual life, possessed a great
attraction for him, for he was more inclined to a contemplative life and to asceticism than was suitable for the
newly-rising Society; and this disposition made him do
things afterwards which gave some trouble, as we shall
see in the sequel of this history.   Having gone after his
recovery to rejoin the rest at Bessano, and comparing
the repose, the peace, and the sweetness of the life he
had left with the cares and labors of his vocation, he
gave way to these thoughts, fell into a profound melancholy, and resolved to return to his hermitage.   He
left the house without saying a word to any one.   But
scarcely had he gone out of it than he met an armed
man, who drew his sword and drove him back in a threatening manner, and every time he made the attempt to
escape the same figure presented itself before him, so
that he took to flight in great fear, to the no small astonishment of those who saw him running like a man dis-
tracted, and knew not what to think of it.   Rodriguez,
perceiving that his design had been a temptation, went
immediately to find Ignatius, who by light from Heaven

had seen all that passed, and received him with sweetness, saying to him the words of Our Lord—"Simon, wherefore didst thou doubt?"

Ignatius, having returned with his companions to Vicenza, recalled his other dispersed disciples to his ruined monastery, that he might deliberate with them what course they should pursue. They had made a vow to wait a whole year for an opportunity of embarking for Palestine. The year was drawing to a close, and the voyage was impossible during the season of winter and under their present circumstances. It remained for them to fulfil the other part of their vow, which was to go to the Pope and put themselves at his disposition. They agreed, however, that they should not all go to Rome at the same time—a decision dictated also by circumstances of the time. They were not sure of succeeding in their object at Rome, and the least ill report might ruin them and destroy their hopes. Besides, there was no necessity of their all going to Rome; they could, on the contrary, exercise their zeal elsewhere, and thus support by the fame of the good they were doing the exertions of Ignatius with the Holy See. The Saint, therefore, left for Rome in company with Faber and Laynez, and sent his other disciples into the towns where there were universities, to hold intercourse with the students and gain some of them for the rising Society. Xavier and Bobadilla went to Bologna, Rodriguez and Le Jay to Ferrara, Salmeron and Brouet to Sienna, Codurius and Hozez to Padua. But before their separation they agreed upon the following points: They were to live on alms, and to have their lodging in the hospitals. Each was to be superior in turn for a week. Their sole endeavor in their sermons was to inspire in their hearers a spirit of penitence, as well as hatred of sin and love of virtue, to explain to them the Catechism, and to move them rather by the power of the Spirit of God than by elaborate discourses. They were, lastly, to assist their neighbor in his spiritual and corporal necessities, in the confessional and in the hospitals, and to propose to themselves, as the only end of this, the glory of God. Having been often asked their name and their Rule, Ignatius desired them all to give the same answer, and if they were asked who they were, they should reply that they belonged to the Society of Jesus; for the Society having taken Jesus for its Chief and Model, he thought it right that, in its labors for the good of souls, it should call itself by His Name.* This name exclusively belongs to Ignatius, nor did he at all consult his companions in its selection, as in other matters he ordinarily did.

Ignatius had upon the road an ecstasy which was of great importance in its consequences for the future, both as to himself and to the Society. He briefly alludes to it in a few words in Gonzalez. At some miles' distance from Rome he entered into a church,† and whilst he was praying he felt himself moved, and as it were transformed, and beyond a doubt he was given to understand that God the Father associated him with His Son, literally "put him with His Son"—*puso con el hijo.* Gonzalez having observed to him that Laynez recounted several particulars of which he himself said nothing, he replied, "Take as certain all that Laynez has told you, for I do not now very well recollect the circumstances. Of this only am I sure, that when I narrated to him what passed, I said to him nothing but what was true." Laynez' report is as follows—

During our journey from Sienna to Rome the Father had many spiritual emotions, especially at the time of Communion. Faber and I every day said Mass, while he was content with communicating; and he told me that God had imprinted on his mind these words—"I will be favorable to you at Rome." As our Father did not comprehend the full meaning of these words, he said to me, "I do not know what is reserved for us, perhaps we shall be crucified at Rome." He told me, moreover, that Jesus Christ had appeared to him, carrying the Cross aloft in His arms, and that beside Him was the Eternal Father, Who said to Our Lord, "I will that Thou take this man for Thy servant." Jesus took him and said to him, "I will that thou serve Me."

To understand the full meaning of this vision, we must

---

* The word *compania* signifies in Spanish, in its second principal sense, a company or regiment of soldiers. Bartoli was the first to give this anecdote in the life of the Saint, which doubtless he had taken from reliable sources. Orlandini says the same, that it is to Ignatius alone the Society owes its name.

† At La Storta.

consider it in relation with the other facts of the life of Ignatius.  He would at first have gone to Jerusalem, but circumstances showed him in an evident manner that this was not what God wished of him.  He had made a vow, in case he could not go to the Holy Land, to put himself at the disposal of the Vicar of Jesus Christ.  We must imagine his position, and the uncertainty of the future which was opening upon him ; the difficulties that awaited him, and which he could not be ignorant of ; the doubt he was in whether they would accept at Rome the idea of the Society of Jesus, which he had endeavored hitherto to realize at the cost of such sacrifices and sufferings.  These considerations, and many more besides, must have weighed heavily upon his mind, for, although he was a saint, we must not suppose that all was easy to him, and that, like Cæsar, he had only to say, " I came, I saw, I conquered."  His distinctive character as a saint is his constancy, his courage, and his confidence in God. Everything in his life told him that God had given him a mission, that the work which he had undertaken did not come from himself, but from on high.  In the obscurity in which he found himself involved at the moment when his work was to take a new development, along with the sense of his own feebleness, for the saints are not exempt from this unless God enlightens and fortifies them with an extraordinary grace, Ignatius could not do better than fervently implore his Divine Master to take him into His service.

But we are here endeavoring to penetrate fully the meaning of the words which Our Lord addressed to him. The Saint could not have asked Jesus Christ to take him as a servant in the same sense and only to the same degree that every Christian ought to be one, for this is a general obligation, and cannot be made the object of a particular prayer.  What he asked was to serve God as Jesus Christ served His Father and mankind during His mortal life, and, consequently, to be treated as He was treated.  Moreover, Ignatius spoke as founder of a work in which he was but an instrument; he spoke in the name of the Society which he was intending to establish.  In this state of mind he entered into the chapel, and prayed with extraordinary fervor, and fell into an ecstasy. He found himself enlightened and fortified by a vision which took place, not on earth, but in Heaven, in which he saw Jesus Christ holding His Cross aloft and saying, " I will be favorable to you at Rome." God therefore signified to him the place to which he was to go, and assured him at the same time that he would succeed in founding the Society of Jesus, and that Christ Himself would be the true Head and Founder of it, because He made no distinction in favor of Ignatius apart from the rest, for He did not say " to thee," but "to you I will be favorable." Nor is this all : Ignatius asked that he and his might be always special servants of Christ, and it is in this prayer that the gist of the Exercises lies, for they centre in this point, in taking up voluntarily the ignominy of the Cross, and asking of God the grace to be made worthy of this shame, without which that shame will not be the ignominy which Christ bore, but vain pretence and folly in the eyes of God and man. His prayer was heard. Our Lord manifested Himself to him with this sign, which is a folly and a scandal to the world, indicating thereby that crosses should never be wanting to his Society. He took him at the same time for His special servant, and gave him a personal assurance of his election and perseverance. In this point the words of Christ were addressed to Ignatius only, and not to others ; and he who would have them apply to himself must do the same as the Saint has done. By this we see the important bearing of this event upon Ignatius and upon his followers. It only remains to solve the difficulties which present themselves from the two accounts.

When Ignatius said to Father Gonzalez that he did not recollect more exactly the circumstances of the fact, we must not forget that the whole recital which he made to this Father was in a manner wrested from him ; that he omitted throughout a great number of circumstances which he could not have forgotten ; and that in general, where he treated of himself and his work, he used a reserve and a modesty which may be looked upon as excessive. Ignatius says expressly that he understood them in a manner that he could not doubt of—that the

Father had associated him with His Son. Laynez says, on the contrary, that Ignatius did not comprehend these words, " I will be favorable to you at Rome." But when Laynez wrote he was at the time General. Consequently a long period had passed since the event happened. It is an opinion and a conjecture which he expresses, and nothing in his words goes to show that Ignatius himself told him that he did not understand those words. In fact, what he said, " I do not know what is reserved for us, perhaps we shall be crucified at Rome, " have relation to the vision of Christ carrying his Cross and not to what He had said to the Saint, " I will be favorable to you at Rome." Laynez was therefore mistaken, and had not apprehended in their true sense the words of St. Ignatius, for he spoke thus to his companions to prepare them for the sufferings and contradictions which awaited them, and in a manner to prove them, and not because he was uncertain as to what awaited him, since he had received, on the contrary, particular light on this subject. As the true meaning of this circumstance could not be fully understood without putting the whole thing together, I have dwelt on this point longer than I could have wished, and I hope the reader will excuse me. The apparition took place at La Storta, a village about six miles from Rome. Before entering into this town, Ignatius gave, besides, to his companions a notice the meaning of which can never be too much meditated on. After having exhorted them in general to act with prudence, he added, " Let us avoid all relations with women, unless they be of the very highest condition." He meant by this that his followers should not undertake, as confessors or directors, the guidance of women, in order to avoid giving any room for suspicions ; but as this motive could not apply to women of the highest rank, the exception he has made in their favor justifies itself.

He arrived at Rome before Christmas, 1537. Ribadeneyra says otherwise, but he was not aware of the letter which the Saint wrote on the 19th of December, 1538, to Elizabeth Roser, in which he says expressly, " It is now more than a year since we all three arrived at Rome."

Nor do I know on what authority Orlandini sets down that he arrived in the month of October, for he cites none. We are left to conclude, on the contrary, from many positive dates, that he came there in the course of the month of November.

# CHAPTER XIV.

OCCUPATIONS OF ST. IGNATIUS AT ROME. ALL THE MEM-
BERS OF THE SOCIETY ARE SUMMONED THERE. A NEW
PROCESS AGAINST HIM IS SET ON FOOT, AND HE COMES
OUT VICTORIOUS FROM THE TRIAL.

IGNATIUS, as soon as he had arrived in Rome, presented himself with his companions to the Pope; they were already known to him, and that in a favorable light. The Sovereign Pontiff agreed to their petition, and commanded Faber and Laynez to give provisionally public lectures, the first on Holy Scripture, and the second on Dogmatic Theology, at the Sapienza, which is the name of the University of Rome. Ignatius at the same time began to give the Spiritual Exercises publicly to the people, and to several persons in particular, amongst whom was Cardinal Contarini, uncle to Peter Contarini, accounted by Maffei one of the most learned men of the time. This illustrious cardinal took Ignatius for the director of his conscience, and said that he had found in him the guide he had been long seeking for. The Procurator of the Emperor, Peter Ortiz, wished to make trial of the qualities that Contarini praised in the Saint. He retired to Monte Cassino, to go through the Exercises in the most complete solitude, and invited Ignatius to accompany him thither. The impression they made on this celebrated doctor was so strong that he would have entered into the Society of Ignatius, if the latter had not dissuaded him from this step on account of his age and the important commission with which he was charged.

It was during the time Ignatius was at Monte Cassino that he was apprized of the death of James Hozez, who had been the last to enter into the new Society, and was now the first struck down by death. He died at **Padua**, the victim of his zeal, death having found him on that field of battle which he had freely chosen as his portion. At the moment of his death Ignatius saw his soul depart out of this life, surrounded with a marvellous splendor; and another time, while assisting at Mass, at the moment that the Priest said the words, *Confiteor . . . et omnibus Sanctis,* he again saw him in the company of many others. He was in this manner consoled for the loss he had sustained, and had, moreover, the happiness of soon replacing by another disciple the one whom God had taken away from him. On his return to Rome he met a young Spaniard, named Francis Strada, who, having been unsuccessful at Court, had come to Naples to seek his fortune in a military career. But Ignatius having brought him in conversation to more serious thoughts, he enrolled himself as a soldier under the standard of Christ, and rendered most signal services to God in several countries. The Saint himself informs us with great detail, in a letter to Elizabeth Roser, of what he and his companions did at Rome after his return. We here give a translation of the original, which lies in the collection of the Saint's letters at Rome.

I think you are both troubled and surprised at not receiving more frequent letters from me. I would myself write to you more often, persuaded that, if I were to forget all the good which God has done to me through you, with so much goodness and love, His Divine Majesty would also forget me, for you have never ceased to render me service for the love and honor which you bear to Him. If I have delayed to write to you, it is because we hope, from day to day and month to month, to conclude an affair which concerns us, for I wish to inform you exactly of all that is passing here with regard to us.* During eight whole months we have had to sustain the most terrible persecution which we have ever experienced in this life. I do not mean to say that they have troubled us personally, or dragged us before tribunals, but by reports spread in public, and by denunciations the most unheard of, they have rendered us suspected by the faithful, to their great disedification. We have been obliged to present ourselves before the Legate and the Governor of the city, the Pope having gone to Nice, on account of the scandal which numbers took against us. We have named several of those who have opposed us, and called upon them to declare in presence of our superiors what they have remarked reprehensible in our doctrine or our life. And that you may the better understand the matter

* From this we see that the process was begun towards the end of March.

from its commencement, I will here give you some explanations. It is little more than a year since three of us came to Rome, as I remember to have already told you. My two companions began immediately to teach gratuitously at the Sapienza, by order of the Pope—one taking positive and the other scholastic theology. For my part, I employed myself solely in giving the Spiritual Exercises within the city and beyond it. We sought in this manner to gain over, not so much on our own account as for the honor and glory of God, some men of learning and consideration, for our glory and our desire is to praise and serve His Divine Majesty. We hoped in this way to find less opposition among the men of this world, and to be able to preach with more effect the Word of God: for to judge by appearance, we labored in a soil barren of good fruit, and productive only of bad. After having by these Exercises, with the help of God, won in our favor some personages considerable both for rank and learning, we resolved at the end of four months after our arrival to bring all our members together in this same city; * and having all assembled, we asked permission to preach, exhort, and hear confessions. The Legate gave us very extensive powers † in this matter, although many vexatious things were being reported meanwhile to his Vicar against us, and delayed the issuing of our faculties. When we had obtained them, four or five of our number set themselves to preach in different churches on Sundays and holidays, and to give instructions to children in other churches on the Commandments of God, on the deadly sins, etc. The two lectures at the Sapienza and the confessions were also continued. All preached in Italian. I alone preached in Spanish. I had at all my sermons a great crowd of people, and incomparably more than we expected,‡ for three following reasons : (1.) Because it was an extraordinary time, being, in fact, immediately after the Festival of Easter, at the moment when the other preachers of Lent and of the principal Feast had ceased, for it is the custom here to preach only during Lent and Advent ; (2.) because very many people, after the exercises and sermons of Lent, are disposed, in their inclination to sin, rather to return to the pleasures and diversions of the world than continue works of piety ; (3.) because we neglect the ornaments and elegancies of discourse, since we have learned by a number of instances that Our Lord, in His infinite goodness, does not forget us, and is pleased to make use of us, nothwithstanding our littleness, to show through us His mercy to others.

* This reunion took place before the end of March, 1538. St. Ignatius, therefore, arrived in Rome before the end of November, 1537.

† These were given by the Legate in the city, Cardinal Caraffa, in the absense of the Pope, and in virtue of his full powers, on the third of May of that year. They were thereby authorized to exercise everywhere ecclesiastical functions during their life.

‡ The Saint preached in the Church of Our Lady of Mont Serrat, and what was most admired in him was his power of touching the heart and that he spoke as a man who had the power of the Holy Spirit. His auditors were all Spaniards, and among them was Ortiz, the delegate of the Emperor, who used to boast that he had not been absent from one of his sermons during the time he was at Rome.

We appeared then before the tribunal, at which two of our three opponents were cited to appear. One of these having been found by the judge to be quite the reverse of what he expected, the others whom we had begged to present themselves were so alarmed that they had no longer the will nor the courage to appear ; but they obtained against us a decree which forbade us to prosecute the affair before other tribunals. As they were persons of means—one of whom had a thousand and the other six hundred crowns a year, and were besides men belonging to the Court and in office, one especially being a man of great consideration—they represented the matter to the cardinals and other important personages of the Court in such an aspect, that they raised up against us, for a long time, many obstacles during our struggle. At length the two heads of this little cabal presented themselves, at the term fixed, before the Legate and the Governor, and declared that they had heard our sermons and our lectures, etc., and their testimony completely justified our doctrines and our morals. Although the Legate and the Governor had much esteem for us, yet they wished, out of regard for these persons and for others besides, to hush up the affair. We, on the contrary, demanded several times, as appeared to us just, that declaration should be made in an authentic manner whether our doctrine was good or bad, so as to take away all occasion of scandal from the people generally in our regard. We could not, however, obtain this legally and under title of justice. Still, no one durst henceforward speak against us, for fear of the law being invoked against themselves.

As we could not obtain a juridical sentence, one of our friends spoke to the Pope, upon his return from Nice, and besought him to give us the declaration which we desired. He promised to do so ; but as no result came from this, two of Ours again spoke with him on the subject. The Pope having gone shortly after this interview to one of his castles in the environs of Rome, I went there, and spoke alone with His Holiness for a full hour, in his apartment. After having explained to him at length our design and our purposes, I frankly told him how often proceedings had been taken against me in Spain and at Paris, how many times I had been in prison at Alcala and at Salamanca, not wishing that he should hear these things from any other than myself. And with a view to obtain from him an order for an inquiry, that in some way or other we might have a sentence or declaration passed on our doctrine, I told him, in fine, that to preach and exhort the people with fruit we must preserve our reputation, not only before God Our Lord, but also before men; and that, to avoid all suspicion on our doctrine and lives, I begged of His Holiness, in the name of all my companions, that he would be pleased, in order to remedy the evil, to charge an ordinary judge, whom he should choose, to make inquiry into our doctrine and lives, that we might be blamed and punished if they were found fault with—at the same time asking his protection if they were found to be without blame. The Pope, as far as I could conclude from my interview with him, received my request with kindness, and praised our talents and the use we made of them for good.

Some time after, having first spoken with us in terms worthy of a true Pastor, he addressed to the Governor, who was a Bishop and the highest judicial authority, both ecclesiastical and civil, at Rome, an order to prosecute immediately our affair. He began the inquiry anew with all possible care. The Pope having returned to Rome, expressed himself publicly, and to those around him, several times in a manner that was very honorable to us. For every fortnight it is the custom for several persons to meet at the Vatican and to dispute in presence of the Pope during his repast. These favorable words of the Sovereign Pontiff dispelled in great measure the storm, so that the sky became every day more clear for us, and now our affairs, in my opinion, are proceeding as well as we could desire for the service and glory of God Our Lord, since already several bishops beg us earnestly to come and do some good in their dioceses, with the help of God; but we keep ourselves quiet as yet, in hopes of a better future.

By the grace of the Lord Our God, we have at last obtained the sentence which we desired, and it has been attended by a truly wonderful coincidence. You must know that a report was spread here that we had escaped out of several places, among others from Spain, from Paris, and from Venice. Now, precisely at the moment when the sentence was to be given in our affair, God was pleased to send here the President Figueroa, who had once put me in prison at Alcala and had twice proceeded against me, the Vicar General of the Legate at Venice, who had held an inquiry upon me when we began to preach in the Venetian States, the Dr. Ortiz, who had in like manner instituted a process at Paris, and the Bishop of Vicenza, in whose diocese three or four of us had preached. All gave witness in our favor. Besides which, the cities of Sienna, Bologna, and Ferrara sent hither authentic attestations in favor of us. The Duke of Ferrara, not content with doing this, and taking our affairs still more to heart because the honor of God attacked in our persons, wrote also to our Ambassador and deigned to address several letters to our Society, in which he declared that he made our business his own because he knew the good we had done in his city and in others besides, although, on account of the obstacles put in our way, we had much difficulty in remaining at Ferrara. We give thanks to the Lord Our God that up to this time we have not ceased to preach two or three times a day on holidays, and have given two catechisms each day, while the others occupied themselves in hearing confessions and some in giving the Spiritual Exercises. Now, that we have a sentence in our favor, we hope to extend further our preaching and catechisms to the children. Although the soil is dry and barren, and we meet with many contradictions, we cannot, meanwhile, say that we have been in want of work to do, and that God Our Lord has not done more for us than we could have imagined. I will not enter into further detail, being afraid of making this letter too long, but I can say in general that God Our Lord has fully contented us. I cannot, however, refrain from saying that four or five new companions have resolved to join us, and have now persevered in this resolution for some months. We dare not receive them yet; for, besides other things, they have laid to our charge that we wish to found a Congregation or an Order, without authorization of the Holy See. Although we do not yet live in community, we are, nevertheless, all bound under the same kind of life, so as to join in the future, and we hope that the Lord Our God will soon unite us together to His greater glory.

Rome, December 19th, 1538.

P. S.—Whilst I was writing this letter, the Pope has ordeed, through the Governor, that schools be opened for children, according to the manner prescribed by the law, in the city, that we may instruct them in Christian doctrine as we have already begun to do.

That the reader may fully understand all that happened at this time, we will add from other sources some other circumstances, which the Saint has omitted in his letter. It was, it appears, his fellow-countrymen who here again persecuted him, thinking this time to gain the victory on account of the protection which they enjoyed. An Augustinian monk of Piedmont, who by a popular kind of eloquence had gained the applause of the multitude and the esteem of certain personages, was endeavoring to introduce in a secret manner several of the errors in vogue at the time. The companions of St. Ignatius discovered his secret attachment to the new heresy, and set themselves to preach at once in opposition to him, that they might forewarn their hearers against his false doctrines. Provoked at finding himself unmasked, he had recourse to a clever plan—namely, to impute to his accusers the very errors which they laid to his charge, and to represent them publicly and privately as people who had everywhere been prosecuted for heresy, and had escaped by flight from the punishment they deserved. He was aided in this criminal design by the same Michæl Navarro who had purposed to assassinate Ignatius at Paris, but who afterwards for a time had attached himself to him. At Venice he wished to be again admitted among his disciples, but the Saint refused him because he had not the qualities requisite, and because he could not trust him. He now showed himself in his true character.

Three Spaniards, who were held in considerable esteem, joined in this complot, for reasons which do not appear. These where Peter de Castilla, Francis Mudara, and one Berrera. They would not, however, put themselves forward in the business, but contented themselves with compromising Ignatius and his companions with persons of high station by calumnious reports. It was this that retarded the issue of the proceedings at the court, and was nearly the cause of its being left undecided. Michael, suborned by a bribe, promised his accomplices to denounce Ignatius to the Governor, the Bishop Conversini, and to confirm his accusations under oath, thinking that this would be enough to have him condemned. Accordingly, the enemies of the Saint represented him and those with him as men convicted of heresy; and many persons of higher rank, as well as amongst the common people, believed the calumny. Ignatius found himself on a sudden enveloped in the meshes of a dark snare, and loaded with accusations which pressed on him, but were deserved by his enemies. He was, however, well practised in this kind of warfare ; he went straight to the Governor, and expressly demanded an inquiry, summoning his maligners, who kept in the background, to appear openly. The Governor consented, and fixed a time for them to appear.

Meanwhile, Ignatius managed to gain over to his side the Cardinal John de Cupis, who had great influence, and had hitherto opposed him. The Cardinal had a relation named Quirinus Garzonio, who from the first had been a stanch friend of Ignatius, and had given him an asylum, on his first coming to Rome, in a vineyard belonging to him, near the Trinita de Monti. But the Cardinal had found severe fault with him for being so intimate with suspected persons. Garzonio reported this to the Saint, who quietly begged him not to be disturbed about it, for his relative would soon entertain different sentiments. When the Cardinal insisted more strongly on Garzonio to break off all communication with Ignatius, he replied that it was not just to denounce a thing before examining it, and begged him to send for Ignatius himself, and learn from him the state of the case. As this proposal seemed to the Cardinal to be fair, he sent for Ignatius, and had an interview with him for two hours, which opened his eyes, so that from that time forward he became the Saint's protector, and this change had a great moral effect.

A little time before the day fixed for the inquiry,

Ignatius obtained possession of a letter which Michæl, who denounced him, had written to one of his friends, while he was still on good terms with the Saint, in which, saying quite the contrary of what he had affirmed on oath, he expresses himself with regard to him and his companions in the highest praise. The appointed day having come, Ignatius presented to him the letter, and asked of Michæl if he acknowledged having written it. Upon his reply that he had, he read it in public, so that the accuser, being contradicted out of his own mouth, had no more to say. This circumstance, joined to other evidence, proved clearly that Michael was a false accuser, and as such he was punished with exile. Ignatius insisted upon his other maligners being heard, but they, to escape punishment, declared that they knew nothing but what was good of him. By this insufficient apology they thought that they had given satisfaction to the party injured. The Legate and the judges were also of this opinion themselves, and therefore did not push the inquiry further, so that Ignatius did not receive, as he desired, a sentence declarative of his innocence. Many persons, and some of his companions themselves, advised him to let the matter rest there, but he rejected their counsel, which might have had troublesome consequences afterwards. He expresses his thoughts on this subject, in a very proper and honorable manner, in a letter to his friend Contarini, at Venice. It is dated the 2d of December, 1538, and is written in Latin, and is to be found in Menchacha.*

We know [says the Saint in it] that this will not hinder our being blamed in the future, and besides, it is not what we have hitherto had in view. We have only wished to save and protect our honor, and, at the same time, the sound doctrine and manner of life we have embraced. If we are represented as ignorant, stupid people, without eloquence, or even bad, unsettled, or deceivers, with the help of God, we will never complain. But what afflicts us is that they represent the doctrine we preach as erroneous, and the life which we lead as bad : now these two things touch Jesus Christ and His Church.

At the same time he declares that what he sought was

* i., 7.

not the punishment of the guilty, but the acknowledgment of his own innocence.

We have learned from his own account how he obtained what he desired, and we have only to give the contents of the sentence, which is dated the 18th of November. It states that the doctrine and life of Ignatius and his companions having been attentively examined, the accusations and the reports spread about him have been found to be false, and that the faithful ought henceforth to acknowledge them as orthodox. The false accusers were not punished this time, but their own perversity of mind brought upon them afterwards the shame which they deserved, and the Saint was avenged upon them more than he could have wished. We will not now speak of what befell them in the sequel, as it does not belong to our narrative. The sentence contained a remarkable passage, in which it was said that by these denunciations and rumors not only had Ignatius and his companions received no prejudice to their reputation, but that they had made appear more evidently the sanctity of their life and doctrine. In fact, the little Society of Ignatius, the existence of which had hitherto scarce been noticed, was soon known everywhere, and made rapid progress.

A circumstance which gave them an opportunity of showing their charity to their neighbors, without distinction, manifested in a striking way the spirit that animated them. Towards the close of this year a great famine afflicted the city of Rome, and a multitude of poor people, destitute of all means, were seen lying in the streets dying of hunger. In this extreme abandonment, Ignatius and his companions exerted the tenderest care in behalf of the sufferers. They took into their house as many as it could contain, they procured for them beds, or at least straw, to lie on, and went to beg alms for them from door to door, while they themselves were living only upon alms. They gave them clothing to protect them from the cold, and did everything that inventive charity could suggest when it takes the burden upon itself, instead of leaving it to others. They thus received as many as four hundred persons into their care, and, besides, assisted so many others, that the most authentic documents put them at the number of about three thousand, who by the care bestowed on them were enabled to wait till the time of harvest. The rich and the great, seeing that in fact the money they intrusted to their hands was so well employed by these men that they could desire nothing better, put their charities under their management, which was at the same time so prudent and so faithful. They were men who, in advance of their age, and great alike in heart and mind, divined and put into work institutions which charity afterwards developed. While they relieved the wants of the body, they were not negligent of the soul, for these often go together, and both the moral and physical evils are cured by a wise employment of well-adapted means. This was what then took place, and the example they gave led many others to imitate what they had done. Such a public calamity, in which they gave so great proofs of their virtue, drew upon them the esteem and the affection of the inhabitants of Rome of every state and condition. I will only mention in particular the daughter of Charles V., Margaret of Austria, who took an especial part in the works of mercy they practised by the abundant alms she procured for them. She chose Ignatius for her director, and afterwards, when she was married to Octavius Farnese, she seems to have kept up correspondence with him by letter. *

The first efforts of these men of God upon their arrival in Rome procured the establishment in that city of many permanent charitable institutions; for they took charge of abandoned orphans, provided dowries for poor girls, whose poverty exposed them to dangers of sin, they sought to extricate from vice those who had already fallen, and to remove them from occasions, and founded an asylum for Jews converted to Christianity. These works, which were begun by them, gradually developed themselves and were consolidated, and some of them remain to the present day. The newly-born Society had less opportunity of exercising its zeal in other labors. The storm which we have related having passed away, Ignatius

---

* There is the Latin translation of a letter of Ignatius, addressed to her, in Menchacha (i., 27). The Bollandists (sec. xxix.) cite a letter of Margaret to the Saint.

at length celebrated his first Mass, at the end of the year, as appears from a letter of the 15th of February, 1539, written to his brother Martin, in which he says to him, "I have gone at Christmas to St. Mary Major's, and there have said, by the help and grace of God, my first Mass in the chapel which contains the crib in which the Infant Jesus was laid." This letter did not reach his brother, for he had died two months before it arrived, but Ignatius had not yet learned of his death.

# CHAPTER XV.

IN the year 1538 Paul III. had appointed a commission
to inquire into and reform the abuses which had grown
up among the clergy.   This commission declared in its
report that the professors in the universities taught
publicly errors contrary to the faith, and that great
scandals existed in monastic houses.   It proposed to
suppress all the monasteries by forbidding them to receive novices, so that, the present race of religious
being extinct, a new generation might possibly be formed
according to the spirit of the primitive rule.   This project was at once violent and useless for the end proposed,
for without a higher principle of life, which it is out of
the power of man to give, the wisest and most perfect
exterior prescriptions are but a dead letter, and produce
no permanent fruit.   But although the Pope rejected this
proposal, it shows how little he would be disposed to
favor the multiplying of Religious Orders, and how difficult an enterprise it was to establish a new one.   Yet it
was precisely under these circumstances that Ignatius
was about to ask of the Church to acknowledge publicly
and approve of his Society.   The task was indeed an
arduous one, and above mere human strength.   Considering the state of things at the time from this point of
view, it is impossible not to admire the ways of Providence and the wisdom of Ignatius, who remained long
without speaking of founding an Order ; and before
asking the Holy See to approve of his Constitutions,
would in a manner deserve to obtain it by his works and
his prudence, and so lay beforehand the foundations of
the building he intended to raise.   However, events had
now given the necessary maturity to his designs, and the
time was come when he must go boldly forward, for
without that step the union of these admirable men

would have been merely fortuitous, and with no durable results.

When the question was raised among them of founding a new Religious Order, their opinions were divided, and it was first agreed that all should redouble their prayers and penances to learn what was the will of God, after which they should hold a common consultation on what was to be done, and, in order that their apostolical labors might suffer no detriment, these deliberations were to be held by night. In the first meeting they examined the question whether—in case the Pope should, in accordance with their vows, send them into different countries, even out of Europe—each should remain his own master, and independent of the others, or whether, although dispersed, they should continue to form one Society. The question was unanimously resolved in the latter sense, for though they were of different nations and customs, they were united with the closest ties to one another, and to maintain this union they must form one body ; they knew full well, too, that unity would give them more strength than if they were separated. They added, however, not only on this point but upon all the rest also, the clause, " so far as this agrees with the will of God and the intentions of the Holy See."

In the following meetings they considered another question, intimately connected with the first, namely, under what form of government the Society should be established. They put the question to themselves whether, though they had already made the vows of perpetual chastity and poverty to the Legate at Venice, they ought not to make another, of obedience to one among themselves, in order to be able in a more meritorious manner to fulfil the will of God. They had hitherto lived without any fixed head, although they all honored Ignatius as their father, and as he would prescribe nothing upon this point, and none of them could take the initiative, they did not know what to resolve. Ignatius abstained from exercising authority, because he wished that each one should take part in the work according to the lights he had received from God, that so they might be all more strongly united together, and that their resolution might be common to all and inspired by God. Some proposed that they should retire for thirty or forty days into solitude, to pray to God to make known to them His will. Others thought that three or four only among them should do this in the name of the rest. Both these propositions, however, were rejected, for fear of rousing attention and giving room for false reports, and of thus injuring their labors in the service of God and their neighbor, which, at that time, were in such request that, had they been four times the number, they could not have sufficed for all the demands made upon them. They resolved, then, to have recourse to the means prescribed in the Exercises under the name of " Election." But before the common consultation none of them was to advise with another on the point in question, and each one was to seek solely in prayer and meditation the lights which he needed, and then act as if he was entirely a stranger to the Society, and had to give it counsel. They were, in the next conference, to set forth, each in turn, the reasons which militate against subordination under one head, and the inconveniences which, considering the state of things, might result to them from the vow of obedience. All these reasons were put together, and the following were the principal ones. They found that, public opinion being very unfavorable to the then existing Orders, especial prejudice would necessarily attach to any one who should endeavor to found a new one ; secondly, that the vow of obedience would keep away from their undertaking many persons who would otherwise embrace it ; thirdly, that the Pope, whose approbation was necessary for founding a new Order, could refuse it, and send them to join those which already existed in such great numbers.*

In the following conference they discussed the reasons which inclined, on the other hand, to the taking of the

---

* This account is taken from Orlandini and the Bollandists, who, in nn. 280—287, give an exact abridgment of an authentic document which was then to be found in the archives of the Professed House at Rome, and bore these words written on it in the hand of St. Ignatius himself—" 1539. *En tres meses el modo de ordenarse la compania.*" It would be interesting to submit this document to a careful review, as it contains, to a certain point, the protocol of the deliberations.

vow of perpetual obedience. It was represented, first, that among the existing Orders not one answered to the wants of the present time, that all had principally in view the preservation of the faithful from the errors existing in their own day, and that the Pope would, on this account, show himself more disposed to approve of them; thirdly, that, if their Society were established as a Religious Order, many, it is true, might be hindered thereby from entering it, but that this title would attract very many more, who would look upon it as an immense advantage to be entirely dependent, as they would be, on the Pope ; fourthly, that, in fine, a Society composed of men of such distinguished parts, and brought together at the cost of so much labor, could not long subsist without the vow of obedience, and that, without it, the decision which they had last taken would be impossible in its execution. They spent several nights in discussing the reasons for and against, and it was not until they had exhausted all the arguments that could be brought against a Regular Order that it was unanimously resolved to add to the other vows the vow of obedience, and to choose a head. They bound themselves immediately to obedience. The formula, written by the hand of Faber, was approved by all, and each signed his name to it, after having read it during the Mass before Communion. It ran as follows :

I, the undersigned, declare before God Almighty, the Blessed Virgin Mary, and all the court of Heaven, that, after having prayed God and maturely weighed the matter, I have voted with my whole heart for the vow of obedience being taken in the Society, finding it more conducive to the glory of God and the preservation of our Society. I declare also that I have freely decided, but without vow and without any obligation, to enter into this Society, if God permit it to be approved of by the Pope. In proof of this resolution, which, by the grace of God, I have taken as I here declare, I go now to holy Communion though unworthy, with this same intention:

On Thursday, 15th of April, 1539.

| | |
|---|---|
| R. Cacres. | J. Codurius. |
| Laynez. | Salmeron. |
| Bobadilla. | Paschasius Brouet. |
| Francis. | Peter Faber. |
| Ignatius. | Simon Rodriguez. |
| Claude le Jay. | |

Besides these two points, several other rules were adopted by them, pertaining to the end of the Society, and in relation to the development which it had up to this taken. On the 4th of May it was unanimously decided that whoever should henceforth wish to enter into the Society should make, in the person of his Superior, a vow to the Pope of going into all countries in the world as soon as he should receive an order to do so, whether Christian or infidel, and this decision was immediately put in writing. It was also ruled that each member of the Society should explain publicly every year for forty days the Christian doctrine for an hour each day. The assembly wished to make this obligatory by vow, but was prevented by the opposition of Bobadilla. Such a vow might, in fact, have had its inconveniences, for if that to which they wished to bind themselves was at certain times necessary, still this necessity might change, as experience has shown. However, that the opposition of a single member might not, for the future, hold against the consent of all the rest, they decreed that henceforth, in a simular case, account should not be taken of it. It was also established that those who presented themselves for entrance into the Society should make a novitiate, and in particular the Exercises, and that they should be put to the other probations of the Society. On the eve of the octave of Corpus Christi it was decreed that the Society should have a Superior General, and that he should be named for life, always under the restrictions as to this last point which were appointed later. They decided also that, in case they were dispersed into other countries, the resolutions touching the affairs which concerned the whole Society should be taken from the majority of the votes of members residing in Italy, who should be called to Rome for that end, or should send their vote thither by writing, and that these resolu-

---

The name of Father Cacres, which occurs on the preceding page, is found nowhere else among the first Fathers of the Society. Whence we may attribute it to some fault of the copyist in the Bollandists, as there is a similar one in two letters of St. Ignatius of the year 1536, in Menchacha (i., 3, 4), where a certain Carceres is spoken of—or Cazeres, as Menchacha would have it—who is perhaps the same as this Cacres here named.

tions should be obligatory upon all, as if the whole Society had been present. These regulations were approved and subscribed unanimously.

If we cast a glance over the main features of these new Constitutions, we may observe that the nucleus of them and their distinctive mark consists in an obedience inspired by love—not a blind obedience, but vigilant and ever kept awake by the spirit of the entire body, which is alive to what is necessary at each epoch of time, and must consequently have the right of determining, in the person of the superiors, that which circumstances demand, so that life may never become extinct, nor the salt lose its savor. It is on this basis that the rules established by St. Ignatius were founded.

The Society, after having completed the sketch of its Constitutions, laid upon our Saint the task of drawing up a formula to be presented for the approbation of the Holy See. He put together the decisions they had come to in five chapters, and had them presented to Paul III. by Cardinal Contarini, with a petition to confirm them. The Pope sent the formula to be examined by Thomas Badia, the Dominican, Master of the Sacred Palace, who, at the end of two months, sent it back to the Cardinal with a favorable reply. What followed may be gathered from a note of the Cardinal to St. Ignatius—

I received yesterday [he writes] by the Spaniard, Marc Antonio, your rule in brief, with a letter of the Master of the Sacred Palace. I have been to-day to the Pope, and, after having put to him your petition by word of mouth, I have read to His Holiness the five chapters, with which he showed himself highly satisfied, and he has been pleased to approve and confirm them. We shall return to Rome with His Holiness on Friday, and then the Most Honorable Ghinuccio will receive an order to make out the Brief or Bull. I recommend myself to your prayers.

Your most devoted
C. CARDINAL CONTARINI.

Rome, 3d Sept., 1539.

The Pope, according to another most reliable authority, after having examined the formula which had been read to him, remarked, "The finger of God is here." On account, however, of the importance of the matter, he referred the sketch of the Rule to a commission composed of three cardinals, amongst whom was Cardinal Bartholomew Guidiccioni, of Lucca, who shared the views expressed by the committee established the previous year for examining into the abuses of Religious Houses, and of which we have spoken above. His learning, his purity of morals, and the reputation he enjoyed, gave him a superiority over his two colleagues to which it was difficult for them not to bow, and hence a favorable sentence could hardly be expected from this commission. When Guidiccioni had received the formula he would not so much as read it, but gave his formal declaration against the introduction of new Orders. "For," said he, "they become relaxed in time, and when they are old they do more harm to the Church than they did good in their beginning." Whatever truth there may be in this judgment, it rests, nevertheless, upon an argument which may be brought against all human institutions, for these, too, are subject to decline and degeneracy. The Cardinal would certainly have denied the conclusion to which his argument led, namely, that it is better to have no establishments at all, than to have some faulty ones. It is true, on the other hand, that his opposition was unhappily justified by experience, especially at the time in which he lived; so that we must not blame him for it, but rather allow that it was a serious objection, and strengthened by a considerable amount of reason.

Nevertheless, Ignatius and his companions had recourse to Him Who holds the hearts of men in His hand and turns them whither He will. It was the only means to which he could have recourse, and it was the most efficacious one as well. The Cardinal, after having for a long time refused to cast his eye upon the five chapters, on a sudden decided upon having them read to him, though we know neither the reason nor the occasion for this change. On examining them he found them so perfect that he entirely approved of them, and declared that, without departing from his former opinion, he would nevertheless make an exception in favor of this institution. He easily brought over his two colleagues to unite with him in sending a favorable reply to the Pope, who then published the Bull of confirmation, *Regimini militantis ec-*

*clesiæ,* etc., dated September 27th, 1540. The number of the Professed belonging to the new Order was limited, it is true, to sixty, but soon after, when its labors for the Holy Church had become more extensive and efficacious, the same Paul III. took off this restriction by his Bull of the 14th of March, 1543.

Many causes contributed to this happy issue, among the chief of which I reckon the zeal of the Society, the good which it did, and the desire which, contrary to all expectation, the King of Portugal, John III., manifested of seeing it established in his dominions. Towards the close of the year 1539, at the very time when Cardinal Guidiccioni expressed in the strongest manner his opposition to the new Society, Ignatius received a letter from Diego Govéa, then at Paris, who had been a long time his master, and even his opponent. This learned man, who was held in high estimation, wrote to him that God was about to open in the East Indies an entrance for the Gospel and a vast field for him and his companions, and that, if he wished to go into these countries, he would speak for him to the King of Portugal. This proposal could not be otherwise than very pleasing to Ignatius, though he replied, as he was in duty bound to do, that he and his were in the hands of the Pope, and were ready to obey at the least indication of his wish, and to go wherever he should send them ; that therefore Diego could, if he thought fit, make application to the Holy See. Govéa wrote to John III., * to whom he sent the letter of Ignatius, advising him not to let this opportunity escape him, but to ask of the Pope for some of these priests, that they might go as missionaries into the newly-subjected Indian possessions. The King, who from this moment became one of the most faithful and energetic friends of the Society, sent the two letters to his ambassador at Rome, Peter Mascarenha, with instructions to press the matter with Ignatius and with the Pope.

---

* Orlandini, ii., 85. Menchacha proves, in his comments, that this letter of the Saint's, which is not now extant, must have been written before the end of the year 1530. He shows also that Govéa was then at Paris, and not in Portugal, and that he was still dwelling in Paris in 1541.

The ambassador, on the principle of asking for enough—
*pete iniquum et accipies justum*—demanded, in the name of
his master, six priests of the Society.   A negotiation so
zealously urged on his ambassador by a monarch then so
powerful, that he might obtain these particular priests,
while there were plenty of others who could be had, at a
time also when they were suspected at Rome, calumniated, dragged before tribunals, and on the point of being
ship-wrecked in their plans, must have awakened the attention of small and great, and have opened the eyes of
the most prejudiced to see the merit of men who were
sought for from so far.   Ignatius showed in this conjuncture that he had never doubted of the accomplishment of
the promise which Our Lord had made to him, that He
would be favorable to them at Rome.   Although everything seemed turning against him, he still hoped for a
happy issue, and so did not allow himself to be dazzled
by the bright prospect which was opened to him in
Portugal, and declared to Mascarenha that he could not
give him more than two of his companions.   As he continued to persist in asking for six, Ignatius made him this
truly great answer, which was the more remarkable from
the circumstances in which he was placed, " If out of so
small a Society you take six for one kingdom, what will
be left for the rest of the world ? "   The Ambassador
was not more successful with the Pope, to whom he
addressed himself; and in this Ignatius must have recognized a sign of favor to him, for Paul III. left it to his
free choice to determine the number of missioners whom
he would give to the King of Portugal, and Mascarenha
was obliged to be content with two.

Ignatius set apart for this important mission Simon
Rodriguez and Bobadilla.   The former had arrived at
Rome from Sienna, and, though sick of the fever, departed from Rome on the 5th of March, and embarked
at Civita Vecchia for Portugal.   The second came from
Naples, suffering so much from sciatica, that another
had to be chosen in his place, as time pressed and did
not allow of delay till his recovery.   St. Francis Xavier
was chosen in his stead, for God had chosen him to become the apostle of a multitude of nations.   Ignatius

announced his resolution to him on the 15th of March, 1540, and the next day Xavier departed with Mascarenha, taking with him nothing but his cassock, which he had himself mended, and his breviary. He took a letter of Ignatius to his nephew, the lord of Loyola, as in passing he had to go by that place. The letter was as follows :

> Pressed as I am with occupation in sending some of my companions to the Indies, and, at the same time, others to Ireland and Italy, I cannot write to you at the length I would have wished. The bearer of this letter is Master Francis Xavier, son of the Señor de Xavier, and a member of our Society. He goes by order of the Pope, and at the request of the King of Portugal, together with two others,* who are going by sea to the same prince. Master Francis will tell you all that can interest you to know, and I have commissioned him to converse with you on certain affairs, and to treat with you concerning them as if I myself were in person with you. I wish you to know that the Ambassador of the King of Portugal, with whom Master Francis travels, is very much attached to us, and we owe much to him. He hopes to be of use to us as far as he can with the King, his master, and with all others, in all that pertains to the service of God Our Lord. I beg you, therefore, to receive him with all the honor and state you can.
>
> Rome, 16th of March, 1540.

To preserve the thread of the narrative, I may mention that the King wished to keep both priests in Portugal, and this led to several negotiations between him and the Pope, in the course of the summer and autumn. The Pope left the decision of the matter to the King and St. Ignatius, and at length the Saint proposed to John III. to send Xavier to the Indies, and to keep Rodriguez in Portugal, that he might plant there a seminary for the Society, and so provide for the wants of both countries. The King accepted the proposal, and Xavier took his departure alone, as Apostolic Nuncio, on the 7th of April in the following year. In like manner, as Ignatius, in the letter quoted, acknowledged the services which Mascarenha rendered to the Society with the Holy See, for it is of him evidently that mention is made, so he speaks in a more positive manner of the

---

* By this it appears that Ignatius had not given up the idea of sending Bobadilla. I have only read this letter in the Latin translation of Menchacha, on whose fidelity one may rely.

support it derived from the two Contarini, when writing on the 18th of December, 1540, to Peter Contarini at Venice, to inform him of the approbation of the Society. He thanks him for the trouble he had taken with the Cardinal, his uncle, on this score, and tells him that he had been one of the most devoted patrons of this work with the Pope. It is the duty of history to register the names of persons whose services God has employed for the accomplishment of His designs, notwithstanding the opposition of men, and who have thus acquired a just title to our gratitude. And we must not be less ready to acknowledge it than Ignatius, although, among the natural causes which brought about the success of the undertaking, not the least was its own excellence, and the talents of the persons concerned.

In the deliberations which took place on the subject of the Constitutions of the Society, the question of its name was definitively settled. We know, as has been said already, that Ignatius did not wish to be considered as its founder, and hence his manner of proceeding. He had it much at heart that the Order should not take its name from him, or from any subordinate cause, but should be called the Society of Jesus, as being entirely consecrated to the service and imitation of Our Saviour, and as finding in Him the true principle of its life, besides which he acted as one persuaded that he had not himself conceived the form of this institute, but had received it from Jesus Christ. He had already expressed himself in this sense at Vicenza, and his object was recognized by all his companions, and the name of the Society of Jesus was inserted from the first in the brief formula which Paul III. approved. It is in this sense also that he had asked to be admitted into the service and the household of Jesus, not wishing to be himself the head of the Society; thus the words of Our Lord : " I will be favorable to you at Rome" were regarded as an assent to the request that Jesus would vouchsafe to be its true head and founder. Indeed, St. Ignatius says later on, as recorded by Father John de Polanco, the secretary of the Society, that he would have gone against the will of God, and committed a grievous fault, if he had hesitated in the least to give to his institution the title of the Society of Jesus.

This title met with much opposition, though on this subject I need say but little, since at the present day the name, so far from being in the eyes of the world a matter of envy, requires no little virtue in us to bear it now with the same goodwill as our forefathers bore it when an unjust jealousy disputed their right to its possession. At the time that the Sorbonne, in 1554, published its false and violent censure against the Society, Father Michael Torres wrote from Spain to St. Ignatius to tell him of a controversy which he had held on the subject of the Society, and particularly as to its title of the Society of Jesus, to entreat him to consider the point of changing it, in order to avoid scandal and dispute. To this the Saint replied that the name had deeper root than the world imagined, and that the substitution of any other for it was not to be thought of.* Even at Rome the act of the Sorbonne made some impression, as appears from the interview between Cardinal de la Cueva and two members of the Society, in which the former remarked that he did not approve of this title, because it might awaken the jealousy of other Orders. When this conversation was related to the Saint, he replied, " If it is not to be called the Society of Jesus, let it be called the Congregation or Order of Jesus. But I think they will never take from it the name of Jesus."

Nor was this confident hope mistaken, even though the Society was threatened afterwards with the loss of its cherished title. The great Pope Sixtus V. was so prejudiced against the Society's name and some of its rules, that neither the prayers nor the representations of cardinals could turn him from his determination to change them. His objections, however, were worthy neither of himself nor of the important question against which they were directed. He accused the title of being a proud one, and of doing a wrong to the other Orders and to the faithful in general ; he maintained that its use was injurious to Our Lord, because it led to His

* This is taken from Menchacha (Com. prær., 159). The letters are no longer extant.

name being profaned both by the people and by writers ; that the obligation of making a sign of respect while the name of Jesus was pronounced, was a troublesome and inconvenient interruption to pious persons ; and that the Jesuits formed a class apart from other men, and could not be even named except with hat in hand. These, however, were but pretexts, and Sixtus V. concealed the true motives which led him to pursue the course which he did. In order to avoid incurring the odium of the measures he had determined upon, he tried to carry them out through the General of the Society himself. He therefore ordered Father Claudius Aquaviva to write to the Provincials of the Society and forbid their further use of this title, and, as the General could not escape from the painful necessity, he brought to the Pope the form of the decree which he had drawn up. Sixtus V. approved of it, and praised the obedience of the General ; but he appeared content with having taken this first step, as he kept the form beside him without requiring it to be despatched, and his death, which took place soon after, settled the question forever. In fact, his successor, Gregory XIV., approved forever, in his Bull of the 28th June, 1594, of the constitution and name of the Society of Jesus.*

---

* We know that the letters I.H.S. represent the Holy Name ; but, as the letter " H " seemed superfluous, some have taken the monogram to mean *Jesus Hominum Salvator.* Nothing, however, justifies this interpretation, for the name of Jesus is found in very early times almost always written with an " h," and St. Ignatius and his companions never wrote it otherwise than " Ihecus " or " Ihesus," as it is also to be found in the seals used by St. Ignatius. Of these, one used as his private seal has this form—$\frac{\text{I.h.s.}}{\text{Y.}}$, the " Y " underneath being the first letter of the name Ignatius or Ynigo. The second seal, used by him as General of the Society, had this form—$\frac{\text{I.h.s.}}{*(*}$ surrounded with the words *Sigillum præpositi Societatis Jesu.* It is of the size of a crown-piece, and is well engraved. Underneath is the crescent moon between two stars, which was afterwards replaced by three nails joined together, so that the seal of the Society was the same as that of the Gesuati, whose Order was abolished at the beginning of the seventeenth century. The only difference is that they had a small Latin " h," whilst in the seal of the Society the great " H " with the cross above was more generally taken, according to the ancient custom. But it is not yet known for certain how the " h " was in-

St. Ignatius was, indeed, not the first who adopted this name, although he could have known nothing of the attempt which had once been made to found a Society of Jesus.   It is a fact especially ignored in history, and of which no memory remained in his time, nor do any traces of it exist, except in a few ancient documents.   After the conquest of Constantinople by Mahomet II., in 1452, when the whole of Europe uttered a cry of compassion over that unfortunate city, and indignation at the cruelty of its enemies, the popes especially raised their voice and supplicated the princes of Europe to unite their powers to meet the danger.   Calixtus III. made a vow to lead in person a Crusade against the Turks.   But the sovereigns were too much occupied with their wars of selfishness and ambition, to embrace so generous an idea.   Pope Pius II., seeing that the precious time was passing, and that the West was doing nothing to preserve Europe from the perils with which it was threatened, resolved to found an Order of Chivalry, which to the other three vows of the Religious life should add one binding itself to fight always against the Turks.   For this purpose he abolished several smaller Orders, which had at first been erected for the

serted in this name.   It was rejected in the ninth century, and we have an excellent reply of this date, which saves the trouble of philological research on the subject.   In the *Spicilegium* of Archery, iii., 330, a Bishop named Amalaric says to Jeremia, the Archbishop of Sens—"The name of Jesus Our Saviour is written with an aspiration, I do not know why.   Before the last journey the Lord Charles made to Rome, I heard our priests of France pronounce it 'Jisus'; but since that time they say 'Jésus.'   The Greeks write this name with the letters 'I, C,' in this manner—IHCOYC.   It seems to me, then, that we ought to write it with the letters 'I, H, C,' or 'S,' and pronounce it Ihésus.'"   The Archbishop replies to him—"The philosopher Porphyry, who was, as is well known, very skilled in the Greek and Latin tongues, wrote in Latin the name of Jesus in this manner—IHESUS, using the Greek letter 'H,' or long 'E,' which the Greeks always pronounce in their tongue as 'I' *longum*, and the Latins as 'E' *longum*. . .   For our part, imitating the Hebrews, we pronounce 'Jesus' without an aspiration, and we write it with the Greek 'H.'"   The Archbishop, therefore, with reason, rejects the Latin "h," which is nothing else than the Greek *eta*, and which, from the most ancient times, has been used by the Roman writers, not as their "h," but as the Greek *eta*.   I will here observe that the letter cited in this note is a very important testimony to the antiquity of the opinion of those who maintain the *eta* against the "h."

same end, but had afterwards abandoned it, and out of
their remnants he formed his new Society, as appears
from the Bull of its foundation, of the 18th of January,
1459. He calls it in this Bull the Order of the Holy
Virgin Mary of Bethlehem, and gives it for place of residence the Isle of Lemnos, and establishes in it three degrees, namely, Knights, Priests, and Lay-brothers. He
adds also the right of choosing their Grand Master, and
assigns to them the dress of the ancient Templars, which
was a white habit, bearing on it the badge of a red cross.*

The Pope, it is true, does not call this Order in the Bull
the Society of Jesus, but he gives it this name in a letter
dated from Mantua, on the 13th of October of the same
year, at which place he was presiding over an assembly of
princes to arrange the differences which had arisen on
the subject of Naples, and to push on the Crusade. The
letter is addressed to Charles VII., king of France, in
which we read—" We have learned that William de Torret
has made a vow to enter into the Society which bears the
name of Jesus, and which has been of late founded to
fight for the glory of God against the infidels, and that
he will remain there in defence of the Christian faith
against the Turks." He then begs the king to give his
leave to Torret, " whom we have named promoter of the
said Society, on account of his eminent virtues and merits,
and to permit him to enter into the service of the said
Society."† It is evident that the Order spoken of in the
Bull and the Society spoken of in the letter are the same.
The only difference is in the name, which, however, cannot give ground for an objection, since other Orders
have several names, and are almost all founded in honor
of the Blessed Virgin. The Bull makes mention only of
the latter title, which formed, as it were, a general title
common to all Religious bodies. But the name in particular of this new Order must have been that of the Society
of Jesus. Pius II. calls this Society now lately founded,
*noviter instituta*, and therefore it must have been instituted

---

* Raynald, *Ad Ann.* 1459, n. 2 : Leibnitz, *Cod. Diplo.*, i., 418.
† This letter is to be found in the *Spicilegium* of Archery, iii., p. 806.
Paris, 1723. The Bollandists cite it also, but without knowing of the
Bull.

by the Bull of which we have spoken.   He complains of
the inefficiency of the Orders of Chivalry then existing,
and on that account suppresses several which he names.
It is impossible that he could have founded within the
space of two months two different Orders, yet with the
same object of fighting against the Turks.   But since, for
the establishment of a Religious Order, human means,
however great, are not sufficient, the Pope's enterprise did
not succeed, and history has scarcely preserved even the
memory of it.   It may have been that Charles VII. opposed the design.   This attempt, however, places one
very interesting point before us, when it shows for how
long a time the idea was at work in the most eminent
minds of raising up an order which should bear the holy
name of Jesus.

Besides this, several prophecies seem at different times
to have pointed to the Society which Ignatius was to
establish, and these are too clear and distinct to be considered as applied only in an after-thought and by
arbitrary interpretation.   These can be very simply explained by the fact that men who desire to see the
Church most freely develop itself, would naturally desire also to see a particular Order arise in which the
Religious state should realize as closely as possible the
ideal.   This explanation must have its weight even with
those who feel alarm at the thought of any supernatural
inspiration.   In addition to the prophecies related by
Bartoli, and which may all apply to the Society of Jesus,
we will cite one still more ancient, and which gives no
room for doubtful interpretation.   It describes in a very
exact manner, as the distinctive character of the Order
which it foretells, its apostolic zeal, its particular obedience to the Holy See, its science and learning, and
even its title of Jesus.   This is the prophecy of the Abbot
Joachim, of St. John de Fiori, in Calabria, who was
known also to have predicted, in 1190, the ill-success of
the Crusade to King Philip II. and Richard Cœur-de-
Lion, when he plainly told them that the time of the
deliverance of the Holy Land was not yet come.*   He

* See the Chronicle of William de Nangis, in the year 1190, and
that of Nicholas Trivett, in Archery, t. iii.

foretells, in his *Explanation of the Apocalypse,* * " that there will arise a new Order of learned Religious, which will take for its title the name of Jesus; that it will imitate the Apostles, will be under particular obedience to the Pope, will be distinguished for its science, and will impose silence by its labors on false doctrines." †

Whatever we may think of this prediction, there can be no doubt that it is drawn from an authentic source, and that the terms of the prophecy are as formal as possible, while the error of Abbot Joachim with regard to time does not, any more than his other errors, take from the value of the document in itself. Like many other persons, he believed that the end of the world was very near at hand, an opinion which has often appeared again from time to time, even down to our own days.

---

* Capp. x., xiv.

† "Venturum novum ordinem et religionem doctorum designandum ab Jesu; qui clareat sexto ecclesiæ suæ tempore, atque in fine mundi; eumque fore et Apostolicum quique peculiariter subsit obedientiæ summi Pontificis et eruditum, qui tumidis magisteriis studiis suis silentium imponat."

# CHAPTER XVI.

IGNATIUS IS CHOSEN SUPERIOR GENERAL. HE AND HIS
COMPANIONS TAKE THEIR SOLEMN VOWS. HIS MAN-
NER OF LIFE.

THE first draft of the Constitutions of the Order being
approved, and the foundation-stone of the building laid,
the next thing was to develop it in all its parts, and,
above all, to choose a superior. The development of the
Society must needs be the work of time, but it was of
urgent necessity to choose a superior, as several members had already passed beyond the confines of Italy,
and the Pope had the intention of sending others soon
into distant countries. Ignatius, therefore, summoned
to Rome, in the Lent of the year 1541, all the members
dispersed through Italy. Brouet came from Sienna,
Laynez from Parma, Le Jay from Brescia. Bobadilla
was at Bisignano, in the kingdom of Naples, but the inhabitants, afraid of losing him, sent a petition to the
Pope, in answer to which he forbade him to quit the
place, and as very little time remained before the day of
the election, it was not in his power to send his vote
even in writing. A document given by the Bollandists,*
which contains a kind of protocol of the election, affirms
in the most positive manner that, contrary to the opinion
of several writers, Bobadilla took no part in this act of
election. It is in fact there stated:—

The sealed papers having been opened one after another, it was
found that all appointed Ignatius, with the exception of Master Bobadilla, who, being on the point of departure from Bisignano, received
an order from the Pope to remain, and did not send in his vote. As
his Holiness wished that the members present in Rome should be sent
into different countries, they were obliged to finish the election without

* Sec. 34.

Bobadilla, according to the votes given of all members present or absent.

Among these latter were Xavier and Rodriguez, who had left their votes in Rome before leaving for Portugal. Faber sent his from Germany at three separate times for greater security, that, in case of accident, one copy at least might reach its destination.

The companions of Ignatius were all gathered together at a time when it was very well they should meet, for, before choosing a general, it was necessary to trace out, at least in their main outlines, the Constitutions and Rules. For this purpose the Saint presented them, according to the commission given him by them, with a draft of the Constitutions, which was carefully examined and accepted by all as a rule to which they were bound. They wished, by this means, to prevent the leaving all to the free disposal of him who should be elected general, and to oblige him to confine himself to the limits fixed by this plan. This important affair being finished, the election was deferred to the 9th of April, and it was resolved that the three days which preceded and which followed this ceremony should be consecrated to prayer, and that no one should be allowed to deliberate with another on the choice they should make. On the seventh day, the urn, which contained the sealed votes of the members, present and absent, was opened, and Ignatius was unanimously elected General. They acknowledged thereby, not only his piety, but the other qualities besides, which rendered him more fitting than any other for this charge, and, in the circumstances of that time, it required great qualities indeed. We cannot, in fact, suppose that the electors, among whom were men so remarkable, as all allow, made this choice at a venture. Moreover, it must be observed that all the members of the Society were perfectly free to act in this case, and that they did not start with the supposition—which, in the establishment of other religious orders, is an admitted one—that the founder ought to be, during the course of his life, at the head of his work. And further, as we shall see presently, Ignatius would not admit his election. The better to appreciate the motives which determined these men in this important matter, we will give the language in which some recorded their votes :—*

Laynez. I, James Laynez, moved solely by zeal for the glory of Our Lord Jesus Christ and the salvation of souls, choose Master Ignatius of Loyola for my superior and that of the Society of Jesus. In testimony of which I here subscribe my name.
April 4, 1541.

Salmeron. I, Alphonsus Salmeron, most unworthy to belong to this Society, after having prayed God maturely, weighed the matter according to the measure of my judgment, choose and declare as my head and superior, as also of the whole Society, Master Ignatius of Loyola, who, after having, according to the wisdom given him from God, begotten us all in Christ and fed us with milk while we were little, will, now that we are grown greater in Jesus Christ, direct and guide us with the substantial food of obedience into the pastures of Paradise and the well of eternal life.
Rome, this 4th day of April, 1541.

The vote of John Codurius is the longest in its reasons. He says that, being on the point of departing for Ireland, by order of the Pope, and the distance being too great to allow of writing often, he thinks it better to leave in writing before his departure the name of him who, with the approval of the Society, ought, in his opinion, to be appointed superior. He then continues in these terms—

He is the same of whom I declare that I have always known in him the greatest zeal for the glory of God and the salvation of souls. It is he who should be preferred above all, because he has always made himself the least and the servant of all, that is, the venerable Father Master Ignatius of Loyola; and next after him, in my opinion, Master Faber, no less virtuous than the first. †

The vote of St. Francis Xavier contains two declarations. In the first he gives beforehand his assent to all that the Society shall decide regarding its Constitutions, even though there should be only three members of it

* The Bollandists (Sec. 35), give them all, faithfully translated into Latin. The greater part, even that of Faber, was in Spanish.
† The vote is dated the 5th of March, 1540, and he would have left for Ireland afterwards, as is mentioned in the vote. But as he was delayed, Codurius assisted at the election, and remained afterwards near Ignatius, having been chosen his socius on the 4th of May, 1541, and in virtue of this office he was charged with the Society's business, and with making it acquainted with the matters important to be

met together.  In the second he commissions **Laynez** to
make, in his stead, in the hands of the superior who
should be elected, the three vows of Religion which he
ratifies beforehand.   His vote is given in the following
terms—

I, Francis, affirm and confess, *nullo modo suasus ab homine,* and
speaking from my conscience, that, in my opinion, as superior of our
Society, whom all should obey, Master Ignatius, the Father of us all
hitherto, ought to be chosen.   It is he who has gathered us together
at great cost of labor, and he will also know how to keep us, not without his cost, and to govern us and make us progress in virtue, for he
knows each one of us better than any other.   *Et post mortem illius*—I
speak as I feel, from my heart and as if I were at the point of death—
I say that it should be the Father Master Peter Faber.   And *Deus est
mihi testis* that I say here only what I think, and that this is the truth
I here subscribe my hand.

Rome, 15th of March, 1540.

Ignatius named no one in his vote, since he wished to
avoid mentioning any one as considered by him to be
the most worthy.   He therefore submits his judgment
to the majority, and declares that he accepts beforehand
whomsoever it may choose, provided it be not himself.
He could never have acted more humbly, nor, at the
same time, with more tact.   His vote was drawn up
thus—

Excluding myself, I give my voice in Our Lord, for him to be
superior who shall be named by the majority of votes.   I give it in
this indeterminate manner *boni consulendo.*   But if the Society should
consider otherwise, and consider it better and more conducive to the
glory of God that I should name some one, I am ready to do so.

When Ignatius found himself elected superior he was
the only opposer to it, and immediately made known his
resolve to refuse the charge they would confide to him.
He dwelt on his defects and his incapacity, though these
were not the only motives which decided him in this
conjuncture; for deficiencies are the common lot of

known, so that the others might have more time for their spiritual
labors.   He died on the 29th of August of this same year, and Ignatius
knew of his death at the moment that it took place, for he was on his
way to the Church of St. Peter in Montorio, to say Mass for the sick
Father, when, upon the Bridge of St. Sixtus, he turned to his companion
and said, " Let us turn back ; our Father Codurius is dead."

humanity, and he had already shown these to be as little obstacle to good in him as they were in any man. I think that the true motive of his refusal is to be sought in that line of conduct he had always pursued. It is remarkable that, after having won over his companions, and formed them upon the plan of the Society as found in the Exercises, he avoided putting himself forward, and that, when there was question of developing the Society, he acted always in concert with it and as its delegate, never making himself of more account than the rest, never wishing to be considered as its founder. It was precisely this which decided his refusal, and this his companions understood better than we can do, for they had themselves observed how, before the election, they had remained all along without a head, so far was St. Ignatius from himself taking that position amongst them. He desired that this work should be guided and developed by another hand than his own, and that it should appear as little as possible to be his own doing; for he was convinced that, being directed by the guidance and superior power of Providence, it would accomplish its end, whoever should be chosen for its head, and doubtless it would have pleased him better that some one were elected other than himself; therefore did he make every effort to cancel his election. It was not ordinary modesty nor a show of humility which led him to this step, for that inwardly desires what it outwardly refuses; but it was an intimate union with God, and an entire forgetfulness of all purely human interests in that which he had undertaken for the sake of God alone. I do not know, in the lives of the saints, of a similar instance of such greatness of soul and high perfection.

But why did not Ignatius declare before the election that he would refuse the charge of Superior General if they chose him? For, either simplicity or malice might suggest the question. The reply is that such a declaration would have been a very great mistake, for it would have caused serious perplexity to the electors. Who, in fact, would have consented to give his vote, had the highest in consideration among them been beforehand excluded? An act like this would have created a kind of anarchy in the little rising Society ; by it St. Ignatius would have given an example of that very arbitrary proceeding which above all things he wished to avoid, nor could he have prevented many bad interpretations being put upon it.    I am yet more confirmed in my view by the way in which Ignatius endeavored to withdraw himself from the burden laid upon him.    Through the earnestness of his entreaty, he obtained of his companions that they should recommence the election after three days, and should ask meanwhile for light from Heaven to make a good choice.    He hoped that thus every human consideration would be blotted out from the minds of his companions, and that God would hear him and take his part.    But He made it only the more evident how completely he was worthy of the highest duties, and how truly he had all the qualities necessary for fulfilling the charge they were about to intrust to him, while no one else could be put in comparison with him.

The new scrutiny of votes was followed by the same result, but again he was on the point of resisting.    Then Laynez, rising from his place, said with firmness: " Submit, my Father, to the will of God.    If you do not, the Society will be broken up, for I am resolved to recognize no other head than him whom God has chosen."    Ignatius, foreseeing the consequences of longer refusal, proposed to them that the decision should be referred to a third party, promising that, after having opened his whole soul to his confessor, he would leave to him the decision what he ought to do.    They accepted the proposal, well knowing what would be its issue.    His confessor at that time was a Friar Minor, named Theodoric, of the convent of St. Peter in Montorio, and to him the Saint went to make a retreat of three days, that he might the more easily consult with him on this important affair.    After having given an exact account of conscience to this good Father he asked of him whether he ought to accept the charge of superior.    The Father replied in the affirmative, and seeing that he had not yet overcome all his doubts, he bade him plainly to resist no longer the Spirit of God.    Ignatius, acknowledging the authority of God, and perceiving no further escape, yielded, and thus gave an example to all his children that, although ambition should never make them desire a charge so heavy on the conscience, still they should never, when possessing the necessary qualities, be moved by personal motives to withdraw from the burden placed upon them. He, however, once more begged his confessor to communicate his opinion to the electors, and explain to them, if he judged it good, the reason why he thought himself unfit for the charge, that he might thus satisfy their minds. He returned to the house on Easter Sunday, and on Tuesday, the 9th of April, Father Theodoric brought him his written decision, which was read in the assembly. He declared in it that Ignatius ought to submit to the will of his companions and accept the charge of superior.

This affair being settled to the satisfaction of all, it remained for the members of the new Society to bind themselves to it forever by the solemn vows. The time which they chose for this purpose was the Friday following, and the place was the Church of St. Paul, in which, being outside of the walls, they hoped to be more undisturbed. After they had made the Stations in the other churches, Ignatius celebrated the Holy Sacrifice in the chapel of the Basilica dedicated to the Holy Virgin, which was also the chapel of the Blessed Sacrament. Before giving Communion he turned towards his companions, and holding the Host above the paten, read aloud the formula of the vows. He then communicated, and in a similar way gave Communion to the others. The ceremony over, they visited the other altars, after which, coming before the high altar, they embraced Ignatius, shedding tears, and showing their filial veneration by kissing his hand. They then drew up a protocol, which was signed by a clerk of Valencia, Jerome Domenect, acting as secretary, and was afterwards probably presented to the Pope. The superscription is—"Done in the Church of St. Paul. out of the walls, in the year of Our Lord 1541, the 22d of April." In it we read that Ignatius of Loyola, etc., and the others assembled in chapter in the church, and representing the Society of Jesus, lately founded by Pope Paul III., after having invoked the Holy Spirit and offered the Holy Sacrifice, have proceeded, by virtue of the Letters Apostolic, in their own name and in the name and by the commission of those absent, to the election of their superior, and that they have unanimously chosen the venerable Master Ignatius of Loyola as their head and their General ; * that they have made in his hands the perpetual and solemn vows, following the form of their Institute and the manner permitted them in the Letters Apostolic, especially in that which concerns particular obedience to the Pope with regard to missions, and the teaching of youth in the Christian doctrine.

The formula of the vows subscribed by St. Ignatius, and still preserved, is drawn up in the following manner—

I, the undersigned, promise to God Almighty, and to the Pope, His Vicar upon earth, in the presence of the Blessed Virgin His Mother, and in the presence of the Society, perpetual poverty, chastity, and obedience, according to the form contained in the Bull of the Society of Our Lord Jesus Christ, and in the Constitutions already published, or which shall be published afterwards. I promise, moreover, particular obedience to the Pope with regard to the missions spoken of in the Bull. I promise likewise to take care that the youth be instructed in the doctrines of the Faith, according to the same Bull and the Constitutions. Given at Rome, Friday, the 22d of April, in the Church of St. Paul beyond the walls,

IGNATIUS OF LOYOLA.

St. Ignatius thought that he could not better begin the new duties which he had undertaken, than by works of humility and by fulfilling the obligations which their vows laid upon all the members of the Society. He assisted, therefore, for several days in the service of the kitchen, and in the humblest offices of the house, without at the same time neglecting important business. Besides, for the space of forty-six days continuously, he taught catechism in the little church of the Society, called Sta. Maria della Strada; but he found more adults of all ages than children assembled to hear him. The following is the method he pursued. He first explained a mystery of faith, or one of the Commandments, suitably to the in-

* We must admit, according to this, that the election, if it did not, properly speaking, take place in the church, was at least publicly confirmed and solemnly proclaimed there. Faber made his profession at Ratisbon, the 9th of July (Bolland., sec. xxxvi.).

telligence of the most unlearned, repeating the same thing many times to fix it deeper in the mind. He then drew from it practical conclusions or applications useful for conduct, and such particularly as were of a kind to touch the heart, and on these he dwelt the longest. Ribadeneyra, an actual witness of these instructions, says that they were more devotional than studied, that the language was simple and without ornament, and that Ig-natius often employed inaccurate expressions, because he did not know Italian well. But his words were powerful and effective, and touched the heart, leading the hearer to enter into himself, and inspiring penitence. His hearers were to be seen, after he had done speaking, running to the confessionals, and showing by the extra-ordinary contrition they felt the fruit of the exhortations they had heard, so that Laynez in particular was surprised at it. " And yet," says Ribadeneyra, " it does not seem astonishing to me, when I call to mind what I then saw. For I remember well with what force and fire Ignatius used to speak. He seemed like one inflamed with the love of God, so that, even when he was silent, the fire which shone in his countenance enkindled his hearers, and he could do with them what he pleased." He relates afterwards that then, scarcely out of his boyhood, he was appointed by Ignatius to repeat to the people what the Saint had said the night before. And as he was afraid that the beautiful thoughts with which the discourses abounded might be less understood on account of the faulty expressions which Ignatius used, he gave him advice to take more care of his language. Ignatius replied, with his usual humility, "You are right; watch while I speak, and take note of all the mistakes I make, to correct me afterwards." Ribadeneyra did so, and set himself to write down all the solecisms the Saint made use of. But he found so many, that the whole instruction seemed full of Spanish idioms. He told the Saint so, who smiled and replied, "What can we do, my dear Peter, when it is God's doing?" Meaning that he wished to have no more than that which God had given him, and to employ well what he had received from Him.

The following, according to Maffei, was from this

time forward the Saint's order of the day: After he had risen, he spent in meditation the time which he had prescribed for it; this done, he made his preparation for Mass, which he said when not hindered by his infirmities, though this happened but too often. If any business called him abroad, he then went out with a companion ; if not, he received visits of those in the house, or of strangers, in conversation with whom he always showed himself bright, never letting any painful hesitation or suspicious distrust appear, but he was very prudent and circumspect in what he said. After dinner, he took recreation in talking on subjects that were instructive without being fatiguing to the head, or on the manner of dealing with others, or on the different works they had undertaken. After this he entered upon matters of business, put his signature to, or read and corrected, letters, etc. In the evening, after supper, he regulated the labors of the following day, told the superiors of the house what they had to do, and then gave himself to very attentive business with his secretary. As soon as he had quitted him, he paced to and fro a long time, alone and leaning on his staff, absorbed in profound recollection. He slept the remainder of the night, but never more than four hours. This is, I know, only the exterior shell, and, as it were, skeleton of his life, but all this was animated within by an intimate union with God, and in this part of their life the saints can only be revealed to us by themselves.

It may be readily supposed that the piety of the head would naturally communicate itself to the members. In fact, all the accounts we have of the time show that these admirable men led an angelical life, and that minds the most prejudiced against them could not withstand the edifying sight. We will give one example. A young man of talent came to Rome at this period from the furthest North to spread the Lutheran doctrines. He first set himself to attack the morals of the clergy in places of public resort. By little and little he went further, and spoke against Catholic faith, thinking, perhaps, that he had now gained over his listeners. But he was mistaken; he was suddenly seized, and would have been dealt with according to the rigor of the law, had not his worth and talents excited some interest and compassion. He manifested, however, the most obstinate resistance to the efforts of the clergy who visited him and endeavored to bring him to a better state of mind. Discussions, as it almost always happens in such cases, only strengthened him in his opinions, and persuaded him that he had got the best of the argument. A happy thought struck them of placing him in the house of St. Ignatius, and, instead of disputing with him, of leaving him there to see and observe with his own eyes all that passed. The real charity and spirit of the Gospel which he witnessed touched his heart, and he learned that the life and power of the faith show themselves not in controversy, but in practice. He lost by little and little the fanaticism which had clouded his understanding and hardened his heart, and of his own account surrendered himself to the truth which he had found out. Some persons of distinction having asked him afterwards how he had not yielded to the reasons which had been adduced to convince him, he replied that it was not by learned proofs and objections that he had been converted, but by the virtue and sanctity he had seen in the companions of Ignatius; that in beholding them he had come naturally to this conclusion, that it was impossible that the true faith should not be found united to a life so pure and so saintly, to so great charity, and such oneness of heart.

As the last fifteen years of the life of Ignatius belong to the second part of this work, it only remains for us to say a word on the mission to Ireland, which took place during this year. Every one knows what hard treatment the inhabitants of that island have always met with at the hands of the English. Under the reign of Henry VIII., in addition to the evils with which the unfortunate country was already afflicted, were added those of religious persecution, the English nobles of Ireland having joined the schism and acknowledged the King's supremacy, while the people remained faithful to the Church. As relations with Rome were both extremely dangerous and extremely difficult, Robert, the Archbishop of Armagh, had a little time before begged the Pope to send an Apostolic Nuncio, with full powers, to fortify the faithful Catholics, and to grant the necessary dispensations and favors. Paul III. had, in the preceding year, asked Ignatius for one of his companions, and Codurius had been chosen for this mission. But the matter having been delayed, and Codurius having meanwhile died, Salmeron and Brouet were sent out as Nuncios on the 16th of September. They were accompanied by Brother Zapata, who, after having been secretary in one of the Pontifical chanceries, had afterwards entered as a novice into the Society. The two fathers being without money, he was to undertake the charge of the voyage, which presented dangers both by sea and land. As a very severe law had been passed by the King, enjoining that every envoy from Rome found in the island should be seized and sent to England, their stay in this country was very insecure. They were in continual danger of being discovered by the numerous spies of the Government, they were obliged often to change their hiding-place, and could remain for only thirty-four days in the island. To escape the penalty of death pronounced against them, and still more to save the lives of their protectors, they resolved to return into Scotland, whence they had crossed over, after having made, however, frequent and salutary use of their powers during the short space of time they could remain. But even in Scotland they found the roads closed to them, and were obliged to return by way of France, having run the greatest risks and suffered much hardship. This mission furnishes an occasion to set before the reader the instructions which St. Ignatius gave to the two Fathers whom he sent.

When we have to treat of matters of business, particularly with equals or inferiors, we ought to speak little and slowly, having due regard to the distinction of rank and station of each one, and listen readily and patiently until the person addressing us has finished all he wishes to say. Then we should answer each point in particular, and take leave when we have no more to say. If the conversation is continued, we should answer as concisely as possible, and our parting should be brief, but amicable.

When we have business to transact with some great personage, we must study well his natural disposition, and act so as to gain his good will for the greater glory of God our Master. If, for example, he is of a choleric temperament, and speaks quickly and sharply, our manner and tone should be courteous in all things good and holy, nor should we show ourselves too serious, cold, or morose. In our relations with those who, on the contrary, are reserved, are slow in speaking, and grave and measured in their conversation, we too must observe the same manner. This is a means which is sure to please—*Omnia omnibus factus sum.*

When two persons of a choleric temperament have to transact business between them who are not quite of a mind, they run great risk of misunderstanding each other. If one be aware that he is choleric, he ought to study in detail all that concerns his manner of conversing with others, and to prepare himself, if possible, by an attentive self-examination, or by taking a resolution to suffer everything rather than give way in the least to the natural heat of his character, especially if he knows that the person with whom he has to deal is of feeble health. Should he have to treat with a melancholy or phlegmatic person, he runs less risk of making him lose his temper by an inconsiderate expression.

If we observe that a person is tempted or is sad, let us be kind and amiable with him, let us talk readily, and show, both interiorly and exteriorly, much gaiety and pleasantness of manner. To help and console persons of this kind, we should manifest a disposition of mind directly opposed to that which they have themselves. Upon spiritual matters, or where the reconciliation of enemies is involved, we require to be on our guard, bearing in mind that all which we say may be, or probably will of a certainty be, known in public.

In expediting affairs we must be liberal in the time we give to them —that is to say, we must secure that each matter be really settled on the same day, if possible. If you have the administration of money to arrange, it will be well for Master Francis (Zapata), to charge himself with it, that you may the better fulfil your duties in all cases without any of the three touching money. Send it rather to a banker, or let him who applies for a dispensation take the sum to the banker and bring an acquittance in due form, after which the dispensation may be granted; or take any other means you may find most convenient, yet so that in every case each one of you may say that he has not derived a penny from his mission.

# THE LIFE

OF

# ST. IGNATIUS OF LOYOLA.

## The Second Part.

## CHAPTER I.

### IGNATIUS DRAWS UP THE CONSTITUTIONS. THEIR END, AND THE MEANS THEY PRESCRIBE TO ATTAIN IT. THE EXAMINATION AND APPROBATION OF THE RULES.

IN the first part of this history we have spoken of the innumerable sufferings and difficulties in the midst of which the Society of Jesus was founded. We have related how St. Ignatius was led to change the place in which he intended to establish it, and how, in consequence of this important change, by a particular dispensation of Providence and to the great good of the Catholic Church, he carried out his plan, not at Jerusalem, as he had first proposed, but at Rome.

We now proceed, in this second part, to look upon him as the legislator and ruler of the new Society, keeping exclusively to what concerns his personal history, and setting aside all that regards the Society itself as alien to our subject. The order of things, for the better understanding of the whole, obliges us to speak first of what St. Ignatius did for the development of the Society. At the same time, we will give a succinct idea of his Institute as it existed in his mind, and the original draft of it which he conceived. We shall thus refute the false and absurd opinion of those who pretend that he was not the originator and sole founder of the Society of Jesus.

Long before the existence of the Order and of the Constitutions which he gave to it, Ignatius lived according to the rules communicated to him in the Spiritual Exercises at Manresa, and in accordance with the idea of the Society of Jesus which was there imparted to him. We have seen him always acting as a Jesuit, except sacerdotal duties, while he was not yet a priest. He gave to his disciples the same form, so that the essential laws of the Society existed practically in them before the code was written, and the letter served only to establish what was already being done, and to give an embodiment to it. He undertook this work because the Pope had enjoined it in his Bull of 1540 upon the Society, and the Society gave the task of performing it to Ignatius. Now, it is certain on the one hand that it was he who drew up the Constitutions, and on the other that these Constitutions have never been altered. Every one may see this fact for himself by comparing the original Spanish manuscript with the printed Latin translation. It is equally certain that, although he well knew the rules of other Orders, he made no use of them for his own work. We have still in our possession the declaration of Father Annibal Codretti, who, in his early life, was attached to the person of St. Ignatius, while he was engaged upon the Constitutions, and this document is dated in the year 1599. In it we read as follows—" The whole time that the venerable Father Ignatius was composing the Constitutions, during the seven months that I waited on him, I never saw in his room any book but the Missal on the days when he was going to say Mass. After having recommended the subject he was thinking about to God during the night, he wrote in the morning what God had inspired. When the weather was fine, in order to be less disturbed, he went into the garden which a Roman gentleman had lent to him for his use. A table was set there, on which were placed ink and paper, and so he wrote what came to his mind." Ignatius gives his own account in Gonzalez— " This was the manner of his proceeding in the drawing up of the Constitutions. Every day at Mass he presented himself before God, and offered to Him the point he was considering." He treated on this important matter with God alone, employing on his part meditation and prayer as a means to draw down light from heaven.

But what is the principle and the kernel (if we may call it so), the fixed and indestructible portion of these Constitutions? It is clearly the formula which the Society proclaimed in its first assemblage as to the end of the new Order, which it presented to Paul III., and to which he gave his approbation. In this it is said that "whoever wishes to enter into the Society of Jesus, to fight under the standard of the Cross and God and Our Lord Jesus Christ, and to serve the Church, His Spouse, under His Vicar, the Roman Pontiff, must keep in mind that this Society has been established for the defence and propagation of the faith, for the promotion of the salvation of souls, by teaching Christian doctrine and Christian life, by explaining the Word of God, by giving the Spiritual Exercises, by teaching Catechism to the young and ignorant, by the administration of the Sacraments, and especially the Sacrament of Penance. He must keep also in mind that its object is to perform works of mercy, and more particularly for the sick and the imprisoned; and all this is to be done gratuitously and without any earthly recompense." It is first of all and above all things necessary for the attainment of this end, and for the salvation of souls, for the edification of the Church and the greater glory of God, to form and maintain the instruments adapted for this work, that is, the members of the Society.

We have now to examine how far the Society has answered to this project. I am not here speaking of facts, but am only setting forth the theory, and no one, I am sure, will deny that it is holy, and conformable to the end in view.*

The life and principle of the Institute, as we have seen above, spring from the Spiritual Exercises. It is, in fact, by them that each particular Religious receives the formation which the Society requires in all its members

* The following exposition is based upon a work, now of long standing, of Father Achilles Gagliardi, *De plena cognitione Instituti*, which has lately been reprinted in Rome, in 1841.

as suitable to its end. It is by them, in like manner, that it has received the end to which it tends, the means to attain it, and its whole form of government. This end is the sanctification of one's self, and of others, to the greater glory of God, and the means to arrive at it is self-abnegation, a virtue which is the foundation of all other virtues. The meditation of the " Foundation " in the Exercises sets forth the end of the Society, and the meditations of the first week form the novice to self-abnegation; those of the Kingdom of Christ and of the Two Standards, etc., show the degree of perfection to which the Religious should aspire in his fulfilment of the evangelical counsels, and all the Society should accomplish for the good of the Church and our neighbor. Lastly, everything that concerns the Religious in particular is regulated and typified in the meditations " on Election," and in the rules " for the Discernment of Spirits." This interior formation of his Religious is called by St. Ignatius the work of the Holy Ghost; and he attaches to it so great an importance that he prefers it to all exterior prescriptions, and to all his written rules, * and with good reason, because this spirit alone can give the freedom and the vigor which prove interior vitality, and prevent that spiritual death which easily creeps into the soul, so long as men are content with merely observing the outward letter of Christianity.

That we may give the reader a succinct and, at the same time, a tolerably sufficient idea of the Institute, we will consider it in its end, and we will consider the means which it prescribes for arriving at it. All the motives which the Society proposes to itself are concentrated in its ultimate object, which is the greater glory of God. Its members seek to procure this effectually by laboring for their own sanctification and the sanctification of others; and they do this, not by undertaking obligations of any particular kind, but by excluding nothing which is either good in itself or is conformable to the Gospel and to the end of the Society. † It follows from this that the Society embraces every practice of virtue con-

* Procemium Const.
† Const., pt. iii., ch. i., sec. 21 ; pt. vi., ch. i., sec. I.

ducing to its end, since, in everything that is done, the glory of God is proposed as its final object, and it is this which must be the measure of the efforts each individual is to make for his own sanctification and for the sanctification of others.*  It is on this principle that the freedom of the Institute turns; it is the mobile part of it which is incessantly being renewed, and which derives its origin from the will of God.  From this divine will it ever flows anew, according to the knowledge vouchsafed from Heaven that such or such a work can promote His glory.  Hence it follows that the members of the Society of Jesus ought to seek the glory of God for its own sake alone, † not through fear of punishment or hope of reward, but out of pure love; and for this reason the Constitutions do not bind under pain of sin. ‡  He who can rise to this height of perfection is invulnerable.  Safe himself so far as it is possible upon this earth, he is at the same time placed on the most advantageous stand-point for doing good to others.  But this task is one of great difficulty.  There are a thousand obstacles in the way of it, both from without and within.  It is, in fact, a task which human weakness can never completely and fully accomplish.

The members of the Society ought always to have this supreme object alone before their minds—" the greater glory of God," and to wish for nothing else besides.  On the contrary, they should be utterly indifferent as to the means which conduct to this end, unless they be directed in the choice of them by obedience.  If, for example, of these three acts of virtue, prayer, preaching, and hearing confessions, the last contributes most to the glory of God, the other two must be set aside.  The same indifference should be maintained with regard to spiritual lights and consolations, § as also the greater or less degree of advancement or speed in the way of perfection, provided there be no culpable negligence of our own to

---

* Pt. iv., Procem. A; pt. vii., ch. ii., sec. 1, D; pt. iii., ch. i., sec. 21; pt. vi., ch. i., sec. 1; pt. viii., ch. i., sec. 1.
† Pt. iii., ch. i., sec. 26.
‡ Pt. vi., ch. v.
§ Pt. iii., ch. i., sec. 16.

retard its progress. The Society, therefore, prescribes very few fixed rules for the practice of virtues, in order that this end may be the better attained. The principle of the greater glory of God is the rule, and as this requires something more or less, the time, the place, or the person with whom dealing is to be had may require some particular line of conduct, and, consequently, circumstances, of a necessity, must be the guide. It is for this reason, also, that the life of the Religious of the Society of Jesus is an ordinary life. It is in no way distinguished as to the exterior from that of good and pious ecclesiastics, and, at the same time, it has the advantages of community and monastic life.* That no external impediment may hinder the Society from tending towards its end, it must never engage itself in things which would lower to a particular object the general end which it has in view, nor apply to a small number of persons the energy and service which it owes to all. Consequently, it must not, for example, undertake to serve foundations for certain private devotions, such as Masses for the dead, etc. Moreover, it is forbidden ever to receive money for the services it renders, and this forbiddance is an essential point of its Constitutions. In a word, the Society having in view the salvation of souls in general, its members ought to be animated by a spirit, not of a particular, but of a general character, which acts from love, and embraces all that is not contrary to its end. For the attainment of this end, their conduct must be under the constant guidance of the rules of wisdom and prudence.

Such is the end of the Society as laid down in its Constitutions, and it may be said to be identical with that of the Catholic Church, and that the two cannot be distinguished, except by the degree of perfection which they require. The Church, in fact, only demands of the faithful in general the fulfilment of the Commandments, while the members of the Society of Jesus bind themselves to the practice of the counsels, and seek in all things, not only the glory of God, but His greater glory ;

* Exam. ch. i., sec. 6; pt. iii., ch. i., sec. 18; pt. iv., ch. viii., sec. 2.

and it is distinguished from other religious orders precisely by this difference, that it does not propose or practise any virtue in particular as the object of perfection which its members are to aim at, but it considers them all, to the exclusion of none, as means to arrive at its end,—" the greater glory of God."

I have now to show in what manner and in what measure these virtues must be practised in order to arrive at the end of the Society. They must then, in the first place, have this end always fully in view—that is to say, whatever the member of the Society does must always be done with the persuasion that God will draw from thence His "greater glory;" at least, he must exclude from his intention all that can destroy the purity and sincerity of this idea ; in other words, he must seek, as his ultimate object, not his own satisfaction, nor even his own sanctification, but the Kingdom of God and His greater glory, and then all the rest shall be added unto him. Each member ought, it is true, to endeavor to acquire every virtue in an eminent degree ; * but the Constitutions do not fix for their exercise either positive rule, or time, or number. We may take, as an example, there are no definite or fixed practices of mortification,† and the reason for this liberty is as follows : If a fixed measure be prescribed for all, violence is done in a certain degree to the liberty of those who might do more, and to the weakness of those who cannot do as much. Moreover, prescribed acts of virtue lose something of the merit which each individual might gain by the sacrifice of himself in offering to God with generosity the specialty he has to give, and the more so, as in the Society there is gathered together an immense variety of nations, of ages, and of talents. ‡  Thus it is that dispensations from rule, which are almost inevitable in other Religious Orders, and which have ultimately been the ruin of them, are of no use in the Society ; yet this liberty is no hindrance to the practice of mortification : on the contrary,

---

* Pt. vi., ch. i., sec. 1; pt. vii., ch. iv., sec. 2; pt. iii., ch. i., sec. 21 ; pt. vii., ch. i., sec. 1.

† Pt. vi., chs. ii., xv., xvi., and ch. iii., sec. 1.

‡ Pt. vii., chs. i., ii. ; pt. vi., ch. iii., sec. 1.

it is thus that there is imparted to it a freshness and a healthy alacrity, because it springs from charity and is not enjoined by command. One of the principal reasons why the Institute does not prescribe any fixed and regular and exterior practice of penance is, that the members of the Society may have more free access to persons of every state and condition of life, and may be at greater liberty to serve their neighbor according to their vocation. There is no reason to fear, on the other hand, that its members should do too little, or be left entirely to their own individual choice, for the Constitutions have provided for this danger by the Exercises practised in the noviceship, by the customary usages of the Society, by the continual direction which each man receives from his superiors, and by the spirit of his vocation.

We have called attention to the general object and end of the Society ; we must also add another distinctive feature in its character, which is, that it does not look to the exterior, accessory, and material part of virtue so much, as to what we may call the essential and constituent portion of it. It does not, therefore propose, as an end to which everything is to be referred, any particular virtue, such as singing office in choir, silence, the care of the sick, etc., upon which the whole life turns as on a pivot, and to which all other duties are subordinate. The Institute of the Jesuits demands the practice of all virtues, but only as means to an end. It raises none above the others, nor selects any one as of complete merit, but acknowledges in each the value it possesses as a means to attain the end. The practice of virtue is not, therefore, circumscribed by external acts enjoined by such and such a rule, as, for example, to take a discipline every day, to which each Religious is obliged to conform, and which may be said to represent the material part of virtue. The Society follows a more perfect way, for, in all acts of virtue, it considers only the object it has in view, performing or omitting them as reason finds it good. In this manner, the danger is avoided of doing either too much or too little ; virtue retains that loveliness which reason justifies and the conscience approves, and is thus made pleasing to the heart.

It is prescribed, like a wise doctor's dose, according to the wants of each individual. And thus, in the members of the Society, in these external and material practices of virtue, there are differences more or less; but in the formal and spiritual part of it there is the greatest unity among them, for all are tending to perfection, and performing those outward acts of virtue which are dictated by their conscience and allowed of by the direction of their superiors. St. Ignatius requires that his spiritual children should so progress in virtue as to cooperate faithfully with grace, and attribute the whole merit to it; whilst, on the other hand, they are to put forth all their energies as though the whole result depended upon their own exertions, and leave nothing undone which right reason dictates.*

The means recommended by the Society for the acquiring of virtue, both by its own members and by those under their direction, are gentle, and therefore the more efficacious ; and in this way it follows the manner of Our Lord Jesus Christ and of His Apostles, who acted with gentleness and sweetness, just as divine grace also acts upon our souls. It rejects, as opposed to its mission, violent and indiscreet zeal; but it recommends and embraces the zeal which is as far removed from lukewarmness on the one side as it is from extravagance on the other.

To make what we have said in general still more clear, we will apply the doctrine in a more particular manner to some of the main virtues. First we will take penance, because it is the first step to be made in religious life, and we will examine in what way it is practised as a means to arrive at the end which the Society proposes. Penance, as a virtue and as a Sacrament, has for its object and effect the blotting out of our faults, the eradication of sin, and the purifying of the conscience, so that grace may reign and bring forth fruit in the soul from the pure motive of pleasing God.† Confession, there-

---

* Pt. iii., ch. i., sec. 20 ; pt. ix., ch. ii., sec. 1, and ch. vi., A. ch. x., secs. 1, 2. Procem. Const., pt. iv., ch. viii., sec. 8 ; pt. x., secs. 2, 3.

† Exam., ch. iv., sec. 41.

fore, is prescribed at least every eight days, because man is the better disposed to receive the impression of grace the oftener it is imparted to him, and in this manner the acts of penance become easier and more agreeable to him, temptations are avoided or lessened, and the soul, by the help of the prudent directions it receives, is better enabled to escape the dangers to which it is exposed. * For the same end every Jesuit makes an examination of his conscience twice a day, and he frequently makes general confessions, that he may take account of the progress he has made, or see if, instead of advancing, he has on the contrary gone back in virtue. Interior and exterior mortification are both necessary to the virtue of penance, in order to strengthen it when it languishes, and restore it to life when it dies ; and the members of the Society have the more need of them, as they have to do with every kind of person, have endless occasions of distraction of mind, and are so exposed to lose little by little the discipline of religious life. And yet we cannot be occupied a whole lifetime in subjugating the passions and natural inclinations; and consequently our principal intent must be to make of these very dispositions of ours instruments of virtue ; in other words, we must employ mortification simply as a means, so that, far from crushing the vigor of the soul, it may rather augment it. We must be masters of all our tendencies, and make them subserve the end for which we were created, but we must be very far from destroying them entirely.†

There are three principal passions apt to gain dominion over the heart, and put great obstacles in the way of community life. Mortification must regulate these passions. The first is an attachment to the goods of this world. He who enters into the Society does not at first lose, it is true, the right to keep or receive property, but he can no longer make use of it as he pleases. It is only when he has bound himself by the solemn vows that he loses this right. Then, indeed, is he obliged to dispose of what he has, or may hereafter have, before he makes his profession.

* Pt. iii., chs. i., xi., xii. ; pt. vi., ch. iii., A.
† Pt. iii., ch. i., sec. 2.

He must dispossess himself of all things, without any greater regard for his relations than for others, and he must prefer the poor to his kindred, unless they may be in want, according to the words of Jesus Christ, " If thou wilt be perfect, sell what thou hast and give to the poor, and come follow Me." Accordingly, the novices are accustomed from the first to make use of nothing as their own, in order that they may keep their hearts disengaged from every attachment to the things of earth. They must practise entire poverty ; what is granted to them is not their own; they are given what they want, and with this they must be content, and without ever taking, or changing, or lending anything without permission—in a word, without ever acting in any way which shows a right of property.

The second object for mortification are parents, friends, and country. Our Lord has said that he who would be His disciple must hate father and mother, and his own life also, by which is meant that excessive attachment to them is an obstacle to the love of Jesus Christ. These same words are addressed to every one who desires truly to follow him in His Society. The novice must consequently free himself from all overfond attachment and tenderness to his parents and his country. He must not, indeed, transgress his duties in their regard, but he must transform the natural love which he feels for them into a spiritual love; that is, into a love which has always in view the greater good of their souls.

The third object for the appliance of mortification is the passion for dignities and honors. ⸳ In the book of the *Spiritual Exercises*, Ignatius has written a meditation on three degrees of humility. The third and the highest of the degrees teaches the companion of Jesus to choose with Jesus what is mean and contemptible in the eyes of the world, and to fly from seeking or desiring for their own sake the dignities and honors of this life. Amongst the members of the Society the most perfect equality reigns in all that concerns the manner of life, and no one can claim any distinction. They may gain academical honors and dignities, but these give them no exterior mark of distinction, and it is not even permitted to call them by their titles. No sign or title of rank can be accepted without the permission of the General.*

That the very root of ambition may be cut away, St. Ignatius forbids his Religious to accept of any charge or dignity to which honors or revenues are attached, and he punishes those who seek for place either within or without the Society.† For this reason the Professed bind themselves by a vow to accept of no dignity in the Church, unless the Pope commands them to do so by virtue of holy obedience. And one of the reasons why the office of General is for life, instead of being for three years as in other orders, is that all occasion of ambition may be cut off. But it is not enough for the legislating Saint that his Religious shall not be ambitious nor seek any dignities, he will have them give each other honor according to the teaching of the Apostle, take for themselves the worst, and desire to be held in little honor, both within the House and without.‡ It is clear that the merit and the very foundation of this exterior mortification rest upon self-abnegation and the victory over self-love. Apart from this, the motto of the Society of Jesus, " All for the greater glory of God," can have no reality. If, then, it is a necessity and a duty of every Christian to subdue his passions, this obligation is much more strictly binding upon a Religious who is engaged to tend to perfection. This truth holds with special force in the society which, to attain its end, must form a body intimately united by the links of charity ; and charity, we know, can only dwell in hearts where self-love and the passions are under control. For this reason the Society does not admit into its bosom men in whom reign strong passions or bad habits, unless they be such as admit of hope of substantial amendment. Mortification is only to be practised in the measure that is suitable to the end of the Society. For if the want of it favors self-seeking and self-love, the excess of it is no less noxious by injuring the health, and

---

* Rule 62, Offic. Prov. ;  Can. xix., Congr. i., pt. iv., ch. xvi., sec. 8; Can. ii., Congr. ii.

† Pt. x., sec. 6; pt. ix., ch. iv., sec. 5; ch. iii., sec. 13; pt. viii., ch. vii., sec. 2.

‡ Exam., ch. iv., secs. 26, 44, 45.

enfeebling the strength. Both extremes must therefore be avoided.

The next virtue necessary to a Jesuit is a knowledge and love of the Society. By its object and end as an ecclesiastical institution, it is the work of God, and draws its life from the life itself of the Catholic Church. Each member of it, therefore, must be, closely attached to it, and apply himself to the full knowledge of the Institute, and love it as the mother which has given him birth and spiritual formation. But it is here especially that the exterior knowledge of the letter of the law is insufficient, because with very few exceptions almost all the laws of the Society are general, * and because in each particular case they leave to the individual the liberty to do what is most suitable, provided it be in accordance with the spirit of the rule he must fulfil. Each member is therefore obliged to make this spirit his own. Thus the laws have the advantage of being living laws, and no one can become a slave to the letter of them without opening a door to caprice and defects contrary to the rule. Hence there result union and harmony among all the members of the Society, and that which powerfully contributes to this union and harmony is, that there is no dependence upon individual lights. There is a continual recourse to the assistance of others, and especially of superiors. Individual action and mutual dependence are thus reconciled— they regulate and sustain each other; and so it comes to pass that personal activity enjoys the just measure and the wise moderation which constitute perfection. Now this advantage can scarcely be found in the world, for where can two men be found with precisely the same interests? Besides, no one dares take upon himself the responsibility of counselling and directing all his fellow-men.

The love of their Institute has often been made a capital charge against the Jesuits, and it is said that the most of them, seeing nothing else in the world, are consequently incapable of living up to the times and contributing to the progress of mankind. If this were true the accusation might be just, but the supposition rests on

---

* Procem. Const. declar. Gagliardi, p. 49.

some rare individual cases, which have been unreasonably generalized. Now we neither take upon ourselves to refute every unfounded conjecture, nor to defend the faults of which some individuals have been guilty. On the contrary, we should be the first to condemn them. Without entering into any discussion, we will content ourselves here, as we have hitherto done, with stating the simple truth of the matter. Every one must grant that whoever has a vocation to a certain rule of life must have for it a special taste and affection. Without it there is no vocation, and each religious body, without this bond of union, would inevitably fall to pieces. However, the love of a Jesuit for the Society ought not to rest in this love as in its final term. He should love his Order as a means to attain his end, which is to give glory to God on earth. And this is, in fact, the same as the love a man has for the Catholic Church. The Jesuit lives in the Society, not for the sake of the Society, but for the sake of God and the salvation of souls. This point of view at once excludes the selfish and faulty affection which is laid to the charge of the Jesuit. It were a narrow and merely human *esprit de corps* that would say, "I love the Society because I belong to it." The spirit of the Society is the love of the general good. * It is not blind, and knows very well how to distinguish between the faults and errors of individuals and the spirit of the Society at large. Such disinterested love is the more necessary as it is the sole motive which induces the Jesuit to enter the Society, and supports him in fulfilling his duties and labors, for he finds in it none of the means which are usually employed by human prudence to sustain men's weakness. There is neither fear of sin nor of punishment if he transgress the rule, nor hope of earthly reward if he keep it. He has, then, no other motive left to him but the love of the Society of which he is a member.

But since it is impossible that this pure love of God can exist except in one who has attained to a perfect indifference to all things, we will here say something of this last virtue, so eminently necessary for the members of the

* "Spiritus Societatis totus etiam quoad affectum architectonicus esse debet, omnium bonum universe complectens." (Gagliardi, p. 52.)

Society. The man who follows his tastes and humors, so far from being useful to the Order, would be very injurious to it.   If he would give himself to study without the requisite talents for it, or contrary to the wishes of his superiors, if he be discontented with the employment given him or the office he has to fill, he runs the risk of spreading his private dissatisfaction through the whole body. He may, indeed, manifest his wishes, provided he does so with a will indifferent to the result, and with a sincere conviction that there is a special providence over those who submit to obedience for the love of God, and that the issue, whatever it be, will be always most to his own advantage, since no human resolve can hinder the accomplishment of the divine will.   Submission, therefore, is certain to be the best for him, whatever it cost;  and the responsibility, together with the blame which Superiors may incur by their determination, do not fall on him for executing their will.  This indifference is the groundwork of the perfection of a member of the Society of Jesus; and the Order esteems this indifference so absolutely indispensable, that it looks upon a man who does not possess it as injurious to the body,  though he be otherwise most gifted and learned.   The Jesuit begins from his noviceship the work of acquiring it; he is not only taught it, but put through various probations according to the degree of his progress in virtue and the time he has been a novice. After the novitiate, he must exercise it in a still more serious and practical manner, when sent to teach schools, or set to study on his own account.  In both of these occupations opportunities are not wanting for humiliation and self-conquest.   When he has completed his studies, he makes a third year of noviceship to renew in himself the spirit of the Society, and to make his mind a debatable land between science and virtue.*

It is clear that on this indifference not only the good of each individual member, but the continuance and the progress of the whole body in a great degree depend. The mission of the Society in the Church cannot be carried out except by a virtue corresponding with so high a

---

* Pt. x., sec. 2.

vocation; and to attain the end it proposes there must be continual progress. While, then, on the one hand, all depends on the free and living action of the individual, who must run with generosity in the race if he would win the prize, so, on the other hand, the direction and superintendence of superiors is ever following the religious into every detail of life. At one time superiors forestall and warn, at another they repress the inclination of nature for negligence and love of ease; they are always on the alert to hinder members from putting an obstacle to the advance of the whole body. Superiors, however, are cautioned to act with due discretion, to respect each member's individuality as much as is compatible with the good of the Society, and to have a due regard for the weakness of humanity. No one in the Society is deprived of the benefit of direction, not even the superiors themselves, though they hold so important a place in it. They are not, indeed, obliged to follow the advice of others, but all, including the General himself, have their consultors, and a monitor, whose duty it is to notify them of any false steps they may have taken, or may be about to take, and to watch over the maintenance of religious discipline.* That the superior may have the necessary light to guide each one in a manner suitable and commensurate with his condition, every subject is obliged at least once a year to make a manifestation of his conscience to whosoever is placed over him, and to conceal nothing from him that may be either useful or injurious to his direction.† Nor must he be angry if others discover to his superior, as to a spiritual father, his defects and failings, which must be done, not out of dislike or ill-will, but in a spirit of fraternal charity, and for the interests of his eternal salvation.

As to the remaining fundamental virtues which a Jesuit should possess, we will here limit ourselves to those which are required by the three ordinary vows. The first is obedience, the firm foundation on which the solidity of the building rests, and the shortest and surest means whereby every member of the body is to reach

---

* Pt. ix., ch. vi., secs. 10, 14, J.

† Exam., ch. iv., secs. 34, 36; pt. i., ch. iv., sec. 6; pt. iii., ch. i., sec. 12; pt. vi., ch. i., sec. 3.

perfection and his last end.* The root of obedience is
the love of Christ Our Lord, for whose sake the Religious is subject to his superiors, recognizing them and
loving and honoring them as the representatives of God.
It is for the sake of Christ he consents to obey man, and
not for any human motive. This spirit of charity unites
into one the wills of superior and subject. Nor in this
is there any detriment done to the individuality and to
the mind of the subject, for he submits to the will of him
who commands, because he recognizes in it, by the light
of an intimate conviction, the will of God, resistance to
which would be a crime. This obedience, therefore,
springs from pure reason freely accepting its necessity.
In thus obeying, the mind develops its activity in the
noblest of all manners, for it is guided by a principle
incontestably more lofty than the blind desire of man's
own will, which is always so prone to follow the inclination of sense. Obeying God in his representative,
the will freely takes a higher flight and enjoys a greater
security; while the seeker after happiness according
to the dictates of his own capricious reason and will
takes his stand upon the low level of the mere natural
man.

Many false and exaggerated things have been written on
the obedience of subjects to superiors in the Society of
Jesus, without considering that the principles on which it
rests were long ago familiar to the oldest monastic institutions, and that they are founded on the Gospel itself.
Nor is this obedience so alarming a thing in reality as
the imagination or the wilful malice of our opponents has
been pleased to paint it. In fact, on no other point have
greater precautions been taken that reason should come
in to reconcile obedience to the command. In the employments, orders, and commissions given to their Religious, superiors are directed to take into consideration
not only the powers, the talents, and the character, but
even the tastes, of the individual. It is certain that, in
the world, it is often very difficult for those who hold
office under any government to obey the orders of their

---

* *Ibid.*, pt. viii., ch. i., sec. 3, C ; pt. iv., ch. x., sec. 8.

superiors; it is very seldom that their tastes are consulted, or their opinion and wills considered, and yet, in
spite of all this, they have often nothing to do but to
submit. Why, then, is a religious man, who obeys for
conscience' sake, to be reproached for doing what a
soldier is obliged to do for the maintenance of military
discipline, when it is, moreover, his superior's duty to
take into account, as is always done, the strength and
capability of the inferior, and when the relations between
the obeyer and the obeyed are all sweetened by a family
and paternal spirit?

Yet more:—for the good of the individual member and
of the whole Society, St. Ignatius makes it a rule that
the Religious who receives a command shall have not
the liberty only but also the obligation of manifesting,
without any detriment to obedience, the doubts he may
have of the fitness of the order or commission, having first
consulted with God in prayer. Except the imaginary
case that a superior should order something intrinsically
bad (in which case it would be a duty not to obey, since
obedience is a means of perfection, not of perdition), the
thing commanded is either good or doubtful. If it be
good, it is always a duty to obey. Still, in particular
circumstances, it may happen that a thing good in itself
may become bad or dangerous. If, for example, a
Religious commanded to preach has some secret defect
incompatible with preaching, he is obliged to declare it
to his superior, and, supposing the superior thinks that he
has reason to persist in the order he has given, the subject
ought to obey, for he is freed from all responsibility, and
his act is doubly meritorious. In the case of doubtful good
he ought to prefer the judgment of his superior to his
own, because self-love makes a choice of what is best to be
done more difficult to be understood by ourselves than by
one who sees things from a higher and more just point
of view. Thus there are three degrees in obedience:
firstly, the Religious does what is commanded him,
keeping his own judgment; secondly, he renounces his
own judgment; and thirdly, he adheres entirely and
interiorly to the judgment of his superior. It is this
last degree which St. Ignatius would have in his Relig-

ious.    There is no virtue on which he has dwelt so much
at length, or that he has so much exalted and recommended, as obedience, and nothing can be more beautiful and more true than what he has written concerning
this virtue in several of his letters.

When Our Lord sent His Apostles to preach in Galilee,
He forbade them to take anything with them but what
was strictly necessary.    Deprived of all human resources,
they were to abandon themselves to the Providence of
God, and trust in this Providence to provide for all their
wants.    They were to be contented with what was offered
them, and freely give what they had freely received,
grace and spiritual goods.    This is the type on which
Ignatius planned the poverty of his Religious; he would
have them cherish poverty as a mother, and would have
all, at times, experience the effects of it.*    They have no
right of property in anything whatever, and they cannot
use even the most necessary things without leave of the
superior, and then in such a manner and so long only as
he wishes.    St. Ignatius especially recommends that the
command be inviolably kept which was given to the
Apostles—*Gratis accepistis, gratis date.*    Consequently, no
one in the Society can receive any stipend for Mass or
for the administration of the Sacraments. †    The colleges,
it is true, have incomes, because they could not otherwise
teach the students either of the Society or others unless
they were supported.    But the professed Houses cannot
possess any fixed property as their own, not even the
churches which are attached to them.    They can, indeed,
receive donations and legacies to build them, but the
Society has no right to dispose of them nor to take action
concerning them. ‡    For the practical maintenance of
poverty the Professed also bind themselves with a simple
vow, to take care that not only the strictness of poverty
be never suffered to decay, but, if it appear necessary, to
make it still more strict.

It is not difficult to discover the reasons why this virtue
must be practised in its purity by the members of the

* Pt. iii., ch. ii., sec. 25 ; Exam., ch. iv., sec. 2.
† Exam.; ch. i., sec. iii. ; pt. vi., ch. ii., sec. 7, G.
‡ Pt. vi., ch. ii., B, E; Regul. Provinc., 76.

Society. It is reason enough, however, that Christ has put it as the foundation of the apostolic life. The experience of all times proves, moreover, that the preservation of the spirit of religious life is incompatible with personal property, and that, together with it, the spirit of the world enters into the most fervent Communities, and ends by causing their complete ruin. Attachment to the most trifling objects is enough to destroy religious discipline, whereas the individual member may remain truly poor while the body possesses the goods necessary for the attainment of its end, provided always that he keeps his heart in entire detachment from all things. Now the Jesuit is obliged to practise poverty in renouncing his own comforts and in clinging to nothing as his own, that he may give to God alone his whole love and confidence, and fulfil with great liberty and with the purest intention his duties of the apostolic ministry.

In regard to chastity it is worthy of note that, on the one hand, our holy founder speaks on this subject most laconically, and, on the other, the very enemies of the Society have never been able to lay the least charge against it on this ground. And yet Jesuits, from the beginning, have had to mix with persons of all kinds, live in the midst of the world, be exposed continually to the observation of every malevolent eye, and be placed in an infinity of dangers. Notwithstanding all this, St. Ignatius contents himself with saying on the subject of this virtue—"As to what belongs to the vow of chastity, there is no need of explanation. It is evident with what perfection it must be observed, and that we must endeavor to imitate the purity of angels in cleanness of body and soul." † The principles of the Society are so severe on this point that the least exterior action contrary to chastity in one of its members is a reserved case. The theological professors belonging to the Order are forbidden to teach that there can be " any smallness of matter," as it is termed, in sins done with full knowledge and consent contrary to the Sixth Commandment. The Society holds this angelic virtue in such high esteem that the

† Reg. 28, Summ.

General himself would infallibly be deposed from his high office were he to infringe it.

As the Society, in the midst of its dealings with the world, has been enabled by the grace of vocation to preserve so delicate a virtue as purity, so it has preserved, amid occasions and seductions of every kind, the no less difficult virtue of humility. It is natural to man to seek the applause and the esteem of others, especially when, gifted with superior talents, he can lay the flattering unction to his soul that he has distinguished himself above his fellows. It is, therefore, a supernatural virtue neither to be elated by plaudits and eulogies when they are bestowed, nor to be depressed when they are denied. Now this is what the Society has done, pursuing its path with tranquillity in the midst of good and evil report. Besides, it is a principle with it to endeavor, on the one hand, to develop to the full natural talents and capacities, and, on the other, to rise by virtue above these gifts, and not to value them on their own account, but solely as a means to attain to the end it has in view. For this reason the Jesuit is prepared from the very first either to fill the most honorable posts and offices if they be confided to him, or to render the humblest services to others; to ascend the pulpit or to teach the ignorant and children their grammar or their catechism.* A Jesuit may enjoy the highest consideration with princes or with the people, but as soon as he enters the walls of the House he is no more than the last of the Religious. He must wait upon himself and be ready to wait on others. Be he what he may, he must, like the other Religious, tell his faults to the superior, or to the Community. In various ways humility is always kept going, as we may say, without breathing time, and thus it is very difficult for pride or vanity to take possession of the heart. There is nothing to favor, on the other hand, hypocrisy or false humility; their is no mantle of exterior mortification to hide the absence of virtue, while true virtue and real merit are preserved in the Society from the attacks of pride by interior and exterior mortifications. The soul is thus preserved by a well-adjusted counter-

* Exam., ch. iv., sec. 28; pt. iii., ch. i., sec. 22; pt. iv., ch. iii. B.

poise in the proper means, wherein repose, as in their centre, the perfection of virtue and true wisdom.

As for the other virtues which are built upon the Exercises, and which must be practised by members of the Society, such as temperance, guard upon the tongue and senses, and observance of Rule, the same remarks may be made about them as about the virtues which have just been spoken of. It may, then, be said of them in general, that they must be practised in such a manner as to be pleasing to others, and render those who practise them loved by others. They must avoid all appearance of rudeness and repulsiveness, and, on the contrary, always maintain a discreet moderation, as a means of more efficient action.* It is easy to show the relation between the rules of the Society and the Exercises. The Exercises have for their object to decide the doubting and undetermined mind to enlist under the standard of Jesus Christ, and, by the consideration of our Divine Model, to bring the soul to imitate Him as far as possible in all its thoughts and actions, and to copy in its conduct the apostolic life of Our Blessed Lord. The rules of the Society have in like manner for their object to give to the Religious a guidance and precepts which may renew or preserve in him the likeness of Our Saviour. For this reason they prescribe self-abnegation and subjugation of the passions, and propose to him these virtues as the foundation-stones of the spiritual fabric which he must build up in the pursuit of perfection. Human weakness and imperfection must of necessity set limits to this high and holy project, but I repeat it again, no man of understanding can take occasion from this aim to form accusations against the Society, and to deny that such is the end which it proposes to all its members.

St. Ignatius, whilst he was composing the Rule (the most important epoch, perhaps, of all his life), passed his days in an intense thoughtfulness of mind, combined with a marvellous piety and sincerity of purpose. In order to guide, enlarge, and purify as much as possible

* It does not enter into my plan to dwell further upon the exterior constitution and organization of the Society, as this subject has been fully treated in other books. I can here refer the reader to the *History of the Society of Jesus*, by Crétineau-Joly.

his own reason by heavenly wisdom, he had recourse to prayer and the holy sacrifice of the Mass, asking of God without ceasing the necessary light for the knowledge of His will. When he had written anything, after preparation by prayer and meditation, he took the paper and laid it on the altar where he said Mass, as if to offer it to God, that He might give His servant to understand whether what he had decided pleased Him or not. This is affirmed by some of the first Fathers of the Society, and by an eye-witness, John Paul Borelli, who served his Mass.* We can learn more exactly what passed in him at this time from an original document, which has been preserved to us, upon a particular point of the Rule. It was a question with Ignatius whether the churches and the sacristies of the Professed Houses could acquire property or not. For forty days this one point was the object of his prayers and meditations, and was ever before his mind, even during the holy sacrifice of the Mass, so that during the whole of this time he examined and weighed attentively the reasons for and against it. He wrote, as was his custom, day by day, the lights, inspirations, and revelations which he received, and the paper which contains these precious notes is the only one that escaped being burned, for we know that before he died the Saint put into the fire all documents of this kind. Orlandini has translated into Latin a part of this precious document, including the space of two days, and he adds that it is very difficult to preserve the spirit of the original.† We cannot refrain from citing here a passage which more particularly sets forth the motives that determined his decision on the point in question.‡

The Sunday, fifth Mass of the Trinity. At the usual prayer, though at first there was little that was particular, when past the middle of it my soul felt much devotion and great consolation. It also saw a certain object and a figure of very bright light. While the altar was being prepared Jesus became present to my spirit, inviting me to follow. For I am wholly of opinion that He is the Head and Leader of

* Orlandini, 45 ; 54 in the Bollandists, sec. 41.
† Bartoli has also given some extracts from it in his *Life*, but in a less exact manner.
‡ Bolland., sec. 42.

the Society, and on this account, above all others, that it must practise poverty and privation to the highest degree, though there are other reasons also for this which I have taken into consideration in my decision. This thought moved me to devotion and to tears, but also to firmness of purpose, so that, had I been deprived of tears at Mass on this and the following days, the feeling which I had experienced would have been, I think, sufficient to keep me firm and unshaken in time of dryness and desolation. While I turned these thoughts in my mind, as I was vesting for Mass, my feelings of devotion increased, and I saw a complete confirmation of the resolution I had taken, although I had no further consolations. The Holy Trinity seemed itself to confirm my decision by the communication of the Son to me, and I had a recollection of the time when the Father vouchsafed to associate me with His Son. When I was vested the name of Jesus engraved itself more and more within me, and I felt myself fortified against every assault. Then tears and sighs broke from me anew and more vehemently. When I had begun the holy Sacrifice I received many graces and a feeling of devotion with sweet tears, which lasted a long time. As I went on in the Mass I had several inspirations which strengthened me in my decision, and at the elevation of the Sacred Host I heard within me an interior word, as if spoken, and a powerful impulse never to forsake Our Lord in spite of all obstacles, and this was accompanied with new sweetness and renewed emotion. This strong feeling and desire of shedding tears lasted during the rest of the holy Sacrifice and the whole day. Every time that I thought of Jesus this devout emotion and this fixedness of purpose returned to my mind.

The letters of Ignatius acquaint us with the impressions he had in relation to another question. It was about the nomination of superiors to colleges. Although it has been finally reserved to the General by the Constitutions, it appears, from two letters of the Saint, that he was still undecided on this matter in the year 1547, for in several colleges he made trial of electing superiors of the Houses.* In a letter to the members of the Order at Gandia, where the Duke Francis Borgia had founded a university and put it into the hands of the Society, St. Ignatius wrote as follows, July 29, 1547—

With regard to the method of proceeding in the election, let all at Gandia examine the thing attentively for three days, each by himself, without consulting the others whom to choose for superior, and during these three days let them implore with more than usual fervor the aid and assistance of Heaven, both by prayers and public exercises of devotion and by the holy sacrifice of the Mass, which the priests shall

* On this subject Orlandini may be consulted (vii., 10), though he seems to go too far when he says that the superiors were to have been elected in all the colleges about to be founded, a thing which is not confirmed by the words of St. Ignatius nor by the facts.

offer for this intention, that the matter may have happy issue. You must, moreover, examine carefully in your mind who is most suited for this office, having only in view the best manner of governing, the greatest good of the Community, and the greater glory of God, for he who shall be elected will take upon himself a fresh obligation of conscience, which he will have to render an account of to the Supreme Judge at the last great day. After this let each write on a billet the name of him whom he chooses; then put his vote into an urn or other place, fastened up in such a sort that no one can take it out again. On the next day let the votes be removed from the urn in the presence of all, in the manner prescribed, and let him be declared rector or superior who has the greatest number of votes. I approve and confirm this choice beforehand if I do not write to you otherwise, until which time this mode of election may be used among you, as long as there is no one who has taken the solemn vows of Profession, and until the Constitutions of our Society shall be published. *

Later the same year, on the 31st of October, he gave the same recommendations to Father Araoz, the Provincial of Spain—

As to what concerns the mode of election, I wish [he says] to declare to you what I think and judge to be right and fitting in Our Lord. When a superior is to be appointed anywhere, if you know of some one who unites all the necessary qualifications for the office, you must appoint him, without allowing the other Religious of the House to give their opinion, at least, without the supposition that any one except yourself has the right of appointing. If you have a doubt who is the most proper person, you can take the opinion of the Religious of the House individually, and in this case each one shall weigh the matter before God for the space of three days, and if he be a priest he shall recommend it in the holy sacrifice of the Mass. He shall then carefully consider who is the most suitable person for the office, and shall then put in writing what he thinks best for the service of God. The Religious ought not to communicate to each other what they have written, and no one ought to know what another thinks, nor be informed of it in any way whatever. They shall then seal what they have written, and shall give it or send it to you, and you, or whoever holds your place, after having recommended the choice to God and said Mass for this intention, shall, after cognizance of the opinions given, name the person to the office if the greater glory of God so require, and you must not choose him whom you yourself prefer.†
So soon as he shall be declared I acknowledge him as superior, in virtue of the full powers I have received from the Apostolic See, and I would have all acknowledge him as such.

* Menchacha, ii., 19.
† The thought of St. Ignatius in in this place is incomplete. He means to say to Father Araoz that he must not follow in this choice his own judgment, but name him who shall have been elected by the greatest number of voices of the members of the College.

It will suffice to give us an idea of the exactitude and maturity of thought with which St. Ignatius drew up his Constitutions, and the care with which he avoided all precipitation, if we only consider the time he took to make them and the trials to which he subjected them. It was only in the year 1550 that they were so far complete that he could communicate them to an assembly of the Professed, whom he had summoned to Rome, and amongst whom were Laynez and Francis Borgia. He wished to submit them to the assembled Fathers, and to take their advice as to any changes or additions that they thought useful. He would publish nothing until it was in a condition to bear the most severe criticism, and therefore he would not trust his own individual judgment, but asked the advice of others. He would have his work suitable for all without distinction, so that the difference of countries and nations, of manners and characters, should render all exceptions or dispensations unnecessary. For this reason he was not content with the approval of the Fathers assembled at Rome, but he submitted his Constitutions to the judgment of those also who were absent. They examined them with the most minute attention, and St. Ignatius did not publish them until he had made the corrections and additions which had been pointed out to him, or which he himself afterwards judged to be necessary. He sent them into Spain in 1553, and to Portugal and some other provinces, not as a work completed and to serve immediately as an obligatory rule, but upon trial, and to ascertain by experience if they were applicable to different nations; and even in the case that they were found everywhere to be in accordance with the design of the Society, they were not to receive their definite sanction until they had been examined and approved by the whole body. Now this did not happen until after his death, when the General Congregation was held to choose his successor, in the year 1568. This Congregation, as soon as it met, was occupied in revising the Constitutions of Ignatius, and confirmed them with sentiments of the most profound veneration for the work and for the author of it. They were then presented to Paul IV., who appointed a Commission of four cardinals to give

him their opinion about them. After having examined
them anew, the cardinals gave a unanimous approval of
the work, and upon this the Pope confirmed it without
the alteration of a single word.

It will perhaps be asked, What rule had the Society
followed before the publication of these Constitutions ?
The answer may be given, that those who entered the
novitiate in those days learned the Rule by immediate
contact with St. Ignatius himself or from the first members of the Society, for in all its essential parts it existed
before it was written. We see, moreover, from a letter
of St. Ignatius to Laynez, that he had already given to
the Provincials some particular Constitutions, drawn up
by himself and approved of by others, and had already
ordered them to be introduced into various Houses of
the Society. This letter relates to the obligation of
teaching Christian doctrine to the ignorant and to children for forty days every year, and to the habit the
members of the Society should wear.

In conclusion, we have but to add to this long exposition that, besides these authentic Constitutions of St.
Ignatius, there are no others in the Society of Jesus.
Laynez, so far from having given new ones to it, or
having contributed more than the others to the drawing
up of those which were given by our holy founder, had so
high an opinion of them that he was not afraid of saying
to Father Ribadeneyra * that the book of the Constitutions of Father Ignatius would alone be enough to enable
him to govern and reform all the Religious Orders in the
Church.

* He made this declaration under oath, in 1595, in the process taken
at Madrid for the beatification of Ignatius.

# CHAPTER II.

THE year 1542 was a happy one for Ignatius, since it
gave him the opportunity of acting as a mediator between
the Pope and the King of Portugal in an affair which had
caused much angry feeling between them. The whole
cause of the disagreement is not clearly known.* Michael
da Silva, after having been the Portuguese ambassador at
the Court of three Popes, had been made bishop of
Viseux, and privy councillor to King John III. But he
left the King's Court secretly to go to Rome, at which
the King was so angry that he sequestrated the revenues
of the bishopric. Notwithstanding this, he was named a
cardinal, and the Pope then made a complaint to the
King about the sequestration of the revenues of the
bishopric, while the King on his part reproached the
Pope with having raised to the purple a man who had
given offence to himself. Hence there arose a quarrel
and a bitterness of feeling the issue of which it was
difficult to foresee. As St. Ignatius was under great obligations to both of them, and feared some bad results for
the newly-existing Society in consequence of this sad
affair, he had it greatly at heart to effect a reconciliation

* The Portuguese Jesuit, Balthasar Tellez, in his *Chronicles* (tom i.,
ch. xxv.), has some interesting documents on this subject, but I could
not procure the work, and I have taken from Menchacha (p. 32) what
is here said.

between them, and he earnestly recommended the matter to God. He proposed to the Holy Father, for the sake of peace, to give the bishopric of Viseux to Cardinal Alexander Farnese, on the condition of his making over the revenues to the actual holder of the see, Da Silva. Paul III. accepted the means proposed, the success of which depended in a great measure upon the person acting as mediator, and he commissioned Ignatius to make this offer to the King. The Saint wrote accordingly to the Provincial at Lisbon, Father Simon Rodriguez, a letter which the King no doubt read, drawn up in such terms as to make a greater impression on him than any diplomatic negotiations would have done. The issue, in fact, accorded with the wishes of St. Ignatius, and both the Pope and the King expressed their acknowledgments to the Saint. His letter was couched in the following terms *—

Whilst considering, with the help of God's goodness, that ingratitude (saving some better judgment on the matter) is one of the most odious of evils, because it forgets goods and graces and gifts received, and is the cause and source of every other sin and evil, whereas gratitude and thankfulness for goods and gifts received is loved and esteemed alike in Heaven and on earth, I have thought it my duty to call to your recol_ lection that since our arrival in Rome we have been continually favored in many things by the Pope, and have received from His Holiness very special favors. The whole Society also knows, and you know in particular (as you are on the spot) what deep obligations we are under to the King, your master and ours, too, in the Lord. Firstly, on account of the great number of spiritual favors which God, our Master and Creator, has been pleased to bestow on him, exalting him by His grace for His own greater glory, and regarding him as His creature with infinite love, so as to become, all infinite as He is, Man for his sake and to die for him. Secondly, who and whence are we, that God should have arranged matters in so providential a way that so illustrious a prince should have thought of us, and following the impulse of his own heart or the counsel of others, should, at a moment when we least thought of it, and at a time when the Society was not yet approved by the Apostolic See, have asked for some of us so earnestly from the Pope, for his service in the Lord, and have loaded us with favors at a period when many persons suspected our doctrines ? You know all this very well, but I also myself know with what good-

* It is taken from the Archives of Rome. Menchacha gives an imperfect translation of it from Tellez, and was unacquainted with the date. The Bollandists (n. 873) and Orlandini (v., 27) give the date of 1545, which is incorrect.

ness and affection he has cared for you since you have been with him, giving you his countenance and, what is not ordinary in princes, offering with all his heart, on account of his great attachment to us, to found a college and build several houses for this our Society, unworthy as it is in the sight of our great Master in Heaven, and of so great a prince upon earth. Moreover, he goes so far in his kindness to us as to take under his protection all those whom we send hence to Portugal for their studies. I would call these things to your recollection, that all of us, both we here and you there, may keep the same object in view, so that, while we serve ever more and more our Master and Creator, we may remain ever faithful and grateful in all things to the persons to whom we are, by the goodness of God, under such obligations, and endeavor, with all the power given us from on high, to take upon us the griefs which the enemy of mankind has labored to stir up, both in temporal and spiritual matters, between personages of such high importance. Inasmuch as you know as well as we what has happened and is now happening, it remains for us all, both here and there (as it is our duty to do), to betake ourselves to our spiritual armor, since we have renounced all other, and pray without ceasing, particularly at the holy sacrifice of the Mass, beseeching Our Lord most earnestly to be pleased to take in hand this most difficult affair, which with such good reason should be recommended to His boundless mercy. Although I am quite convinced that by the grace of God our enemy will not triumph in this matter, it would be nevertheless a misfortune and a scandal to many souls that we should remain even a few days longer in the present state of things.

I have just been speaking at length on this matter with the Cardinal of Burgos,* who is our special protector in Our Lord, and takes a lively interest in all that concerns us. He said to me, in support of my opinion, what has greatly consoled me. Some one lately made the remark that the king of Portugal seemed to be intending to withdraw himself from the obedience to the Pope, to which the good cardinal with much heat replied quickly, " Who says that ? He would not do it if the Pope were to trample on him. Do you think the people in Portugal are like the people here ? and that the king is like the king of England, who is already half out of the Church before declaring himself against her ? You judge very ill of a prince who is so good a Christian, and has such a tender conscience." I would have written to the King; but I put aside the idea, because I consider how insignificant a being I am in comparison with him, and because you are on the spot, and this is sufficient excuse for me. You must, therefore, in the name of us all and in your own name, tender to him our profound respect for his person. If there is anything else you judge good, I request and desire in Our Lord that you will leave nothing undone by you that is necessary.

Rome, March 18, 1542.

If no mention is made in this letter of the plan of mak-

---

* This was John Alvar, of Toledo, a Dominican. He was called Cardinal of Burgos, because he was archbishop of that town. He was afterwards archbishop of St. James of Compostella.

ing up the difference which had arisen, it is because it had to be communicated to the king, and gave a particular instruction to Rodriguez on the affair in question. It is true that in conclusion the Saint gives him news of several members of the Society, but this would not prevent the letter being perused, as Ignatius well knew the interest he took in such matters.

The following year, 1543, Ignatius occupied himself about a matter of the highest importance, which, owing to the worldly and interested views of some persons concerned, had become a disputed question. His associates, from the commencement of their ministry, had perceived with sorrow that many persons dangerously sick waited until it was too late to ask for spiritual attendance. The Council of Lateran, under Innocent III., by its Twenty-second Canon, had forbidden physicians to visit the sick in cases of danger until they had been to confession. Ignatius resolved to restore the practice of this decree, of such importance for the salvation of souls. Several medical men saw with regret that the confessors of the Society put in force this law, and found fault with them in consequence. The Saint then had recourse to Cardinal Carpi, at that time Legate, during the absence of the Pope.* Ignatius addressed to his Eminence a supplication, together with a theological disquisition drawn up by himself, in which he refuted the objections of the physicians. In his letter he says—

Many sick persons die without the helps of religion, either without confession altogether, or with confessions badly made. They ought to have timely notice before the sickness becomes dangerous, otherwise they either have not the strength to make a good confession, or even to confess at all; and so their death is hastened by speaking to them of the obligation. These evils would be avoided if they made this confession at the beginning of their sickness, for besides the security to the soul, this practice gives ease to the body, and greatly contributes to its cure, for we know that bodily ailments are often the effects of sin. For these reasons, your Eminence would wish to put in force, as you have done in your own diocese, the decree of the Lateran Council, with this mod-

---

* Paul III. left Rome on the 26th of February for Buseto, where he had an interview with Charles V. The Pope arrived there on the 21st of June, and the Emperor on the next day. But they parted on the 16th of July, little pleased with one another. Paul returned to Bologna, and Charles went to the Netherlands.

ification, that the physicians can make one visit or two, but no more, to the sick who have not made their confession. But notwithstanding this concession, several physicians have done all in their power to prevent so holy a practice, while others are in favor of it. The objectors say that it is a sin against charity to let a sick man die unattended by a doctor if he positively refuses to make his confession, for they add, if he live, he may afterwards be converted and be saved. But all reasonable men would reply, that laws are made for the general good, and that no fault is to be found with them if they sometimes result in evils to some particular persons. Thus, for example, the law of Moses commanded the keeping of the Sabbath day, and bid the man be stoned who gathered sticks upon it, that, being enforced by this severity, it might be observed for the general good. If the objection they make had any force, it might be said of Ananias and Sapphira, that they also, if they had been left alive, might have repented. In short, the best theologians and canonists, after a minute examination of the question, have declared for the enforcing of the law, as your Eminence will see by the paper I send. His Holiness, when acquainted with it, will certainly receive the proposal with favor. But as the physicians of this city raise such a clamor about it, and, it may be presumed, will try with all their power to prevent the execution of this holy enactment (even when the law shall have been promulgated and enforced anew), I enclose to your Eminence a dissertation approved by the learned in canon law, refuting the objections and setting forth the whole matter clearly.

In this document, written throughout in St. Ignatius' own hand, the extraordinary opinion of the physicians of the time at Rome is refuted, pretending that the decretal of Innocent III. is contrary to charity. Ignatius adduces four reasons against them. If a sick person refuses to make his confession, the laws and canons justly prefer the general good to the evil of one who makes himself an exception. Again, if the help of medical aid cannot be refused to an obstinate sinner, the malefactor cannot justly be punished in other cases, and so all justice will be done away with. Thirdly, the law of God is pure and undefiled, and yet it ordained the punishment of death to many, as to Dathan and Abiron, without giving them time for repentance. Lastly, the decree of a General Council under the inspiration of the Holy Ghost makes this provision, first for the all-important care of the salvation of the soul of the sick man, then for the cure of his body. *

The Cardinal Legate referred the matter to the Pope,

* The two documents here cited are to be found in the Bollandists, sec. 36, nn. 374—378.

as appears from a letter of Ignatius to Cardinal Cervini. *
And although he does not seem to have gained the
results of his endeavors in his own life, they afterwards,
however, bore fruit ; for Pope Pius V. renewed the
decree of Innocent III., and forbade physicians, under
pain of excommunication reserved to the Pope, to visit
more than twice persons dangerously sick who refused
to confess, and this decree was again confirmed in 1725,
by Benedict XIII., in a Council held at Rome.

A much more important matter for the constitution of
the Society is the care that Ignatius took to avoid from
the beginning two causes of ruin. He obtained for it
exemption from ecclesiastical offices and dignities, and
from the ordinary direction of convents of women. With
respect to the dignities, the first attempt was made in
Germany to have bishops from the members of the
Society. In fact, many sees were vacant there, because
men were not to be found capable of filling them, and
the good of religion required for such posts persons
equal to the difficulties of the times. King Ferdinand I.
cast his eyes on Bobadilla, who was at Ingolstadt, and
offered him the bishopric of Trieste, as appears from a
letter he wrote to Ignatius on the 5th of September,
1546. "A Secretary," he says, "of the King of the
Romans has come to this Court, and begged me to
accept the bishopric of Trieste. But I made answer to
him that we were called to poverty and not to honors."
Then Ferdinand, through his confessor, the Bishop of
Laybach, made an offer of this see to Father Le Jay.
Le Jay refused it ; but this time the affair was one of
greater difficulty. He wrote immediately from Venice
to Ignatius on this subject a letter, dated the 13th of
September, and another, on the 25th, to the King. Then,
having learned the steps the King was taking at Rome,
he wrote to him again from Trieste on the 10th of
December, entreating him to desist from his design.
Ferdinand had commissioned his ambassador at Rome,
James Lasso, to obtain Le Jay's nomination. Ignatius
was thus directly involved in this business, and he put

* Menchacha, p. 299, 24th June, 1543.

forth his energies to withstand it. His friend, Maffei, Private Secretary to the Pope, who was afterwards Cardinal, communicated to him the letter in which King Ferdinand put before the Pope, in the most pressing manner, the reasons for his conduct. Ignatius hastened to the Ambassador, who showed him the letter, nearly all written in the King's own hand, giving him the orders to act as we have said above. All the Saint's representations were in vain. The Ambassador would not and could not enter into his views. Ignatius then went to the Pope, and laid before him, with expressions of grief, the reasons which obliged him to entreat of His Holiness not to allow the members of the newly-risen Society to accept of bishoprics. But the Pope had already received with favor the nomination of Le Jay, and had decided to confirm it. He replied to Ignatius with the text of Holy Scripture, that " the heart of kings is in the hands of the Lord," and that Ferdinand had been guided by God in this affair. He added, however, in dismissing the Saint, that he would consult with God, and recommended him to do the same. Ignatius tried the force of his reasonings with the cardinals who were his friends, and endeavored to bring them to his side ; and Cardinal Carpi, the Protector of the Society, actually wrote in his favor to Ferdinand on the 4th of December. But notwithstanding all, the matter went on just as before, and the day for the Consistory was fixed. Ignatius in this extremity had recourse to Margaret of Austria, a penitent of his, and besought her to use her influence with the Pope to induce him to defer his decision until he had written himself to Ferdinand and received his answer. The devout Princess complied with the rèquest of Ignatius, and succeeded in her negotiation. The Saint then wrote to the King the following letter—*

I am well aware of the goodwill of your Majesty towards the Society, and of your zeal for the salvation of the people committed to your care. I give thanks to God for it, and would that I could thank Him suffi-

* The Latin original is probably in the archives at Vienna. We give it from Orlandini (vi., 34), who seems to have corrected the style of it. The date is wanting ; but the letter was certainly written in the latter part of December.

ciently, whilst I beseech His infinite wisdom and goodness to grant to your Majesty the means of accomplishing your pious and zealous projects. The greatest benefit and the highest favor you can confer on us is to aid us to walk faithfully and with sincerity in the path of our vocation. I am so fully persuaded that honors and dignities are a hindrance to us, that I do not hesitate to say, in the most absolute manner and with perfect assurance, that no more certain means of the ruin of our Order can be devised than to force upon us the acceptance of bishoprics. All, in fact, who have entered into this Society have done so with the intent of going into each and every country of the world where the good of religion may call us, and where the Pope commands it. The true and primitive spirit of this Company is, in all simplicity and humility, to go from city to city, and from country to country, for the greater glory of God and the salvation of souls, and not to confine its action to any one particular province. Now, not only has the Apostolic See confirmed this our rule and manner of life, but God Himself has shown most clearly that it is pleasing to Him, by blessing the labors of our Society in promoting holiness of life. And whereas the preservation of its first spirit is the soul of all Religious Societies, it is most certain that, if we keep ours, our Company will be preserved, but if we lose it, it will infallibly come to ruin. Besides, it is easy to see with what dangers it will be threatened if we accept bishoprics. We are, in fact, as yet only nine Professed, and out of this number there are four or five who have been offered episcopal sees, which they have refused with the greatest firmness. Now, if one of them had yielded, the others might have thought they could do the same, and this Society would not only degenerate from its first spirit, but it would, moreover, fall into complete dissolution by the dispersion of its members. In conclusion, this least of all Orders has hitherto done much good by giving an example of humility and poverty, but were they now to see us in riches and honor, they would lose the esteem they have for us; many would be scandalized, and we should no longer exercise our zeal for their salvation so successfully as heretofore. I need not adduce any further reasons. We address ourselves to your Majesty's wisdom and goodness, and we abandon ourselves to your honor and to your protection. And whereas I hold for certain that what is proposed would be an occasion of ruin to our Society, I most earnestly entreat your Majesty to be pleased to follow the impulse which your kindness and conscience would dictate, and remove from us these dangers, looking upon this our little new-born flock as your own, and preserving it intact, for the greater glory of God's eternal majesty; and I pray that He may protect your Majesty in your pious endeavors, and ever adorn you more and more copiously with an abundance of heavenly gifts.

This letter had the desired effect, thanks to the prayers of Ignatius. Ferdinand sent orders to his ambassador at Rome to desist from urging the request, and the Pope had no further reason to refuse the Saint his petition. Upon this he ordered Masses of thanksgiving to be said and the *Te Deum* to be sung throughout the whole Order.

He had fresh alarms of the same kind in regard to Father Canisius, who was several times offered ecclesiastical dignities. The first of these attempts was made by Albert, Duke of Bavaria, who wrote to the Saint on the 25th of July, 1551, to beg of him to allow this Father to accept the office of Vice-Chancellor of the University, and also of a Prebend. Ignatius could without much difficulty give a refusal to this request; * but he was far more seriously embarrassed when Ferdinand asked for the same Canisius as Bishop of Vienna, and persisted in the demand for many years. Ignatius, however, resisted with courage all the efforts of Lasso, the Ambassador at Rome, and the representations of the Pope's Nuncio at Vienna, Ferdinand Martinengo. Lasso did his utmost to induce the Pope to oblige Canisius, under virtue of holy obedience, to accept this dignity ; and, as he afterwards admitted, Ferdinand had promised him a bishopric if he succeeded. Julius III. said in reply that he would be very glad to oblige the King, but that he did not wish to disoblige the Society : he would willingly give his consent if Lasso could obtain the consent of Ignatius. The Ambassador answered—" Most Holy Father, it is certain that he will never give it. If

---

* The Duke's letter is to be found in the Bollandists, p. 501. The reasons for the refusal are set forth in the following portion of the letter of Ignatius to the Duke. The first is—" The dignity and honor attached to this office, which, as far as lies in us, we must avoid. The second is, that we renounce all temporal profit and emolument in the exercise of spiritual duties and works undertaken for the good of our neighbor, so that, even the shadow of covetousness being removed, we may seek with greater purity the glory of God and the good of souls. The third reason is, that the office, being in its nature fixed and perpetual, would, in a manner, oblige Dr. Canisius to remain tied to this University, whereas he was bound by a solemn vow to go wherever the Pope should send him for the good of the Catholic faith." Then he adds—" Hence the King of the Romans, after having offered the bishopric of Trieste to some of Ours, gave up his design. The Duke of Ferrara, in like manner, who had wished for a confessor of the Society to stay with him, and the Duke of Gandia, who asked for a Father to direct a convent of Nuns founded by his sister, both met with refusals from Ignatius; and yet they all remained friends of the Society."

the thing cannot be done without his consent, it will never be done." "Well," said the Pope, "we are in much want of these Fathers, and I say again, I cannot disoblige them. Find some means for them to comply with the King's wishes without their accepting the bishopric, and they will do it." By this he gave a hint of the method they must pursue ; and the matter ended by an agreement that Canisius should undertake the duties of the bishopric for a year, without receiving the revenues or binding himself to a longer time.

A similar but still greater difficulty presented itself in the case of St. Francis Borgia. Although he had become a member of the Society in 1548, he had obtained a dispensation from the Pope to remain for three years in the world. Being at Rome for the Jubilee of 1550, he learned at the commencement of the following year that Charles V. had asked the Pope to give him a cardinal's hat. To avoid what he considered so great a misfortune, he left the city in all haste on the night of the 4th of February, having first sent to several persons of distinction a declaration of his religious vow, which he had up to this time carefully kept a profound secret. He went as quickly as possible to Oñate, in the Basque provinces, and there having made a formal renunciation of his possessions, he was ordained a priest, and immediately began his apostolic labors. However, the negotiations at Rome went on as before, and two letters of St. Ignatius tell us of their advance and progress. John Polanco, his secretary, writes the first in the name of his master. The Saint himself writes the second ; both are dated the 1st of June, 1552.

Polanco writes—

About a fortnight ago Cardinal Cueva, on coming out of the Consistory, sent to our Father to say that you were to be made a cardinal. Cardinal Maffei, whom I went to see the same day, told me the same with much joy, and when I said that our rule forbade us to accept of this dignity, he replied, " For my part, I should wish to see your Order become a seminary for bishops and cardinals." Our Father had an interview with Cardinal Cueva, and having heard his reasons and those of several others, resolved to go to the Pope. In short, he pleaded his cause so well with His Holiness, that the Pope gave him clearly to understand that he acknowledged that your present manner of life is of greater advantage to the glory of God than the dignity of a cardinal. He added, moreover, that he would prefer our kind of life and that of any member of our Society to his own of Sovereign Pontiff. "For," said he, "you have no other thought or care but to serve God, and we are involved in many things which turn away our mind from Him." It was agreed not to send you the hat against your will, but only on the assurance that you are willing to accept it.

The letter of St. Ignatius was couched in the following terms—

With regard to the cardinal's hat, I think myself bound, for the greater glory of God, to give you an account of what I think and feel upon the matter, according to my conscience. So soon as I learned that the Emperor wished to make you cardinal, and that the Pope consented to it, I immediately resolved to do all in my power to hinder it. However, as there were many strong reasons on both sides, and I was not quite assured of the divine will, I ordered all the priests of the House to say Mass, and all the Brothers to pray for three days, that I might be guided in this affair for the greater glory of God. During these three days, while at certain times I weighed and considered the matter attentively, I felt in myself some hesitation, or at least I did not feel that assurance and liberty of spirit which I wanted in order to decide how to act, and I said to myself, How can I know what is the will of Our Lord God, while I do not feel in myself the certainty that I ought to put myself into opposition with the Emperor's intentions ? At other times, when I returned to my usual prayers, and recommended the proposal to God Our Lord, my troubles disappeared. After having several times experienced this combat and trouble, divided between fear and hope, at last, on the third day, both during and after my usual prayer, my doubts disappeared, and I found myself firmly resolved to labor with all my power with the Pope and the cardinals to stop the proceeding. I was then and am still assured that if I did otherwise I should have to give one day a severe account of my conduct to God. I thought, and I still think, that I can most undoubtedly and without opposition to the divine will, take all measures to hinder their giving you the purple, while others, on the contrary, do all they can to obtain it for you. For it is possible that God is moving me to act thus upon certain strong reasons, while he is moving others by opposite reasons to act otherwise, in order that the Emperor's wish may be finally carried into effect. May God Our Lord grant that all of us may wholly and more and more promote His glory and praise. I think it is right that you should reply to the letter that Master Polanco has written to you in my name on this affair, and that you declare the sentiments and the wishes with which God has inspired you, or shall further inspire you with, on this subject. But your answer must be put in such form as may be shown to every one if it be necessary to do so. But you must earnestly recommend all to God Our Lord, in order that in all His most holy will may be done, for the greater glory of His Divine Majesty. *

* Menchacha, iii., nn. 15, 16.

We see from all this with what circumspection Ignatius proceeded in this question. At first sight it might be supposed that, having the Pope and the Emperor's ambassador on his side, all difficulties would be smoothed over, and that, as Francis Borgia had made to him a solemn vow of obedience as a professed of the Society, he had only to forbid him to accept the purple, and there would be an end of the business. But Ignatius could not act in this authoritative way in the present case, for on the one hand he wished to avoid giving offence to the Emperor, whose mind was bent on having Borgia for a cardinal, and, on the other hand, he had to protect the religious vocation of his subject as well as the rule of the Order forbidding its members to accept of such dignities; and it was a rule which had cost him an immensity of trouble to establish. Under these circumstances, then, the best method of proceeding was to leave Borgia his own free choice to take the course he judged best, after Ignatius himself smoothed the chief difficulties at Rome. He thus contrived to meet all parties and interests. It was a delicate trial for Borgia's virtues, but he came victoriously out of the ordeal. The same danger was renewed again two years later, when Philip, son of Charles V., wished to procure a cardinal's hat for the same Saint. The Prince was then in England, and his sister Joanna was regent of Spain in his stead. Ignatius and Borgia addressed themselves to this protectress of the Society, begging her by their letters to turn away her brother from the design he entertained, and they succeeded in gaining the object which both of them so ardently desired. Joanna wrote with her own hand to St. Ignatius to congratulate him on the constancy with which he kept the Society free from ecclesiastical dignities. "God," said she to him, "gives to every Order a special spirit, and it cannot depart from it without great prejudice to itself."

Ignatius was so entirely persuaded of this truth, that "he would never have ceased," these were his words, "to have opposed the elevation of his Religious to dignities and high offices, though all the world should have gone upon its knees to ask him." And at a later period, having understood that Paul IV. intended to make Laynez a cardinal, he said to a Father of the House, "Perhaps in a day or two we shall see Laynez a cardinal, but if it take place I will make such a noise that the whole world shall know how the Society accepts such an honor." Lastly, with the approbation of the Holy See, he forbids in his Constitutions the members of the Society to accept of any dignity without the authorization of the General, who ought not on any account to grant it without an express order from the Pope. The elevation of three Jesuits to dignities, when Julius III. somewhat later made one of them a patriarch, and two others his suffragans, for Ethiopia, may seem an exception to the rule; but on the one hand, the request was made by the king of Portugal, backed with an order from the Pope, and on the other, the reason of the Rule did not hold good in this case, for, instead of revenues and honors, there was nothing to expect in the acceptance of the offices but dangers, sufferings, and privations.

Some were for extending this law, founded upon an essential principle of the Society, to the prohibition of its members becoming confessors to princes, but Ignatius would not consent to this prohibition, because the zeal of the Society for the salvation of souls excludes no man, nor any condition of life, and there is no parallel between such duties as these and ecclesiastical dignities. The Jesuits have often been accused on this head, but let the accusers take the pains to examine the grounds on which Ignatius decided this question, and they will be satisfied; yet more, they will be obliged to own that the Society has always been faithful to the principle laid down by its founder. John III., King of Portugal, was the first prince who asked for a priest of the Society to be his director. He had first addressed himself to Father Louis Gonzalez de Camara, the biographer of St. Ignatius. After awhile the Father declined this task. The King then chose the Provincial, Father James Miron, for his confessor. He also excused himself, saying that this office was contrary to his vocation, on account of the honor and consideration attached to it. Ignatius being informed of the conduct of these two Religious, disapproved of it. He wrote at once to Father Gonzalez, August 9th, 1552, saying that he was edified indeed at his refusal of a duty which many other men ardently desired, but that he thought, nevertheless, the King's request should be complied with, and that there could be no difficulty in undertaking the direction of a conscience so upright and pure as His Majesty's. Moreover, he added that there was no reason to fear lest the acceptance of this office might lead to other dignities, since he could not receive anything of the kind without the consent both of himself and of the Society. If the living at court was a cross to him, he must bear it patiently, remembering that what is done by obedience is in conformity with the will of God, which all should endeavor to accomplish everywhere and in all things. Afterwards he declared his opinion on this subject in a still more explicit manner, by a letter of February 1st, 1553, written to Father Miron, in which he says to him, among other things, that the general good of men and the glory of God must needs be advanced by this proceeding, for the good of the head is the good of all the members, and subjects participate in that of their prince; so spiritual succor can never be better bestowed than upon such as them. The Religious of the Society ought not in this to look only to the security of their own conscience, for if they kept this alone in view, and omitted on that account to do the good that comes in their way, they ought on the same principle to fly from all commerce with the world; whereas their Institute does not allow of this flying from others, but, on the contrary, obliges them to become all to all. They must not disquiet themselves if the world condemns their conduct, and accuses them of seeking honor and influence, but take care to refute these charges by the innocence of their lives. Ignatius at the same time enjoined the Religious whom the King and Queen should choose as their confessor to accept the duty immediately. Miron was instructed to inform the King of this decision, and even to show him the letter if he required it.*

Hence it is clear that princes themselves were the first to seek Jesuits for their confessors, and no discredit can attach to Ignatius for having broken down the opposition

* Menchacha, iii., 20, 27.

of his followers in this point. For it was above all things necessary for the Company, in the fulfilling of its mission of regenerating social life, to renovate the hearts of princes with the spirit of Catholicity, that so the good example might descend to others. The principle here set forth by St. Ignatius is not only undeserving of censure, but was demanded by the state of general society. It is not enough to say in vague terms that it was afterwards abused, which is the common phrase of calumniators, but it must be shown by well-authenticated facts that the abuse has really taken place.

The series of charges laid against the Society is not yet concluded. John III., who had befriended it so well, for a long time entertained a desire of having Jesuits for judges of the tribunal of the Inquisition, and the more so because, when he established it at Lisbon, it was through St. Ignatius at Rome that he obtained from the Holy See the necessary powers and Bulls. This fact is gathered from two passages of the Saint's letters to Simon Rodriguez. *

At the same time, when King John chose Father Miron for his confessor, he proposed to him and to another member of the Society to become judges of the Court of the Inquisition at Lisbon. The Provincial declared that he must refer the matter to Ignatius, and he replied that he forbade them to accept of this employment, for, said he, the Society had for its mission the assistance of our neighbor by preaching and by the duties of the confes-

---

* The first is of the date of December 14, 1545. It appears from the contents that St. Ignatius was at the same time employed to negotiate the nomination of the Infante Don Henry, Archbishop of Evora, to the cardinalate. The second is dated August 19, 1546, and shows that the propositions made with regard to the Inquisition have not yet been definitively accepted, and that the wish of Rome is that the Inquisition of Portugal should fix a term of four months for baptized Saracens and Jews, during which they may decide, either to remain in the country and live as true Christians, or to quit it if they prefer their false religion. It is also apparent that the wish of Rome is that the Inquisition deal mercifully and with indulgence towards those who have been accused before its tribunal on any account whatever. From this it is pretty manifest what the Pope thought of the conduct of the Holy Office in the Peninsula of Spain. The two letters are in the collection at Rome.

sional, but looked upon all eminent posts and charges which lead to bishoprics as alien to its object ; that, moreover, he did not wish its members to have power to punish heretics with death, but that, on the contrary, their duty was to endeavor to console with kindness these unfortunate men, and, in the spirit of the humble Religious, to prefer these lowly services to the employments which bring with them consideration and authority. But the King did not abandon his project, and renewed his request through means of Miron. It seems that Ignatius found difficulty in refusing the request of the Prince, for it appears by a letter written to Miron that he gave up his own opinion in deference to the advice of others, and on account of the circumstances of the case. The letter is couched in the following terms—

I am informed, by your letter of the 4th of May, of the desire expressed by His Royal Highness to have a Religious of our Society appointed Inquisitor at Lisbon, under the direction of the Cardinal the Infante, if the thing is not contrary to the spirit of our Institute, as the occupant of this post is dead. You also inform me what reply you have made to His Royal Highness. This affair requires much consideration, because there are very strong reasons both for and against it ; and so, after having thought much upon it, and recommended it to the Lord Our God, I gave orders to six others, namely, Master Laynez, Masters Salmeron and Bobadilla, the Doctors Olave and Madrid, and Master Polanco, to say Mass for three days for this intention, and, after having conferred with Louis Gonzalez on the matter, and being fully informed of what you have written from Portugal, to weigh the thing maturely and take counsel together, and then give me their opinion in writing. We have at last decided in Our Lord to leave the thing in the hands of His Highness, and to do what he shall judge best for the glory of Our Divine Lord. As, in fact, this charge is not directly contrary to the spirit of our Institute, there is no reason why the Society should seek to withdraw itself from the trouble of it, for it is decidedly a matter which nearly concerns the interests of religion in that kingdom. But in order to avoid many inconveniences, we think it would be good for His Majesty to write to the Pope, requesting him to give us an order under obedience to accept of this charge, for then it would be on the express command of His Holiness as Dean of the Cardinals, the Inquisitors, that the Society would undertake the office, and so all would be done with the Pope's full approbation. It would also be good for the King to write a letter to our Protector, Cardinal Carpi, the acting Dean of the Inquisitors, and another to his ambassador, to push on the affair. If His Majesty shall not think proper to write, we shall nevertheless be ready to comply with his commands to the greater glory of God. And if he should oblige us to accept of this charge, we will make some propositions to him which, without prejudice in any way to the end which this holy work proposes, will contribute to put the Society in a condition to undertake it with greater advantage and edification. If His Majesty thinks that we should not wait for the Pope's reply to begin, one or two of Ours can undertake the office provisionally, until such time as an official appointment from the Pope shall be made. Whatever may be the case, we will do in all things (as I have already written) what is most agreeable to His Majesty. *

Rome, June 20, 1555.

Hence it appears that St. Ignatius, though adhering to his first opinion, would not decide by himself, and that he yielded to the desires of the ruling authorities, as he often did when he could do so without infringing the principles of the Society. And this is a sufficient answer to the injurious sarcasms of some past and present writers, who wilfully or ignorantly misrepresented him as a blinded fanatic. The letter also indicates that he had the intention of proposing to the King some abatement of the rigor of the tribunal of the Inquisition. Had the matter been proceeded with, the Inquisition in Portugal would have been more lenient, and perhaps have taken for a model the Roman one, which was much more just and merciful than the others. But whether it was from some disagreement at Lisbon with the wishes of the Saint, or whether it was that the King's death prevented it, the Society remained always a stranger to the Inquisition, and has reason to be glad that it has done so.

The saintly founders of the great Orders of the thirteenth century, St. Francis and St. Dominic, thought it necessary for attaining their end to admit women to their Institute, as had been done by religious societies in the foregoing ages. St. Ignatius had very soon to examine the question whether the Society of Jesus could be extended also so as to include them. We have already seen

---

* This letter has been hitherto unknown to all the writers of the life of St. Ignatius, with the exception of the Portuguese, Antonio Franca, in his *Synopsis Annalium S. J. in Lusitania,* published in the last century. He gives a Latin translation of it. It is taken from a copy of the original preserved in the chapel of Loyola, which we have translated. It serves to rectify all the old biographies of the Saint—Orlandini (15, 19), the Bollandists, Tellez, and even Menchacha (nn. 140, 180), who with one accord assure us that Ignatius twice positively refused the King's offers. It is natural enough that those who have come after Orlandini should have followed him in this error, but it is hard to discover upon what ground Orlandini based his assertion.

in the course of this history that women from the very first
declared themselves in his favor, approved of his manner
of life, and put themselves under his direction.  His
letters, and the circumstances of his life, have brought
before us the names of many ladies of high rank, and of
others, especially of Nuns, who kept up correspondence
with him, either by letter or otherwise, in order to be
directed by him in spiritual matters.  There are some
who made the Exercises under his guidance.  It cannot,
however, be said that he sought for this kind of ministry ;
it came to him spontaneously, and the Saint, who felt
himself called to do good to all without distinction, would
not refuse to accept it; but put it in practice as occasions
offered, when he was not hindered from so doing by more
important and more general duties.  Some of these pious
women seemed to have supposed that Ignatius would go
a step further, and admit them too into his Order.  But
he was far from having any such intention ; and, in fact,
an institution whose distinctive character is the apostolic
ministry, could not possibly receive women into its body,
for its end and place in the Church are, as must be allowed,
quite incompatible with the duties and position of the
weaker sex.

Ignatius, out of regard for his old relations with
Elizabeth Roser, yielded at last to her earnest solicita-
tions, and he permitted her, after the loss of her husband,
to take a simple vow of obedience to him in matters of
conscience and eternal salvation.  But many other women
in Spain desired to place themselves under obedience
to the members of the Society, and several ladies of
high position in the world begged to be admitted into
the Order; that is, they wished to found convents of
Nuns living according to the rule of the Institute.  We
cannot resist quoting a supplication of this kind, of extraordinary warmth and eloquence, for such a monument
of pure and noble sentiments ought not to pass into
oblivion.  It is the supplication of Donna Joanna, of the
ducal family of Cordona.  Her husband died at Valencia
by the hands of an assassin, and early in life she became
a widow.  In the delirium of her grief she repaired to
the Court to demand justice on the murderers.  Return-

ing to Valencia, she became acquainted with Father Miron of the Society, and under his direction made the first week of the Spiritual Exercises, which produced in her so powerful an effect, that, after a renunciation of her possessions in favor of her children, she retired with some friends into an alms-house, and gave herself to the care of the sick. In this hospital she died, March 13th, 1547, in the odor of sanctity, faithful to the resolution she had taken. It was in the year 1546 that Ignatius obtained from the Holy See a decree by which the Society was freed from undertaking the perpetual direction of religious women, and it was in the same year Joanna wrote to him a letter in which she asked of him much more than this. She says—

One who prays with great faith does not cease to pray, though his prayers are not heard. I shall do the same, most dear Father in Our Lord ; for, although I have written to you many times, and have received lately but one reply, still I do not doubt of your affection. My desire is only the more lively, and my faith is so strong, that I think in my heart that it is with you as with Our Lord, Who, pressed by the crowd, felt that some one had touched the hem of His garment. Would that you, my dear Father and my lord, could feel that I have touched the hem of yours. It is in this hope that I begged my confessor, Master Miron, to give me the Spiritual Exercises, and he has done so with much charity. But whether in the Exercises or out of them—whether in the midst of temptations, or sadness, or darkness, I have and have had no other thought in Our Lord than the continued feeling of the vocation to enter into the camp and under the standard of the Society of the name of Jesus; and so my heart is ready, most dear Father and lord—my heart is ready; humbly prostrate at your feet, it will never rise, and, like the Cananean woman, I will cry to you until you give me my soul's salvation, which is signified by the Cananean's daughter. My need is no less than hers, and my hope is accompanied with a faith equal to hers. In this faith I have quitted children and goods, friends and relatives, and renounced all that I possessed; and by this faith I regard all that is dear to the flesh with aversion, as the enemy of my soul. I have withdrawn myself from all others to serve the poor of Jesus Christ; and in these occupations I begin to possess the treasure of poverty, and keep myself in an entire indifference to all things, that the will of the Lord may be done in me through you. Would you have me go to Rome? I will go. But if I am unworthy to see you and receive your blessing, bid me go to the Indies, or elsewhere, or to remain here, it matters not, I will obey you to the death. One who, moved by a strong natural affection, made a journey of more than a thousand leagues to demand justice, will not be prevented by any difficulty, and will make, if need be, a longer journey, or travel in pilgrimage all the rest of her life, to find

mercy, and for the love of Him to Whom she and all things else belong, and Who quitted all for all of us.  Since your heart, so full of tenderness, is open to others, and so ready to receive them, do not, most
honored Father and lord—do not close it to me, unworthy servant of
the servants of Jesus.  Full of confidence in Him, my good Master,
and in your kindness, I will wait for your reply, which I beseech you
in all possible humility to give me as speedily as you can. *

To anticipate all difficulties that might arise from other
requests of this kind, St. Ignatius addressed the following supplication to Pope Paul III.

Most Holy Father,—We the undersigned, the General and priests of
the Society of Jesus, erected and approved by your Holiness in this
holy city, use their continual endeavors, according to their poor means,
to serve the Church of God and Our Lord Jesus Christ, and, consequently, your Holiness, his Vicar upon earth.   But whereas the said
priests are solicited by many personages of consideration, and especially
in Spain, to take the direction of religious sisterhoods, and women
who desire to serve God in a life of piety ;  and as they are convinced
that this would be a great obstacle to the other duties which they have
to fulfil in the service of God, according to the Constitutions given to
their Institute by your Holiness ; as, in a word, this ministry which is
sought to be laid upon them may easily, even at the commencement,
lead to a deviation from their path, and, in lapse of time, become a
serious impediment, the same priests, humbly prostrate at your feet, ask,
as a special grace, that your Holiness would be pleased to declare and
pronounce that the direction of religious sisterhoods or other women,
and the power of receiving vows of obedience from them, is incompatible
with the other duties of the Society, according to the Constitutions
given by your Holiness to the Institute ;  that it is not fit that they
should be held bound to take upon themselves this charge, and that such
an obligation is contrary to the Constitution of the Society, such as it
has been approved.   Your Holiness could then cite word for word the
approbation which you have been pleased to give us on this subject.†

At the same time, Ignatius prayed the Pope to dispense
Elizabeth Roser from the simple vow which she had made
to him, and the Pope granted his request.   This pious
lady had come to Rome with exaggerated ideas of the
rights she supposed she had with regard to Ignatius, as

* She had written to him another letter, thus—" I most earnestly
beg of you to receive me into this holy Society and the Order of the
sweet and holy name of Jesus, for this sacred name has ever been
engraved in the very depth of my heart, from my infancy and ever since
I came to the use of reason."  We owe the preservation of these two
letters to Menchacha (bk. ii., nn. 4, 6).  He also gives us some information regarding this admirable woman (Com. Prœv., n. 38).

† The Bollandists, sec. 40.   The date is not given.

we shall see presently. However, her conduct perfectly justified the resolution which the Saint had taken, and which undoubtedly is to be reckoned one of the wisest measures with which God inspired him. This procedure with regard to a person to whom he owed so much must have been a painful one to him; but in his position he could not have regard to personal feelings, and he did all that was in his power to make the blow fall as gently as possible. He communicated his resolution to her by a letter, in which he says—

It is true that I could have wished to comply with your desires, for the greater glory of God, and to continue to guide you under vow of obedience as I have hitherto done, watching over your soul for its greater good and for your greater perfection. I feel, however, that I have not the strength I should require for it, being much hindered by my infirmities, and busied by affairs of high obligation in the sight of our Lord God and the Pope, His Vicar. Moreover, being conscientiously persuaded that the particular direction of women under vow of obedience is contrary to the end of this little Society, according as I have declared to His Holiness about six months since, I have considered it most conducive to the glory of God to withdraw myself entirely from this care and to keep you no longer under my obedience as my spiritual daughter, but to think of you rather as a good mother to me, as you have been for a long time, to the greater glory of the Divine goodness. I therefore remit you, as entirely as I can, always without prejudice to every higher authority, under the all-wise judgment of Heaven, to what shall be the decision of His Holiness, that so your soul may be entirely tranquillized and consoled, to the greater glory of God.[*]
Rome, October 1, 1546.

The Poor Clares of Barcelona having, after this time, begged of him, through the mediation of Father Araoz, to be pleased to confide their spiritual direction to one of his Religious, he refused them in the most positive manner, and even censured the Father who had pleaded for them. In the same manner, he rejected the demands of this kind made to him by several Religious Sisters in particular, grounding his refusal on the decree of the Holy See. He wanted, even, to make this exclusion a part of the Constitutions. We will not speak here of the attempt made in much later times, but in vain, by the foundress of the Sisterhood of English Ladies, to affiliate her Con-

---

[*] Ribadeneyra and Menchacha, who had not the original to refer to, have not given it exactly. This copy of it has been taken from the collection at Rome.

gregation to the Society, nor of the Institute of the Jesuit-esses suppressed by Urban VIII., in 1631.

Such were some of the contests which St. Ignatius had to sustain for the preservation of the primitive idea of the Society in its purity. It required gigantic strength of soul to put his resolve into execution in spite of all the difficulties which surrounded him, and to keep him from yielding to false and illusive appearances of good.

# CHAPTER III.

RENEWED CALUMNIES AGAINST IGNATIUS. HE TRIUM-
PHANTLY REFUTES THEM BEFORE THE TRIBUNALS.
UNFOUNDED CLAIMS OF ELIZABETH ROSER UPON HIM.
HE WISHES TO ABDICATE THE OFFICE OF GENERAL.

IGNATIUS, after some years of repose, exempt from
persecutions and calumnies, was again subjected, in 1536,
to this kind of trial.  It is painful to the historian to have
so repeatedly to record such persecutions, and to the
reader to peruse them, although the Saint came forth
from the ordeal with glory.  It is, however, the duty of
the chronicler to relate the facts as they occur, that the
truth may not suffer.  Ignatius was attacked from three
several quarters at once.  The first of these trials of his
patience came from a man holding a high post at St.
Cassian.  His name was Matthias, a man of very violent
passions, who had seduced the wife of another, and lived
with her publicly at Rome.  She was brought to repentance, and had retired to St. Martha, the house for
penitents, through the efforts of Ignatius. Matthias, transported with rage at the news, tried to break into the
house by night, but having failed in his attempt, he
spread through the city the vilest reports against the
character of the Jesuits, renewing the old story that they
had driven them from Paris on a charge of heresy.  It
was an old accusation, which had been already often and
juridically refuted.  By these reports, and by written
libels which reached even the Pope's ears, he raised such
a prejudice against Ignatius and his companions, to the
detriment of their ministrations and their reputation, that
the Saint thought himself obliged to address a supplication to Paul III.  In it he prayed the Pope to be pleased
to name judges who should inquire into the charges laid
against them.  Paul deferred the matter until his Vicar,
who was an invalid, had recovered his health.  Ignatius
then renewed his demand through the Bishop of Cesena,

who presented a memorial to the Pontiff on the part of the Society, which he styles the holy company of Jesus.

The Pope intrusted the examination to his Vicar, Archinti, and to the Governor of the city, Franzini. The Vicar twice visited the Convent of St. Martha, to take the depositions of the inmates, and made a searching inquiry into the life and doctrines of the Jesuits. The 3d of July was appointed for the two parties to appear before the judges; but the plaintiff had not the courage to present himself either on the day or afterwards, not even at the declaration of the verdict. He secretly tried to make a compromise with St. Ignatius, as is evident from a letter of the Saint, dated the 9th of October, addressed to Dr. Torres, in which he says—

Our good friend, Matthias, has entreated Doña Eleonora Osorio * not to take part against him in this business, telling her that he will apologize to me, and will everywhere speak in our favor if she wishes it. Her Grace sent for me, two days since, to the Campo-Fiori, to tell me that she and her husband were of opinion that I ought to accept of the compromise offered by Matthias ; but I contended against this opinion with such strong reasons, that I succeeded in convincing her that I ought to do no such thing. I represented to her that, according to my views, there could not possibly be any compromise between me and Matthias, that I did not wish for his apology, nor that the decision of the trial should be brought about by anybody's mediation, or that any one should trouble himself about it. I was certain that the sentence would be in conformity with right and justice, and would end to the greater glory of God. Her Grace was clearly made to understand that this way was far preferable to the other. Matthias went yesterday to meet the Pope's Vicar, and said much in our favor and to his own damage. He tried to make friends, for fear the matter might turn out badly for him, as might easily be the case. God grant that all may be done to His greater glory.

Some days later he writes again to the same—" Matthias has presented to the Pope's Vicar a testimonial in our favor, in which he pleads guilty, and declares that he wishes to make peace with me." †

* She was the wife of John de Vega, Viceroy of Sicily, of whom we shall speak presently. She and her husband were both great friends and benefactors of the Society. They founded five Jesuit Colleges.

† These two letters are to be found in Menchacha, ii., 11, 12. They prove that the date of August 11th, given by Ribadeneyra for the passing of the sentence, is not exact, for Matthias was still endeavoring to effect a compromise in the month of October. (These letters also conclude the acts of the Bollandists, sec. 38).

The sentence of the Tribunal declares, after a short *resumé* of the inquiry, that the imputations laid against Ignatius are false, mendacious, and calumnious ; that the accused priests and their congregation are irreproachable in their lives, their conduct, their faith, and their doctrines ; that for many years past they have produced abundant fruit in the vineyard of the Lord ; that they are held in high esteem and consideration by all ; and that they have always shown themselves above all suspicion and calumny, and in particular and especially their General, the venerable Master Ignatius of Loyola. The judges imposed silence on Matthias, threatening him with the loss of his post and sequestration of his goods without further informations, if he continued to calumniate these honorable men. They reserved to themselves to declare the penalty he had incurred, with the costs of the process, which they would inform him of at their pleasure. This indulgence was owing to the interposition of Ignatius, who obtained the remission of the penalty, and by this act of kindness the Saint gained the friendship of Matthias, so that afterwards he became one of the benefactors of the Society.

A priest named John de Torano, superior of the house of catechumens or Jewish Proselytes, entitled St. John de Mercato, conceiving a feeling of jealousy because the authorities had followed the advice of St. Ignatius for the good of that establishment, which the Saint himself had founded, allowed himself to be so far carried away by this vile passion that he publicly calumniated Ignatius and his companions. He even presented a memorial to the Pope, accusing them of heresy and of violating the seal of confession. In the blindness of his anger he provoked an inquiry, which turned to his own confusion, and his other misdeeds, which he had concealed under the mask of hypocrisy, came thus to light. The Cardinal del Monte, who conducted the inquiry, gave judgment against him, suspending him from the exercise of his priestly office, as guilty and convicted of calumny by his own confession. He was also, at the same time, deprived of his benefices and his place, and his goods were confiscated. The culprit was also condemned to imprisonment for life, a punishment which was afterwards changed to exile, probably at the entreaty of Ignatius.

At the same time, a Spanish monk, named Barberan, set himself in opposition to the Saint, for reasons which are now unknown, and he, too, as if all the adversaries of Ignatius had agreed together, presented a complaint to the Pope, the import of which is given in a letter of the Saint, dated the 18th of October. He writes as follows :

> Barberan has raised a complaint against the house of St. Martha. His Holiness has placed the matter in the hands of Cardinal Crescenti. The Cardinal told me, in an interview yesterday, that the charge is utterly groundless. To give me an idea of the frivolous nature of the imputations against us, he said that we are accused of superintending the house of St. Martha without having received powers from the Holy See, that we pretend to reform the whole world, and teach that all the married women of Rome who are guilty of adultery should be put to death, and other such-like silly stories. The Cardinal, who is aware of all the circumstances, has advised me himself how to proceed, so that the whole thing may be cleared up to the satisfaction of His Holiness.

Not content with thus addressing the Pope, Barberan, moreover, sent to Ignatius an abusive letter by the hands of a third party. The Saint replied by the bearer in a truly Christian and characteristic manner. His answer runs as follows, addressed to the messenger :—

> August 10, 1546.
> Sir :—Tell Father Barberan that, if he wishes, as he says, to have a number of Ours burned from Perpignan to Seville, that I also wish that he and all his friends, with all that belong to them, not only from Perpignan to Seville, but throughout all the world, were consumed with the fire of the Holy Ghost, in such a manner as that they might be led to the height of perfection, and be made great promoters of the glory of God. Tell him also that the Governor and the Vicar of His Holiness are making a judicial inquiry into our concerns,* and that the sentence will soon be pronounced. If, then, he has anything against me, he can address himself to them, and present his proofs, so that, if I am guilty in any point, I alone may be punished, for I would prefer to suffer in my own person, rather than see all my companions burned, from Perpignan to Seville, without the slightest fault committed on their part. †
> Rome, near Sta. Maria della Strada.

* He speaks of the proceedings of Matthias.

† Menchacha, ii., 9.  I cannot refrain from putting beside this letter of Ignatius another letter of Luther's, which puts in a clear light the difference of the spirit which animated these two men.  The well-known reformer, Schwenkfeld, had sent him, in the year 1543, some writings

Thus far the persecutions we have recounted were inspired by bad motives, and the life their authors led was such as to take away all credit from their imputations. This was not the case in the instance which now follows, and it is only to be regretted that the noblest dispositions are not exempt from the weakness of human instability, but allow themselves to be drawn by it into unjust and unreasonable conduct. Elizabeth Roser, of whom we have spoken above, began a lawsuit against Ignatius, for reasons which are not clearly intelligible, from a want of sufficient documents. It is, however, very certain that she was very much aggrieved at being compelled to renounce the spiritual relationship which she had heretofore held with him, and that she could not at all acquiesce in the grave considerations which led him to this determination. There are also some indications that her nephews, and in particular one Dr. Ferrer, undertook to reclaim money from him, but on what title does not appear. The Saint makes mention of this affair in several letters, and tells us how it ended. The following is what he wrote to Dr. Torres, on the 18th of the October of this year, 1546, in which he was exposed to so many storms—

Señora Roser asks for two things. First, she wishes me to give her in writing an assurance that I will not, seeing that she has so great an attachment to me, dismiss her on account of her defects. Secondly,

by a messenger, asking his opinion and judgment upon them. As Luther was angered with him for thinking differently from himself on the Eucharist, he did not answer a word to him directly, but, addressing the bearer in an open note which he sent back by him, he said thus:—
" My dear fellow, tell thy master, Gaspar Schwenkfeld, that I have received the books and the letters thou hast brought me. Would to God he would stop his doings, for he has lit up an incendiary's fire against the Lord's Supper in Silesia, which is not put out yet nor ever will be. Besides, he still propagates his Eutychian doctrines and troubles the churches, without having received orders or mission. The old fool is possessed by the devil and does not understand a word he says. If he will not be quiet and let me alone with his books, may the devil spit and , . . through him. Here is my final sentence upon him :—May the Lord punish Satan in thee and in thy spirit, which has driven thee and the life thou leadest, and all those who have anything in common with thee, Sacramentarians, Eutychians, etc. May He confound thee and thy-blasphemies, as it is written : ' They have run and I have not sent them, they have spoken and I bade them not.' The 6th of December, 1543." (Dollinger's *Reformation*, t. i., p. 238).

she raises an objection to a settlement of some temporal matters, made in presence of Doña Eleanora, herself (Elizabeth Roser), John Bosch, and myself, together with another, a stranger. She now demurs to this settlement, because, three or four days after the agreement, she looked through her account, and found, as she says, that our house owes her a considerable sum. I have refused to yield in this case until a new inquiry has been made, being convinced that the right is on our side. I had great difficulty to prevail upon her by my entreaties to name some one to act for her while I did the same to act for me, on condition that, if these two referees could not agree, we should submit the case to the judgment of some learned and important person or other, for example, to an auditor of the Rota, and so, the question being once for all ended, the Pope's Vicar might give a definite sentence and all scandal be avoided. *

Ignatius could not satisfy this lady, who was blinded by the excitement of her feelings, until the justice of her claims had been proved or disproved, and the more so as she and her nephews spoke both against him and the Society. He did what every man of sense must have done in his place. In advising her to refer the matter to arbitration he acted more in her interests than his own, as the sequel proved. This proposition was agreed to by all, and Cardinal Carpi was chosen by both parties, and heard their depositions under oath. But the adverse party, foreseeing an unfavorable issue, carried the matter before the representative of the Pope's Vicar, who was prejudiced in favor of Elizabeth Roser, and therefore they hoped to get a favorable sentence from him. He, however, having accurately examined the question, was obliged to reject the claims of the lady Roser as untenable, and imposed on her strict silence, declaring that her pretensions had no foundation whatever. When the inquiry was concluded, he publicly avowed that the tears of Señora Roser had touched him and prejudiced him in her favor, but that now he was convinced that Ignatius had the right on his side. Through this affair, however, certain calumnies spread against Ignatius by Dr. Ferrer, one of the nephews of Elizabeth, were brought under examination, and on the 2d of June, 1547, the Doctor was condemned to ask pardon of the Saint publicly, and the judge remarked that he was treated thus leniently because, before the sentence was passed, he had retracted

* Menchacha, ii., 19.

his charges against Ignatius in the presence of the persons before whom he had expressed them. The Saint was still most careful of the character of his kind old friend, and forbade all of the Society in Spain to speak of the past except in case of necessity. It does not appear that the friendly relations between them were ever broken off. *

The Saint's patience was sorely tested by all these trials. If it be asked whether he ought to have yielded to his opponents with ill-advised humility, and let the storm pass, we answer he could not do so, for in his position he had the choice of encountering the persecution with firmness, or else of being completely beaten by his adversaries. In fact, although the first three attacks seem to have proceeded from feelings of personal resentment against him, still the individuals from whom they originated were not alone. Their sentiments were shared by many others; they were only the representatives of that numerous class who do not wish to allow Christianity to exercise a practical influence on their life. They found support and encouragement in the secret approbation of all those who favored the new errors, as the accusation of heresy so constantly repeated against Ignatius and his companions proves. But from this time forward, these false charges fell to the ground, and, silenced by so many triumphant refutations, could never be reproduced with any shadow of success. Thanks to the courage and patience of Ignatius, his innocence was acknowledged by all, and he came forth victorious from all the trials to which he had been put by the malice of his enemies.

Nevertheless, it is not surprising that, with all his firmness, he secretly desired to abdicate the post of General, which brought upon him so many troubles and annoyances, for, besides these vexations, he had reasons which, in his eyes, were of the greatest cogency. This desire is found expressed, for the first time, in a letter written to Laynez at Bologna, where the Council was then being held, in the spring of the year 1547. He says—

---

* There is a fragment of a letter to be found in Menchacha (n. 105 of his Comment.) written by St. Ignatius in the year 1551, which Menchacha thinks was addressed to Elizabeth Roser.

If the Society, or only the half of its members, consent to it, I give you my vote, if that is possibly of any weight, and with all my heart and the joy of my soul remit into your hands the post which I occupy. I choose you not only as worthy of this charge, but if you refuse it I choose in your stead whomsoever either you or any other shall appoint, for I think that, were it so settled, it would be to the greater glory of God Our Lord, and to the great consolation of my soul's spiritual state before His Divine Majesty. The truth is, and I cannot conceal it, that I desire to lay down this burden and retire into humble life. But, setting aside my own poor judgment, I hold, and hope I shall always hold, that to be best which you, or the Society, or a moiety of its members, shall decide, as I have already said, and by these presents I approve and confirm whatever shall be so decided in this matter, and attest it by my hand.*

It seems very probable that the representations of Laynez induced him for the time being to set aside the execution of his wishes, but he kept them within his bosom until the end of the year 1550, when he summoned to Rome the principal members of the Society, to communicate to them the Constitutions he had drawn up. But falling very sick on Christmas Day, after the second Mass, he could not declare in person his intention to the assembled Fathers, but sent them under seal the following letter in Spanish, dated the 30th of January, 1551—†

To my very dear brothers in Our Lord, the members of the Society of Jesus,—In the presence of my Creator and Master, Who will one day pass judgment on me for eternity, I wish now to declare to you, according to the truth and in all tranquillity of mind, what I believe most to the advantage of the glory and praise of His divine Majesty, after a deliberation of many months and years, in which I have followed no interior or exterior impulse. Thinking over my numerous sins and defects, and my infirmities of body and soul, I have often come to the conviction that I fall short, so to speak, infinitely, of the strength which I need to bear the burden which the Society has laid upon my shoulders. I desire, then, that the matter be maturely considered in Our Lord, and that a man be chosen in my place capable of governing the Company better, or at least not so badly, as myself, and that this office be con-

* The Bollandists (sec. 42, n. 437) have given this fragment translated from the original Spanish.

† This date, which the Bollandists have been the first to give, corrects Ribadeneyra and Orlandini, who put the attempt to resign of St. Ignatius in 1550.   Mariani made use of the Bollandists, but it is clear that he took no care to study the dates, for, like all those who preceded him, he places the sickness of Ignatius after receiving the reply of the Fathers.   But as both Ribadeneyra and Orlandini say expressly that Ignatius fell sick at Christmas, and that his letter is dated the 30th of January, 1551, he could not have fallen sick after receiving their answer.

fided to him. Besides this my desire, I am persuaded, even though he who shall be chosen in my place should do neither better nor less bad than myself, that, nevertheless, this burden ought to be removed from me and put upon him. All this maturely considered, I lay down my office, and make my renunciation of it, without condition or reserve, in the name of the Father, of the Son, and of the Holy Ghost, one God, my Creator. And I pray and conjure in Our Lord, with all my soul, the Professed Fathers, and all those whom they shall think ought to be taken into their consultation, to be pleased to receive my proposition with favor, for it is certainly acceptable to the Divine Majesty. And should there be any difference of opinion among those who shall consider this matter, I beseech them, for the love and regard of God Our Lord, to recommend the matter earnestly to His Divine Majesty, that His most holy will may be wholly done, for His greater glory, the greater good of souls, and of all the Society, and that all may ever and always tend to the greater praise and glory of God.

In compliance with the Saint's desires the assembly put his proposal to the vote, although it was beforehand fully resolved not to accept of his resignation. It was unanimously rejected. This decision was very painful to Ignatius, and he now put all his hopes in the sickness from which he suffered, thinking that death would deliver him from the burden he found so heavy. But he was still necessary for the development of the work he had begun, and God, by leaving him upon earth, willed that he should still for a season bear the yoke. He did so with patience, setting a firm foot to meet the new trials which were reserved for him to encounter.

# CHAPTER IV.

IGNATIUS APPEASES THE ARCHBISHOP OF TOLEDO, WHO HAD SUSPENDED THE SOCIETY IN HIS DIOCESE. THE FAULTS OF SIMON RODRIGUEZ, PROVINCIAL OF PORTUGAL.

THE Society had founded a college at the University of Alcala, and the Fathers of that house had labored in tranquillity to the satisfaction of all parties, from the year 1544, in which it was first established, to 1551, when Cardinal John Siliceo, the archbishop of Toledo, very suddenly and without any cause, suspended them from the priestly functions which they exercised in virtue of the powers granted them by the Pope. An account of the whole proceeding is preserved, written by the secretary Polanco in the name of Ignatius. The Archbishop ordered his Vicar at Alcala to publish from all the pulpits a decree by which, under pain of censure, he forbade the priests of the Society to preach, hear confessions, administer any Sacraments, or even to say Mass. The Fathers, on whom the blow was inflicted, were only apprised of it just before the publication of the decree. They immediately took the necessary step of showing the Vicar-General the powers they had received from the Holy See. As the Vicar-General was their friend, he asked for a copy of the document, and sent it immediately by a courier to the Archbishop. Notwithstanding this representation, he gave a fresh order for the publication of his decree, to the great scandal of almost the whole diocese. The superiors of the Society sent an account of the transaction to Ignatius, and at the same time memorialized the Castilian Council of State, showing the powers they had received from Rome. The Council immediately gave orders to all the officials of the govern-

ment in Spain to support the Society in the exercise of
its privileges, and commissioned the Governor of Toledo
to communicate to the Archbishop the apostolic powers
bestowed upon the Company. Upon the receipt of this
decree of the Council of Castile, the Jesuits, who had left
Alcala, returned and presented it to the Chapter, which
forthwith placed its church at the disposal of the Fathers,
with full leave to exercise in it all their priestly functions.
But neither the order of the Council nor the letters of
the highest personages in favor of the Society made any
impression on the Archbishop; they had only the effect
of increasing his ill-will against it. In this extremity,
Ignatius was obliged to have recourse to Pope Julius
III., and beg him to assist the Society in whatever
manner he should judge most convenient. The Pope,
at first, would not employ any vigorous measures; he
merely wrote by his Secretary of State, Cardinal Maffei,
to the Archbishop and to Cardinal Poggi, his Legate in
Spain. In his letter to the Archbishop he spoke words
of commendation of the Order, saying that it was "beloved, cherished, and esteemed by all the present Christian world." But all this gentle dealing only met with
a rude opposition from the prelate, who continued to
resist the will of the Pope and the request of Philip II.,
as far as he could without coming to an open rupture.
At last he yielded, but not before Poggi threatened
him with the severest measures. He then published a
decree in which, without any indication of his regret
for what he had done, he menaced with ecclesiastical
punishment all who should trouble members of the Society of Jesus in the exercise of the functions which they
were authorized to discharge by the Holy See. Ignatius
had foreseen the issue of this affair, and upon the first
news he had of it said to Ribadeneyra, with his usual
calmness: "This contradiction is for our good, for we
have not deserved it. It shows that Our Lord intends
the Society to produce much fruit, for where we have
done the most good, we have the most suffered. The
Archbishop is old, and the Society is young; it will, in
the natural course of things, live longer than he." *

* Ribadeneyra, iv., 4.

As soon as he learned the happy issue of this difference, he wrote immediately to the Archbishop, to the Legate, and to Philip, to thank them, and, at the same time, to Father Villanova, the rector of the College at Alcala, to advise him not to make use of the privileges of the Society, without the approbation of the Prelate, a rule so much recommended by St. Francis Xavier.    The letter to Siliceo was couched in the following terms:—

Although it may seem somewhat singular in me to write to your Eminence, it cannot be considered a singular thing for a person who has received benefits to feel and to show lively sentiments of gratitude. Being informed that your Eminence has been pleased of late to do honor to our little Society, I consider myself bound to pray the infinite goodness of God to repay you liberally and to give you an eternal recompense.    Besides acknowledging the debt of gratitude, which I must leave to Him to repay for Whose love you have done us this good, I have deemed it my duty to write to you and to declare that the benefits your Eminence has conferred upon us shall not find us ungrateful. And although the services which our poor Society can offer to one in so high a place in the Church of the Lord our God are but insignificant, I humbly beg your Eminence to consider us as entirely yours in Our Lord, and to make use of us as such for the greater glory of His Divine Majesty.    We look upon you, and shall always look upon you, as our lord and our father ; and as a proof of these sentiments, I have written to our Fathers, both at Alcala and elsewhere in Spain, not to receive any person into the Society without the approbation and consent of your Eminence.    Although the Apostolic See has granted us many favors to aid us in procuring the salvation of souls, I have nevertheless written to our Fathers not to make use of them except so far as you shall see good to call them to your assistance and to share with them the heavy burden which God has laid upon you.    As I attribute to your high understanding and zeal for the glory of God the measures which your Eminence has taken against us before you were well acquainted with us, so I am persuaded that for the same motives, now that we are better known to you, your Eminence will become our protector, our lord, and our father, and will more than all the prelates of the realm aid us to fulfil the pious projects which the Author of all good shall give us to perform for the glory of God and the salvation of souls.
    Rome, June 1st, 1552.

Ignatius wrote also to Philip II. a few lines of acknowledgment, which we cannot omit.    He says—

The love which I owe to your Majesty, and the desire I have to serve you, oblige me daily to have you in remembrance before God, our Master and our Creator.    But I have thought it my duty to write to you especially on this occasion, in all humility to express my thanks to your Majesty for the favors you have done us all, not only in past times, but also for protecting us in the difference we have had with my Lord Archbishop. May your Majesty have, for your blessed and everlasting reward, God, the eternal and sovereign good. It was for His glory that your royal and Christian heart has already honored us. I hope that your Majesty will continue with fervor and kindness to honor this little Society of ours, which is entirely and altogether God's own.*

Ignatius also writes to the Rector Villanova the following letter—

As the privileges accorded to our Society by the Holy See are employed with greater fruit to souls when we take the precaution to act in concert with the Pastors of them, and as this precaution ought to be specially observed in the diocese of Toledo, whose prelate, as I do not doubt, will regard favorably all that is done for the greater glory of Our Lord God, I think it my duty to recommend to you by this present letter, to depart in nothing from the intentions of his Eminence in preaching, administering Sacraments, or other functions which concern the good of our neighbor. In the hope that the Lord Archbishop will prove to you a father and a master, and will support you in all that can serve to the increase of our Institute, and to the glory of God, I wish that no one whosoever be received into the Society in Spain contrary to the will and the judgment of his Eminence. I charge you with the execution of this order. You must take care to comply with it.†

June 1st, 1552.

This trial came from without, and although it was painful, it cost him much less time and trouble than one which came to him from Portugal on the part of Father Simon Rodriguez. With good intention, no doubt, Rodriguez had introduced a method of spiritual conduct among the Religious whom he governed with the best of intentions, but it departed from the spirit of Ignatius. The Saint had summoned Rodriguez to Rome in 1545, and again in 1550, to give an account of the state of things in Portugal, and to take back with him the manner of life and the method of government practised in Rome, under the eyes and direction of Ignatius himself. Accordingly he wrote in the summer of 1549 to John III., to be pleased to allow Master Simon to absent himself from the August of that year until the month of April in the year following. But

---

* I have translated this letter from a fresh copy of the original preserved in the royal archives of Simancas. I must, however, observe that the rough draft of it found in the collection at Rome differs in many places from this copy.

† This letter is found in the collection at Rome, and in the *Varia Historia*, p. 102.

the King would not allow him to leave before the commencement of 1550, because he required him until that
time for the education of his son, the Prince and heir-
apparent.　Father Louis Gonzalez took his place in this
important charge.　It was very natural that Ignatius
should wish, after so many years, to see again his old companion, and again in some sort to renew his acquaintance
with him.　He wished to learn from a personal interview
with Rodriguez what principles he followed in the government of the important province of Portugal, especially
as he was well aware of the peculiarities of his character,
which had at a former time nearly caused him to quit the
Society.　Ignatius eventually thought it necessary to deprive Rodriguez of the post which he occupied, though
he did not carry his purpose into execution until the
following year.

Rodriguez had trained and formed the greater number
of the members of the Society in Portugal ; they were too
much accustomed to him and his method, and it was time
to put an end to his too great personal influence.　Moreover, Ignatius desired to introduce into Portugal the
Constitutions which had been lately approved.　Many
customs authorized or established by Rodriguez were in
opposition to his own Constitutions.　This divergence of
laws between the Society at Rome and the Society in
Portugal was a grave inconvenience.　Now Rodriguez did
not seem to be the man to whom the making of this change
could be confided.　Moreover, it would show a consideration for the good name of Rodriguez to intrust this
business to the hands of another.　Besides, he had been
superior and provincial in Portugal more than twelve
years, and the Constitutions forbade superiors to be left
in office more than three, consequently he had no right to
keep his place any longer.　Ignatius well knew the state
of the province, but he did not know whether the King
would give his support to any changes ; in fact, he
thought it possible that very disagreeable results might
follow.　Although he did not, indeed, fear the difficulties,
yet he took his measures with the greatest prudence and
consideration.　He wrote to John III. and several members of the royal family, communicating his design to

them, and the motives which had determined him in the action he was taking, so that he might have them on his side. He gave free choice to Rodriguez either to go to the Brazils (as he had himself previously requested) or to Aragon as superior, and he named Father James Miron provincial of Portugal in his place. He put the execution of this order into the hands of Father Michael Torres at Salamanca, and of St. Francis Borgia, whom he commissioned to go from Guipuscoa for the purpose. He sent to Father Torres credentials to present to the King, and a number of blank papers signed, to make use of as occasion required. But as the King entered perfectly into the views of St. Ignatius, and understood the necessity of the appointment of another provincial, and as Father Rodriguez at first submitted with every sign of the most perfect obedience, and resigned the province into the hands of Father Miron, there was no occasion at this time for the two commissioners to undertake the journey.

All this took place in the month of May, 1552. But it was not long before a change came over Father Rodriguez, and, under the pretext that Ignatius had once recommended him to do nothing but with the King's consent, he addressed himself to him, and asked if he consented to this change. The King replied in the affirmative, upon which he put forward the plea of health, which, he said, prevented him from going to the Brazils or Aragon. He left Lisbon, however, for Coimbra, where the Jesuits had a large college. No sooner was he there, than he manifested great discontent, which was increased by the imprudence of the Superior, and which greatly disturbed the order of the House. Upon this, Father Torres went thither, and commanded the ex-Provincial to leave immediately for Aragon. The King wrote at the same time to induce him to do so; he obeyed, and quitted Coimbra in the month of August. All difficulties now seemed at an end, and Torres was already on his way back to Salamanca, when Father Gomez, a companion of Rodriguez, repaired to the Court with some other malcontents, and set on foot measures to obtain, by the intervention of the King and other great persons, the

restoration of the old provincial.   In order to attain this
end, they tried to represent the measures which St. Ignatius had taken as pernicious, and they strove to throw
discredit on his prudence.   But they did not meet with
the reception they had expected from King John, who
sent for Torres and St. Francis Borgia to Portugal.   The
schism which threatened to disturb the Society in its
early years was stifled in its birth by the firmness of the
King and the wise precautions of St. Ignatius, who with
a firm hand laid open the hidden sore and prevented it
from sinking deeper into the body.   He wrote the
following letter of thanks to the King, his friend and
protector—

Ever since the Lord our God has inspired your Highness to take
under your protection this, our little Society, which is entirely devoted
to you in Our Lord, you have always shown yourself not only as a
royal prince towards it in the care you have taken of it, but also as a
true father.   I have been informed by Ours of the late conduct of your
Majesty, with regard to the government of the Society, and in circumstances in which it was most nearly interested.   I rejoice that all has
turned out for the best by the assistance of the Holy Ghost, Who has
chosen your Majesty as the instrument by which to effect this good.
I and all of us have felt ourselves under the deepest obligations to your
Majesty ; but the kindness and the goodness which you have lately
shown us have increased this obligation to an extent which I cannot
express.   May Our Lord Jesus Christ, whose divine love has inspired
your Majesty's most Christian heart, give to you a foretaste in this life
of the recompense He will render to you in life eternal. *
Rome, September 24, 1552.

Rodriguez had no sooner arrived at Aragon than he
plied St. Ignatius with letter upon letter to allow him to
return to Portugal.   Ignatius acted towards him with
the greatest consideration, and, after a little while,
granted him his request in the following letter, which is,
on many accounts, most worthy of being written here in
this history—

I see, [he says] by your letter of the 26th, that you are ill at ease in
the country where you are, on account of your infirmities, and that
your office is a source to you of many annoyances ; and therefore you
ask me, for these two reasons, to allow you to return to Portugal,
even without any office.   I am so willing to do everything I can in
Our Lord to give you satisfaction, that I find no difficulty in granting

* Collection at Rome.

what **may** content you. I think I am the more bound to do so, and to spare you the exterior inconveniences of which you complain, by reason of your corporal infirmities being so very serious. I give you, therefore, permission to return to Portugal, and to breathe your native air, which will re-establish your health, and to live there without the charge of any office, as you desire. However, as you have hitherto served the Society by your cares and exterior labors, so it is to be looked for from your charity, during the time it shall please Our Lord God to preserve you upon earth, that you should aid it by your prayers and fervent desires, asking of God to promote by it His own glory and the salvation of souls. It is in this sense that I grant to you the time you ask for thinking on your own salvation, without any charge or office. After what I have said, I think that you will find St. Felix *quite the place to suit you, where you will find the air, the water, and the site all that you can desire. At the same time, whilst you have the leisure which you ask for, to give your soul spiritual entertainment, you will also have opportunity, if you choose, to assist your neighbor in the vicinity. To facilitate your return to Portugal, I have written to the Provincial to procure for you every kind of convenience for your bodily comfort, so that nothing may be wanting to you, and for the rest to leave you to do whatever it shall please you in Our Lord, without imposing on you any penance or mortification, but at the same time without the power of permitting you to change your place of residence. I think I have thus satisfied the desire you have expressed of not being subject to any one except to me. As to the false reports which, you say, they have sent me from Portugal, and which you ask to be informed of, I think it is better not to attach importance to things of this kind, and to bury the past in oblivion, when there is explanation to be made on both sides; for it is not pleasant for a Father to be told about his children, or for children to be told about their Father, things that it would give them pain to know. What I can truly tell you is that, according to the news I have from Portugal, you are beloved by all; and that is enough. †

When St. Ignatius wrote this letter, he knew nothing at all of the false step taken by Father Gomez. He soon received the account of it, however, from Father Michael Torres, who informed him of the true state of things. In consequence of this communication, Ignatius changed his resolution, and on the 17th of December wrote to Rodriguez, saying that he must submit to the decision which the Provincial of Portugal, together with the three or four other Fathers, should make in his regard. These Fathers should be nominated by Ignatius himself, and the orders they should give must be regarded by

* The name of the country house belonging to the College of Coimbra.
† Collection at Rome.

Rodriguez as a command from himself. They would assign to him the place they thought the best for him, either in one of the Houses in Portugal, or elsewhere. Meantime he commissioned Father Miron, the Provincial, to send to Rome all those who should refuse to submit to the new order of things. We give an exact translation of this characteristic letter—

By the information of Dr. Torres, whom I have sent in my place to visit you in Our Lord, I have learned that some, yea, even a considerable number among you, are wanting in that virtue which is the most necessary and most essential to our Society—a virtue in which we ought to be distinguished, because the Vicar of Christ, in the Bulls of our Institute, recommends it to us in the most forcible manner ; I mean honor, respect, and perfect obedience to superiors, who hold over you the place of Jesus Christ. You may well imagine from what you have heard from me that I heartily desire this virtue to be practised by my brethren, as I myself am bound to practise it. How great would have been my satisfaction to learn that there is not one among you who would have been so disrespectful to his superiors as to say, " You have no right to command me this," or "it is not proper that I should do that : " and to know that there are none who refuse to do what is commanded them. How glad I should be if you did not show by signs and acts (as I hear some of you now do) the little respect you have for *him* whom you ought to honor as the representative of Our Lord Jesus Christ, and to whom you ought to humble yourselves in all things in the presence of His Divine Majesty. This insubordination comes from the fault, I think, of *one* (Rodriguez) who has not employed the necessary remedies to put a stop to the evil, as it was his duty to have done. May God Our Lord pardon him. It would have been better to lop off from the body of the Society some rotten members, and so save the sound ones, rather than expose the good to the contagion of so great an evil by keeping the bad. I have informed you some time since that it was a thing very agreeable to me to hear that Master Leonard (Kessel) at Cologne had dismissed nine or ten individuals who were not conducting themselves as they ought. He dismissed as many more a second time, and I again approved of it, although it would, perhaps, have been enough to send away one or two at first if the evil had been withstood at the beginning. Though the remedy be employed too late, it is better late than never.

If there be any among you who refuse to obey, not only yourself, but any others of the local superiors or rectors in Portugal, I command you, by virtue of holy obedience, and as you shall answer to me for the execution of this order, to dismiss them from the Society, or else to send them to Rome, in case you shall think that the subject may be bettered by this change, and may so become a true servant of Our Lord Jesus Christ. Communicate to their Royal Highnesses, if requisite, this order, and I do not doubt they will approve of it according to the spirit and goodwill which the Lord Our God has given them. In fact, to keep men who are not true children of obedience is not for the good of their realm ; and we must not think that such Religious will save the souls of others when their own is so dead, nor that God will make use of them as instruments of His glory. Experience proves that men of moderate or even inferior talents are often the best instruments, and produce more abundant and more supernatural fruit, because, being sincerely obedient, they allow themselves to be conducted and directed by the almighty hand of the Giver of all good. On the other side, we see men of talent labor much and produce little fruit, because they are guided by themselves, or by their own self-love, or, at least, will not allow themselves to be directed by God through obedience to their superiors. Therefore they produce fruit accordingly, not with the almighty hand of God Our Lord, Who will not have them as instruments, but only with their own hand, which is weak and feeble.*

Rome, December 18, 1552.

Somewhat later Ignatius thought it best to summon Simon Rodriguez to Rome, for after all that had passed he found himself in a false position, and could be no longer of any use in Portugal. Ignatius informed him of his resolution in the most affectionate manner, and Rodriguez accepted his invitation. The following is the letter which the Saint wrote to him.—

Master Simon Rodriguez,—My dearly beloved son in Our Lord, I have read and attentively considered your letters of the 10th of February, the 23d and 26th of March, and the 12th of April, and many others which you have written to me before. I am of opinion, yea, I am quite satisfied, that your presence here is necessary for the repose and spiritual consolation of the members of our Society in Portugal. I have, moreover, need of you to consult with you on measures concerning the good of the whole Society, and I cannot treat of these things with you by letter. I have, therefore, resolved in Our Lord to command you to come to Rome, notwithstanding the fatigue to which the journey will expose you. And as the matter is of importance, I order you, on the part of Our Lord Jesus Christ, and in virtue of holy obedience, to come either by sea or land, as you shall think more convenient, and to come as speedily as possible. You will have, therefore, to put yourself on the way eight days after the receipt of this letter, and to continue your journey without delay: and I pray God to accompany and conduct you on the way.

My son Simon, believe me, your arrival here will be a source of consolation to your soul and to mine in Our Lord, and all what we both desire for the greater glory of God will be accomplished. Meanwhile, keep fervently before you the object we both have in view ; and if your sentiment of piety is not yet such as it ought to be, the Lord Our God will give it increase, provided you let nothing hinder you from the journey I bid you undertake. Remember, when I had no authority over you, you left for Portugal without delay at my proposal, though

* Collection at Rome.

you had upon you the quartan fever, and God restored to you your health.   How much more will this voyage be beneficial which you make under obedience, and when you are not so sick as you were then ?   Master Simon, take your departure immediately, as I have said, and be sure that we shall find here both spiritual and bodily health to the greater glory of God.   Leave all in perfect confidence to me, and you shall find yourself entirely content in Our Lord.*

Rome, June 12, 1553.

This circumstance gave occasion to Ignatius to compose his celebrated letter on obedience, which he addressed to the members of the College of Coimbra, on the 26th of March, 1553.   It is a letter which, however often it may be heard or read, supplies new lessons for our guidance in life.   It has been often printed, both in the original and in a translation, and we need say no more about it here.   On the same occasion Ignatius wrote a circular to the superiors of the Society, to recommend them to dismiss without delay all subjects of an intractable disposition; and, by a remarkable coincidence, St. Francis Xavier, in another part of the world, and without being acquainted with the circumstances we have just related, was doing the same thing the very same year.   It was in consequence of the occurrences in Portugal that Ignatius decided upon the recall of St. Francis Xavier from the great spiritual conquests he was making in the East.   He came to this resolution induced by grave motives, which he set forth in a letter addressed to Xavier about this time.   Francis Xavier, however, was already dead, and he could not obey the call.

* Collection at Rome.

# CHAPTER V.

THOUGHTS OF ST. IGNATIUS ON THE PROPAGATION OF
THE FAITH BY DESTROYING THE CORSAIRS AND THE
MARITIME POWER OF THE TURKS. THE CARE HE
HAD FOR THE EAST, AND PARTICULARLY FOR THE
HOLY LAND. NEGOTIATIONS ON THE SUBJECT WITH
THE LATIN PATRIARCHATE OF ABYSSINIA.

THE history of this epoch continually makes mention of
the ravages and the audacity of the Mediterranean pirates,
whose plunderings and incursions menaced perpetually
the coasts of that sea. The two brothers Horuc and
Heiradin having by treachery gained possession of the
States of Tunis and Algiers, created for the Turks a kind
of empire over the Mediterranean Sea. The Emperor
Charles V. undertook, in 1555, an expedition against
Tunis, and though it was successful, the piracies did not
cease, and commerce was almost paralyzed. From all
parts there came a universal cry for help, and Charles,
to satisfy the request, made a second expedition against
Algiers, which, it is well known, unhappily failed. This
defeat naturally increased the audacity of the Moors, and
they took vengeance, with more cruelty than ever, on the
defenceless coasts. The Emperor ruled over the most
extensive empire that ever existed in the world, yet its
strength was frittered away by his wars with France, whose
increasing power awakened both his jealousy and fears.
He was indeed victorious, but his victories crippled his resources. He left unsolved the great problems of the day,
and he suffered the German empire to fall into anarchy.
The piratical Turks, who were but as a miserable handful in
comparison with his own vast armies, set him at defiance ;
his subjects were pillaged, and many of them were dragged
away into slavery, losing not only their liberty, but what

is more, their faith. Could the wise men of the time blindly shut their eyes to the danger and disgrace which such a state of things involved? Ought not the great and eminent minds of the time, if they could not actually solve the questions, take them at least under their serious consideration? We are not, then, surprised to find that Ignatius, whose solicitude for the good of his brethren and the advancement of the Kingdom of God was so ardent, should turn his thoughts to the solution of a difficulty involving the salvation of so many souls. The affairs of this world were to him a matter of perfect indifference; his eyes were fixed on eternal goods. He was blind to political questions, and he forbade his followers to mix in them, but he could not be insensible to the sufferings and dangers to which immortal souls were exposed, nor to the hindrances put by the passions of men to the progress of the Kingdom of God. In such a crisis he neither could nor ought to have been indifferent ; he burnt the rather with an earnest desire to contribute all he could to the true advancement of civilization and the welfare of humanity. Urged by such high motives to consider the question of the States of Barbary, he conceived a plan which, had it been put in execution, would have infallibly succeeded. Its object was to secure the preponderance of Christian Europe over the power of the Turks, and to give to some particular States a new political condition. It was like the last reflection of the ideas of the Crusades, but accompanied with a more perfect and sure knowledge of the means by which a successful result was to be obtained.

The plan of Ignatius, the purport of which was to combat the Turks and destroy the pirates, was written by his secretary, Polanco, and addressed to the Provincial of Sicily, Father Jerome Natal, who was commissioned to go, in 1552, to Portugal and Spain. Ignatius wished to have his opinion before taking any steps with the Emperor. As no written document is extant on the matter, it seems probable that Ignatius did not proceed further in this affair. We will give a brief and exact analysis of the projected scheme.

The Saint first remarks that he wishes to know Father

Natal's opinion, because he does not feel in himself the confidence necessary for setting his project on foot, adding that, if he had this assurance, he would ask counsel of no one, but would employ the rest of his life in carrying it out, would confer personally with the Emperor upon it, and would not be prevented from his purpose by any inconvenience that should arise. Nine reasons are given in justification of the enterprise, and then he develops the means for organizing a maritime power which should render success certain, with less expense to the Emperor than the measures which had been hitherto taken, but which had all proved unavailing. The first reason is the good of the Catholic faith, which is so seriously injured by the ravages of the corsairs; many of the captives deny their religion while they are in slavery, and so lose their immortal souls. The second is the responsibility incurred by potentates, who will have to give an account to God for the loss of these souls, and for the sufferings their subjects endure in a horrible captivity. They will repent, he says, at the Day of Judgment, for having preferred their revenues and their treasures to the souls and bodies of so many thousands of men for whom Christ died. Thirdly, the Turks, who formerly were but an insignificant maritime power, are now beginning to possess a formidable navy. They will infallibly ravage the rest of Europe, as they have already ravaged Greece; they will form alliances with individual States, as they have already done with France, and so weaken and subdue one by the other. Now this danger cannot be avoided without a considerable fleet. Fourthly, this fleet will deprive the Neapolitan revolutionists of the hope of support from the Ottoman Power and of succors from France, and will thus secure the western coast of Italy. Fifthly, France, by being kept within its natural bounds, will become more disposed for peace.* Sixthly, a stop

* It must be remembered that this paper was written the same year in which the Prince of Salerno, the leader of the Neapolitan malcontents, fled into France, and persuaded Henry II. to march against Spain. As this prince was too weak in power to undertake the expedition without support, he had recourse to Soliman, his ally, and induced him to send to the shores of Southern Italy a fleet of 150 galleys, under Dragut, which landed in Calabria and carried off much

will be thus put to the ravages of the Turks by their yearly descents upon the shore, and the expense of the coastguard in Spain and Italy be saved, which must now be kept up everywhere, in the uncertainty of the point on which the incursion will be made. Seventhly, the passage by sea between Spain and Italy would be secured. Eighthly, by the aid of this fleet the Emperor could obtain the dominion of the sea, the recovery of the coast of Africa, the liberty of Greece and the Isles, make new acquisitions in the East, and open its shores to Christianity; whereas, without a fleet, there was fresh danger of important countries being lost to Christendom, as is clear from the capture of Tripoli, not many years before. The ninth and last reason is that this fleet will sustain the honor and influence of the Emperor, both among Christians and infidels; it will place him in a position to carry the war into the enemy's country, instead of standing on the defensive at home; and it will secure that authority which is necessary for the protection of his own subjects in a considerable part of his dominions.

After having given the reasons for the equipment of a fleet, he shows the means by which it is to be raised and maintained. The Emperor, he says, cannot be in want of men, for he has a greater number than any prince in the world. He can procure the money requisite in many various ways. In the first place, the opulent Orders in his States, who had much more wealth than their wants required, could arm a considerable number of galleys.* Then the bishoprics and chapters could supply a large sum of money to fit out a mighty flotilla for the defence of Christianity. The four Orders of Knights were, by virtue of their foundations, obliged to contribute to these expeditions, both by supplies and personal aid, and negotiations might be entered into with the Pope on this

---

spoil. But it sailed away without having effected anything, after waiting a long time in the Gulf of Naples for the French fleet, which arrived too late. This unnatural alliance of France with the Turks drew upon it the just reproaches of Christendom.

* We know that the great Archbishop of Toledo, Cardinal Ximenès, equipped at his expense, for this same object, a fleet and an army (*History of Cardinal Ximenès*. Translated from the German by MM. Charles de Sainte-Foi and De Bermond, ch. xx.).

matter, since it concerned the general good of Christendom. Another source of revenue could be obtained from the contributions of other cavaliers and nobles, to whose honor it would redound to spend a part of their superfluities for so glorious an object, instead of wasting it in uselesss pomp and prodigality. The merchants would be willing to partake in the good work, for the sake of the security to commerce, and the maritime towns, as most exposed to danger, would naturally take part, together with the great cities generally, in fitting out and maintaining the maritime power. It would surely be more to their advantage to employ their wealth in such a way rather than let it be taken from them by the corsairs. The parties most interested in the measure ought to contribute the most towards it. Besides, the Emperor would find allies in the Kingdom of Portugal, the States of Genoa, Lucca, Florence, and Siena, who might supply their own proportionate contingents. And lastly, the Pope would in all probability unite with the Emperor, and thus there might easily be gathered two or three hundred sail to put to sea. So writes Ignatius.

This plan, which was not then made public, nor communicated to the princes of the states named above, was afterwards found to be a matter of absolute necessity. The time and occasion were for the present allowed to pass by. The alliance of Pope Pius V. with Spain and Venice only imperfectly fulfilled the desire of the General of the Jesuits. The proposal of Ignatius was the only one that could have accomplished the desired object, but the East, and especially the land of Palestine, has been at all times under a peculiar dispensation of Providence, and is a country that is still waiting for a master to govern it. Ignatius was warned, either by his conscience or by an interior admonition, that his pious purpose was not in accordance with the divine decrees, and he therefore abstained from taking the steps which were necessary for the execution of his plan. He acted wisely in so doing, for, apart from this consideration, the Emperor was no longer in a condition to realize this grand thought, and his political schemes were not of a character to rise to so lofty a view.

Ignatius himself had to experience, in 1554, the effects

of those evils which he had proposed to remedy. A member of the Society, John Gudani, a native of France, being on a voyage from Crete to Italy, was taken by Algerian corsairs off the coast of Sicily, and carried away to Africa. So soon as Ignatius was informed of this, he ordered the superiors in Sicily to make every effort and every sacrifice to ransom the captive Father, and to give him an account every week of the steps they were taking to obtain the freedom of the prisoner. He wrote also to the Viceroy, John de Vega, and requested his support. But this great solicitude only awakened the cupidity of the pirates, who increased the stipulated ransom, and so the deliverance of the captive was deferred rather than promoted by the means that were taken to secure it speedily.

We have seen from the first how Ignatius believed himself particularly called to act upon the destinies of the East, and especially of Jerusalem. Even after the guidance of the hand of Providence had fixed him in the West, and at Rome, he did not altogether abandon the cherished idea of his earlier years. Whoever is acquainted with history must acknowledge that there is no country more important in its bearings upon Europe than the coast of Syria. There are times when the most considerable questions of our politics here take their rise, and find, at is were, their centre in this spot. These questions are never definitively settled. Now Ignatius wished to awaken the dormant sympathies of Christendom for these countries, and to restore to Catholic unity the various sects which divide them. He was persuaded that this was the only means of giving these nations, which had fallen so low under the hand of the oppressors, a rallying point, to make a stand against the intolerable tyranny of Islamism. A gleam of hope shot before his eyes in the pious and persevering enthusiasm of a Spanish gentleman. Don Pedro de Zarata de Bermeo, Commander of the Knights of the Holy Sepulchre at Jerusalem, zealously endeavored to promote the interests of Christianity in the Holy Land. For this intent he addressed himself to Pope Julius III., from whom he obtained, in the year 1554, a Bull authorizing him to found, in the name of the Society of Jesus, three colleges in the East, which should belong to that Order, one at Jerusalem, one at Constantinople, and the third at Cyprus. The Pope, at the same time, erected an Archconfraternity of the Holy Sepulchre.* The following is a letter on the subject written shortly after this by Polanco, the secretary of Ignatius, to the Fathers at Louvain.

As yet no one has been sent to Jerusalem. However, three colleges of the Society are to be founded by the authority of the Pope, one at Jerusalem, which is to be the head-quarters, one in the island of Cyprus, and the third at Constantinople. In due time Fathers will be sent thither, and already many are eagerly asking to go. A few months since the Pope sent a patriarch to convert the Nestorians, who are very numerous in the East, and on the same occasion he declared in the Consistory that he purposed to despatch some of our Society to aid the patriarch. But since it is understood that access can be had to those parts through the Indies, it has been resolved to send succor from those quarters. It is probable that both the Nestorians and other sects will readily enter into relations with us when we have a college at Jerusalem, for it must be remembered that they flock from all parts to the sepulchre of Our Lord.

Ignatius supported with all his power the efforts of Zarata; but the object of the enterprise was too far away to interest the rich and powerful in Europe. Their minds were too narrow to comprehend the greatness of the idea; they had no heart to look forward into futurity, they were wholly absorbed by the special wants of their own homes. Such as had the power and the will to do anything at all asked at most for a college in the country or town in which they themselves dwelt. However, so soon as he received powers from the Holy See, Zarata repaired, with letters of introduction from St. Ignatius, to the Kings of Portugal and Spain, and to Francis Borgia, that he might assist him at the Court of Philip. Ignatius wrote to Philip the following letter—

The Cardinals, the Protectors of the Archconfraternity of the Holy Sepulchre, have begged me to send a letter along with the credentials which Peter de Zarata, Knight of the Holy Sepulchre, will present to your Majesty.* Their Eminences are of opinion that this letter may be of some use, on account of the favor your Majesty has always been pleased to show towards our little Society, though in truth the undertaking itself is a work of such excellent charity, that it recommends itself to all who have the least zeal for the glory of Our Lord Jesus

* Raynaldus, *Annal.*, an. 1554, n. 22.
† Philip was now king of Naples, at the date of this letter.

Christ and the good of souls, which He, as your Majesty well knows, loved so dearly. Any other recommendation, then, may seem superfluous. Our Holy Father, too, the Pope, shows, by the establishment of the confraternity, by the numerous spiritual graces conferred upon its members, by inscribing his own name the very first on the list, and by his zeal in promoting the work both at Rome and elsewhere, how much he has it at heart. He knows how it will serve to advance the service of God in the holy places, build churches, and afford many spiritual benefits to the Christians who come to them from all parts. It seems therefore certain that this work will eminently contribute to the glory of Our Lord Jesus Christ, for His Vicar upon earth so positively assures us that it will be certain to do so.

The said Knight of the Holy Sepulchre, who has obtained the Bull for this holy enterprise, has edified all here who have ever been acquainted with him by his virtues and integrity, and he has put himself at the head of this work without having in view any temporal interest, either present or future. On the contrary, it has cost him considerable expense and long labors. In our House, where he is well known, he is much esteemed, both for his own sake and for his zeal for the glory of Our Lord Jesus Christ.

I have no more to add to this statement than humbly to pray your Majesty to recommend the affair in which this good Knight is engaged throughout your kingdom and dominions as a pious and useful work to the greater glory of God and the public good. These my views and opinions I submit to your Majesty's judgment and to the line of conduct which the Eternal Wisdom shall inspire you to adopt, with the hope that, receiving from above abundant light from Heaven, you may do in all things whatever may promote God's greater glory. This is the only end which we all desire.*

Rome, October 26, 1554.

Ignatius adopted Salmeron's proposal of sending Simon Rodriguez with a companion to Jerusalem, after his summons to Rome in the year 1553. He was to wait there until a favorable opportunity presented itself of establishing the intended college. Rodriguez went no further than Venice, where he fell so sick that he was utterly unable to continue his voyage.

Philip II. gave the proposed plan to some commissioners to examine, as appears from a letter of Ignatius to Zarata, dated April 18, 1556, and the Saint concluded

---

* Collection at Rome. It appears from the date and contents of these letters that the Bull was given in the year 1554, according to the conjecture of Menchacha (p. 209), and not in 1553, as Orlandini pretends (xiii., 1). It must be added that this Bull is not to be found in any printed collection, not even in the Pope's Archives, having been lost, like many other documents, through the negligence of the librarians.

from it that the King was disposed to support the enterprise. The business, however, was dragging on slowly, when the King left for the Low Countries. The indefatigable Zarata followed him thither. Nor was this the only difficulty in the way. Jealousy in other quarters raised obstacles to the execution of the plan, as is proved by the fragment of a letter of Ignatius to Zarata, dated June 9, 1556, given in the Bollandists.* It is said there that certain Religious (the Franciscans) had made a request that the Saint would renounce in juridical form the right which by the Bull of Julius III. to Zarata had been given to him of founding a college at Jerusalem. He declined to do anything of the sort, on the ground that, an annual income of five hundred crowns for the support of a college in that city having already been bequeathed to him, it was unreasonable to ask him to renounce it. " Moreover," adds the Saint, " as we do not know what God Our Lord may be pleased to do through the poor instrumentality of this little Society, it does not seem to me to be right, or conformable to the spirit of God, to consent to the closing of the prospect of having a college in the Holy Land. And even were I to renounce it, this act would not bind the Society in any future time. But I do not think I can consent with a free conscience to a renunciation of this kind, even though it should appear unlikely that we should found a college there during my life. It is, of course, quite possible that this design may never be carried into execution, but we must not engage ourselves by a promise that it shall not be done." These words of the letter were prophetic, for his successors have made no more use of the Pope's permission than he made of it. As for himself, not many days passed away before he exchanged the earthly for the heavenly Jerusalem, that blessed abode for which he sighed to the very last moment of his life.

In connection with this subject we will place another event, though of a preceding date and with a different object in view, we mean the sending of a patriarch of the Society into Abyssinia. The Portuguese had established

* N. 876.

themselves on the coasts of the Red Sea, and had acquired great influence in Christian Abyssinia, which was torn into factions by civil wars. But just as in the Indies, so also here, the Portuguese looked to little else beyond their commerce and the wealth they amassed by it. Led by a spirit of avarice, they only sought to enrich themselves; neither did they give a single thought to any higher policy. They never even dreamt of civilizing the people that had fallen so low down in the scale of humanity, nor of forming with them relations of any lasting beneficence. Thus they were neither acquainted with their qualities, good or bad, nor with their wants and necessities. Their influence over the natives extended no further than their superior prowess in war. Relations of this kind must naturally produce on the one side contempt and oppression, and on the other a profound hatred of the powerful and conquering stranger, and a dislike of everything the selfish aliens would impose upon the conquered. St. Francis Xavier often complains of these evils in the most energetic terms, because they are the source of such woes to religion. The Court of Portugal did not know and was not willing to learn the extent of the mischief, for the reason that it did not think itself in a state capable of applying a remedy to it. The piety of the King and Queen was desirous of ending, or at least of alleviating, the miseries of the injured peoples, by procuring for them the blessings of Christianity; but they forgot that one of the greatest of earthly blessings is to elevate the mind of subject nations by a gentle and paternal government, and thus develop their good qualities, instead of treating them as a mere matter of barter and traffic, and consequently only imparting to them the vices of civilization. For this reason the Gospel made such little progress among these nations, and in Abyssinia the reunion with the Catholic Church, and the consequent restoration of Christianity, was only looked upon by princes as a political measure, inspired by a fear similar to that which arose in the Indies. The manners and conduct of Christians were far from corresponding with the truths they taught. The Society has shown at a later period to what extent the practice of the Christian faith can elevate and civilize the most ignorant and barbarous people.

John III. most sincerely desired, as we have said, to propagate the Christian faith, and so to heal the wounds of the wretched Gentile nations ; and he did what he could to further this object. Abyssinia also moved his compassion, and so early as the year 1546 he begged of Ignatius to send thither some of his Society to convert the native Christians and reunite the Church, debased by error and superstition, to the Holy See. Ignatius joyfully consented, and at once set himself to the task of writing rules with consummate wisdom for the conduct of the missionaries in case the project should be carried into immediate execution. He chose for this important affair Paschasius Brouet, in whom alone he found the qualities required for this expedition, as he says in a confidential letter to Father Rodriguez, which we here give—

If it be the will of God Our Lord that one of Ours go to Ethiopia, I think the lot will fall on Master Paschasius. If I had to choose, after having considered both in general and in particular, there is no other whom I should select. Now, supposing that a Professed Father alone were fitting for this post, which I do not, however, think necessary, in any case, he to whom it is confided ought to possess three qualifications, namely, virtue, learning, and imposing exterior, a robust health, and be of middle age. Now I think of no one who combines these three things so well as Brouet. Le Jay is too old, Master Laynez, though he is very virtuous, has no great personal presence, and is too delicate in health. Master Salmeron is too young, and still looks almost as young as when you knew him. Master Bobadilla is very subject to maladies, and, besides, is not very suitable for this work. The nine Professed Fathers of the Society, all of whom you know, are indeed fitted by their qualifications for the duties proposed to us, but Paschasius seems to me to combine them all in the highest degree. First of all, he is so good that we all look upon him in the Society as an angel. Besides his great learning, he has had much experience in the reform of dioceses and monasteries. While he was nuncio in Ireland, he was employed in this business more than any other of the Society has ever been, and he acquitted himself of it with wonderful ability, giving excellent decisions upon all questions proposed to him, for he is naturally very studious and laborious. He has always a number of cases, both reserved and not reserved, to solve, and he will find abundance of such sort of work in Abyssinia. He is, besides, of an imposing presence, of a strong and portly frame, and about forty years of age. May God Our Lord, through His goodness and infinite mercy, conduct and guide the whole affair, and settle it with His own directing hand as shall be most agreeable to His greater service and honor, and to the greater glory of His Divine Majesty.

Rome, October 26, 1547.*

The matter was protracted for many years without any serious measure being taken by the King to promote it. Ignatius more than once complained of this delay. For instance, in a letter of the 17th of January, 1549, which he addressed to a nobleman of the Court at Lisbon, he reminds him that the choice of a patriarch has been put off for three years, and observes that this measure would increase the influence and authority of the kings of Portugal by placing in their hands the choice of this prelate, chiefly on account of the vicinity of Abyssinia to their Indian possessions. He adds, "If grave reasons have hitherto hindered the King, it is impossible not to be moved to compassion at the sight of so many souls, who are neglected for so long a time. This consideration obliges all here (at Rome) who desire the consummation of the plan, to make every effort to promote it." However, the King took no serious steps till the year 1553.† He then wrote to Ignatius, begging him to choose twelve priests of the Society, one of whom should be patriarch, and another his coadjutor with right of succession. The Saint gives the following reply to the King—

I have received at the same time two letters from your Majesty by the hands of the Grand Commander, ‡ the first dated July 25th, and the second, September 30th, in which your Majesty requests us to send into the States of Prester John § a patriarch and coadjutor, with ten other Religious of the Society. And, indeed, the enterprise seems to us most worthy of your royal heart and of the zeal for the glory and service of God Our Master and Creator with which He has inspired your soul, for the propagation of the holy faith and the Christian religion. It has pleased His goodness and His providence to choose you as an

* Collection at Rome. Menchacha says (p. 176) that the Portuguese historian Tellez places the King's proposal in the year 1554, whilst Orlandini puts it back to the year 1546. The date of this letter shows that Orlandini is more correct.

† Orlandini (14, n. 112) is wrong in placing this event in 1554. This date does not accord with those of the following letters. At the same time it places beyond dispute the number of the missionaries.

‡ Don Alonzo, who was the Portuguese Ambassador at Rome.

§ The imaginary personage of the middle ages, for whom sometimes the Great Khan of Tartary and sometimes the Kings of Abyssinia were taken.

instrument to bring so many nations to His knowledge and service and lead them into the way of salvation. I cannot doubt that a crown of immortal glory is reserved for you in Heaven as well as on earth for this work, which is above all the other great things you have done.

I am not surprised that your Majesty has been pleased to make use of the members of our Society for this enterprise, and that you look upon them as something belonging to yourself. This employment is surely calculated to advance the glory of God. Would that we had (if it so pleased God) greater power and virtue to correspond with the high idea you have of it, and that we were more capable of carrying into effect the holy desires which the Giver of all good inspires into your heart for the conversion of nations. But He, through His divine power and goodness, will supply for our feebleness. I have named twelve persons, according to your Majesty's commands, and you will find in the letter of information which I send in this enclosure the judgment we form concerning them, and our opinion regarding the other points on which your Majesty wishes me to make proposals to you. The whole is in your Majesty's hands, and the wisdom of God will inspire you with thoughts which will best conduce to His service and glory, which is our only end. I have ordered this House and all the colleges in Rome to offer all the masses and prayers for five days with the intention of obtaining of God for me the grace of making a good choice, and I have commissioned those who are most enlightened to examine the matter most carefully. After having taken their advice about the smallest points, I have decided on proposing to you those whose names you will find in the information appended. Nevertheless, whatever your Majesty shall decide will be accounted by us as the best and most expedient, for the heart of the King is in the hands of the Lord. And I hope that the Lord Our God will take under His special guidance this enterprise, which is wholly for Him, and that He will direct your Majesty in mind and heart. I humbly beseech Him to cause your Majesty to make your decision as speedily as possible. You can do as we have done here, should it accord with your pious feelings—take five days to consider on the matter, and during that time bid all the members of our Society and other religious Houses to recommend this choice to God in their prayers and the holy sacrifice of the Mass. We shall thus receive many graces and consolations, besides the many others which your Majesty has conferred upon this our least Society, which is entirely at your disposal.

Rome, December 28, 1553.*

The mission of a patriarch of the Catholic Church into Abyssinia, suffering as it was from the ravages of schism and superstition, being decided upon, in accordance with the desire of the Sovereign of the country, it became the duty of Ignatius, in the interests of the Holy See and of his own Order, to take care that this prelate remained faithful and obedient, both to the Pope and to the Society.

* Collection at Rome.

This was the more necessary, because the only means of passing into the country at that period was by doubling the Cape of Good Hope. Besides, little trust could be placed in the dispositions of the princes who governed it, and there was reason to apprehend that they would make every endeavor to bring under their influence the stranger sent to be their patriarch, and that he would be liable to make a bad use of his position. To anticipate this inconvenience, Ignatius at first thought of putting the patriarch under obedience to a commissioner in the East, whose duty it should be to visit him from time to time. For this end, he took counsel on the matter with the most eminent ecclesiastics at Rome. He thought it also good to give to the patriarch two coadjutors with the episcopal character, with the right of succession to the see after his death. He did this on account of the distance and difficulty of access to those countries, which seemed to require the presence of a Bishop simultaneously at several different points. Now it is seldom that the inspiration of the moment can supply the superior with the necessary human prudence and attentive examination of circumstances and means, and it is still more rare to find instruments to his hand who can secure the accomplishment of the enterprises he would undertake. We cannot, therefore, be surprised that Ignatius, as he always did in matters of such great importance, gave to it such long and serious reflection, and put his hand to the work with extreme prudence and precaution, making use of every human means, as the letter proves which we shall presently cite, as well as the letter which Polanco afterwards wrote to King John, giving him information of the persons whom Ignatius had consulted. Two points, however, presented difficulties at Rome. It was thought strange and inconsistent with the dignity of a patriarch that he should be subjected to a commissary of the Order and to the visit of a superior. Objections were also raised to the number of coadjutors, because heretofore never more than one had been appointed to any bishop. As to the first point, not one of the members of the Society would accept of the dignity of patriarch unless he remained under the obedience of the

Order; and the advantages of this were so much in favor of the interests of the Church, that they compensated for the apparent irregularity. The second proposition of Ignatius with regard to the coadjutors was also adopted. He chose, then, for patriarch, the Portuguese Father, John Nuñez Barreto, and for his coadjutors, Melchior Carnerio, another Portuguese, and Andrew Oviedo, a Spaniard. Ignatius contented himself, however, with merely putting before the King these three Fathers for the first places, leaving to him the choice of the patriarch. The King, agreeing with the Saint, chose Nuñez. When the matter was so far in progress that they only waited for the expediting of the Bulls, Ignatius wrote to the King, to give him an account of the negotiations, the following letter—

In my last letter, of the 23d of July, I informed your Majesty that the eight priests of our little Society who are under orders to go from Rome and Castile, according to your commands, to consecrate themselves to the service of God in Abyssinia, were ready any day to set out. As to the business with which your Majesty has been pleased to intrust me, according to the habitual desire which the Lord Our God has given you of showing the interest you have in all that concerns us, I have thought it best in Our Lord that your ambassador would do well were he to push on the negotiations with His Holiness, and to press the expediting of the Bulls and Briefs, because he represents the person of your Majesty, and in that capacity has the greatest power with every one here. The second reason is, that in this matter we are treating about dignities. Every one knows what this word signifies when the honor alone is considered, without the appendages, which make the counterpoise; and therefore it seemed to me more convenient that the negotiations should be transacted rather by him than by us. We make use, therefore, of the commission which your Majesty has given him, and we leave the whole affair in his hands to ensure its success, for he is, in all that concerns the service of Our Lord and of your Majesty, both able and expeditious. He has willingly consented to undertake it, and we on our part will be careful to point out to him what shall seem advantageous for the progress of this work, which is of such moment for the glory of God and the salvation of souls.

It appears that upon expediting the papers, the Committee made some difficulties as to the number of coadjutors, saying that it was a new thing to name two. We are not surprised at this objection. However, as they are ordinarily given for countries very near, it seems that two can very well be allowed for such distant lands, and that the novelty in canon law can be admitted in so novel a case. It has also been observed that the nomination of a commissary, who shall reside in the Indies and visit the patriarch, is not necessary for the present. We allow this to be true, but if a commissary be appointed now, when it is not necessary, the precedent will be established in case that it should be necessary to name one at some future time. The thing will not then seem a novelty, and the patriarch cannot be offended, nor complain that they have sent a Visitor because they are displeased with him. This would always be a check upon those who should require it, for they would know that there is some one near them who can visit them, and he who should not require it would lose nothing by having him as a witness of his good administration. The matter presents the less difficulty, inasmuch as he who is designated by your Majesty as patriarch desires to have a commissioner given him. Other objections besides these have been raised, as is always the case where something new is proposed. But as your Majesty's ambassador will write to you on this subject in detail, I will say no more, and will only beseech your Majesty to be pleased to make known to us your decision as soon as possible, that the papers may be expedited in due time. And if in these difficulties, or any others that may arise, your Majesty would be pleased to refer them to your ambassador, I am persuaded that God has given him such zeal and ability in Our Lord in all that concerns His holy service and yours, that he will always know how to proceed for the best, both for the one and the other. In any case, our Fathers will take their departure in the month of September, as the ambassador is of opinion that they should not wait for the expediting of the Bulls, and I am of the same opinion.*

Rome, August 27, 1554.

In fact, Oviedo and Carnerio, with several others, set out from Rome about the middle of September, for the letter of recommendation written by Ignatius to the King is dated the 15th of that month. These two Fathers and Nuñez were not consecrated bishops until the following year, at Lisbon. Ignatius wrote to Nuñez to say that he granted him, according to his request, another priest for the mission of Ethiopia—provided the King thought it good—so that he should take with him twelve companions, over whom he was to have authority as his own representative, as well as over all the members of the Society who should be sent into that country. But for the present he would not have a commissary named to whom the patriarch should be subject. He contented himself with the appointment of a Visitor, not by a Papal Brief, but by his own nomination, by virtue of a verbal concession granted him by the Pope. The Saint also sent a letter † to the so-called Prester

* Collection at Rome.
† This letter, dated February 23, 1555, is to be found in Menchacha (iv., 13).

John, the King of Abyssinia, whose real name was Claudius. We here give this remarkable document and memorial of the faith of Ignatius, and our reason for doing so is the more necessary, because the translations which have been made of it into various languages do not perfectly nor exactly render the original Spanish.

The most illustrious King of Portugal, moved by the great zeal imparted to him by God, our Master and Creator, for the glory of His holy name, and for the salvation of souls purchased by the precious blood and the death of His only Son, has informed me by his letters at various times, and by his ambassador, of his desire that I should name twelve Religious of our least Society, called the Society of Jesus, of whom two should be coadjutor bishops, and the third should bear the title of patriarch. They are to labor for the reunion of your church and kingdom to the Church of Rome. In all this we are guided by the direction of His Royal Majesty, who is moved by his earnest zeal to send them to you. On account of the obligations which bind this new Society to the service of His Majesty, I have given him the religious men whom he has requested, and have also, by his ambassador, prayed our Holy Father, Julius III., Pope of Rome, and Vicar of Christ upon earth, to be pleased to grant to them the powers and authority which they require for the exercise of their office in the dominions of your Majesty. I have, therefore, obeyed the command of the most illustrious King John, and have chosen purposely the number twelve, to represent the Apostolic College of Christ Our Saviour, for there are twelve Fathers besides the patriarch. Being unable to take the journey myself, I am happy to see them depart to consecrate their lives to God in the service of your Majesty, and to impart the light of faith to the souls who are subject to your kingdom and your crown. Although the will of the most illustrious King of Portugal was sufficient of itself to make me obey his wishes, I am induced also by the thought that our Society may be able to render some services to your Majesty, whose interests we recommend to God in our humble prayers more than we do our own. We also give thanks to His Divine Majesty because, surrounded as you are by so many infidel nations and the enemies of the Christian name, you have, notwithstanding, so great a solicitude for the honor and glory of God, and because you endeavor, after the example of your forefathers, not only to preserve the faith, but to carry it to complete perfection.

It is, therefore, by a particular providence of God that, according to the pious and ardent desires of your Majesty, these Fathers come to the succor of your people, that, with full and legitimate powers from the Apostolic See, they may put an end to the division which has disturbed the harmony, in matters of faith, with Rome, the Mother of all the churches of the world. God has put in His own place upon earth His Vicar, for it is certain that the two keys of the Kingdom of Heaven which Christ gave to St. Peter are the symbol of the authority which He conferred upon him when He said to him, as we are taught by the Evangelist, St, Matthew, "I say to thee, thou art Peter, and upon this rock will I build my Church, and I will give to thee the keys of the Kingdom of Heaven; and whatsoever thou shalt bind upon earth shall be bound also in Heaven, and whatsoever thou shalt loose on earth shall be loosed also in Heaven." He promised him the keys, and He has fulfilled His promise. After His glorious and triumphant resurrection, before His ascension into Heaven, He asked of Peter three times, as we are assured by the Evangelist St. John, "Simon, son of John, lovest thou Me more than these?" and after each reply he added "Feed my sheep," * giving to him not only a portion of His sheep, but the whole flock, with unlimited power to feed the faithful with the food of life, and to pasture them and to guide them to the heavenly joys of eternal felicity. Christ has given to the other Apostles a limited power only, whereas He has given to St. Peter and his successors a full and unlimited authority, so that the other pastors of souls should receive from their Sovereign Pastor, as from a fountain-head, their share of authority, power, and jurisdiction, each according to the degree of the hierarchy which he holds in the Church militant.

Our Lord seems long since to have expressed this truth by the Prophet Isaias, regarding the Roman Pontiff, when He says, "I will put upon his shoulders the keys of the house of David: he shall open, and there shall be none to shut; he shall shut, and there shall be none to open." This prophetic image represents evidently the Apostle Peter and his successors, the Roman Pontiffs; for the keys which signify this power and supreme jurisdiction declare that they have received full and unlimited authority in Heaven and on earth. This being certain and without all doubt, your Majesty has reason to give thanks to God Our Lord that it has pleased Him to send in the happy days of your reign to your good people true pastors of their souls who are dependent upon the Sovereign Pastor and Vicar of Jesus Christ left in His place on earth. Now this Chief Shepherd has given to the Fathers I send to you the fullest powers, His Holiness having been pleased to cast his eyes upon them with a most particular zeal and intention, and to choose them for an enterprise which so much concerns the service of God, the good of your Majesty and of your kingdoms. All this being so, it is not without reason that the father and grandfather of your Majesty would not recognize the authority of the Patriarch of Alexandria in spiritual things, who, like a rotten and lopped-off branch of the mystical body of the Church, has neither received nor can receive life or vigor from this sacred body. For being a schismatic and separated

---

* Menchacha remarks that this passage is taken from the Abyssinian translation, which was "Feed my sheep," and not "Feed my lambs;" and that the well-known Greek Codex of Canterbury, in the 15th verse, gives the word "sheep" instead of "lambs." He proves from St. Augustine (*Tract* 123 *in Joan.*, cap. xxi.), and from passages of the Evangelists themselves, that the Vulgate makes no distinction between these two words, and that the lambs as well as the sheep may be in reference to the Apostles. In fact, St. Matthew (x. 16) says—"Behold, I send you as sheep," whereas St. Luke (x. 3) says, "as lambs;" and the Codex of Oxford has also, at verse 15, "as sheep."

from the Holy Apostolic See, which is the Head of the whole Church, he cannot lawfully communicate the life of grace nor the office and dignity of pastor, which he has not himself received, and which, therefore, he cannot legitimately give to others.

The Holy Catholic Church is, in fact, One throughout the whole world. It is One, and therefore it is impossible to acknowledge at the same time the Roman Pontiff and the Patriarch of Alexandria, as though the Church were in them both at once—in the one limited, and without limit in the other. As Jesus Christ, her Spouse, is One, so also the Church, His Bride, has ever been and still is One. It is of her that the wise King Solomon says in the Canticle, speaking in the Person of Our Lord Jesus Christ, " My dove is one." It is of her that the Prophet Osee speaks in a still more express manner—" The children of Israel and the children of Juda shall assemble together, and shall choose one head." And a long time after, Our Lord, in St. John, expressed the same sentiment when He said, " There shall be one fold and one shepherd." We read also in Holy Scripture that there was but one ark of Noe in which men could find safety, and that out of it no flesh could be saved ; that Moses raised but one tabernacle ; that Solomon built at Jerusalem but one temple, in which the law commanded that sacrifice and worship should be paid to God, and forbade it elsewhere ; that there was but one synagogue, the decrees and authority of which bound the others. All this is a clear and precise image of the unity of the Church, out of which there is nothing that is good, nothing that can live. For whosoever is not united to this mystical body cannot receive from Jesus Christ, its Head, the strength and grace necessary to obtain everlasting happiness. And in order that this unity of the Church may be still more evident, we recite the article of the Creed—" I believe in One, Holy, Catholic, and Apostolic Church."

That there can be particular churches, numerically and essentially distinct, is an opinion which has been condemned as an error and sin against faith by all the holy Councils which have been held upon this one foundation of the Church, under the special assistance of the Holy Ghost. It is therefore an error to say that the churches of Alexandria, of Constantinople, of Antioch, and Jerusalem, and other patriarchal churches, have or can have particular distinctions and privileges while they are not united with the supreme head of all the churches, that is, with the Roman Pontiffs, the successors of St. Peter, who by a particular command of God chose the city of Rome for his seat and consecrated it with his blood, as the holy Pope and Martyr Marcellus declares.\* The Bishops of Rome are acknowledged without dispute as

---

\* The letter to the people of Antioch attributed to St. Marcellus was held for authentic in the time of St. Ignatius, and it was only later that criticism tried to prove that the letter was not his. As to the phrase to which Ignatius alludes, it is supported on tradition ; and a purely subjective criticism, which sets itself to deny everything, cannot hinder the truth from being truth. Moreover, St. Leo the Great says (*Serm.* v. *de SS. AA. Petro et Paulo*)—" Thou didst bear within the walls of Rome the trophy of the Cross of Christ," etc.

Popes and Vicars of Jesus Christ, according to the prescriptions of the Catholic Church, by all the holy Doctors, both Greek and Latin. This faith is confirmed by a multitude of nations, of pious solitaries, of bishops, and an innumerable host of Confessors, by signs and miracles without number, and, in fine, by the testimony of the martyrs who have died for Christ and have confessed the unity of the Roman Church, on the solid rock of which their blood has been spilt for a witness.

It is in accordance with this faith that the holy Fathers, the bishops and prelates assembled in the Ecumenical Council of Chalcedon, with unanimous voice gave to Pope Leo, the most holy successor of the Apostles, the title of Ecumenical. The General Council of Constance has also condemned the error of those who denied the primacy of the Bishop of Rome over each of the other churches, and over all the churches of the world. To these holy and authentic decisions is to be added the authority of the Council of Florence, presided over by His Holiness Pope Eugenius IV., who at that time sat in the chair of St. Peter. There were present at this Council, among other nations, the Greeks, the Armenians, and the Jacobites; and all of them, with universal acclamation, and under the particular inspiration of the Holy Spirit, decided this article of faith, which they formulated in the following terms—" We declare that the Holy Apostolic See and the Bishop of Rome have the primacy over all the world, that the Pope is the successor of St. Peter, the true Vicar of Christ, the Supreme Head of all the Church, the Pastor and Doctor of all the faithful. We declare that Our Lord Jesus Christ has given him, in the person of St. Peter, authority over the whole Church, and the right to govern and to feed it with the plenitude of power." It is therefore with good reason that your Majesty's father, the most illustrious King David, through his ambassador, whom he sent to declare his submission to the Roman Pontiff, acknowledged this Holy See to be the mother and head of all the churches. Now, among all the great actions which preserve the memory of your illustrious father and of your Majesty, his worthy son, this is the principal one and the foundation of all the rest; it will make them endure forever, so that they shall never be forgotten. The subjects of your Majesty's vast dominions are bound to give perpetual thanks to God for the benefits they have received from you both, whose pains, courage, and zeal for the public good have been truly marvellous. It was your father who was the first to fling himself at the feet of the Pope, and to acknowledge him as a Pastor and Father; and you, in like manner, have been the first for the good of your realm to demand and obtain of the Vicar of Christ a patriarch who is a legitimate son of this Holy See.

If it be, as it surely is, a special and most precious grace to be united in the mystical body of the Catholic Church, which is animated and governed by the Holy Spirit, and this same Spirit, according to the testimony of St. Paul and the Evangelist St. John, teaches and suggests to this Church all truth; if it be a most precious gift to possess the light of the true doctrine, and to obey the commandments and the holy prescriptions of the Church, which the Apostle, writing to his disciple Timothy, styles " the house of God, and the pillar and ground of truth " —to which, moreover, Our Lord Jesus Christ has promised His assistance for all times when He says, by His Evangelist St. Matthew, " Behold, I am with you always, even to the end of the world ; " then these far-distant lands have surely great reason to render thanks to God, our Master and our Creator, for having granted them such a benefit by His divine mercy, through the liberality of this Holy See, the zeal of King David, your father, and your own distinguished piety and holy desires. And the more so, inasmuch as it may be justly hoped that this union and reconciliation will, by the divine favor, cause an increase of good, not only spiritual but temporal, by the aggrandizement of your already powerful kingdom and by the humiliation of your Majesty's enemies.

The priests who are setting out upon this holy enterprise, and especially the patriarch and his two coadjutors and successors, are men of a holy and irreproachable life. They have passed through all the probations of this our least Society, and they have been chosen for this work on account of their singular charity and profound learning. They have also the courage which is derived from hope founded in Heaven. Supported by this hope, they will be enabled to endure the pains and labors which they will encounter on their road, and even death itself, and by it they will make a sacrifice of all things for the glory of Our Lord Jesus Christ, the service of your Majesty, and the salvation of souls. They are moved by the sincere desire of making every possible effort for the salvation and regeneration of mankind, in imitation of the example of Christ Our Saviour, Who, for the ransom of the world, of His own will, endured sufferings, shame, and death, and has said to us, by His well-beloved Disciple and Evangelist, " I am the Good Shepherd ; the Good Shepherd giveth His life for the sheep." Moved by the example of their Master, these good priests and Fathers take their journey, eager to succor those who are in danger of losing their faith, not only by their words and by the good counsels and spiritual blessings which, with the grace of God, they take with them, but also, if occasion require, by their death, and so to seal with their blood their doctrine and their holy desires. I hope in Our Lord that, thanks to your goodwill, you will receive them with the greater favor, inasmuch as, both in private interviews or in public instructions, they can expound the truths of the faith as legates of the Holy See. Your Majesty may especially rely upon what the patriarch shall declare to you, for he holds the place of our Holy Father, the Pope. Whoever rests his faith upon the patriarch and those who are with him, rests his faith also upon the Catholic Church, in the name of which they interpret the Word of God. As it is right and necessary that all the faithful humbly bow their head to the sweet yoke of the Church, in obeying her decrees and ordinances, and in submitting their difficulties to the servants whom she has chosen to resolve them, I do not doubt that your Majesty's distinguished piety will take measures in all your states, so that all, of whatever rank and condition they be, shall accept without hesitation the prescriptions and decisions of the patriarch and of his representatives and companions.

The Book of Deuteronomy relates that it was the custom in the Old Law to have recourse to the Synagogue, which was a figure of the Church, in all doubtful and difficult cases. And the words of Our

Saviour declare the same—" The Doctors of the Law and the Pharisees sit upon the chair of Moses." Solomon says the same in the Proverbs —" Depart not from the teaching of thy mother," that is, of the holy Church; and again—" Transgress not the ancient landmarks which thy fathers "—that is, the bishops—" have set." In short, Our Lord Jesus Christ has in so express a manner commanded us to submit to the sentence of the Church, that the Evangelist St. Luke says—" He that heareth you heareth Me, and he that despiseth you despiseth Me." St. Matthew says, still more clearly—" He that heareth not the Church let him be to thee as a heathen and a publican." It follows from all this that we must neither listen to nor believe those who advance any assertion contrary to the sense of the Catholic Church, as St. Paul says very markedly in the Epistle to the Galatians—" Though an angel from Heaven preach a Gospel to you besides that which we have preached to you, let him be anathema." In one word, this doctrine is taught and established by the holy Doctors of the Church, by the decisions of Councils, and the general sentiment of all the faithful. The patriarch, then, and his companions, come to you in the assurance that your Majesty will receive them, as far as possible, with your accustomed piety, and with Christian deference and respect. As for us, the members of this least Society, who live in various parts of many countries, we offer ourselves to your Majesty as your spiritual servants in Jesus Christ forever, and we beg you to reckon us as such. We will entreat of the Lord Our God, in our prayers and at the altars, as we are on other accounts bound to do, that He may preserve your royal person and your vast dominions, with your good people, in the obedience and love of Jesus Christ, and that He will grant you so to use temporal goods as not to lose eternal ones. May the Lord Our God assist us all to do His holy will, and to walk with piety and devotion in the path of truth, giving us, in His infinite mercy, peace and strength so to continue forever. *

Rome, Feb. 16, 1555.

This letter, the incontestable truth of which is but too well confirmed by the lamentable state of all the churches separated from Rome, made a great impression upon

---

\* Collection at Rome. The Latin text of this letter, which Maffei first published in his *History of the Indies* (t. xvi.), seems to be only a translation, though all those who have published it since, and Menchacha too, have taken it for the original, because the Spanish text was unknown to them. I cannot, however, decide whether Maffei gives his own translation, or whether he has only reproduced a translation already existing. It is still more difficult to fix precisely the date of this letter, the original being long since lost in Abyssinia, but it must have been written between the 16th and 23d of February. Menchacha observes (p. 81) that the first and best editions of this letter bear the date of the 23d, but Father Tellez, the Portuguese historian, cited by Menchacha himself, gives the 16th of February in his *History of Abyssinia* (ii., 22), and so does the copy of the Spanish text in the collection of letters at Rome, from which we have given this translation.

John III., who would have it read to him, and extolled its principles and lessons with the highest encomiums. We shall say no more of the result of this mission in the sequel, as it does not come within the scope of our history.

# CHAPTER VI.

IGNATIUS REFUSES THE REQUEST OF THE BARNABITES TO
BE INCORPORATED INTO HIS SOCIETY. HIS RELA-
TIONS WITH THE CARTHUSIANS, ESPECIALLY WITH
THE PRIOR OF COLOGNE. THE CARE WHICH HE
TOOK IN THE REFORM OF CONVENTS AT BARCELONA.

THE Congregation of Clerks Regular of St. Paul and
St. Barnabas, commonly called Barnabites, had not long
before been founded at Milan. Laboring zealously and
successfully in their vocation, they felt the need of extending the narrow circle of their ministry, and of
attaching themselves to the Society of Jesus, a Company
yet younger than themselves, but whose progress was
drawing the eyes of the world upon it. There existed
already amicable relations between them and St. Ignatius.
These relations had been brought about by the charitable
care with which the Barnabites had entertained in their
house Father Miron of the Society, when he fell sick at
Milan, on his journey from Paris to Rome. Ignatius had
shown his gratitude for this kindness by services which
he had rendered in return; and thus in, 1552, they further
begged him, through the Archbishop of Genoa, Jerome
Sauli, to receive them into his Order. Ignatius replied to
the prelate that he fully acknowledged and appreciated
the good qualities and the good desire of the Congregation, but that he was persuaded it was more to the glory
of God, that the two Orders, united in heart, should remain separate in body, and, each apart, follow its first vocation.* This refusal was only natural, for every Jesuit
goes through a long training, and one peculiar to the
Institute. It could, therefore, be only prejudicial to the
Society (in which agreement and uniformity are an essen-

* Orlandini, xii., 13.

318

tial condition of existence) to admit into its body a number of men, many of whom were already old, and had followed a different kind of direction. Besides, Ignatius was no longer in a position to consent to this request. He had already twice refused an offer of the same kind, made by the Theatines, and had he consented to the admission of the Barnabites, the Theatines, who had so powerful a protector in Cardinal Caraffa, might not unreasonably have been offended.

The close union which had begun to exist at a very early date between Ignatius and the Carthusians had still greater value in his eyes. During the stay of Faber at Cologne, in 1543, this Father was received in the most kindly manner by the Prior of the Carthusians in that town, Gerard Hamonton, and his Monks, who, out of zeal for the Catholic faith, were most anxious to support its new defenders. Faber had given them the Spiritual Exercises, and continued after his departure to correspond with the Prior, who was not content with protecting the Society in Cologne. but endeavored to spread throughout his Order the sentiments of affection with which he himself was animated towards it. It was at his proposition that the General Assembly of the Order, held at the Grand Chartreuse, in 1554, passed a resolution to admit the new Society to the participation of all the merits of the Carthusians, and to join the two Orders together by the ties of a common fraternity. The Prior of the Grand Chartreuse, Peter de Leyde, communicated this their decision to St. Ignatius, in the name of the Chapter General, in the following letter—

Dearly beloved brothers in Our Lord,—We have heard of the good report of your exemplary lives and salutary doctrine, of your voluntary poverty and other virtues, by which you shine as lights in the midst of the darkness of our deplorable times, by which you recall back to the narrow path of salvation those who wander in the ways of perdition, by which you support the feeble and encourage the strong in the progress to perfection, and by which you thus produce, in Our Lord, much fruit for the Catholic Church. We rejoice in Our Lord and give Him thanks that, in the midst of the persecution under which the Church groans, and which afflicts us to the heart, He has remembered His mercy, and has been pleased to raise up and send new laborers into His vineyard. Desirous of aiding you in this holy work, according to our feeble powers, we conjure you, by the love of Him Who has given His life for us,

not to receive the grace of God in vain, but to persevere in your holy
purpose, and to show yourselves true servants of God in much patience,
and not to faint in the labors, dangers, and persecutions which are the
lot of those who live piously in the Lord, for you will one day reap, not
failing. For our part, dearly beloved brothers, if we can assist you in
anything before the Lord, we will support your pious labors in Him
by the offering of the Holy Sacrifice, by our prayers, our fasts, and our
other holy practices, of which we grant to you a special portion, to you
and to your successors, both in life and after death; desiring that you,
on your part, will make us participators in your spiritual goods and
your prayers, to which we commend ourselves.

Given at the Grand Chartreuse, 1544, Thursday after Cantate
Sunday.*

Ignatius, without doubt, sent a suitable reply to this
affectionate letter, but it seems to have been irrecover-
ably lost. The Prior of Cologne and the Saint continued
to correspond with much interchange of friendship, and
the Prior labored with great zeal to establish a college of
the society at Cologne, and assisted its members in that
city with abundant alms. Ignatius, whose poverty could
make no other return, sent to him from time to time, at
his request, some rosary beads indulgenced by the Pope,
recommending him to exhort those to whom he distributed them to practise their religious duties. He imparted to the Carthusians, in the same manner, a participation in the merits of the Society, as appears from
Orlandini, † who gives the date of 1548 to this correspondence. In the year 1549, Ignatius wrote the following
letter to the Prior—

To those who are united by the bonds of charity in Our Lord Jesus
Christ, and by the desire of procuring the honor and glory of God, the
most pleasing epistles are those which the Holy Ghost writes in their
hearts by mutual prayer. This notwithstanding, I have thought it
my duty to take advantage of the journey of our Brother Adrian, to
write to you and refresh your memory of us by him, and to ask of you,
in the name of Jesus Christ, for our little Society, which is yours also,
the prayers of your holy Community, in which we have such great confidence in Our Lord. I send you also twelve rosaries blessed by the
Vicar of Christ and enriched with very great indulgences, as Master
Adrian will fully declare to you, to distribute among your good Brothers
for the good of souls. I send you also a copy of the *Spiritual Exercises,* as I am assured by Master Adrian that this present, though
small in itself, will be acceptable to your charity and piety. He will
communicate to you more in detail all that you wish to know concern-

* This day fell that year on the 3d of May.        † ix., 74.

ing our Society. I salute you in Our Lord Jesus Christ, beseeching Him to grant us in His infinite goodness the grace to know and perfectly accomplish His will. Amen.*

Rome, March 28, 1549.

The friendship of the Prior reached as far as Rome in giving aid to Ignatius and the Society at a time of need, for at a moment of extreme necessity the Saint received from him a hundred crowns, for which he expresses his gratitude in the following letter—

May the boundless grace and eternal love of God and Our Lord repay your paternity and your pious community, making you increase in spiritual gifts. Although we have seldom written to your paternity of these late years, yet we have often held communion with you in prayer, and we have seen in the course of time that our reciprocal love, one for the other, so far from diminishing, has rather increased. We see it, on our part, in the lively remembrance we have of you and the ever-increasing regard we have for you, and we perceive that it is the same on your part, not only by the letters of our Fathers, who speak of the benefits continually conferred upon them by your paternity, but by the experience we have ourselves of your beneficence, which reaches us even at Rome, for which we give thanks to God, the Author of all good, and to your paternity. Your liberality has come in a time of need for the support of this college, and this testimony of your great affection has bound with closer ties our mutual friendship. May Our Lord Jesus Christ vouchsafe to repay you according to the riches of His infinite goodness for this benefit as well as for all the others which you have bestowed abundantly on His poor. Our Brothers at Rome are all well. The Lord has visited me with a sickness for six months, but I am somewhat better. Your paternity will be informed of the rest from our Brothers, to whom I write more in detail. We humbly commend ourselves to your paternity's prayers, and those of your venerable brethren, who are ours also, and more especially to your holy sacrifices of the Mass. We salute you in Our Lord Jesus Christ, Who is the life and the eternal good of all. Amen.

Rome, August 21, 1554.

The pious and liberal Prior answered the Saint in the following letter—

Fight the good fight with the armor of justice on the right hand and on the left, my venerable Father, whom I embrace in the arms of charity. I have received your letter, and I see that your health is somewhat restored, and that you are good enough to make me, sinner as I am, participator in the prayers and Masses of your holy community, to which I recommend myself and my brethren. I will never forget you, so great is the love with which the Lord has inspired me for you

* Collection at Rome. This letter was unknown both to the Bollandists and to Menchacha.

long since, through Master Faber, of holy memory. The small present I have sent you does not deserve thanks. I wish that the misery of the times permitted me to satisfy my inclination, and that I could find means to employ our superfluity in favor of your Society, which, I see, increases and continues in the good which it has begun. However, to do something, and to profit by the occasion which is offered me, I send you five hundred gold florins, for which I ask neither reply nor thanks, but silence and prayers, for I know you clerks (the Jesuits) live by the alms of the faithful, and that one is bound to dispense in good works our superfluity, as I propose to do, with the help of God, until my death, for the peace of my conscience, so long as I shall have, against my will, the government of this house Would that I could see before my death a college of your Society at Cologne. I have spoken much on this subject with the prelates and magistrates of the city, but these last have made difficulty. May God have mercy on us, and preserve your paternity with your holy Society as long as possible, to carry on the pious enterprise which you have begun for the good of His afflicted Church.

Sept. 27, 1554.

Ignatius had relations of a very different kind with other Religious Houses, not in maintaining, as above, an interchange of goodwill with a flourishing Order, but in restoring conventual discipline which had fallen into decay. A long time before, as we have seen, he had reformed a convent of Nuns at Barcelona. Francis Borgia, being appointed viceroy of Catalonia, followed in the steps of the Saint, and conceived a plan for the reformation of the Orders of religious women in all the province, and especially at Barcelona. He proposed the matter to Prince Philip, who wrote two letters to Ignatius, in 1546, to beg him to obtain the necessary powers at Rome. They were granted that same year for the city of Barcelona, and, at the beginning of 1549, for the whole province, as appears from the two following letters of Ignatius to the Prince—*

John de Vega, the Viceroy of Sicily, is writing to your Royal Highness, and sending the Bull for the reform of the convents of Barcelona. He is writing also to the bishops who are specially charged with this work, and he gives them all the necessary informatiom. But as the matter is one of great importance, and it is good that your Royal Highness should write with much warmth and charitable kindness to all the persons who are engaged in the work of this holy reform, and give them your command, it seems to me that your Royal Highness

* Orlandini (vii., 45) relates that the reform took place in Catalonia in the year 1547; but it was not completed in 1552.

ought to be informed of some particular circumstances to further the success of the business. As to the matters on which the Bishop of Barcelona has written to me, Dr. Torres, the procurator of the University of Alcala, who was at Rome when the Bull was expedited, to whom I have written all at length, will give your Royal Highness some information tending to the happy and holy issue of the undertaking, such as the unworthy and devoted servants of your Royal Highness desire, for the greater glory of God and yours. May God, of his immense and infinite goodness, give you recompense on earth, to His greater glory, and give you still greater in Heaven.

Rome, December 26, 1546.

## In a second letter he wrote as follows—

Your Royal Highness will receive with this letter the Briefs which you have requested for the reform of the convents of Catalonia, according to the pious and Christian desires which God Our Lord has given you. The ambassador of His Imperial Majesty (Charles V.), and of your Royal Highness has spoken with much warmth to the Pope on the subject of the expediting of these Bulls, and has shown the zeal in the matter which it so justly deserved, and which had been commended to him by your Royal Highness. The cardinals to whom your Highness wrote have done the same. Accordingly, the Brief is considered here very favorable and very effectual for the purpose in view, agreeably to the usages of this Court. We hope and pray that He Who has been pleased to grant your Highness the grace to begin this good work as well as so many others, will continue to assist you so as to complete it, for the honor and glory of His Divine Majesty, and for the necessities of so many souls. If it should be necessary that any other clauses be added to the Brief to attain the result more fully, it will always be possible to obtain them. And in so holy a thing set on foot by your Royal Highness, all those who have hitherto been employed, as well as others, if required, will not fail to labor with zeal in all that shall be considered best for God's service and the service of your Royal Highness.

Rome, Feb. 28, 1548.

Philip put the execution of the Pope's Briefs for the restoration of conventual discipline into the hands of Father Araoz, who, without doubt, conferred with his superior, Ignatius, on the matter, giving him an account of all that took place, and receiving from him the necessary instructions.

From this it appears what zealous efforts were made to restore and renew the vigor of ecclesiastical discipline, a work which all must allow to be one of far greater difficulty than to throw it overboard altogether, as the Protestants did, together with all other decrees of the Church which were obnoxious to the votaries of sensuality.

# CHAPTER VII.

## ORDINANCES OF IGNATIUS REGARDING SCHOOLS. THE FOUNDATION OF THE GERMAN COLLEGE AT ROME.

IT is not our intention to examine here in detail what was the constitution of schools in general at the time of Ignatius, or of the schools of the Jesuits in particular, nor the method followed in them and the matters which they taught. It is enough for us to observe that the Society pursued the usual method of teaching in all Catholic schools, and especially that of Paris, in humanities, philosophy, and theology, excepting only some special arrangements with regard to the system of education. A work drawn up by Ignatius himself, and addressed to a person who desired some instruction on the subject, gives us an idea, though it is, indeed, an incomplete one, of the manner of teaching used at that time in the Society. It is a short and simple notice of the rules for day scholars, and it runs as follows—

1. Every one, rich or poor, shall be admitted gratuitously for charity, and no retribution can be received for the lessons or scientific lectures.

2. Those who are in a state of pupilage cannot be admitted, except through those who have the care over them: and if they wish to pursue their studies, they must be asked whether they are resolved to obey their masters in all that concerns their lessons and good behavior, to be docile, abstain from all bad language, and observe the rules of modesty in all things. If they answer in the affirmative, their names shall be inscribed on the books, and they shall be applied to study, and shall conduct themselves as belonging to the House.

3. They must, if possible, hear Mass daily, and attend sermons when given, and the explanation of Christian doctrine on all Sundays and holidays, and go to confession every month. They must be accustomed to recommend themselves often to God; and great care must be had in general of their studies and piety.

4. For the young boys who cannot be kept in order by words only, a corrector shall be maintained at the expense of the House, who shall be present at the lessons, and shall keep them in fear, and punish them when he shall receive orders from the Master. Recourse,

however, must not be had to corporal punishment, except when all other means are found insufficient. Lastly, if any are found to be quite incorrigible, they are to be expelled.

5. As to the matter taught in the different classes or schools, the lessons must be proportioned to the abilities of the learners; the ancient languages, Latin and Greek, and even Hebrew, shall be taught when they can be learnt by the scholars. Logic and philosophy shall be also taught, if there be a sufficient number of young persons formed to literary studies, and if it be not thought more convenient to send them elsewhere. The Society shall supply professors to teach the whole course of philosophy and theology, as is done at Paris. The professors shall not confine themselves to giving their lectures, but shall take care to practise their scholars in written compositions, in disputations, and conferences, which are, perhaps, more useful than the explanations of the Master.

Teaching is a thing of experience, from which alone just and proper rules can be drawn. It is the result of the experience of ages, and, like all other human things, has its traditions. To pay no attention to these traditions, and to build on mere abstract principles, is to take away from teaching all its strength and sinews, and to follow an end different from the very end of all education. Ignatius had, therefore, no need to make long theories : he and his Society attached themselves to that which was already in existence, and the principal point in every matter is always the practical part of it. What Ignatius wished was that the teaching in our schools should never be separated from the education of life, and this is what the Society has always observed. It was, indeed, impossible, with so great a variety of talents, and in consequence of the general progress of human knowledge among civilized nations, that there should be no attempt to extend and perfect teaching, both in matter and form. Improvements, consequently, were introduced, and were embodied in a plan, which was adopted by the Society in every country. This plan is called the *Ratio Studiorum*, and the main features of it have always been kept in all Jesuit schools. This plan has two invaluable qualities ; it has escaped the inconstancy which is the characteristic of modern systems, and it has long since been in possession of most of the advantages which they present. But experience alone can give a just idea of it, and many false judgments have been passed on it because people have discarded all the teachings of experience. It is a plan which admits of every legitimate progress and perfection, and what Ignatius said of the Society may be applied to it, namely, that it ought to suit itself to the times and comply with them, and not make the times suit themselves to it. *

St. Ignatius, being called by God to renovate Christian life, must needs have had at heart the care that youth, while receiving a classical education, should not lose the substantial good for the sake of an accessory, and that the loose reading of Pagan authors should not impart to young minds a taste for Pagan manners. He considered for many years, as he himself writes to a friend, the means of obviating this danger—

When [says he] I consider that the young receive and retain so easily their first impressions, for vice or virtue, and that the first notions, lessons, and examples, whether good or bad, are of such great importance for all the rest of their life ; and when, on the other hand, I consider that the books, and especially the classics, which are explained to the young, such as Terence, Virgil, and others, together with many things useful for instruction and for life, contain others which are very bad and very dangerous, which cannot be heard without injurious effect, (for the thoughts and the heart of man, says Holy Scripture, are inclined to evil from youth), still more when these things are presented to them in books which they read or study continually, and which they have habitually in their hands—when, I say, I consider all this, it seems to me, and always has seemed to me, that it would be a very good thing to expunge from the classical authors all that might scandalize, or be injurious, and to replace it by edifying matter, or else, if nothing must be added, then simply retain what is good, leaving out what is bad. This method has occurred to me, during these latter years, as a thing of the greatest utility for the leading of Christian life and the good education of youth. But I did not see how it could be put in practice, and I limited myself to simply desiring it. However, now that I see that Our Lord blesses our Society, which is His work, not only by giving it colleges, but also universities, such as Gandia and Messina, it may be more easily carried into execution, at least in the places where the Society has the direction of the studies. It will be, nevertheless, much to my satisfaction to know your most reverend Lordship's thoughts upon this subject, for, if you should agree with me on this point, it will be a very happy thing, for the glory of God, as I will more fully set before you hereafter.†

* Galiardi, p. 115.
† This letter, taken from the collection at Rome, is without address and without date; but it appears to be written to a prelate, or, perhaps, to a cardinal. It must have been written after 1551, since the universities spoken of were not established until after that year.

It is well known that this idea of St. Ignatius was afterwards realized, and that for a long period it bore very happy fruit. We leave to more competent judges to decide how far it is suitable, or possible, at the present day. But the saintly originator of the measure must meet with the approbation of every impartial man, both for the idea itself, and for the good results that have followed its realization. Still, it must not be forgotten, when we would carry into effect such a rule as this, that St. Ignatius most wisely said, all times are not convenient for realizing an idea which, taken absolutely, is the best.

Ignatius turned all his thoughts to the Roman College, which was opened in 1551. It was small in its commencement ; but, in spite of numerous difficulties raised by the jealousy of those who held public schools, and in spite of its poverty and the want of proper buildings, it not only maintained itself, but, by the persevering energy of the Saint, made rapid progress. He wished it to be a seminary of the Order ; and it has always kept this character, for, up to the present day, the Society sends to it students from all quarters of the world. Several masters of schools who made their living by teaching, seeing their interests threatened by the Jesuits, who taught gratuitously, made their way on a certain day into the college, and, mixing with the auditory during a lecture, railed roundly at the Jesuit who was giving it. Ignatius, who always sought to conciliate every mind, and to meet each rising difficulty by sweetness, when the nature of the case admitted it, wrote on this occasion to the rectors of the colleges in Italy, through his secretary, informing them what they were to do on similar occasions.

" If," says he, " foreign masters pretend that the professors of our colleges are ignorant men, they must humbly avow that they know far less than they would desire, but that they serve God with the poor talents which the Father of all good has given them. It is in this manner they must by their modesty triumph over the prejudices against them." He also forbids them to receive students into the Society without the consent of their parents. He showed himself very severe on this point, and opposed with great energy the indiscreet zeal of some of the Society.    In the previous year the superior of Louvain, having received a student of the University against the will of his tutor, excited the anger of the professor against the Society.    Ignatius blamed the rector's conduct, and ordered him to ask the professor's pardon.

But another case, in which he himself was implicated, gave him occasion to forbid by a general ordinance all admissions of this kind.    In the year 1553 there was a young man named Octavius Cesar, who had entered the Society in Sicily, and his father, the secretary of the Duke of Monte Leone, had given his consent after it was done. But Octavius being summoned to Rome by Ignatius, the father changed his mind, and followed his son thither. He obtained an audience of Pope Julius III., and pretending that his son had entered the Society against his will, demanded an inquiry, which was intrusted to Cardinal Caraffa.    The young man's mother, meanwhile, came also to Rome, and with all the passionate vehemence of her countrywomen, flew from house to house, complaining of her wrongs and exciting compassion by her cries and tears.    The Cardinal himself, moved by her lamentations, without a full examination of the facts, gave orders to Ignatius, under pain of censure, to give back the son to his parents, although he had voluntarily followed his vocation and entered into the Society.    As the truth had been garbled, the Saint did not think it his duty to yield. He had recourse to the Pope, who, being informed of the true state of the case, annulled the sentence of Caraffa and decided that Octavius had been admitted in a regular manner.    At the same time he named a committee of cardinals to examine into cases of the kind which should arise for the future.*

In consequence of this occurrence, Ignatius addressed a circular to the Society in the following terms—

As it is our intention that youth should be formed to knowledge and good manners in our colleges and schools, and that the parents should derive therefrom the fruits of edification, in the same manner as from the other works of charity practised by the Society, namely, preaching, confessions, and the rest, we judge it to be proper in Our Lord to issue an express command to all on the part of God our Master, that no young

* Orlandini, xiv., 12.

man, living under the care of his parents or tutors be admitted into our Order, either in the college of the town where he resides, or in any other place, without the will and consent of those under whose care he is. Still less ought students to be allured to enter into the Society. For, as it is allowable and praiseworthy in itself to push on and to assist those who have reached the years of maturity to embrace a state of perfection, that is, to enter into a religious life, to do so in our schools is not agreeable to the greater glory of God and the general good, which we ought to have a greater regard for than our own particular good. This is nothing but reasonable. We give you notice that we have issued this command to all the colleges of our Society.

It was in Italy especially, where minds are very impressionable, that a fear had arisen lest the schools of the Jesuits should become a means of drawing the young to enter into the Order. This command, therefore, created a very favorable impression, and the effects of it were soon seen at Perugia, where a great number of parents, who previously would not trust their sons to the Jesuits, immediately sent them to their schools with joy.

It is natural to speak here of the foundation of the German College at Rome, because it was established at the same time as the Roman College, and, besides, it is connected with the present history. As it was but too evident that the disorders of the clergy had been the principal cause of the miseries of the Church in Germany, and that the evil would always remain the same so long as there were no means taken to remedy it, Ignatius wished to raise a supply of good missioners, capable of meeting the want, and the more so, as there were very few Jesuits in Germany, and these few were unable to meet the demands that were made on them from all sides. He thought, moreover, that, on account of the prejudices against the Holy See, the members of the Society, for the most part foreigners and bound by a particular vow to the Pope, would be less favorably received than others. To meet all these difficulties, he believed it expedient to found at Rome itself a college for the training of young Germans for the service of the Church, and to meet the wants of the age; so that, after having acquired a profound knowledge of doctrines, rites, and discipline, and drunk in deeply the love of their vocation, without which the ministry of the Church is barren, they might issue from this Seminary, and, returning to their country, re-

store in it the true spirit of the Church by their doctrine
and example as preachers, pastors, professors, and prelates, combat all erroneous teaching, and dissipate the
prejudices which existed there.

Germany at this period showed little prospect of supplying these wants.   With the exception of Cologne and
Ingolstadt, where John Eck had successfully maintained
the ancient traditions, the Catholic schools were almost
destroyed, and the clergy held in contempt, while the
schools, almost without exception, were imbued with the
novelties of Luther, which, taking away from the sciences
the proofs on which they are founded, leaves them to
be the sport of the caprice of the imagination.   This
calamitous method has its attractions for the spirit of
idleness and levity, and there is a reason for its success.
Luther had banished logic from philosophy and theology,
because he knew that it could not agree with his asser-
tions ; and, unfortunately, even to the present day, the
Catholic schools in Germany, especially in the northern
parts, make too little use of the rigorous method of
proof, to which so much importance was attached in
former times.   The consequence of this negligence, then,
was a lamentable ignorance among the clergy, which the
reformers regarded with joy, because they found in it a
means of spreading the infection of their errors.   Besides all this, as Religious Orders were held in detesta-
tion in these countries, Ignatius thought that secular
priests would find an easier access to them, and his idea
of a German College was to form a seminary to train
them.

This plan was in his thoughts long before he had an
opportunity of carrying it into execution.   One day,
Cardinal John Moroni, who had been the Pope's nuncio
in Germany, and knew the state of things there very
well, in the year 1552, during an interview with the
Saint, said to him, without knowing anything of his project, that he ought to bring some young Germans to
Rome to train them for the priesthood.   They both
thought that the Pope should be made acquainted with
the design, in order to secure his approbation and assistance.   Moroni succeeded in interesting Cardinal Cervini,

who was very influential with the Pope, in the matter, and these two proposed the idea to Julius III. He at first made some difficulties, on account of the expenses it would involve, for the treasury was exhausted. But as they represented to him that cardinals, among whom there were many both rich and munificent, would not fail to contribute to an undertaking of such great importance, he gave them his permission to sound the dispositions of the Sacred College, promising his support if they were found to be favorable. After they had mooted the matter, Julius III. called a Consistory, and Moroni, supported by Cervini, made an eloquent discourse in favor of the enterprise. As the greater number of the cardinals were already prepared, they readily gave their consent, and some even proposed to fix a sum which they should contribute yearly to it, but the Pope rejected this motion. He himself subscribed to it in these terms · " As it is right that we should give an example in so pious and praiseworthy a thing, we will pay to it every year the sum of five hundred crowns in gold." It was resolved at the same time to put the arrangement and the direction of the new college into the hands of Ignatius and of the Society, and to commission him to draw up the statutes. These resolutions were communicated to Ignatius in the Pope's name, and, with his usual activity, he set himself to the work immediately, so that by the 29th of July he sent the plan of the statutes he had drawn up to Cardinal Carpi, then at Viterbo, with the following letter—

We hope, my most reverend lord, that you will, please God, soon return to Rome and give your help to the establishment of the German College, which you have so much at heart, both on account of your usual great charity and by a special inspiration of God. Nevertheless, as the month of October is drawing near, and at that time some young students may arrive from Germany to commence the work, the most reverend Cardinal of Augsburg has counselled me to write to you, my most reverend lord, in his name and in my own, and to send you the statutes of the College, so that, after you have looked over them, and added or struck out what your wisdom shall deem necessary, we may, upon information of it, draw them up in a definitive form. Meanwhile, the reverend Cardinal of Augsburg, who is so full of zeal for this pious work, will undertake the task of obtaining from the Pope Briefs for bishops and other principal persons in Germany, and will write himself to that country to obtain scholars for the college. But whereas it may happen that several of the commissioners in Germany who were employed ,by their princes to further the undertaking may write at any moment that all is ready, and there may be very little time before the arrival of the young students, the Cardinal has thought it best that the most reverend the Patrons should contribute a certain sum for the good of the holy work, so as to encourage others by their example to do the same. Thus the expenses of the journey may be defrayed for some, and the house and furnishing be got ready. I am writing the same to the other most reverend Patrons. So soon as the most necessary measures shall have been taken, I will write to our Fathers at Cologne and Vienna, by direct post to each, if your most reverend lordship approves of it, as well as to the Cardinal of Augsburg, to take upon themselves to send thence young Germans for the new college, and I hope that we shall have a certain number of them by October next, and that we may be able then to begin this holy undertaking. May it please Our Lord, by means of your most reverend lordship and your colleagues, to conduct the whole in the manner that shall be most to His own divine glory, to the public good in general, and that of Germany in particular.

Rome, July 29, 1552.

He wrote at the same time to the superiors of the colleges in Germany, and one of these letters is preserved to us, addressed to Le Jay, at Vienna, which we here give—

Dearly beloved brothers in Christ—You have heard speak, I think, more than once, of the project of establishing a German college here at Rome for the reception of chosen young men of pious dispositions, of whom there is good hope that they will make progress in Christian virtue and piety, as well as in the study of the sciences. They will live under the patronage of the Pope and five cardinals, and under the direction of our Society, so that nothing shall be wanting to them of what is necessary for food, clothing, lodging, books—in a word, for all that is useful and convenient for students. Those who shall have made considerable progress in science and virtue shall return to Germany with ecclesiastical benefices, and those who shall have distinguished themselves in a very special manner shall be promoted to bishoprics or even to more exalted dignities. All who desire the salvation of Germany think that the most effectual human means, and perhaps the only one to support religion in the countries where it is on its decline and falling to ruins, or to raise it up again where it is completely fallen, is to send on the mission as many men of ability as can be found belonging to the nation and speaking the language, so that these, exerting the influence of a holy life and sound doctrine, may, by preaching and explaining Holy Scripture, or by private conversation, dissipate the cloud of ignorance and vice which blinds their fellow-countrymen, and open their eyes to the Catholic faith. Accordingly, the students who shall come to this college, founded for the good of Germany, as the copy of the Apostolic Brief which I send with this letter declares, will find here masters to teach them Latin, Greek, and Hebrew.   Those who have already studied their humanities will be taught logic, physics, and the other sciences, and finally theology, by means of public lectures and continual exercises.   They will find, also, masters who will watch carefully over their morals, and over the whole service of the house, and govern the college.   These pious and learned men, selected from the Society of Jesus, must be as far as possible Germans, or at least from the adjoining countries.   In order that this excellent work may be begun this year, the cardinals, the Patrons of the College, and especially the Cardinal of Augsburg, who has interested himself in this matter with a charity and zeal truly admirable, have decided that we should write a circular letter to you and to Dr. Canisius and the other Fathers of our Society at Vienna, recommending you to send as soon as possible to Rome some young students who are Germans both by birth and language, so that they may be here in the month of October, or at least in the month of November.   In consequence of this decision having of our own accord taken this burden upon ourselves, and moved by our zeal for the salvation of souls, as we are in duty bound, we must earnestly commend to you this work, desiring you to employ in the choosing and sending of these young men the same care and zeal that you would have in a matter of the highest importance for the glory of God and the salvation of souls.*

July 30th, 1552.

The Bull of the erection of the College was given by the Pope on the 31st of August; it conferred on the rector the right of giving the doctor's cap.   The first rector named by St. Ignatius was Father Fruste, a learned Frenchman.   He would have preferred a German, but had not one at his disposal.   The appointment, however, justified the hopes of Ignatius.   On the 21st of November, the first new students who had come from Germany bound themselves in a written form to remain faithful to the ancient faith of their fathers, so that this day may be considered as the opening of the college.   The students attended the lessons of the Roman College, but as philosophy and theology were not yet taught there, Ignatius asked permission of the Pope to erect in it chairs of both these faculties.   The Pope willingly granted the request, and from that time forward the college acquired that importance which it has ever since maintained.   Ignatius saw with much satisfaction the progress of this work, and a few months afterwards he expressed his joy in the following letter to Cardinal Moroni—

* The original, in Latin, is to be found in Menchacha (iii.,19).

As your return to the city, most reverend lord, is delayed longer than was expected, I have thought it my duty to write to give you news of the German College, which your lordship is pleased to hold in special affection, as it is your work, and is, moreover, of sovereign importance for the service of God and the restoration of the Church in Germany and in the North. The establishment consists as yet of two houses near to our college ; but we are endeavoring to find larger ones, as the number of students increases and will increase every day. It is composed of twenty young Germans, exclusive of the rector, who is one of our Society, and two other learned and exemplary men, who are engaged to administer to their spiritual wants, and to direct them. Besides these, there are four paid servants employed in the exterior service of the house, who discharge their duty very efficiently. Some of the scholars are already well instructed in philosophy ; and as they will continue their exercises to the October of this year, in the study of languages, logic, and philosophy, which they have already studied at Louvain, Cologne, and Vienna, they will be in a condition to enter upon the lectures in theology. The others will continue their studies of languages or of philosophy, as shall be found good for them. They are exemplary in their conduct and morals, and we hope that they will become, both by life and doctrine, good laborers in the vineyard of the Lord. We have already selected several professors of languages for them, and have others ready for logic and physics, that they may conduct the classes according to the greater or less capacity of the students. They will also have to engage in concertations with each other, and the course of philosophy will comprise three years, as at Paris and Louvain, and other famous universities. In the month of October, we shall appoint some professors of theology, both of dogma and exegesis, and these, as well as the others, will be the best that can be found in our Society, and we have taken them from other colleges, being of opinion that this college is of a greater and more general utility for the glory of God Our Lord.*

Rome, February 25, 1553.

This seminary was the first establishment of the kind, so that the commencement of such useful and salutary establishments is due to Ignatius. It is true that Laynez, some time before, had proposed to the bishops assembled in the Council of Trent to establish houses of this kind in their dioceses. Perhaps he had taken the idea from his conversations with St. Ignatius. But his proposal did not meet with a favorable reception at that time from the holy Synod. It was afterwards that Cardinal Maroni, when president of the Council, renewed this proposition, and insisted on its acceptance. The German College was at that time already in existence, and could be pointed out as a model. During the first three

* Collection at Rome.

years this establishment made extraordinary progress, but under Paul IV. the aspect of things was changed. Considering the German College to be inadequate to its purpose, he took away from it his support. Some of the cardinals, following his example, withdrew their patronage, so that, being deprived of the necessary resources, it was soon reduced to a very precarious condition. But Ignatius never lost courage; he ordered quests to be made for alms, and bore the burden alone. This perseverance and disinterested charity gave such satisfaction to King Ferdinand that he paid from his exchequer 400 gold florins yearly to the German college.

However, as all good things are strengthened amid contradictions and persecutions, the lot of this rising college was no exception to the rule. A student dismissed for bad conduct, out of revenge, disseminated false accusations against the house, pretending that the discipline was too severe, and that the food was bad and insufficient. Those who from the first had endeavored to ruin it took advantage of this circumstance, and exaggerated these false reports in order to prejudice and drive away the ignorant. Canisius wrote on this subject to Ignatius, and the Saint exposed the falsehood of these reports in a letter, from which the historian of the German College gives the following passage—*

The report that the German College will not succeed can only come from the devil. The truth is that, with the help of God, it prospers as much as can be desired. During these unfortunate times the students are in want of nothing, either as regards necessaries for the body, or for what will assist their progress in science and virtue. The college numbers at present thirty scholars in several classes, according to the different subject-matter of their studies, and we have good hope that they will distinguish themselves hereafter to the greater glory of God. It is our ardent desire to increase the number of the good. One had been admitted of a disobedient and mutinous spirit, and he has been dismissed. Choose for us some young men with good dispositions and send them to us. They are treated here, firmly I believe, with so much gentleness, that I am surprised any one can regard the discipline as too severe. They go twice a week for recreation to the villa-house. So far from the least rigor being used in their regard, they are treated with the greatest sweetness of government so long as they are willing to observe an edifying behavior.

* *Colleg. Germ. Hist.*, auctore Jul. Cordara, S.J. Rome, 1770. The date he gives is incorrect; the letter was written in 1555.

If the constancy of Ignatius was not shaken by these
calumnies, it was no less unmoved by the storms which
burst in the wars between Paul IV. and Philip II., and
which threatened the very existence of the Roman College, which was the Saint's favorite work.  Rome, in fact,
was at the point of being besieged and taken for the second time during the century, for the Spaniards marched
to the gates of Rome, and the city prepared for its defence.  Famine soon succeeded, and Ignatius found it
impossible to give food to his German students, but for
all that he did not dismiss them—he divided them among
the different houses of the Society which were nearest to
Rome.  In this extremity all thought the establishment
undone forever, and even the Cardinal of Augsburg,
Otho Truchses, wrote to the Saint to say that there was no
other alternative but to give up an undertaking which
for four years had struggled against so many difficulties,
that he had done all that man could do, and that he
must take occasion of the war to free himself from these
cares and annoyances.  But Ignatius declared that they
who were weary of the cares and trouble which this
work had cost might lay them upon him, for that his resolution was unshaken, and that, so long as he lived, he
would support this college, and rather sell himself than
abandon his Germans; that the help of man was of little
account, and greater must be the trust put in God.  And
God recompensed this admirable confidence by favoring
him with a prophetic light, by which he predicted in the
most positive manner that there would be one day a
Pope who should be the founder of this college.  Gregory. XIII. accomplished this prophecy in the fullest
manner.  However, the precarious condition of the German College continued until the death of Ignatius, which
took place in this disastrous war between Spain and
Paul IV., who took the side of France.

# CHAPTER VIII.

## OF THE ZEAL AND CHARITY OF ST. IGNATIUS FOR GERMANY.

ALTHOUGH Le Jay had for some time been teaching theology at the University of Ingolstadt, no member of the Society had been invited to Germany to found a college there, or fill a professor's chair in a permanent official capacity, until the year 1549. In this year William, Duke of Bavaria, the first of all the German princes to do so, preferred a request to Pope Paul III. for two professors of theology to teach in the schools of Ingolstadt. The Pope commissioned the Cardinals Ste. Croix and Maffei to communicate this request to St. Ignatius. But he replied that he could employ the Religious of his Order in a manner far more useful for the general good than by sending them to fill for a time a chair in the universities; that, if the duke had a mind to render great services to religion, he could do as the King of Portugal had done, who, having at first only two members of the Society, had established afterwards a seminary in his country, so that there were now 250 Religious, who could do good in all the vast dominions of that prince; that he would consent to send the duke the Fathers he asked for, but upon condition that he would found a college of the Society in which natives of the country might be educated. This condition being approved of by the Pope and cardinals, and agreed to by the duke,* Ignatius sent for Fathers Canisius and Salmeron to Rome, and, at the express desire of the Duke William, for Father Le Jay also. They were to stop on their way at Bologna, to take the degree

---

* No writer of the Society has, as far as I am aware, made mention of these negotiations.

of doctors in theology, because much is thought in Germany of that title. Ignatius, in sending the duke the two men he asked for, wrote him the following letter, in which he alludes to the agreement made between them—

The two theologians whom I have promised, according to the order of our Holy Father, will present your Excellency with this letter. One of them is Alphonsus Salmeron, a Spaniard, the other, Peter Canisius, of Gueldres ; I have summoned them both from Sicily. They are distinguished for their irreproachable life and profound knowledge of Holy Scripture, with a cultivation of mind of the highest Christian character. They are both priests of the Order known by the name of the Society of Jesus. Our Holy Father has not the least doubt that they will fully answer to the views of your Excellency, and that they will give instructions in a most effectual manner, throughout your great country, by their lives as well as by their doctrines. I also send the excellent theologian, Dr. Claude, whom your Excellency asked for by name. Although he cannot remain with you very long,* he will nevertheless be of great assistance to you for some days or months, to aid in founding this excellent and useful establishment. The college of the Society has but one sole object in its studies, labors, and cares—to amend the corrupt morals of the age, to convert hearts by example, to promote the sanctification of souls, and, by learning and science founded on the pure and true faith and the sacred teaching of Jesus Christ, to bring men back from the peinicious seductions of pleasure to a good and holy life, from the flesh to the spirit, from the world to God. In these our times, and especially in Germany, where a wild boar would uproot and a savage beast trample on the vine which the hand of the Lord has planted, can there be a teaching more suitable than this to strengthen the souls of the good in their sentiments of piety, and to restore the wandering sheep to the fold of Christ ? May it please your Excellency to receive these Fathers, in so many ways worthy of all respect, with special friendship and goodwill. As the rule of their Order requires that they look to no temporal interests of their own, but only to those of Jesus Christ, and that they live on voluntary alms, full of confidence in their Lord and Master and in the greatness of your goodness, they are convinced that they will want for nothing of the necessaries of life. It is, moreover, just that they who sow in spiritual things should reap what is requisite for the body. There is every reason to hope that souls will be found which, filled with admiration for so perfect a life and such holy rules, will give themselves up to the direction of these Fathers. If this be the case, and the Lord look upon His vineyard, your Excellency will honor these new laborers with your favors and graces, and will be rejoiced to see their number increase. How great will be your merits before God and His holy Church when this vineyard, cultivated by the new seminary and watered by the pious liberality of your Excellency, shall produce new buds and shoots ! Our Holy Father the Pope has a special interest in this matter, and it will be very pleasing

* He was the confessor of Hercules, Duke of Ferrara, who would only consent to part with him for a time.

to him to hear that these three Fathers—men of such piety and learning—have been treated by your Excellency with all possible affection and goodness.*

Rome, 1549.

Salmeron could not long remain at Ingolstadt, for Ignatius received orders from Pope Julius III. to send him to the Bishop of Verona, who had asked the Pope for him. The Saint acquainted the Duke Albert, who had lately succeeded his father William in the government, with this new appointment. He informed Salmeron of it also, though he says at the same time that he would have preferred to leave him in the post which he occupied. He adds that he would not willingly offend the duke in anything, and that he is willing to take any pains to win his favor and good will; that he does not wish to do any injury to that famous university, but rather to render it any service; and, therefore, that he sends Dr. Gaudan and Father Schorich to replace Salmeron. He wrote also to the Duke to explain all that had passed, and to recommend to him the new professor, who, being born in Flanders, belonged to Germany, and might be very useful for public lectures and sermons. He added that, if the college intended by his father were established, he would send professors of the other faculties, so that the Society might contribute its aid to the pious undertakings of the duke for the good of his country and of the whole of Germany.†

Things remained in this condition until the year 1551, and the project which had been first agreed upon at Rome seemed to be abandoned ; for the duke always delayed the foundation of the promised college, and so the Society was baulked of its object. In fact, if the Company could not propagate in the country, it could not be expected to take away some of its most distinguished members from other parts and employ them in a place where they must remain without producing fruit for the

* This letter is to be found in the collection at Rome, but it bears no date of the day or of the month. It must have been written in the month of August, or, at the latest, in September, since it was sent by these three Fathers, who received their Doctor's degrees at Bologna October 4th (Orlandini, ix., 51).

† Collection at Rome.

body, or making it any compensation for its sacrifice of them. The Fathers, therefore, made it be understood that, in this case, their recall would be inevitable. But the Bishop of Eichstadt, in whose diocese the town of Ingolstadt is situated, would not hear of this, and wrote accordingly to St. Ignatius. The Saint, in his reply, saying nothing of the delay in the fulfilment of the promise made to him at first, contents himself with observing to the Bishop that the vow of the members of the Society to the Holy See does not allow of their being determinately attached to fixed places, and refers him in his letter to Le Jay. Polanco, the secretary, writes to Le Jay, in the name of Ignatius, and takes a retrospect of the negotiations first made, and of the agreement which had been guaranteed by the Holy See. Then coming to the change of views that had taken place since, he declares that Ignatius cannot allow his Religious to be limited to the teaching of students who do not belong to the Company, but are destined to fill benefices afterwards, and that, if they do not keep to the agreement of establishing the promised college for the Society, they must not be offended if Ignatius does on his part what the good of the Order requires, and the more so, as colleges are asked for in different parts of the world, and he is in want of subjects to send to them.*

In fact, Ferdinand, King of the Romans, besides other princes, had asked Ignatius for two theologians for the University of Vienna, where he wished to establish a college. Le Jay had shown himself to be very useful at Augsburg during the holding of the Diet, and the Bishop of Laybach, Ferdinand's confessor, had by his counsel decided the king upon calling in the Jesuits. He immediately wrote from Augsburg, on the 11th of December, to the Pope and St. Ignatius. In his letter the pious king says "that, seeing the good that is being everywhere done by the colleges of the Society, he has resolved to found one in Vienna as soon as possible : that, meanwhile, he asks for two Fathers for the university of that city to give lectures on the interpretation of Scripture," and

---

* Collection at Rome.

specially mentions Le Jay, whom he knew personally.* In his reply to the king, Ignatius says "that a Christian prince cannot bestow his pains on a better object than the promotion and increase of religion, and that he can only bless God for inspiring the design which his Majesty has formed for the cure of the wounds of the Church in Germany, and pray that He may preserve in him these pious sentiments ; that one of these means is to have a university supplied with men of a character to edify others by their example and orthodox teaching ; and that he is ready, on his part, to contribute to this work as far as his powers will allow, and according to the request of the king's ambassador at Rome, he will send him, as soon as possible, two theologians and some students to Vienna, to found a college there ; that Le Jay, if the king wished it, should present himself there before them." † In fact, that Father received orders at Ingolstadt to go to Vienna with Father Schorich,‡ and both arrived there at the end of June, 1551. The question of the method of teaching at the time could not long remain without serious discussion. At that troubled period, when the taste for the severe studies had almost disappeared in Germany, and both in science and religion fancy reigned uncontrolled, and when there was no teaching body to form a learned and faithful clergy, it was in vain to endeavor to raise the standard of theological study by merely naming some able professors, if there were only to be a few hearers to attend their lectures, and the more especially if these few were without the preparation of preliminary studies. And yet, this was the means to which the counsel taken by princes seemed to confine their designs. It was owing to this mistake that such long delays were made in founding a college of the Society in Bavaria, and it was this that impelled Ferdinand to write to Ignatius through Le Jay, in 1551, saying that

* The Bollandists (secs. 44, 45) give eight letters from the king to St. Ignatius, and, consequently, the correspondence on this affair must necessarily comprise a greater number of the Saint's letters than the few I have been able to procure.

† Collection at Rome. The date of this letter is wanting, but it must have been written in January or February of 1551.

‡ Query Storch.

he desired to raise the standard of the studies in the universities by bringing the young people from the provinces to be taught their theology there by the Jesuits.    Albert of Bavaria made the same proposal at the same time. Ignatius endeavored to combat this opinion, which well-intentioned advisers, but little conversant in these matters, had counselled these princes to adopt, and he wrote as follows to Le Jay, by his secretary, Polanco.    He says " that this plan was no expedient for the end in view, but was subject to great inconveniences ; for the young men whom they wished to attract to the universities would come there without preparation, and with that profound dislike for scholastic studies which was so prevalent in Germany.    This dislike would take from the teaching begun under such circumstances all its efficiency for good, for if the students at the universities were to have to go through the necessary course of philology and philosophy, they would have to spend from four to six years before entering upon theology at all, besides which, he adds, it did not properly belong to universities to teach the inferior branches of learning.    From all this it would follow that philosophy and theology must be left as they are.    The Jesuits there must begin by undertaking preparatory teaching with professors capable of inspiring, little by little, in their young scholars, a taste for theology."    Ignatius concludes by recommending Le Jay to communicate this plan, first to the Bishop of Laybach, and, if it meet with his approval, then to the king himself.*

The reply of Ignatius to Duke Albert, dated Sept. 22, 1551, is still extant, and we give it almost entire.  He says—

With regard to the proposed college, it is my opinion that it should be founded not only for the higher studies, but for the lower schools, with masters who shall not be merely content with giving their written lectures, but shall endeavor to instil into their scholars moral instruction and education, and to make them both pious and learned.

He then continues in the following terms—

For although our end in teaching the other sciences is theology, we think that for its restoration in Germany, where at present it is almost

* This fragment of the letter to Le Jay is to be found in the collection at Rome.

utterly lost, it is useless to provide masters unless the scholars also receive some preparatory course, and unless the young are previously formed with a will disposed to enter zealously and devotedly upon this sacred science, and with a mind cultivated by lower studies, so as to be capable of making progress in it. But how many youths will be found so disposed among all the students of theology at Ingolstadt? I am told, and I write it with sorrow, that there are very many who are wanting in one of these things, if not in both; for, either they have no taste for theology, or else they have not received a sufficiently solid basis in the lower studies, so as to be able to make sound progress in this science. For the revival of theological studies, the following is our proposed plan, as we have said to the most illustrious king of the Romans. We must first, as we have done in our other colleges, choose masters for the study of languages capable of instructing the youth in classical literature by lessons *viva voce* and written exercises, and of forming them to piety and good manners by instructions, frequentation of the Sacraments, and good example. When they shall have made sufficient progress, and shall be in sufficient number to begin a course of philosophy, we will give them a professor of logic, and in the following years a master of philosophy, so that every year there shall be some to pass from humanities to logic, and from logic to other parts of philosophy. All these masters shall give their endeavors to enkindle in the hearts of the young scholars a gradual fire, by which they shall be more and more inflamed with a love for theology, and bend all their efforts towards it, as the end of their studies, before ever they come to it. Then, after having concluded their course of philosophy, and being formed in the lower sciences, considerable numbers will possibly enter the school of theology with great earnestness. We will take care to provide them with masters under whom they may study it with all serious application and with the full exercise of all their mental faculties, and so ensure a rapid progress in it. By proceeding in this manner, most illustrious Prince, we can have a host of theologians well versed in this science as well as in the lower kinds of knowledge, and capable of confronting the Reformers and confirming the faith of Catholics, of preaching with fruit and filling the positions of the pastoral ministry in all Bavaria. There will then be an inexhaustible seminary at Ingolstadt of pious and learned men, and the University will flourish in science and virtue; for in our colleges we apply ourselves alike to the formation and education of life and to the cultivation of science.

The Saint then comes to the request which the Duke had made to him at various times, that he would send to him more professors of theology, and he excuses himself for not having done it for want of men, having been only able to find with great difficulty, in the space of a month, priests enough to send two to Pisa and to Naples, to found colleges in those places. Nevertheless, he promises to do all that he can, so that the studies may suffer no detriment at Ingolstadt.

Ferdinand soon perceived that two Jesuits were not enough at Vienna, and that they would infallibly succumb under the burden. He therefore wrote in the month of December in the same year, 1551, both to the Pope and to St. Ignatius, to ask for some more Fathers. "He had been informed," he says, "that Ignatius intended to withdraw from Ingolstadt two learned theologians, Germans by birth, and therefore he asked for them for the college at Vienna, which he had lately founded. It was, he thought, the more necessary, as Le Jay was very much occupied with compiling a manual of theology." *

Ignatius was at a loss whom to send to Vienna, having no men at his disposal who were suitable for the purpose, except Canisius and Gaudan, who were at Ingolstadt. And though the establishment of the college they came to found was delayed, they were exercising a most salutary influence upon that city, and it was very difficult to withdraw them. St. Ignatius informed the king of his embarrassment, adding that the Pope absolutely commanded him to attend to the prince's request, and that he had no other course to pursue than to recall these two Fathers from Ingolstadt. He wrote the same day, January 12, 1552, to Duke Albert this decision of the Sovereign Pontiff, and said to him, that "the king of the Romans had some little time before asked of him two theologians of the Society for a most important work, but that, notwithstanding the obligations he was under to him, he had replied, as he had done to the duke, that he had no theologian to send him. The Pope, however, willing to satisfy the request of the king, had thought that he could give him the two theologians who were at Ingolstadt, and had declared to him his intentions in this regard by a message through a cardinal." He added, "that, though members of the Society were bound by a vow to go wherever the Pope should send them, he thought he might venture to represent to the Sovereign

* The work spoken of here is the *Summary of Christian Doctrine* which Canisius published three years afterwards. It appears that it was begun by Le Jay, of whose labors the venerable Canisius made use. Orlandini is therefore mistaken when he says (xiv., 43) that Le Jay died before putting his hand to this work.

Pontiff that these two Fathers had gone to Ingolstadt to found a college there. He had done so, and had thus obtained of His Holiness that they should be only lent for a time for the king's use, and should return to Ingolstadt as soon as ever the college at Vienna was established." He therefore begs the duke to allow these two Fathers to go where obedience calls them, and promising that they should be at his command, as well as others, as soon as it should be necessary. *

Although Duke Albert was sorry to see these two Fathers take their leave, and the University as well as the people of the city deeply regretted their absence, this measure was justified by its necessity, and all parties understood that they must submit to it. The two Fathers arrived at Vienna in the month of March of this year, where they waited for two other companions whom Ignatius had sent them from Rome. They immediately opened a numerously attended school, the results of which were most successful. King Ferdinand was delighted, but thinking he had reason to fear that Ignatius would recall some of his subjects from Vienna, he wrote to him on the subject. The Saint replied that many, indeed, were of opinion that one of the Fathers at Vienna should be recalled and sent elsewhere, but that he himself thought of increasing the Vienna college, rather than of diminishing it. The Society's members were too few to fill all the colleges that were asked for, it was true, but he would prefer to neglect in some degree other colleges, in order to be enabled in due time to strengthen that at Vienna. He concluded with a promise that none of the Fathers should be called away without His Majesty's consent.

The following year, on May 20th, 1554, the duke of Bavaria addressed another letter to the Pope and to St. Ignatius, asking for Canisius and some more Fathers for the college of the Society which he had established at the University of Ingolstadt. He observes at the same time that the departure of the Jesuits had given him much pain, and that the cause of the delay in founding the college which he had promised had solely arisen

* Collection at Rome.

from the wars and calamities of the times. * He refers Ignatius to his private secretary, Henry Schwickhard, whom he sends to Rome with full powers to treat of this affair, and to communicate to the Saint his master's plans more in detail. Father Cordara, in his *History of the German College at Rome,* † gives us some information on this subject. The duke had heard speak of this institution, and approved of it so highly that he thought of establishing a similar one in his own country, for the education of a body of learned clergy. Schwickhard was to confer with Ignatius upon this matter, and obtain from him the necessary information. The Saint was very much disposed to support this proposal, and let the duke see the Bull of the Institution of Julius III., and the Statutes of the German College. However, this plan was never carried into effect, because, from the moment that the Society had undertaken the education of youth, and the bishops had established seminaries in their dioceses, the want of such an institution was no longer felt. It was different with the German College at Rome, which had a higher object, and was destined for those who were intended to occupy more elevated positions in the Church, and who required a more careful education.

It seems probable that there was the intention of uniting the proposed seminary with the college about to be founded, for in a letter written later, May 6th, 1556, by the duke to St. Ignatius, he says that he had not given up the project of a seminary, but that, as his Paternity had informed him that the Constitutions and the customs of the Society did not allow him to accept of an endowment with clauses and conditions, he thought that neither party was bound except by the articles which they had agreed upon. With regard to these articles, as in Germany at that period nothing could be done without endless conferences and writings on the model of the formulas of the empire,

---

* The wars in question are those which were waged by Maurice of Saxony against the Emperor, and by Albert, Margrave of Brandenburg, against some of the States of the Empire. The letter of the duke is to be found in the Bollandists, nn. 501 and 502.

† L. xvi.

the duke had entered into correspondence with Canisius, who had gone for the purpose from Prague to Munich in the autumn of 1555.*

The duke had put a stop to certain arrangements that were being made relative to the foundation of a college at Ingolstadt, and he sent certain points of difference, with a letter of explanation, to Rome, dated December 12, by the hands of Canisius himself.† In this letter he begs St. Ignatius to confirm the proposed articles, promising on his part to do all he had engaged. But as the request was for two things, a college of the Society, and a seminary for the secular clergy in union with the college, which was contrary to the rules of the Order, the establishment of the first was deferred. Ignatius had hitherto kept quiet, and borne with admirable patience the delays and difficulties of the duke's advisers. But at length, with his characteristic greatness of mind, he appealed to the duke's own magnanimity, sending him the portion of the Constitution which treats of the foundation of colleges, and wrote to him at the same time, saying that he left the whole to his decision. This course had more effect than all the representations and negotiations which had hitherto been employed. The duke made an end of all difficulties, and the business proceeded quickly, to the satisfaction of all parties. This result appears evident from the duke's letter of the 5th of May, cited above ; and June 8th, 1556, Ignatius wrote to Schwickhard the following letter—‡

I have not been able to reply to your lordship's letter of the 10th of March, both on account of my bad health, and because there was no necessity, as your letter was an answer to mine. I have, however, sent the duke's letter to the Pope by one of our Fathers, and he received it graciously.§ But as the Pope did not read it in his presence, we have nothing to write on the subject, though we have not failed on every proper occasion to express, as we ought to do, our sentiments with regard to so pious a prince, who takes up so vigorously the de-

* The letter in which Ignatius made the declaration here alluded to is not to be found, as well as several others relating to this subject. The originals are probably in the archives of Munich.

† Bolland., *Ibid.* I have nowhere found the articles in question.

‡ Oddi, in *Vita Canisii*, cap. ix. ; Menchacha. p. 193.

§ The Pope was Paul IV., and the Father mentioned must have been Laynez. The letter is to be found in Menchacha, iv., 32.

fence of the Catholic faith.   We have come to the determination of sending the Fathers who are to compose the college before the heats of summer begin, for this reason, amongst others, that this fact may dissipate some false rumors spread at Augsburg after the holding of the Diet, and some conjectures raised by persons of consideration.   For when it is understood that the most illustrious Duke of Bavaria is inviting the members of our Society and establishing a college for them at Ingolstadt, these persons will perceive how far they have been wrong in their conjectures.   I have therefore obtained an audience of the Pope for the members who will compose the college, and whilst they kissed the feet of His Holiness, and received his Apostolical benediction, two of our Fathers who accompanied them, James Laynez and John Polanco, spoke much to the Holy Father of the pious desires of the Duke of Bavaria to protect the Catholic faith, and how they have led him to form the design of founding a seminary of ecclesiastics who shall be faithful to the Holy See.   The Pope seemed much pleased, and after having questioned the Fathers going to Ingolstadt, and having given them many recommendations, he dismissed them with orders that they should be supplied with money for their journey.   But our Fathers having replied that they only needed the blessing of His Holiness, and that the duke had liberally provided for their journey, the Pope seemed pleased and edified, as were also all those around him.   Thereupon they were presented to some of the principal cardinals ; and thus their departure for the college at Ingolstadt has been made sufficiently known to the glory of God, and has had the effect of calming some disturbed minds.   I have no more to add but to recommend the new college to your charity and goodness.

Ignatius also informed the duke of the coming of the members of the college which he had so long desired to establish.   After reference to the preceding letter, he continues as follows—

Besides the rector, Master Thomas,* who is a doctor of theology, there are two other doctors, who will be professors of theology ; amongst the others there are some who have taken Master's degrees, and have begun their theology; there are also some masters of humanities.   They are for the most part of Upper and Lower Germany, but all full of zeal for the Catholic faith, and trained in the practice of religious virtues.   I offer them for the service of your Grace, and for the glory of God, with the same feelings that I would offer myself if my health and the duties of my office would allow me. I have recommended them to observe fully all that is contained in our articles of agreement, and not to go beyond them, and I am convinced that your Grace and your successors will give your protection and favor to the college, so long as these Fathers shall show themselves useful for the public good.†   And I hope that they will not only

* His surname was Lentulus, or, in German, Lange.
† The sovereigns of Bavaria have done so until the suppression of the Order, and have deserved the blessing that Heaven bestows upon

never cease to be useful, but will ever be so more and more, as is usually the case with our Society. We have heard with much pleasure that the most illustrious king of the Romans has given permission to Father Canisius to be present at Ingolstadt to assist at the opening of the college, and I have written to him to go there as soon as possible. In order that he may take a more lively interest in the success of the new college, I appoint him Provincial of Upper Germany, Bohemia, and Austria." *

Meanwhile Ferdinand I. had been so struck with the success of the Jesuits at Vienna, although they had been there so short a time, that he desired, as he himself expresses it, "to propagate this holy Order in the other parts of his states." Accordingly he wrote to Ignatius, October 20, 1554, to ask him if he could send twelve Fathers of the Society to found a college at Prague, adding that, if he could, " he would receive them with all royal favor, as became a pious and Christian prince." He desired to have at least two professors of theology. Ignatius replied to him on the 22d of November (as appears from a later letter of Ferdinand, dated Augsburg, February 28, 1555), saying that the missioners he had lately supplied to various countries had taken all the subjects he had at his disposal, and that he could not satisfy His Majesty's request, but that he would, as in duty bound, keep it in mind. Thereupon Ferdinand wrote to him that he felt very great joy, because he could henceforward hope " that God had chosen this Order, which was so highly to be commended, and whose members led such holy lives, to work much good in these latter times, and to give to Christendom a proof of His mercy. Dr. Canisius," continues His Majesty, " had lately gone to Prague to take a survey of the place and of the means of establishing and maintaining a college there, and this same Father will write to Ignatius shortly on the subject, with the hope that some of the Fathers may speedily be sent thither."

fidelity in keeping promises. The Saint, when about to quit this world, recommended to them this fidelity in the most touching manner, hoping that the Society would show itself just and faithful to them, as in fact it has done, for these princes have never had occasion to doubt of the fidelity of its services to them.

* This letter, dated June 9, 1556, and the preceding letter, are in Menchacha, iv., 32, 33.

The king intended the House of St. Clement, which the Dominicans had almost abandoned, for a college of the Society. The few remaining Fathers consented to exchange this house for the Convent of the Poor Clares, which was empty. As the approbation of the Holy See was required for this transaction, Ferdinand, on the 3d of August, commissioned Ignatius to press the business actively with the Cardinals Moroni and Truchses. But by the order of Paul IV., as appears from a letter of Ferdinand, dated November 22, 1555, the departure of the twelve Fathers from Rome was delayed, for unknown reasons, until the end of January, 1556. When they took their leave of the Pope, he addressed to them a long allocution, which he did with much pleasure. As they travelled during the time of Lent, and almost always on foot, they arrived at Prague, much exhausted, on April 21st. Canisius was waiting for them in that city. He received from them the letter which named him Provincial. Full of consternation at the appointment, he hastened to conjure Ignatius to spare him this burden, saying that he had no qualities for the government of others. But the Saint replied that he must bow his head to the yoke of obedience, and have confidence in God, Who had chosen him to do great things for His glory, and would assist him with His grace in all things necessary. Canisius represented to the Saint that he had long since made a vow of making no choice, either of place or of anything else, for his own use, and that he could not fulfil this vow in his new office. Ignatius took away this scruple by telling him that the vows which a Religious takes without the knowledge of his superior are invalid. The new Provincial went from Prague to Ingolstadt, as we have seen above. Thus the college of Prague was one of the last founded by St. Ignatius, and it soon became so flourishing that the Society had none that surpassed it in prosperity.

Ignatius, at the same time, thought of erecting a new province of the Order in Lower Germany, of which Belgium then formed a part, and he named as superior Father Bernard Olivier; but as he had died a little time before, Polanco wrote, in the name of Ignatius, February

4, 1556, that each of the three colleges of Louvain, Cologne, and Tournay were to choose two or three Fathers fit to fill the place of Provincial. The votes were to be given by each separately and in writing, without previous consultation, and then to be sent to Rome, that Ignatius might choose the most eligible. But the post remained a long time vacant, owing to the death of the Saint.*

It is known that St. Ignatius appeared, while living, to Father Leonard Kessel, rector of Cologne, by virtue of a phenomenon known in hagiography as bilocation. It is most probable, according to Menchacha's account, that this miracle took place in the year 1550. In a fragment of a letter written by Polanco, July 22, 1550, which has been preserved to us,† he says that Ignatius did not approve at the time of the desire that Kessel had of going to Rome. Now it was the ordinary custom of Polanco to add a letter of his own to the letters written by Ignatius, and we may therefore conclude that Ignatius' letter to Kessel, in which he says that " perhaps he will see him in another manner " is of the same date. When the same Father Kessel left Cologne, in 1553, on account of the unfavorable dispositions of the authorities of the town, Ignatius wrote to him thus—" That, under the circumstances, he approved of his making a short excursion throughout the province, provided he and his companions were not long absent from the city, and did not sacrifice the main thing to what was accessory; but that he did not give them permission to fix their abode out of the town, because places of less importance give fewer occasions of gathering the desired fruit, and besides that, they must not leave so famous a university ; that their exertions would be more useful for the good of religion in forming scholars to become priests and officials of the state, than all the pains they should bestow on the inhabitants of the small towns and villages." By following these prescriptions of Ignatius, Kessel and his companions succeeded by degrees in smoothing all difficulties, and the college of

* Reifenburg, *Hist. Prov. Germ.*, inf., cited by Menchacha, p. 565. This serves to correct Orlandini, xvi., 2.
† Ibid., l. ii., cap. 2.

Cologne was established that year, as we learn from a letter of St. Ignatius, April 3, 1556, written to Ribadeneyra, whom he had sent on a message to the Court of Philip II., at Brussels—

They are asking of me most earnestly at 'Cologne men who shall be capable of contributing to the general good of that city, by preaching, explaining Scripture, and teaching other sciences. Although that city perseveres, in fact, in the Catholic faith, it contains many men who are disseminating evil doctrines, and few that teach good doctrines. We are informed, indeed, by letter that there is not one who teaches any theology at all. And though I am thinking of sending thither a number of Fathers, sufficient for the commencement of a college, which they wish to have established, I wish that, meanwhile, three or four days after the receipt of this letter, you should go to Cologne, unless his Majesty or the Count Ruy Gomez command the contrary, and there employ yourself in preaching in Latin, or in giving lectures on some passages of Holy Scripture, as you shall judge most convenient for the edification of the city.

We have other instances besides these to give of the interest Ignatius took in the welfare of Germany. In 1553, Canisius, seeing the sad condition of religion in that country, besought him to order each priest of the Society to say every month a Mass, that God might grant to that people the light of the Catholic faith, and each of those who were not priests to pray for the same intention. The Saint found this request to be quite in accordance with the spirit of the Society, and after no long delay published the following encyclical, which we give more fully than is given by Bartoli—

Jesus. Ignatius of Loyola, Superior General of the Society of Jesus, to his well-beloved brothers in Jesus Christ, the superiors and members of the Society of Jesus, salutation in Our Lord. As the true charity, which obliges us to embrace the whole body of the Church in Jesus Christ its Head, requires us to apply more especially remedies to those portions of this same body which are suffering from dangerous sickness, we have thought it right that our Society should devote itself with particular attention, according to the feeble measures of our powers, to the succor of Germany and the Northern nations, whom the malady of heresy exposes to the greatest dangers. And although in other ways we discharge this duty, and many amongst us endeavor to give succor to these countries by our prayers and the holy sacrifice of the Mass, nevertheless, in order that this duty of charity to our neighbor may be exercised for a longer time and in a more extensive sphere, we give orders to all our brothers, both to those who are under our immediate rule, and those who are placed under the authority of rectors and other superiors appointed to govern, to say, if they are priests, every month a Mass, and if they are not priests, to recite prayers for the spiritual wants of Germany : that the Lord may be pleased at last to have mercy upon that nation and the other lands which heresy has infected by its contagion, and to bring them back by His grace to the purity of the Catholic faith and true religion. And we wish that they should continue to do so, as long as the want of these countries shall remain. We wish also that wherever the Society is established, no province, though it were at the furthest extremities of the Indies, be exempt from this duty of charity.

Rome, July 25, 1553.

The Saint says, moreover, in a letter to the Margrave of Berg, " As for what concerns myself, He Who knows all things, even the secret of hearts, and has given to me of His free gift the desire of the salvation and perfection of souls, He knows what lively interest I take in Germany and Flanders, and particularly in the people of the country of Berg and the other subjects of your Excellency. Accordingly, as I shall have power and opportunity, I will do for them all that I can." *

* Collection at Rome.

# CHAPTER IX.

WE would not have made any mention here of the persecutions the Society had to undergo from the University of Paris (as this subject has been treated of not long since by Cretineau Joli in the first volume of his *History of the Society of Jesus*), were it not that much remains to be said to complete his account of it. We are, moreover, obliged to take a hasty view of what occurred in this matter, in order to fill up our sketch of the life of Ignatius. The decree of the Faculty of Theology of Paris was dated December 1, 1544, but the Provincial, Paschasius Brouet, was not made acquainted with it until the commencement of the following year. This war against the Society, which was still so young, and had very few members in France, was awakened by the antipathy of the Bishop of Paris, who wished to subject the Jesuits to his jurisdiction as completely as if they were secular priests. Moreover, he could not forgive the Society for having received his nephew into their Order in spite of him. Besides this, the professors of the university (many of whom belonged to various Religious Orders), thought the interests of their respective Communities threatened by the new Society, although, in truth, it had, on the contrary, given occasion to many Religious Communities to return to their ancient vigor and discipline. The sophistries and calumnies invented at this period took root in France. They were studiously disseminated by the Jansenists, and so at last became current among the clergy. Thence they spread into the cabinets and Councils of Ministers of State. It is a remarkable fact that, as a general rule, opposition to the Society manifested itself from the first in some particular phase in each country, and took a kind of traditional shape in its history, and this has lasted down to the present day.

The Bishop of Paris supplied the object of the complaint, which was partly a fabrication and partly a misrepresentation and distortion of facts. Hence many of the professors, who did not share in the prejudices of their contemporaries, refused their signature, whilst others, without entering deeply into the question, declared that they merely followed the judgment of the majority. When the decree was made known at Rome, several of the most eminent of the Society advised Ignatius to have it refuted, but he replied, with a smile, " My Fathers, remember that Christ said to His Disciples, when leaving this world—' My peace I give to you, My peace I leave you.' Take these words to yourselves in this case. We must not write nor do anything which may cause any bitterness. It is sometimes better to be silent than to speak. There is no need of taking up the pen to defend the truth when the truth speaks for itself. The authority of the theologians of Paris is assuredly great, and we ought the more to respect it, without letting ourselves be cast down by it. The truth is never overcome for a long time—it can be combated, but not extinguished. We will take some other means, if it be necessary, although I think it is not, to cure this wound, which is not so dangerous as you think."

But although he would not permit any particular persons to undertake to refute, in the name of the Society, the calumnies uttered against it, knowing well that this course would only provoke new attacks from its adversaries, still he did not remain inactive. He wrote to all the superiors of the Society to ask of the princes, both ecclesiastical and secular, and the authorities of the places where they lived, an authenticated testimonial of their conduct, doctrines, and Institute, and to send it to him, that the prejudices of those who had declared themselves against the Society, in a spirit of party and through want of information, might be answered by the

universal judgment of almost every country.	He ad-
dressed himself to some of the patrons of the Society to
ask their support, and we subjoin the letter which he
wrote on this matter to the duke of Ferrara—

As your Excellency has from the first shown yourself a patron and
zealous defender of our little Society, you will not be surprised if we
have recourse to you in a circumstance where there is question of
removing obstacles put in our way to hinder the service of God; and
even if we had not already experienced your Excellency's good-will,
the care which you take in things of this kind, as becomes a truly
Christian prince, would embolden us to ask your aid and protection in
this matter, for the greater glory of the most high and divine majesty
of God.	Our brother, Master John Pelletier, is instructed to give you
information on the subject of some difficulties which have arisen at
Paris against the Constitutions of our Society, which have been established and observed hitherto for the glory of God and the salvation of
souls.	We therefore humbly beg of your Excellency, if it seems good
to you for the glory of God, which is the sole end we have in view, to
take the trouble to write to the most Christian king.	Some persons,
in fact, endeavor by sinister reports to take away from him his good
dispositions in our regard, although I hope, in the divine goodness,
that the opposition raised against us in that city will contribute to make
more evident the excellence of this enterprise, which God Our Lord has
Himself begun by us, His weak instruments, and that it will happen
at Paris as it happened to us at Rome, where your Excellency was
pleased to give your assistance to aid the interposition of Divine Providence in our favor.*

The certificates asked for by Ignatius arrived from all
parts, drawn up in terms reflecting the greatest honor
upon the Society.	We will content ourselves with giving
some few of them.	The Inquisitor of Ferrara, Jerome
Papin, of the Order of St. Dominic, attests, March 21,
1555, that the rector, John Pelletier, a Frenchman, and
the Fathers his subjects, have conducted themselves
with so much piety and prudence that not a word has
been ever said against them; that in filling the professors'
chairs, and in doing other public offices, they have be-
haved in so exemplary and so discreet a manner, that they
have been of great utility to the students of the university, both in regard to morality and instruction in learning.
The rector and thirty-two professors of the university
of this same city addressed, on their part, a certificate to

* Menchacha, iv., 20.	The testimonials which follow are to be
found in the Bollandists, secs. 47, 48.

the University of Paris, and especially to the faculty of theology, and after an eulogy of the Society in the most flattering terms, they say that "the schools and the Society of Jesus, like all others, ought to be judged by their works, and these works are truly admirable. The Jesuits," they say, "teach humanities gratuitously, and, at the same time, form their scholars in good morals; they preach and explain Holy Scripture, and leave nothing undone that relates to the service of religion, visiting the hospitals, and giving consolation to the sick. On these accounts, far from being deserving of expulsion, they ought rather by all means to have been invited to Ferrara, if they had not been already there."

Giles, Bishop of Modena, attests that "the Society of Jesus, at Modena, and in other cities of Italy, exercises so happy án influence on their inhabitants, by the purity of its morals, its piety, good examples, and holy lessons, that all those who follow its directions make daily progress in virtue; that he says this not out of flattery, God forbid, but to declare to the glory of God what he has seen and known, because a tree is known by its fruits, and every man will be judged at last, not by the reckoning of men, but by the things he has done; that he limits himself to these few words in favor of a Society which he looks upon with reason as worthy of all praise and recommendation everywhere."

The Vicar General of the Archbishop of Florence, commissioner of the Inquisition, together with his colleagues, certifies that the Society is very devoted to all the orders approved of by Holy Church, and that it is particularly careful to preserve peace and true union with all.

We pass over in silence the testimonials sent from Spain and Portugal, and in particular from the universities of Valladolid, Lisbon, and Coimbra, as well as the two letters of the King of Portugal to the Pope relative to this affair. The university of Louvain, in Belgium, also raised its voice against the censure of the Sorbonne, which thus found itself in a manner completely isolated. Almost all those who had authority to speak in the whole of Europe blamed its conduct, and this must have been a very pleasing triumph for St. Ignatius. He made, however, no further use of these testimonials, for the cabal at Paris broke up of itself, as he had foreseen. But the pamphlet of the faculty of theology was censured by the Inquisition of Spain at Saragossa. The decree was drawn up with all the respect due to the Society. It declares—" Ill-disposed men having spread a report that a foreign university had designated the Society of Jesus as dangerous to the faith, as troubling the peace and quiet of the Church, and as injurious to the existing Religious Orders, the Inquisition declares that these propositions are false and injurious to the Apostolic See, and orders, under pain of excommunication, that all writings on this subject be given up to it, and that persons evilly disposed towards the Society should be denounced to it in the space of three days, and that silence be kept on this subject for the future." This unsuccessful campaign against the Company only hastened the foundation of two of its colleges in France.

In Belgium the Society met with difficulties on the part of the government with regard to the rights which are essential for its existence, viz., the rights of acquiring and possessing property for the maintenance of its colleges and of the exercise of the functions which are proper to the Institute. It was pretended that no new Order could be introduced without the royal authority. Here, as elsewhere, the opposition first arose from the clergy, who were displeased that the Jesuits exercised ministerial duties gratuitously, and Robert de Croy, Bishop of Cambrai, was their mouth-piece. In the year 1554 he suspended the Jesuits in his diocese from all sacerdotal functions. The Nuncio Apostolic at Brussels and the English Cardinal Pole endeavored in vain to induce him to retract this measure, which clearly went beyond his powers. However, Ignatius ordered the Fathers in Belgium to conduct themselves with the greatest prudence, and to make no use of the powers they had received from the Holy See against the orders of the Bishop. But as the Society, in consequence of the suspension, was reduced almost to a state of inactivity in that country, it was necessary that something should be done. Philip II. having come to Belgium to receive from his father the states he was resigning, Ignatius thought it a favorable opportunity for obtaining from the new king some better conditions. Accordingly, he sent Father Ribadeneyra, who was still young, to the Court of Brussels, and gave him the following letter to Philip.*

When we were apprized here of the resignation of his Imperial Highness, our Lord the emperor, made in favor of your Majesty, of the German Low Countries, and his other states in those parts, we all felt great joy in Our Lord, both on account of the example of piety given by your Majesty on this occasion, and because we hope it will please the Divine Majesty to prosper these States in committing them to your hands. And this we beg of Him, without ceasing in our poor prayers and in the holy sacrifice of the Mass. Whereas we desire to serve your Majesty with all our power in Our Lord, not only in this but in all other things according to our weak ability, as we are in duty bound, and whereas we are convinced that it is advantageous, both to the glory of God and the good of your Majesty, that some of our Fathers, Germans by birth and language, should employ the talents Our Lord has intrusted to them in the Low Countries, which, on account of their vicinity and relations with Germany, are more exposed to suffer harm, to the detriment of God's honor and your Majesty's service, I have resolved in Our Lord to send to your Majesty Master Ribadeneyra, who is the bearer of this letter, and who will explain *viva voce* the grounds of my opinion, so that, if your Majesty judges that the project will contribute to the service of God and yours, you will be pleased to take under your protection this our little Society in those countries, as you have designed to do elsewhere, and to grant it powers to found colleges in them, so that it may be able to employ in the gaining of souls those little talents which Our Lord has intrusted to it, as it has done in the other dominions and estates belonging to your Majesty. It will thus be enabled to offer to your Majesty, in those countries which have the most need of them, the services which it owes to you, for the greater

* As this letter is dated October 23, 1555, and it speaks of the resignation of the Low Countries by Charles V. as an accomplished fact, and as, on the other hand, the chronology of this event, though so near our times, is very uncertain, Menchacha finds here a difficulty he cannot solve. But it arises from his being led into a mistake by Ferreolus Locrius (*Chron. Belg. Atrebati*, 1616), who, confounding this resignation with the homage of the States paid to Philip, acknowledging him as their future prince, places it in 1549. If Ignatius speaks of the resignation as already made, it is because he wrote of it as it was spoken of in Rome—as a thing shortly about to take place. However, Menchacha cites a Spanish historian of the times, Gonzalez Illescas, who gives (*Hist. Pontif.*, vi., 3, sec. i.) October 28, 1555, as the day on which Charles V. publicly resigned the Low Countries, and January 17, 1555, as the day on which he resigned his other dominions. Sandoval (vii., 592), Illescas, and Thou (*Hist.*, xvi., near the end), agree in giving October 28. Herrera and Pallavicini give the 17th of January. The acts are dated October 25, 1555, and January 16, 1556.

glory of God, our Master and Creator, and the good of the people whom he has confided to your care. Master Ribadeneyra will explain all fully to you. You can place in him the same trust and confidence which you would in myself. And I conclude by humbly beseeching Our Lord to grant you His perfect grace.

Rome, Oct. 23, 1555.*

Philip, notwithstanding his goodwill to the Society, was obliged in the beginning of his reign to conciliate the minds of his ministers in Belgium, and he could not therefore use his power and authority by a decisive step, especially since his Belgian advisers thought and spoke a different language from his Spanish counsellors. The negotiations were therefore long protracted, the king having put the affair into the hands of the Bishop of Arras and the president of the Council, Vigilius Zwichen, who was a declared opponent of the Jesuits. Both raised difficulties, according to Ribadeneyra's account, because the bishops and parish priests were not willing to allow the Fathers of the Society to preach and hear confessions. We have already seen that Ignatius gave orders to his envoy to retire for a time to Cologne. But shortly after this Polanco wrote to him, in the name of Ignatius, to make a declaration that the Society had no interests in the matter of establishing itself in Belgium, and only desired to enter there because it was necessary that able laborers—learned and truly Catholic men—should be employed in that country, in which heresy had already made much progress, and that this was a point which concerned, not only the honor and wisdom, but the conscience also of those who were called to the government of those countries; that, as for the opponents of the Society, they were either persons infected with the contagion of error, or else ecclesiastics who, instead of supporting the Jesuits in their ministry, as it was their duty to do, opposed them because they thought their interests at stake, on account of the rule of the Society to give freely what it had freely received. † But the Saint

---

* Collection at Rome. Menchacha (iv., 25) gives a translation of this letter, taken from the *Imago primi Sæculi Societatis* (p. 737), but it is not exactly rendered, and does not give the peculiarities of the style of St. Ignatius.

† Ibid.

did not live to see the result of his labors. The influence of the Count de Feria, * and of Mary, the king's sister, obtained thus much, that the Society should be acknowledged and allowed in Belgium, although under many restrictions, which Philip afterwards removed. The terms of agreement were settled three days after the death of Ignatius.

Ribadeneyra was also commissioned to explain in the colleges of Lower Germany the true sense of the Constitutions, and to put them into force. Ignatius informed the Fathers of the Society in that country of this by a letter, which at the same time accredited Ribadeneyra to the performance of this duty. This letter deserves a place in this history. In it, then, the Saint writes thus—

As it is absolutely necessary that the members of our Society should be animated with the same spirit and observe the same manners of conduct, according to the prescriptions of our Institute, and the more so as they live very far separated from one another, and in distant countries, and as our dear brother in Jesus Christ, Peter Ribadeneyra, knows perfectly our thoughts concerning the Constitutions and customs introduced into our Society for the glory of God and our own spiritual progress and that of our neighbor, we have thought it good to send him to you for our mutual consolation, and to bind still closer the ties which unite us. As the spirit of our vocation is the same, and makes us all tend to the same end—the glory of God and the salvation of souls, so we ought all to be agreed, both in our manner of acting, and, as far as is possible, in the means we employ. You will therefore receive him with all the kindness and affection that you can, and will repose an entire confidence in all that he shall say to you in my name, with regard to the Constitutions, the Statutes, and all other things. †

Rome, Oct. 20, 1555.

* His son Antonio, whom Charles V. wished to propose as a cardinal in 1552, became a Jesuit this same year.

† This letter is taken from the manuscript life of Father Ribadeneyra.

# CHAPTER X.

## DEATH OF ST. IGNATIUS.

WE have come to the last days of the life of St. Ignatius. But before relating his death we must touch on several points concerning him. His health had always been very weak. In the autumn of 1554 it began to cause alarm; and as his occupations increased, his Consultors begged him to choose an assistant to share his labors. He had already earnestly demanded to be freed from his office, but now they wished to give him a Vicar without his asking for one. At first he refused, foreseeing that an associate, unless he took upon him the whole of the business, would give him little alleviation. However, as he was so humble and so detached from self-will, he very soon returned to the first resolution and accepted the proposition made to him. A letter of Polanco to Jerome Domenech, the Provincial of Sicily, gives us information on this subject—

Father Natalis [he says] is expected with impatience by our Father, and by us in particular, who compose the council for the general good of the Society; for on the one hand the multiplicity of business consequent on the increase of the Society, and on the other the frequent and almost continual indisposition of our Father, who for the most part has kept his bed for nearly a year, makes us desire more ease and help for him than he has had hitherto. We have therefore given him notice that it seemed convenient that he should choose some one to govern the Society in his place. He ordered all the Priests we have at Rome, with the exception of two or three who are novices, to assemble together, and after being informed of the necessity of choosing some one to assist our Father, to say Mass thrice for his intention, and say also other additional prayers for the same end. He wished also that each one should have liberty to consult others and take the necessary informations, after which they should all write on a billet the name of him whom they elected. He wished that the Lay-brothers should also assemble and name four Fathers as electors to vote in their stead. We assembled on All Saints' Day to the number of thirty-four, out of whom thirty or thirty-two elected Father Natalis. Our Father confirmed the election, and Father Natalis began to fulfil the duties of his office, to the satisfaction of all, easing our Father of the burden of affairs which he had borne upon his shoulders.*

Natalis, with great discretion, would accept of no title, so as to preserve the authority of the General intact. Indeed, Ignatius soon recovered his health; sufficiently so, at least, as to be able to dispense with his services, and to employ him for the ensuing autumn in a more useful manner in Spain. We have seen with what activity and energy the Saint continued to expedite business during the last year of his life. The only alleviation which he allowed himself was to name, in the month of March, 1555, Father Pazzano Procurator General of the Professed House at Rome, and to hand over to him the temporal administration of that House. But early in the summer of 1556 his malady began to increase in such a manner that it was evident he had not much longer to live. He himself was well aware of this, and wrote to his friend Doña Elenora Mascareña to this effect, in reply to her request that he would pray earnestly for Philip II., whom she had nursed in his infancy. He answered her that, while Philip was a young prince, he had prayed for him every day, but that, since he had succeeded to the throne of his father, he had redoubled his prayers for him. Then he adds, " This is the last letter I shall write to you. I shall soon pray to the Lord for you in Heaven." He announced to some of those about him, though in a less positive manner, his approaching end, when in a conversation one day with them he said, " I have desired above all others three things, and, thanks be to God, I see them all accomplished—that the Company should be confirmed by the Pope, that the book of the *Spiritual Exercises* should be approved by the Holy See, and thirdly, that the Constitutions should be completed and observed in the whole Society." His hearers fully understood what he meant by these words He showed by another incident that he knew that his end was near, for, wishing to receive among the Professed Father Wirik, who had displayed his zeal in the foundation of colleges in Sicily, he did not,

* Collection at Rome.

as was his custom in all such cases, make him come to Rome, but commissioned Father Domenech, the Provincial, to receive his profession, saying that he must not be called away from Catana. However, he had made others come from much greater distances, and this was not the real reason for his resolution. He foresaw that this Father would not find him alive if he came to Rome.

A little time before his death, he abandoned the government of the Society to three Fathers, John Polanco, Christopher Madrid, and Jerome Natalis, and retired to the villa which he had built for the sick and the recreation of the students, near the Baths of Antoninus. But the excessive heats of the summer made him very ill, and after having been taken with the fever two or three days, he wished to be carried back to the Professed House. The circumstances of his death are related in the account sent by Father Polanco to the Provincials. It is the recital of an eye-witness and has all the freshness of such a narrative, and therefore is best fitted to give us a faithful picture of the last moments of the Saint.

The peace of Christ. I announce by these present letters to your reverence and all the Brothers under your care, that it has pleased God on Friday, the last day of July, to call to Himself our blessed Father, Master Ignatius. On the eve of St. Peter ad Vincula, God has broken the bonds which kept him prisoner in this mortal flesh, in order to admit him to the liberty of the elect, having thus heard at last the prayers of his servant. For although he bore with much patience and courage the pains of his pilgrimage and the burdens which he sustained upon his shoulders, nevertheless he long since desired to praise and contemplate in the heavenly home his Master and Creator, Who by His divine providence has left him to us up to this time, that this little Society, which He Himself begun by his means, might enjoy the benefit of his example, his wisdom, authority, and prayers. But now that its roots have to all appearance struck deep, He has removed him to Heaven, that, being more closely united to Himself, the Plenitude of all Good, he may obtain for us a more abundant measure of grace, and that this plant may increase and grow abundantly, together with its fruit, in the various countries of the world.

It is true that the loss of the presence of so good a Father must needs be painfully felt in this House and all the colleges of the Society, but this feeling of deprivation is without pain; and in the tears which we have shed, as orphans who have lost our father, there is a sweet affection, an assured hope, and a more than usual fervor of spirit. If we look to ourselves it seems that, so far from having lost him, we hope that he will aid us more than ever by his ardent love, and that the divine mercy by his intercession will increase, for the general good of the Church, the number and the benefactors of our Society.

Your Reverence desires without doubt to learn some details of the passage of our Father who is now in glory. You must know, then, that his death was a very sweet one, and his agony did not last an hour. We had many sick in the house, and among them Master Laynez, John de Mendoza, and some others dangerously sick. Our Father had also a slight indisposition, and suffered a little from fever for four or five days. We did not know whether he was still suffering from it or not, although he was very weak, as he had been at other times before. In this state he sent for me on Wednesday, and bid me tell Dr. Torres to attend him the same as the other sick. In fact, as we did not think his sickness dangerous, less attention was given to him than to the others. Dr. Torres did as he was requested, and another doctor of high reputation, a friend of ours, Master Alexander, came to see him every day. On Thursday, about the twentieth hour (that is four of the afternoon) he sent for me, and after dismissing from his room the persons who attended him, he said to me that it was time to send a message to His Holiness that he was dying, and there was no further hope of his life; and that he asked His Holiness for his blessing, for himself and for Master Laynez, who was also in danger of death, and that, if God Our Lord granted them the grace to call them to heaven, they would pray there for His Holiness as they had done every day whilst in this world.* I replied to him, "My Father, the doctors do not think your sickness dangerous, and as for me, I hope that God will leave us your Reverence for some years longer. Are you then," said I, "so ill as he?" meaning Laynez. He replied, "I am so ill, that nothing further remains but to give up my soul." I expressed the hope which I really felt, that he would live a long time yet, but assured him at the same time that I would execute his commission. I then asked him if he could wait until Friday, as I wished to send letters the same evening to Spain by Genoa, and the post left on Thursday. "I should prefer," he replied, "to-day rather than to-morrow." Or, "The sooner it is done, the better; however, do as it seems good to you. I leave myself entirely to you."

Wishing to know whether the physicians thought his case dangerous, I begged the chief of them, Master Alexander, to tell me frankly whether our Father was in danger of death, because he had told me to announce this to the Pope. He answered, "To-day I can pronounce nothing on the danger of his state, I will do so to-morrow."

In these circumstances, and as the Father had left it to me, I thought I could wait until the Friday to have the opinion of the doctors, acting

---

* What Polanco says here of Laynez was a conjecture on his part, for Ignatius did not name the other sick person for whom he asked the Apostolic blessing. Polanco has corrected this error in the third volume of the *History of the Society*. Although Laynez was prepared for death, he recovered two days afterwards. Ignatius meant Father Olave, which Polanco could not then know, as he was not sick until after the 6th of August, but died shortly after.

entirely in a human manner. The same Thursday, in the evening, at one o'clock (that is at eight in the evening according to our manner of reckoning), Dr. Madrid and I were present at our Father's supper, who ate well as usual and conversed with us, so that I retired to my room, not thinking that the sickness was dangerous. In the morning at sunrise we found our Father in his agony, and I hastened immediately to the Vatican. The Pope showed the most sincere sorrow at the news, and gave the sick Father his blessing with all possible affection.* Thus he gave up his soul with the greatest calm into the hands of his Creator, before the second hour after sunrise, in the presence of the Father Dr. Madrid and Master Andrew Frusius. We could but remark here the humility of the holy old man. He was convinced that he was dying, as he had made known to us the evening before, and I never remember to have heard him predict anything with so much assurance as he did this, except only a year ago, when he promised us at Rome that Providence would come to our aid, as It did at the time he designated; and yet, notwithstanding this assurance, he would not have us called to give us his blessing, and he did none of those things which servants of God are used to do at such a time. For he thought of himself with such humility that he did not wish the Society to put any confidence in any other than God alone, and therefore in dying he avoided everything that might seem extraordinary. Perhaps he had obtained of God, Whose glory he ever had in his thoughts, that nothing remarkable should be done at his death, as in his life he had made it a law in himself to keep concealed the gifts of God, except some of those which ought to be disclosed for the edification of others.

When our Father had departed from this world, it was thought proper, for the preservation of the body, to take out the intestines and to embalm it in the best manner in our power. The circumstances attending this operation were very edifying, and excited our admiration, for the bowels and stomach were shrunk and contracted, which was attributed by the medical men to the long fasts he had practised during so many years, and to the ardor and firmness of his character, which made him undertake with cheerfulness and equanimity, notwithstanding his extreme feebleness of body, things which required great exertion. Three little gall stones were found in his liver,† testifying his long abstinences, so that the good old man, James d'Eguia, had good reason to say that our Father had long since been kept alive only by a miracle. I, for my part, cannot understand how he could have lived naturally any length of time with a liver in such a state,

---

* This could not have been communicated by Polanco to the Saint, for he died between five and six in the morning. The attendant watching by him says that he had spoken to himself until midnight, as he had done through the whole of his sickness. After that he became quieter, and called his attendant less frequently, but he often exclaimed, *Ay Dios*—" O my God! " He did not receive Extreme Unction.

† They were in the main artery, as the anatomist, Realdus Columbus, reports in his work *De Anatomia* (Bolland., sec. 53).

unless God Our Lord had supplied the want, and so preserved him for the Society to which he was necessary.

We put off the sepulture of his blessed remains until Sunday after Vespers. Although he was left in the room in which he died, the concourse and devotion of the faithful was very great. Some kissed his hands or feet, or touched his body; we did all we could to prevent portions of his habit being taken, or anything that belonged to him. Some painters took his portrait, a thing he would never permit during his life, though he had been often entreated to have it done. We made a little grave in the great chapel of our church on the Gospel side, and we lowered the body into it, enclosed in a coffin, and after having recited the Office as usual, we placed over it a large stone, which can be removed at pleasure. He will remain there, as we may say, awaiting his destination elsewhere. Dr. Olave went to the Pope to announce his death, and His Holiness, on hearing it, showed himself a truly good father, and testified the affection which he had always felt for the Society in all the stages of its progress. Some of the most influential cardinals did the same, as did other friends who offered their services to the Society. Praise be to the Lord Our God, for He is our strength and our hope. We have offered the holy sacrifice of the Mass for three days for our Father, though many felt the pious wish to recommend their souls to his prayers rather than to commend his soul to God Our Lord. We must, however, observe everywhere what reason dictates, both with regard to the three Masses and the prayers of the Brothers who are not yet priests.

Rome, August 6, 1566.

The congregation assembled for the choice of a Vicar announced in like manner the death of St. Ignatius to the foreign princes who had protected the Society, and we will here give the letter which was written to Albert, Duke of Bavaria—

Considering the special love and duty shown by our most dear Father, Master Ignatius, of holy memory, to your Excellency, though our whole Society also regards you with particular affection as its most assured protector, not only at Ingolstadt, but also elsewhere, we thought we should be wanting in our duty if we did not announce to your Excellency the death of our Father, the first General and Founder of our Society, whom the Divine Infinite Goodness has summoned out of this life to that blessed eternal life for which he long ago ardently sighed. He supported, it is true, his continual infirmities with that strength of mind and constancy for which he was ever remarkable; but for many years he languished with a holy desire of being united to his Creator, and of praising Him perfectly in His heavenly kingdom. Blessed be the name of the Lord Jesus, Who has given us and taken from us such a Father.

Although deprived of the corporal presence of this admirable man, the Divine Goodness gives us the certain hope that our Father will aid us more powerfully in heaven than he could have done upon earth,

And so we have not lost courage since his death, and far from being despondent with regard to the Society, we feel greater zeal and joy with respect to all that concerns our Institute. Since, in fact, our Father has exchanged this earthly life for a heavenly one, we look for succor from him so much the greater and more powerful, as he is nearer to the Source of all spiritual graces and all good. We do not doubt that, having prayed to God so often for your Excellency and all Bavaria while he was living here on earth, he will do so now with greater fervor in the heavenly country, and that he will be heard still more in his prayers.

We, the Fathers who have the right of naming the future General of the Society, which is spread almost everywhere in Christendom, and numbers thirteen provinces,* being assembled together, have chosen as Vicar General the Provincial of Italy (Laynez). Though he is sick, he earnestly entreats your Excellency, as we all do, to maintain your favorable dispositions towards us, and to be persuaded that we will not degenerate from our Father, and that we shall be always ready, within the compass of our Institute and our powers, to serve in all things, both yourself and your Excellency's successors, for the honor and glory of Our Lord Jesus Christ.

Rome, August 14, 1556.

* Abyssinia is here reckoned as one, but afterwards it ceased forever to be a province.

# CHAPTER XI.

ALTHOUGH our work seems naturally to end at the death of Ignatius and with our endeavor to present the facts of his life in their historical unity as exactly as possible, still several things remain to be said which could not well find their place in the narrative, and still which contain very valuable information for the perfect knowledge of the Saint; and though this appendix seems somewhat irregular in form, its eminent importance must plead my excuse. What we have to add relates to the conduct of Ignatius, according to authenticated testimonials, in his interior and exterior government of the Society, and his relations with princes.

The first point we shall dwell on is that of asceticism, which necessarily plays so important a part in the life of all Christians in general, and more particularly of those who make profession of a closer imitation of Our Lord Jesus Christ. Ignatius seems to us a most accomplished master in this science of spiritual life, and to have carried it to the highest degree of perfection which it has ever attained. We have shown in the chapter treating on the Exercises what influence these have had upon it. We will now put together several things regarding the theory of asceticism as held and applied by St. Ignatius. He had learned by his own experience the true principles of that asceticism which perfects the moral nature without ruining the body, which carefully avoids all imperfect and false direction in the spiritual career, and which never allows the sentiment of feeling to predominate at the expense of reason and understanding. He used to say that, in the first days of conversion, men ought to lead a more severe life, but from the time that the soul has come to a state of greater purity from its stains, exterior mortification should be somewhat diminished. We will cite here one example. He allowed St. Francis Borgia at the beginning of his conversion, and while he was still viceroy of Catalonia, to follow the inspiration which led him to penitential austerities, but when he considered that he had done enough, and that he seemed to attach too much importance to practices of this kind, from the love of the contemplative to the prejudice of the active life, he interposed his authority, and regulated the practice of his spiritual exercises. We fortunately possess a letter in which he gives his saintly disciple principles of the greatest wisdom, to teach him the just mean between excess and defect in this difficult path. Borgia had made his profession as a member of the Society of Jesus on February 1st, 1548, in the hands of the Provincial, Father Araoz, although he still remained exteriorly in the world, with the right (by dispensation from the Pope) of administering his goods, and for the purpose of concealing from the knowledge of the world that he had taken vows. But in all that concerned the things pertaining to the salvation of the soul he was no longer master of his person or his actions. In these Ignatius had the right, and was in duty bound, to guide him, as Borgia fully acknowledged. On this very account he asked Ignatius to give him rules for his conduct. On this request being made, Ignatius wrote to him as follows—

When I was informed of the conduct you have prescribed to yourself in spiritual things, and in your external life, for the perfection of your soul, I have found, it is most true, new motives for rejoicing in the Lord. I thank the Eternal Majesty a thousand times over, and can only attribute your holy practices to the Divine Goodness, the Source of every good. However, as I consider in Our Lord that certain spiritual and corporal exercises are necessary at one time, and are not so at another time, and that, after having been useful to us, they are not so useful in the sequel, I wish to say to you, in the presence of the Divine Majesty, that which presents itself to my mind with regard to this matter, since your lordship desires to know my opinion.

First, as to what concerns the time you have prescribed to yourself for these interior and exterior practices of prayer and penance, I think that one half of them might be retrenched. For if, in proportion as our thoughts are carried away, either by our own evil inclinations, or by the devil, to vain and unlawful things, and if again, in proportion as we feel ourselves the more disposed to be attached to these unlawful things, we ought to multiply our practices of penance, so as to overcome our propensities, each one according to his dispositions, or according to the variety of his thoughts and temptations, that the will may take no pleasure in them nor consent to them; so, on the contrary, in proportion as these thoughts are dissipated and give place to holy inspirations, it is our duty to give entrance to such inspirations into our mind, and to open wide to them the gates of our soul. And, therefore, as you have no longer need of so much defensive armor for the conquest of the enemy, I think in Our Lord that you will do better to employ the half of that time in the government of your estates and in spiritual conferences and studies; for in the future acquired science will be more necessary to you, and more useful, than infused knowledge. But, at the same time, endeavor to keep your soul in peace and repose, and ready to receive all the workings of Our Lord in it. For it is the sign of a greater virtue and a greater grace, to be able to enjoy the presence of God in a multiplicity of employments, and in many places rather than in one only; and we ought to do all we can to arrive at this end through the divine goodness of Our God.

In the second place, with regard to fasting and abstinence, I think that it is better for the glory of Our Lord to preserve and strengthen the stomach and other powers of nature, than it is to debilitate them; for when we have the fixed resolution rather to die than of deliberate purpose to commit the least offence against the Divine Majesty, and when we are not attacked by any particular temptation from the devil, the world, or the flesh, exterior mortification is no longer necessary. Now I am convinced that you are in this disposition of which I have been speaking, and that you are free from temptations. I desire, therefore, that you will fully master this thought—that the soul and body both are the gift of God, Our Master and Creator, and that you will have to give Him a strict account of both, and that for His sake you ought not to enfeeble your bodily nature, because, if you take away its strength, the spiritual nature cannot act any longer with the same energy. If I have gladly seen you for some time fast and practise a rigorous abstinence, I cannot do so for the future; because I see that these fasts and abstinences prevent the stomach from performing its usual functions, and even from digesting the most simple aliment necessary for the support of the body. I rather feel myself inclined to advise you to eat all that is allowed, and as often as you find want of it, without scandal to others, for we ought so much more to love the body, and to wish it well, the more it obeys and serves the soul; and the soul in its turn finds in this obedience and assistance of the body increased strength and energy to serve and glorify God, our Master and Creator.

As to the third point, namely, the chastisements which you inflict upon your body, I would avoid, for Our Lord's sake, to spill even the least drop of blood. If hitherto the Divine Majesty has given you, as I am convinced He has, a particular grace and attraction to this practice, as well as to the other holy practices mentioned above, I do not hesitate to affirm, without giving reasons for what I say, that it is better for the future to leave off these things, and, instead of trying to draw a little blood, to seek to unite yourself more closely with the Lord of all, asking of Him more precious gifts, as, for example, the grace to shed a fountain of tears, or, at least, some few drops, whether it be for your own sins, or for those of others, or whether it be in contemplating the mysteries of Our Lord Jesus Christ in this life or in the next, or in considering and loving the divine perfections; and these tears will be the more precious and meritorious as the thoughts and meditations which make them flow shall be more elevated. And although in these several objects the third is in itself more perfect than the second, and the second than the first, nevertheless, that is the best for each individual in which the Lord Our God the more abundantly communicates Himself to him, and gives him a greater abundance of His holy gifts and spiritual graces; for He knows and sees what is the most advantageous to him, and shows him the way which he ought to keep—for He knows all things. But, in order that we may discover this by His grace, it is very useful to prove and try many ways, so that we may choose the one that is the safest and the best for us in this life, and the most conducive to life eternal. Now, among these gifts, I reckon those which it is not in our power to be possessed of at our will, but which are simply bestowed upon us by the Giver of all good, such as are those which have a more immediate relation with His Divine Majesty, namely, actual faith, hope, and charity—spiritual peace and joy, tears, interior consolations, elevation of soul, divine impulses and lights, together with all other spiritual impressions and joys, having always regard to the due subordination between these gifts, and manifesting all respect and humble obedience to our holy mother the Church, and to those who are appointed rulers and doctors in it. There is not one of these spiritual gifts that ought not to be preferred above all corporal austerities, which are only good so far as they have the end in view, which is, to acquire these spiritual goods, or, at least, some portion of them. I do not mean to say by this that we ought to seek them simply for the pleasure they give us, still, all our thoughts, words, and actions, which without them are cold, confused, and disorderly, would through them become, to the greater glory of God, fervent, enlightened, and just. And when the body finds that it is in peril through its excessive exertions, the best thing to be done is to seek for these gifts by spiritual acts and other exercises taken in moderation. It will then come to pass that not only the soul will be in a sound state, but there will be a sound mind dwelling in a sound body, and the whole man will be the more healthy and better disposed for the service of God. As to the special conduct you should observe in other matters, I have not thought it good in Our Lord to enter at length into the subject, trusting that the same Divine Spirit which has hitherto conducted your lordship will continue to guide and govern you, to the greater glory of the Divine Majesty. *

* This letter has been translated from an ancient copy in the Imperial College of Madrid. It is also in the collection at Rome. The date is wanting. Orlandini puts it in 1548, for clearly the contents of the letter he cites are the same with the above, and many passages are word for word. We must not be surprised that Ignatius gives Borgia the title of your lordship, for he does so in letters certainly of a later date.

We have another instance which shows how much Ignatius was opposed to all extravagance in piety, and with what care he endeavored to banish it from the Society. He could not endure devotion which consists in excitement, and which, as soon as the real or apparent heats of fervor are passed, leaves only a void at the very best. Such devotion often exposes the subject of its delusions to fall into palpable errors, and to lose his vocation. At Gandia, the residence of St. Francis Borgia, the rector of the college, Andrew Oviedo, and one of the professors of the university, Francis Humphrey,* yielding themselves to the contemplative life more than was suitable to the spirit and end of the Society, conceived an idea, in the year 1549, that, in order to attain a higher degree of perfection, they ought to retire to the abode of a hermit whom they knew, and give themselves entirely for seven years to ascetical exercises. Oviedo wrote to this effect to Ignatius, his superior, and asked for permission to carry out his purpose, declaring, at the same time, his readiness to submit to his will. Ignatius, at once perceiving the illusion, wrote, by Polanco, to Borgia, to send the rector to him at Rome, and to send Humphrey to Ferrara, to Salmeron.† Borgia replied that this measure did not seem to him necessary, because both the Fathers were waiting for the reply in much tranquillity and with a readiness to obey in all humility; that he had been acquainted with their proposed plan by Oviedo, and that, without disapproving of the thing in itself, he had represented to them that the active life in the Society which they had vowed did not deprive them of the merits of the contemplative. Ignatius had a purpose in using Borgia as the medium of communication in this business, for he was aware that he partook of the tendencies of these two Fathers. Consequently, Borgia's reply by no means quieted his anxiety. However, he did not at the moment insist on the execution of his orders, but he wrote to Borgia a very severe letter, in which he let him see that the dismissal of these two Fathers, whom he designates by the letters B and C, would be an inevitable result, unless

---

* Spanish writers call him Onfroy. In Latin the name is Onufrius.
† This letter is to be found in the collection at Rome.

they corrected their false ideas once for all.   He writes
thus—

It we can believe what has 'been communicated to us, it seems that
the two Fathers B. and C., the one more and the other less, have
found the desert they are seeking, and are making themselves ready to
retire into another, which may be a much more complete one than the
first, unless they humble themselves and allow themselves to be guided,
as every one is bound to do according to his vocation.   The remedies
they are in need of can be administered to them directly or indirectly
by those who have the power and the will to do so.   The first consist
in prayer and the holy sacrifice of the Mass, which we will offer to the
Divine Goodness, but the second will be applied to them by some
other means, with the help of God's grace.   Your lordship can do
much in this case by your presence and your authority.   As for me, I
know to what my conscience obliges me, and I firmly believe, without
a shadow of doubt, and solemnly declare before the judgment-seat of
Christ, our Master and Creator, Who will one day judge us for eternity,
that these Religious are astray from the right road, that they are deceived
and mistaken, both in the things that are otherwise right and in those
that are wrong.   They are seduced by the father of lies, who divines
or suggests one or two truths in order to end by an imposture and to
make them fall into it.   In this assurance I beg of your lordship, for
the love and regard of God Our Lord, first to recommend this business
to His great goodness, and then to pay an exact attention to this matter, and to watch and take the necessary measures, without permitting
anything which may cause scandal and be extremely prejudicial to all
of us, but which may cause the thing to take altogether another shape.
God grant it may be so, as well as in all that regards His honor.   And
may God also grant that you see to these Fathers being completely
cured of their malady, for His own greater service and His praise and
glory forever.

    Rome, July 25, 1549.*

In general, when there was question of any essential
point, or when there was a necessity for his giving a just
reprimand, the words of Ignatius were so powerful that
no one could make the least attempt to answer them.   A
man of high consideration, who had entered into the
Society, was of so passionate a temper that it was resolved to dismiss him.   Ignatius had often sought to
correct him by kind and gentle remonstrances.   Seeing
that all was in vain, he at last spoke to him with such
terrible energy that the very walls of the room seemed to
shake, and those who were present trembled for very
fear.   The culprit was seized with such a dread that he

* This fragment of a letter is taken from the *Life of St. Ignatius,*
by Father Andrew Lucas, v., 24.

fell into a sort of swoon at his feet and promised amendment.

The practice of peculiar mortifications without the direction of an able and experienced guide was, in his judgment, more injurious than useful. When Simon Rodriguez endeavored to introduce into Portugal a spirit of self-willed piety, little in accordance with the end of the Society, he set himself to oppose it with all his might before it had openly displayed itself. He wrote in consequence a letter to the college of Coimbra, in which he says, among other things—" the enemy of human nature is rejoiced when he sees a soul walk indiscreetly and without a guide by high and sublime paths, because he hopes to find occasion to destroy it and make it fall, and the zeal which, under direction of obedience, would have been holy and salutary, becomes in the hands of the devil an instrument and a most effectual weapon for the ruin of true charity in the heart, and, consequently, of the spiritual life." *

He wished, as we have already said, that the exercises of piety, whether of soul or body, should be only employed as a means of solid progress in virtue, which makes the evangelical laborer more capable of working the conversion of men, and he could not endure that one should be reduced to incapability of action by weakening soul and body with immoderate asceticism. He rejected alike indiscreet penitences and sublime contemplations, into which illusion so easily enters, being persuaded that simple prayer and meditation are sufficient to obtain for all the one principal thing, namely, the acquisition of virtue. He often recommended his Religious to preserve their health, both for the service of God and that they might be able to take great care of the sick. We will cite only two testimonials of his vigilance on this point. The first is a circular addressed to all superiors in his name by the Secretary Polanco. In it he says—

---

* This letter, which is without date, and of which a copy is to be found in the collection at Rome, treats of obedience. This is the subject he loved to treat on, and I, for my part, know of five letters in which he speaks of it. The letter here in question begins with these words —"Aunque de las causas necessarias," etc.

Our Father, considering that he will have to give an account to God not only of the souls but of the bodies which He has confided to his care, wishes to acquit himself of his duty in this matter in other places as he has done here at Rome, following always the advice of the physician. He wishes that all should conform themselves to the doctor's opinion in all that regards the quantity and quality of their food, their sleep, and their clothing, departing in nothing from the prescriptions given for the preservation of health and strength necessary for the brethren. Your Reverence will therefore take care to have this rule observed, and it will be better to diminish by one or two the number of Religious in a house if the orders of the physician cannot otherwise be attended to, so that the rest may want nothing that is necessary. And should the revenues be insufficient—either on the part of the college, or the town, or the prelate, or other persons who, for the sake of serving God, have undertaken to provide for the necessities of the community—let recourse be had to those who have superfluity in Our Lord, by asking alms, so as not to surcharge the ordinary benefactors of the Society, and yet not to permit the members of Our Lord Jesus Christ to suffer hardship, who have need to preserve their health and strength for His service, although they, on their part, be ready to support all privations for the love of Christ.*

Rome, Nov. 2, 1552.

His nephew Araoz being enfeebled by excessive labors, which obliged him to go for a time to breathe his native air, according to medical advice, he wrote to him as follows—

I recommend to you moderation in your labors, and to treat your body better, which belongs to Christ and the Society more than to you. And since this is so, you ought to try to preserve it, and not to destroy it as if it were your own. Although it be charity which leads you to undertake labors above your strength, obedience obliges you to moderate them so that your health may last the longer for the service of God.†

He himself set the example in this matter, in not keeping to any unreasonable or indiscreet practice of piety. One time he fell sick of fever in Holy Week, after having fasted all the Lent. His medical attendant, the celebrated Alexander Petroni, told him to take at night some chicken broth, with a doubt in his own mind whether he would obey the order. The next day he asked the Saint whether he had done what he had told him. The reply was that he had. He said to Ignatius —"There are many who do not keep the Lent and yet refuse to eat meat during these three days, even when

* Collection at Rome.　　　　　† Collection at Rome.

they are sick and it is prescribed for them, because they think it a sin to do so. But you have kept the Lent and obeyed my prescription notwithstanding. I sincerely own, my Father, that I cannot tell you how much I admire this conduct." Ignatius graciously replied—" We must be obedient." The doctor would often recount this fact in after-time, as showing, in his opinion, the true piety of his patient.

Ribadeneyra tells us of himself that, the physician having forbidden him to fast, he expressed to the Saint his desire not to be dispensed with, for fear of giving scandal. St. Ignatius said,—" Who could be scandalized at that, when he ought to thank God that he has not the same need as you?" Having been informed the year following, viz., in 1546, that a Father was in fact scandalized on this account, Ignatius showed that he was very indignant, and threatened to dismiss from the Society one who took scandal at so legitimate a dispensation.

Eye-witnesses declare that he used himself to sweep out the rooms of the sick, to make their beds, and wait upon them as a servant. "If our Father was so full of tenderness for all his children," says Ribadeneyra on this subject, " they, on their part, were docile and obedient to him, and gave him their hearts, so that he could do with them as he pleased without ever meeting in them any resistance, for in his extraordinary love for them he was not only their Father, but their servant. As he watched over them, no one took thought for himself; they labored to their utmost, without regard to their health, because he cared for them. If they needed any alleviation they were sure it would be given them. There was a holy contest between the Father and the children—these to go beyond their strength in their labors, while they honored and obeyed with religious emulation their beloved Father, and he, on his part, treated them as his children with so vigilant and tender a love that no words can express it." *

The following anecdotes are characteristic, and prove in the same manner his solicitude for those confided to his care and his reliance upon Divine Providence. They

* Bolland., n. 820.

are related by a contemporary eye-witness, and thus are perfectly certified. "He had so great a confidence in God," writes Father Manareo, "that he left nothing that was necessary undone, however great the expense might be and however scanty the resources of the House. For example, the blessed Father Ignatius had ordered rooms and furniture to be prepared in the Roman College, of which he was rector, and where we were only as yet twenty-eight in number, as he intended to increase the inmates to a hundred, although there were in the Professed House and the College only five ducats, which Father John Polanco was keeping for the buildings. These, however, he offered me, saying it was all that he had. I felt much reluctance to take them, on account of the extensive buildings which were in progress in the Professed House, in the College, and in the Villa of St. Balbina. We at last came to the conclusion that he should endeavor to procure money by begging, and that I should hire the necessary furniture. Our blessed 'Father, meanwhile, came to see the arrangements in the College for the Brothers whom he intended to receive. Perceiving a large apartment full of wooden beds and chairs, and little tables for writing at, and having surveyed all with much attention, he turned to Father Polanco and said to him, 'What? are our Brothers to lodge here, and be exposed to the severities of the winter which is coming on? Where is the ceiling? Are the Brothers to live under the tiles?' Father Polanco replied, 'My Reverend Father, there is no more money, and we cannot borrow it.' He replied, 'The ceiling must be done, Father Polanco, and the Brothers must not sleep here. God will provide for his servants.' Polanco obeyed, though the house was only rented, but Father Ignatius had ordered it, and experience had already more than once shown that he ordered nothing without reflection. In fact, the next day, Polanco having gone out to borrow money from friends or take it up at interest, met with an archdeacon of Navarre, whom I knew, named Mandragon. He begged the Father to keep for him in deposit five hundred gold crowns, which he would ask for again as he wanted them. Moreover, a Portuguese procurator of the Order of the Hieronymites gave him a still more considerable sum to keep, with leave to use it and repay it by instalments at different times. Soon after the benefactors of the Society sent abundant alms, so that not only was there enough to restore these sums, but also to pay all the debts and the current expenses, all which can only be attributed to the merits and the prayers of our dearly beloved Father. Almost at the same time Father Guido Roilitz, rector of the German College, finding himself in great distress, had recourse to Ignatius. He, having listened to the lamentations of Father Roilitz on the necessities in which he found himself, said, with a smile, 'Master Guido, will the students of the German College have some better cheer at Christmas-time?' 'O my Father,' he replied, 'they scarcely have bread, for the baker will send them no more.' 'Very well,' said the Saint, 'be of good courage. God will help us. Meanwhile, buy for these young men some venison and some other things to give them a treat, and leave the rest to God.' Thereupon he left him comforted and consoled. The next day Julius III. sent our Father five hundred crowns, which he divided, giving half to the Roman College and half to the German."

# CHAPTER XII.

IGNATIUS possessed in a high degree the talent for government. Although this was acknowledged by his contemporaries, and appears evident from all the history of his life, we think it our duty to enter into some details on this head. He especially endeavored to encourage among his children the ardent desire of doing good, to make them capable of undertaking the most difficult things in the service of God. He sought in like manner to inculcate on superiors a spirit of love and sweetness ; and therefore he made no difficulty in changing the rectors of the Roman College until he had found one who had this kindly and maternal tenderness which he considered necessary for those who govern. He avoided with the greatest care all preference and partiality, and often, instead of himself naming persons to certain offices which had exterior advantages attached to them, he left this to the care of his Consultors, after having indicated the qualities which he thought requisite for such charges. As for himself, he had the art of making his authority sweet and amiable to all, avoiding in everything an air of command and an exterior of too great severity. He not only consulted the strength and talents of each one, but, moreover, when he had to issue an order, or to give a reprimand, he told them the reasons why he did so in terms so simple and equitable, that he always carried persuasion into the hearts of those to whom he spoke. He was equally affable to those who returned from any mission. He received them with an air of welcome. " You are welcome back," he would say; " how have things gone on—has such a thing succeeded ? " and the like, thus anticipating what they had to say ; and if the issue had been successful, he wished them joy of it, praised their conduct, and manifested his pleasure, proposed them as an example to others, and showed his acknowledgment by services of all kinds. If the result had not corresponded to their efforts, he consoled them, and exhorted them not to lose courage. He used to have the letters read which he received from members of the Society employed elsewhere upon missions, giving an account of what they had done, so as to encourage others to imitate them.

He chose those for offices and business whom he thought most adapted to the duty ; and in order to give them confidence and no way to discontent them, he avoided any vexatious interference with them, leaving them all necessary freedom of action. He expressed these his principles in a letter of December 22, 1552, to James Miron, the Provincial of Portugal. He says to him—

The Provincial or the General ought not to enter into childish details, nor wish to regulate the minutest matters. It is more becoming their dignity, and safer for their own repose of mind, to leave these things to subordinate superiors, and, when the business is done, to ask an account of it. This is what I do in my office as General, and I derive every day more advantage from this method, because I thus spare myself much labor and pains. I recommend you, then, to direct your thoughts and your cares principally to the good of the whole province. Occupy yourself in regulating details when it is necessary, and then ask the advice of men whom you think the most experienced; but otherwise abstain as much as possible from putting your hand to particular affairs and being occupied with them. You ought to be in your province the mainspring of the machinery, and move the subordinate wheels of it. These will then work as the proximate cause, and produce the effect which belongs to them. By this manner of proceeding you will do more, and without noise and fuss ; you will have no scruples of mind, and you will act in a manner more conformable to your office. This conduct has, besides, another advantage, that, if there be any fault in what is done, the blame will rest rather on your assistants than on you. And it is better for you to have to find fault with the errors they have committed than to expose yourself to be blamed by your inferiors if you are mistaken, which may easily be the case when one will be busy with all things and enter into the least details.*

Father Oliver Manareo relates to this purpose what happened to himself as follows—

When he sent me to Loretto to take the direction of the college, he was content with giving me some advice as to the manner in which I

* Bolland., sec. 81.

was to conduct myself with regard to the governor, the canons, and other externs. I asked him what rules I must observe, remarking that those of the Roman College were for the most part unsuitable, because the place was a much-frequented pilgrimage, and that it was the same with regard to the rules of the Professed House, and consequently it would be very difficult to observe them at Loretto. He replied, "Oliver, do as shall seem best to you, and as God shall inspire you. Try to apply the rules to the place the best you can." I asked him with regard to the persons whom he gave me, how I was severally to employ each of them. He merely replied with the Spanish proverb, "'Cut your coat according to your cloth,' and give me an account of what you have done and how you have done it." It afterwards happened that I did not take account of what he ordered me by a letter. And I wrote to him to say that I had acted as I had done, because I had imagined him to be present beside me and saying; "Do as you have intended to do, for if I were with you, I should order you to do so." He wrote back to say that I had perfectly entered into his intentions. It is man, he said, who appoints to offices, but God who gives prudence and ability to fulfil them. I wish you to act without hesitation for the future, as you think that you ought to do, after having well weighed the circumstances, without attending to the rules or recommendations which I have given you.

He wishes in the Constitution,\* that the superiors of the Society should be a model for others, and that they should mortify in themselves all the bad inclinations of nature, be well exercised in obedience and humility, and in spiritual things, having the gift of discretion, able in government and in the management of affairs, and that they should know how, according to time and place, to join severity to sweetness.

He had a particular care in the formation of novices. His most ardent desire was to see before he died the discipline of the novitiate solidly established according to the spirit of the Institute, so that it might serve as a rule for the time to come. The following is what he said to Father Polanco on the subject.†

He said that if anything could make him wish to live a longer time, though in this he did not desire to have any will of his own, it would be in order that he might be very severe in admitting members to the Society. In those who offered themselves he looked less to purely natural goodness than to firmness of character and ability for business,

---

\* iv., cap. 10, n. 4.

† In a manuscript entitled *Dichos y hechos*, which may be called "*memorabilia* of St. Ignatius." It contains the recollections of some of his most intimate associates.

for he was of opinion that those who were not fit for public business were not adapted for filling offices in the Society. Those whom he had once admitted he employed at first in the service of their neighbor, until they had given sufficient proof of their aptitude and virtue. His solicitude in this matter increased from day to day, and he rather chose to refuse princes and bishops the men they asked for, excusing himself for want of subjects, than to send them such as were not yet sufficiently formed, or such as, not answering to the end of the Society, would have compromised its reputation. He often said on this point that he loved better to see the Society rich in virtues than in numbers, and that it was better to distinguish itself by its acts than by its exterior importance. It is not surely necessary, after all we have written above, to add that he would not permit the heart and spirit of the novices to be crushed out of them.*

For these reasons, also, he dismissed without hesitation those who did not continue to keep the dispositions necessary for members of the Society ; and we have already seen the principles which guided him in these circumstances.† But when any one wished to leave of his own accord and without reason, he prayed, and made those of the House pray, that he might be delivered from the snare in which he was in danger of being caught. He sent for him, spoke to him with kindness, inquired into the causes of his change, made him consider the consequences, begged of him not to be in haste, and to wait some days, during which he might live as he pleased. If he persisted in his purpose, he assembled the greater number of the members of the House, and asked him for what reasons he wished to leave them. When he had given his reasons he asked of the other Religious what they thought of them. And it almost always happened in this manner that the poor novice whom the devil was tempting, acknowledging that he had no reason for leaving, with tears and confusion asked to be allowed to remain. He only had recourse to this method when those who wished to leave were acting, not from want of vocation, but from some passing caprice, and who in leaving would be sure of doing injury to themselves—for to many the religious state is as necessary to salvation as it is to others to live in the world. When a novice of this kind, yielding to temptation, left the Society, if he afterwards acknowledged his fault and returned with a penitent heart,

* Bolland., sec. 82.    † Chapter iv.

Ignatius did not shut the gate to him. We will cite as an example the case of a noble young Portuguese, Antonio Moniz, or Munis, who shortly after his admission, in 1545, lost his first fervor and his taste for religious life, and quitted the House of Valencia, being unable to sacrifice his own will. But as he had made a vow to consecrate himself to the service of God, in order to stifle the reproaches of his conscience, he thought he could reconcile the love of liberty and the keeping of his promise by spending his life in pious pilgrimages. His director, perceiving the illusion he was under, tried to bring him back to other thoughts by sending him to Coimbra, where Father Peter Faber was at that time. But Munis, secretly leaving the House, went on a pilgrimage to St. James of Compostella and the Convent of Mont Serrat. However, it was not long before he became weary of this erratic life, and seeing that he had let himself be deluded by a too lively imagination, he took the resolution of entering again into the Society. In the depth of winter, stripped of all, he set out for Rome, passing through France, and after remaining a long time sick at Avignon, he arrived at Rome; but not daring to present himself before Ignatius, he wrote to him the following letter—

I perceive myself so guilty, that, looking upon myself as unworthy to speak to your Reverence, this first time at least, "face to face," I wish to appear before you as a sinner, "through a glass in a dark manner," that is, by letter, to inform you that I have arrived in this city, and am utterly good for nothing, as I admit. But I have come hither to put myself again into the hands of your Reverence, and under the obedience from which I have so long withdrawn myself; for, finding myself sad and lost in the world, I have entered into myself and have said, "I will go to my Father." May your Reverence, then, vouchsafe, for the love of Our Lord, to show yourself merciful in my regard, and permit me to come and see you, otherwise I should not dare to appear before you, "for fear and trembling are come upon me, and darkness hath covered me," as I know how severely, and with reason, your Reverence punishes faults of this kind. I will tell you the rest at the House, if I may come to it, for I am so troubled that I do not even know how to write this letter to you. If I have done wrong in doing so, the reason is the terror I feel, not daring to appear before you without previously announcing it. I remain at the Hospital of St. Antony, hoping for mercy, which may God grant to me and to all sinners.

The following letter to the Duke Francis Borgia shows

us how Ignatius conducted himself with regard to Munis:

I have heard that Munis, a relative of Madame the Duchess, arrived at Rome on April 12th, in a coarse and singular dress, as a hermit, without shoes, and in a complete state of destitution, and that he had taken up his lodgings in the Hospital of St. Antony, belonging to the Portuguese. Thence he wrote me a letter, which I enclose. I have sent for him, and placed him in a house which is dependent on ours, where I have given him all things necessary, without allowing him to eat or sleep with us. I have killed for him the fatted calf, "for he was lost, and is found again." I have refused hitherto to speak with him, and this is for his good. Full of repentance, however, he has made, unknown to me (though I am well informed of it all), the Stations of the churches, naked to the waist, and taking the discipline without any mercy, and, as they tell me, to blood. He has after this asked to be allowed to preach, and to go from house to house asking alms. Being acquainted with all this, I sent to him to say that I would speak to him to-morrow or some other day. I hope in Our Lord, if I may judge of him from the former knowledge I had of him, that the Divine Majesty will assist him, and will cause him again to make progress in good.

He acted very differently when the fault arose from any one who had a long time walked in the way of perfection, or who held important places, and whose conduct might involve serious evil consequences. He showed himself then the more severe, the more gifted they were and the more they were dear in his sight. He found himself in this position with regard to Laynez, in 1552, when he, having been made Provincial of Italy in the place of Brouet, and taking too narrow a view of things, more than once found fault with a measure of Ignatius agreeable to the more extended interests of the whole Society. The question was about bringing to Rome several of the best subjects from some of the colleges of his province. Laynez thought the measure detrimental to the Society. We will give here the reply of Ignatius. It will be seen from it that Laynez, who is often praised at the expense of the Saint, and is represented as having exercised very great influence over him, was his inferior in point of intellect. It matters little to the question that this letter is not Ignatius's own, but his secretary's, for the contents are evidently his own, and in causing it to be written by another, he added to the severity of the reprimand.

My Father, it is not Polanco, your Reverence's child, full of respect and affection for you, who writes this, but it is the instrument and pen of our Father, who has ordered me to say to you what is contained in this letter. He wished me to write to you some time ago, but, being informed that you were suffering from fever, he waited until you were quite well. Our Father is highly displeased with you, because the faults of those whom he loves most are the most keenly felt by him. They are also the more painful to his heart when they come from those from whom he has less reason to expect them. He has therefore ordered me to write to you on several subjects, that you may acknowledge your faults and amend them, and this you will do readily and with ease by the goodwill which God Our Lord has given you.

He touches then on three points, showing how he has failed in each of them, but as the matter treats of things and names to which interest no longer attaches, we will only cite the close of the letter—

It does not become any one to write to his superior with such a tone of authority, and in that respect he disapproves of your conduct and desires me to give you notice to look to the office with which you are invested, and to tell you that, if you discharge the duties of it as you ought, you will have much to account for. But do not take the trouble to give him your advice, as to what he ought to do himself, unless he asks you to do so, and this he will do less now than he did before you entered upon your office, for the manner in which you have conducted yourself in it does not give him a high idea of your ability. Consider over these faults in the presence of God Our Lord, and pray for that end during three days. You will then write to say whether you acknowledge that you have been wrong or mistaken, and what punishment you deserve. You must not, however, do any penance before receiving the reply of our Father.*

It was difficult in these first days of the Society to keep alive the spirit of fraternal charity, on account of the difference of nationalities, and the separation of its members, who, few in number, were already spread throughout the whole world. Ignatius sought to avoid this twofold inconvenience by keeping up with them a constant correspondence, and by recommending them, in a circular letter which we give here, to apply themselves to learning the language of the country.

The edification and advantage of the people among whom the Society is placed, as well as the union of its members and the increase of charity and goodwill which they should have for one another, seem to require that every one in those places where there is a college or a House should learn the language of the country if he does not know it already, and should make use of it in daily conversation, for confusion

* Menchacha, iii., p. 466.

and division would be inevitable if, among Religious of different nations, every one wished to speak his own language. It is for this reason that our Father orders that, in every country where the Society is established, all speak the language of that country—Spanish in Spain, French in France, German in Germany, Italian in Italy, etc. He wishes that at Rome every one should speak Italian, and that those who do not know it should learn it, and for that purpose a lesson is given every day in Italian grammar, and it is not allowed to any one to speak except in Italian, except where, for the better understanding of some words, translation is made into another language. He orders, also, that a sermon in Italian be given once a week in the refectory during dinner or supper, and that some one who knows this language very well be appointed to assist the preacher in his work. Whoever is negligent in performing this order shall receive a good penance. Our Father wishes that this order be communicated to all of ours, and be observed throughout the Society as far as possible, with due regard to places and persons.

Rome, Jan. 1, 1556.*

From the very commencement he had it much at heart to maintain a regular correspondence with the different Houses of the Society, and it was a point on which he never ceased to insist, as appears from a letter written to Faber and to others, in which he says—" I hold to the custom of writing duplicates of important letters, and I myself have written this one twice. With how much more reason ought every member of the Society to do so, for you have to write but to one, and I have to write to you all? And I can assure you in truth, that last night we found that the number of letters we are now sending out to different places amounted to two hundred and fifty. However much the other members of the Society may be occupied, I think that I am not the least so, and that, too, with the weakest of health." †

But if it be asked what were the points on which Ignatius required that information should be given him, and what were the principles he followed in general in the government of his Religious, we must read a letter written by Polanco in his name, and by his orders, in the year 1551, to the rector of the college of Coimbra—

Your Reverence must know that our Father wishes that an account be given to him not only of things that serve to edification and spiritual good, such as the preaching, confessions, etc., for it is enough to write to him on this subject every four months, as has been hitherto done ; but he desires to know as far as possible all that is necessary, that he

* Collection at Rome.      † Bolland., n. 859.

may apply a remedy where it is needed, and so fulfil the duties of the office which God has laid upon him. However, as there are a multitude of things of less importance, and all cannot be written, and as, besides, the local superiors and the Provincial are sufficient for cases of this kind, our Father desires that an account be given him only of the greater and more difficult affairs. He wishes to know the number of Brothers who enter and leave or are dismissed. And therefore he wishes that every four months you send to him a catalogue in which the names and dispositions of each one are written down. When once this has been made out and sent hither, it will suffice to add to it afterwards every four months whatever new additions are to be made for that time.

He desires to know the chief points with regard to the Brothers, as, for example, what progress they make in their studies and in spiritual life, if they are violently assaulted by such and such a temptation, and by what means they are succored, and whether they advance resolutely in the service of God. It will be good also briefly to indicate what mortifications each one is in the habit of practising for the cure of such and such a bad inclination, and what results he obtains from them, but all this must be declared in general, without entering into collateral matters and details. He wishes also to know who those are who distinguish themselves in the sciences and in preaching ; those who, after the completion of their studies, can be sent into various countries; those who, without having yet finished them, can be sent for a time by way of trial, or in order to satisfy the requests of those whom we cannot refuse ; and so for other objects, on which I have written a little book which may serve as a guide.

Your Reverence desires me to send you in writing some thoughts or principles upon the manner of good government, and other things besides, but I do not find myself in a state to speak of the least things, and much less of things so important. May the Holy Spirit, Who teaches all things to those who prepare themselves to receive His holy lights—especially in what concerns the duty of their office—vouchsafe to enlighten your Reverence. And I hope that He will do so, inasmuch as He has given you the goodwill to consecrate yourself with full purpose and deliberation to His greater glory. However, as I do not wish entirely to leave your request unfulfilled, I subjoin here some things which I have learned regarding the views and the practice of our Father.

I think I may remark, by way of preface, that he desires, above all things, men of good natural dispositions and capacities, either for study of the sciences, or for exterior works, and who have a zeal for both. And first, if one be found of no aptitude for science, but of whom good results might be expected for exterior things, such as, for example, the material management of a House, he would prefer him to one who, with no taste or ability for these things, had some moderate talents for the sciences. Secondly, he would wish to have young men who have passed their boyhood, and are of the height in stature which I send you, except they be of extraordinary parts, or there be some particular motive for receiving them. They ought, also, to have an agreeable exterior, as our kind of life and the relations we have with our neighbor require it. On this account, he does not wish to have those who have any exterior deformity, unless they are distinguished by some particular gift of God which compensates for it, and makes them useful for the good of others. Thirdly, he does not wish young novices to be received of delicate health. He makes less difficulty on this point where they are already well educated or endowed with extraordinary intelligence, for these, though half dead, may still be of service. Fourthly, as to those already admitted, I remark that there is one point on which he is very particular, and which he is very indignant not to see observed. It concerns obedience. I do not speak of great sin, for it is to be presumed that things of this kind will not be committed, but it concerns that kind of obedience which is not merely contented with doing what is commanded, but which makes the will one with that of the superior, and fully accords with it in all that is not sin. He looks, in fact, upon the obedience of a Religious as imperfect when he merely wills and does what is ordered him, but does not think, at the same time, that the thing ought to be done so, which, if he did, would gain a victory over his own judgment, and bring it captive under the yoke of holy obedience, so far, be it understood, as the will can act upon the understanding in things which are not so clearly evident that they practically determine the agent. Fifthly, he cannot endure those who are fixed and opinionated in their judgments, and, by their obstinacy, disturb and trouble others, even though it be in the least things. I remark, moreover, that he desires the employment by preference of such mortifications, for repressing the passions, as keep down pride and self-esteem, and that he makes far more account of them than of those that chastise the body, as fasting, hairshirts, and disciplines, unless a person be troubled by temptations of the flesh and in danger of falling: not only does he not urge his Religious to the practice of these exterior mortifications, but he endeavors, on the contrary, to restrain their fervor within just limits in this respect, especially when they are devoted to study. He thinks that students, when they make due progress in the sciences and in virtue, without giving scandal by their behavior, ought to be left to their studies, and that the time which precedes or follows is more convenient for corporal austerities. Sixthly, as to prayer and meditation, setting aside those who are troubled with dangerous temptations, I remark that he prefers intention to please and serve God in all that is done to long prayers. He would desire that all the members of the Society were so disposed, that they could feel as much devotion in every act of charity to their neighbor, or of obedience, as in meditation and prayer, because they ought to do all solely for the love and glory of God Our Lord, preferring always that which they are commanded to do, because they cannot doubt then but that this is the will of God.

We pass over the three following numbers, which relate to the studies, because they are identical with what we have said above on this subject.

Tenthly, he wishes that all perfectly apply themselves to purifying their intention in all their actions, both corporal and spiritual, seeking in them the glory of God and the means of being useful to their neighbor, either by themselves or by others, to some in one way, to some in another, and preferring always the general to the particular good. Eleventhly, for those who are devoted to some determinate object, as, for example, to the study of the sciences, if they have some aptitude for it, but, at the same time, such study be prejudicial to them, our Father has made it a rule to turn them from it. He acts thus on this principle, that it is more important that they should make progress in virtue than in learning, when the two cannot be had together. For this reason he has prevented a great many from study, because it took away the peace of their souls, and hindered them from walking in the path of perfection. It is the same in other things. Our Father does not require the strict observation of the Rules of the House in those who, for some particular reason, as from sickness, or the occupations of their office, cannot fulfil them all; and he dispenses at times with his usual prudence. But he is very severe on this point with those who have no legitimate reason to excuse them. He requires of them the observance of all the rules, and if they fail to observe them he gives them penances for their correction and as a warning to others. In fact, as there is no sin in transgressing the Rule (and yet it is right that it should be kept), those who break it must be penanced. However, these penances are light for unimportant things, and in general are not severe, except in what concerns obedience.*

Rome, July 1, 1551.

* This important letter has been already printed in the *Historia Provinciæ Toletanæ, S. J.* Madrid, 1710. By Father Balth. Aleazar, and is to be found in Latin in Menchacha (iii., 6).

# CHAPTER XIII.

## ST. IGNATIUS IN RELATION WITH PRINCES.

It is undeniable that St. Ignatius, by his Institute, was a support and rampart to royalty. This was in a great measure due to circumstances. The Protestant doctrine had broken the old ties between princes and peoples, although it was compelled, contrary to its own principles, to accord for a considerable time to the sovereigns attached to it an extension of power hitherto unknown and impossible, namely, territorial supremacy in spiritual things. England and Germany were not long in experiencing the fatal results of this disastrous legacy. It was a natural consequence, for this exorbitant power was the fruit of a revolution in a domain which should be sacred to all, and the product of such a foul usurpation is poisonous to generations to come. The action of the principles of Ignatius could only be conservative. Add to this that his Order, embracing in its Institute the solution of the highest questions that interest mankind, drew to itself, notwithstanding its personal poverty and the exact obedience it required, the noblest and most highly cultivated minds, and men distinguished for learning and for birth. But the conservative action of the Society came especially from this—that every distinction of birth and fortune disappeared within its bosom; and if, on the one hand, its members labored with an admirable devotion to raise and regenerate the lowest ranks of society, they appeared also with authority in the courts of princes, and spoke to them with a perfect evangelical liberty. They sought to reunite in the bonds of the religion of Jesus Christ the ties of affection between sovereigns and their subjects, for their mutual advantage. The first prince who comprehended this mission

of the Society was John III. of Portugal.    The acquaintance he had made with two disciples of the Saint,
Xavier and Rodriguez, led him to desire to know their
master.    Ignatius anticipated the wish, and his first letter
to John, which is still extant, gives us some information
on some passages of his life, although he only speaks of
things that would have been to his disadvantage if he
had not been innocent.    He says—

Many indications and conjectures (as Our Lord knows) lead me to
suppose that your Royal Highness will hear, if you have not heard
already, some circumstances of my former life which do not concern
myself so much as God's glory, Who is worthy of all praise forever.
Now, as I would wish always, not for my own sake, but for my Master's and Creator's, to glory in these things, I think I shall do well in
briefly declaring them to your Most Christian Majesty, to whom we are
forever so much indebted.    After my return from Jerusalem, I was put
in prison at Alcala de Henares, in consequence of a threefold inquiry
about me by my superiors, and I remained in it twenty-four days.    At
Salamanca, a new inquiry was made, and I was put in fetters in a
prison, where I remained twenty-two days.    At Paris, where I resided
to continue my studies, there was a new inquisition made into my
conduct.    In these five processes and these two imprisonments, I
never would take, thanks be to God, nor did I take, any other advocate
or resource for aid but Him in Whom, by His divine grace and favor,
I have placed all my hopes, both present and to come.    Seven years
after this, another process was taken against me in the same University
of Paris, and again at Venice; and finally, at Rome, against our whole
Society.    As in these three last affairs I was not alone, but together
with all who belong to the Society, we insisted on justice taking its
course, that God might not be injured by the calumny.    Now there
were precisely present at Rome, in this last process, three judges who
had received information against me, one at Alcala, another at Paris,
and the third at Venice.    Neither in these eight trials, nor since,
thanks to the Divine Mercy alone, have I ever been condemned for a
single proposition, or even for a single syllable ; and I have never
received the least punishment, nor been banished from any country.
If your Majesty desires to be informed why so many inquests have
been held upon me, I can assure you that it is not because I belonged
to the Schismatics, the Lutherans, or the Illuminati, for I never had
any relations with them, nor have known any of them, but because
they were astonished, especially in Spain, that, having never studied, I
allowed myself to speak at length and discourse on spiritual things.    I
protest and call God Our Lord to witness, Who is my Creator and will
be my Judge for all eternity, that I would not wish, for all the treasures and temporal power under heaven, that these things had not at
all happened to me.    Nay, more ; I desire that much more than all
this might happen to me again, for the greater glory of the Divine
Majesty.    Most gracious sir and master in Our Lord, if any news of
this kind reaches you, you will know how, with the grace and mercy of

God, to distinguish between good and evil, and make use of all to your profit. The more, in fact, we desire to be clothed, without scandal, and for the good of our neighbor, with the livery of Jesus Christ, Who was always the mark for scorn, false witnesses, and affronts of all kinds, the more we shall make progress, and the more we shall acquire those spiritual treasures with which our souls, if we are of one and the same spirit, would wish to be adorned and satiated. *

Rome, March 15, 1545.

We have had occasion more than once in the course of this history to see what care and precaution Ignatius took in his relations with princes when any difficulty arose. We will relate to this purport the following fact. John III. held so much at heart the increase of the Society in Portugal, both in numbers and action, that, in order to prevent any from being sent away elsewhere, he forbade the colleges of the country to send into foreign parts either subjects or money. This prohibition, so far as it concerned the members of the body, might become very prejudicial to the general good of the Society ; for, taken in a literal sense, it would have separated this portion of it from the whole, contrary to the king's intention, who wished, indeed, to guard himself from all injury, but not to put limits to the government of St. Ignatius. In this sense the Saint understood it, and wrote the following letter to the king—

I have received your Majesty's letter by the hands of Father Louis Gonzalez, who, thanks to God, arrived in good health at Rome on the 23d of last month. This letter, in which your Majesty expresses your joy with regard to the change of the Provincial, and the communications of Gonzalez, to whom your Majesty desires me to give entire confidence in all that he shall say to me on your part, confirm me in the persuasion I have always had concerning your Majesty. In fact, as Our Divine Lord has willed that you should be the first among Christian princes and the principal instrument of His providence to begin and increase this Society, which is wholly your Majesty's devoted servant, so it will, I am convinced, prevail upon you to content yourself in its advancement and prosperity with all that is convenient for it, since you seek with so much zeal and sincerity to promote the glory of God and the good of souls, His property, which is the sole end of all our efforts.

With regard to the communication made to me by Father Gonzalez, namely, that your Majesty desires that neither men nor money be drawn from the colleges in Portugal, your Majesty may rest assured that your will shall be followed in every point, not only during my

* Collection at Rome.

life, but even after my death. For, as to money, our Constitutions forbid us to take it away, and as to the persons, I am much more disposed to send them to Portugal and to the Indies, than to diminish the number of those that are there already. However, it would be, in my opinion, a very advantageous thing for the service of your Majesty and the Lord Our God, if some Portuguese were educated in other kingdoms, so as to be sent back when they are formed, and that there should be some foreigners among those who are educated in Portugal, that they may mutually aid one another. However, we will do nothing without the approbation and full consent of your Majesty.

Ignatius had also frequent relations with Philip II., afterwards king of Spain, though he was never so intimately connected with him as with John III. Feelings of antipathy have contributed to render this Spanish Prince an object of dislike, and party passion has judged him with too great a severity. His melancholy and somber character was inherited from his grandmother Joanna, and if a place among great kings is refused him, at least he ought to have the merit of a sincere goodwill and a constancy of soul amid the political mishaps which befell him during his life. There are few men on whom it is more difficult to pronounce with safety. However, we do not wish to justify him in all his acts as a king. It was a task beyond his power to take in hand the inheritance left him by Charles V. But he was yet young, his administration in Spain had gained him the affections of the people, and gave hopes at the time that he would do still more in the future. Spain was at this period the first political power and the representative of Catholic interests. Soon after this it fell from its high estate, but this is not the place to enter into the cause of its fall. We can, however, say that nothing then gave reason to anticipate such a result, and St. Ignatius, finding in Philip a prince truly devoted to the service of God, supposed him to be also a good king ; and in this, without doubt, he had good reasons, for rectitude in spiritual things implies rectitude in temporal things in a well regulated mind. Perhaps Ignatius had these hopes when he wrote to him the following letter, the occasion of which is not known. Philip was then in the Low Countries.

May the sovereign grace and eternal love of Our Lord Jesus Christ give greeting to your Majesty, and visit you with all holy gifts and spiritual graces. Possessing a soul so highly privileged and illuminated with invaluable gifts and spiritual graces, you rule and govern your interior faculties with a marvellous facility, and thus submitting your understanding, your knowledge, and your will to the Supreme Wisdom and Infinite Goodness, you are disposed to allow yourself to be guided and conducted by your Master and Creator. It is, therefore, very just and right that the Divine Majesty should continually impart to your soul heavenly delights and shed on it the most holy consolations, that you may produce perfect spiritual fruit in abundance and with a continual increase, for the greater glory of the Divine Goodness. I see and hear from all sides that your Majesty edifies your people by the good odor of your virtues, and I confide that they are not mistaken in the good opinion they have of you. I perceive each day new motives to make me ardently desire that all the undertakings of your Majesty may have the most complete success, to the greater glory of the Master of all, and I do not cease to recommend them in my poor and unworthy prayers to the Divine Goodness, Who can by His aid do what I have asked of Him daily for so many years. If this letter appear to you too long, or too bold, please to pardon me for the love and regard of God Our Lord. But after having had an interview with Don Diego de Azevedo, to pay him my homage as your Majesty's representative, and otherwise urged by my devotedness to you, I could not refrain from writing to you and declaring my thoughts and desires for the greater glory of God, our Master and Creator.

Rome, February 18, 1549.

He had particularly at heart, after the vacancy of the Holy See, that a Pope should be chosen capable of encountering the difficulties of the times, and we have preserved to us a letter addressed to the members of the Society in Belgium, in which he orders them, as he had done already at other times, to pray for a happy choice of a successor to Paul III. He wrote himself on this subject to St. Francis Borgia. He says : " The vacancy of the Holy See makes us ardently desirous of seeing elected a truly apostolic pastor. May God be pleased to have pity upon His Church, and give it a head who may be as good for it in general as he will be, we may reasonably hope, for this our little Society, whoever he may be that shall be named."

He exacted from his associates the same course of conduct. Thus, in a letter to Le Jay, who had been sent by the Pope's orders to Hercules, Duke of Ferrara, and who wrote for advice how to conduct himself, he says to him, "that he desires both he himself, as well as all the Society, to be useful to the duke, who has been one of the first of all secular princes to show himself favorable

to it, and that he rejoices in having an opportunity of
showing his gratitude to him. He wishes that Le Jay
should consider himself as entirely dependent upon the
orders of the duke, and that, while he is at Ferrara, he
should look upon him as his superior, whenever he should
have recourse to him, either for the promotion of the
glory of God, or for his own advantage and that of his
subjects.*

In order to avoid all conflict between his duty and the
requests of powerful and influential personages, he forbade all the Religious of the Society to write to him
through the mediation of any secular or ecclesiastical
lord, to obtain by this means any office or mission whatever; he wished thus to avoid the danger of offending a
powerful intercessor, in case he could not comply with
his request. This measure was not inspired by the design of gaining the favor of the great or their influence,
but by the same thought which made him forbid all his
Religious to mix in politics, so that, being free from all
worldly cares, they might with greater purity and freedom fulfil the mission they had received from God. Thus,
when it happened that any of the Society said or did a
thing that might compromise the keeping of so wise a
rule, he showed himself more severe upon it than on any
other fault. He acted thus with regard to Laynez in a
circumstance which we will narrate. Laynez was preaching one day at St. Paul's in the presence of Ignatius and
some Spaniards who were at Rome, and allowed himself
to make some allusions to a case of simony which had
been made public. The Saint, much displeased, gave
him a severe reprimand on the way back to the House,
and threatened to give him a severe penance for not
having been able to refrain his tongue, adding that indiscreet words of this kind uttered from the pulpit would
be easily misinterpreted and make people believe that
they wished to accuse the Pope's officials.

He showed in a still more striking manner his displeasure with Bobadilla, who had taken in the dispute on
the subject of the *interim* in Germany a more active part
than became a member of the Society. The opposition

* Orlandini, vii., 35.

which he had shown to this political expedient adopted by Charles V. was so displeasing to Charles's Minister, that, in spite of the authority he had at Court, he obtained an order from the emperor commanding Bobadilla to quit Germany.

It is true that this false peace imposed on the Church by the temporal power was disapproved of at Rome, and satisfied no one. But Ignatius was much displeased with the conduct of Bobadilla in the matter, and that all the world might know it, he would not admit him into the House upon his return, so as to give some kind of satisfaction to the emperor, and lest the emperor might hinder the other members of the Society in the exercise of their ministry.

We close here the documents which may serve to characterize St. Ignatius. But we must be allowed in conclusion to cast a parting glance upon the remarkable man whom we have endeavored to portray chiefly from his own writings. Two periods are clearly discernible in his life ; the decisive moment between the two was that when, giving up the idea of founding a Religious Order for the East, and more especially for Palestine, he took up his abode at Rome. From that day forward a remarkable development of the character and capacities of the Saint becomes visible. His natural powers took a fresh and higher flight ; for the experience he had acquired, and which had been so necessary for him, enabled him to use to greater advantage the noble qualities he had received from God, and to direct them to an end which embraced in its scope the gravest interests of mankind. Reuniting in a whole with a wonderful harmony the inspirations he had first received and the purely natural gifts bestowed on him by Providence, he applied them to the founding of an Institute corresponding admirably to the wants of the age, and offering the guarantees of a long duration. With unexampled strength of mind, and in the most unfavorable circumstances, he passed through a course of painful study in order to apply for the good of the Church this powerful engine of civilization to the world, and to unite in closer bonds faith and science, between which heresy has in all times endeavored to make a complete separation. He extended to poor heathen nations the blessings of Christian life, and if the rulers of these countries have not been wise enough to make use of his zeal for the regeneration and social progress of these countries, it has not been his fault, nor that of the Fathers whom he has sent on those missions.

But St. Ignatius contributed, besides, to the development of charitable institutions for the relief of the needy of every kind ; and these owe to him a method of more appropriate application to the various wants of humanity. He at first gave his attention to the relief of the poor, the sick, and the imprisoned, that he might draw them forth out of that state of moral and corporal misery in which they had been left to languish. It was this spirit of his that afterwards raised up holy Communities which devoted themselves exclusively to these important duties. It was he and his associates who sowed the first seeds of those ameliorations and the progress of humane institutions which are a feature of our times. Whoever is willing to agree with truth and justice cannot deny what we here say, nor dispute the influence which St. Ignatius has exerted on modern times as a benefactor of humanity. Urban VIII., in the Bull of the Saint's canonization, has taken pains to set forth his merits in this regard, and we think we cannot better conclude this work than by quoting the words of this Pope, which gives a kind of *resumé* of the life of Ignatius as the founder of the Society—

He ceased not to succor the poor and sick in the hospitals, distributing to them the alms he had received from charitable persons ; and from the commencement of his conversion he gave himself, in a most especial manner, to the catechising of children and the ignorant. It was he who, by his example, introduced the custom of visiting and consoling the imprisoned. He founded missions in all the countries of the world, built churches and colleges, especially in the city of Rome, where, without counting the public school, in which all frequenters of it are gratuitously taught, he established the German College, the Homes for Orphans and Catechumens, the convents of St. Martha and St. Catherine, and other pious institutions. He settled disputes, gave wise counsel, composed the *Spiritual Exercises*, exhorted the faithful to frequent the Sacraments, reconciled enemies, and made them pray for one another. All these things evidently show how much he loved his neighbor for the sake of God.